POTTERY IN MEDIEVAL SOUTHAMPTON

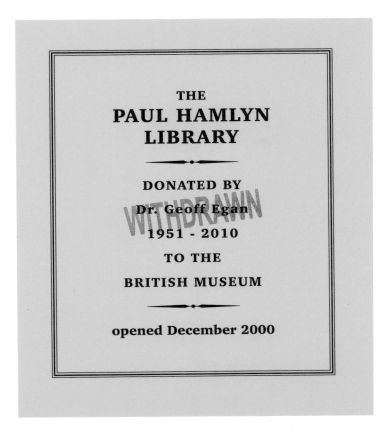

POTTERY IN MEDIEVAL SOUTHAMPTON, *c* 1066–1510

Duncan H Brown

Southampton Archaeology Monographs 8
CBA Research Report 133
Council for British Archaeology
2002

Published in 2002 by the Council for British Archaeology
Bowes Morrell House, 111 Walmgate, York, Y01 9WA

Copyright © 2002 Author and Council for British Archaeology

British Library Cataloguing in Publication Data
A catalogue record for this book is available from the British Library

ISBN 1-902771-30-3

Cover and text designed and typeset in Adobe Garamond by
Carnegie Publishing Ltd, Lancaster
Printed by The Alden Press, Oxford

The CBA acknowledges with gratitude a grant from English Heritage towards the publication of this volume

Front cover: Allegory of Winter, by Cesar Boetius Van Everdingen (courtesy of Southampton City Art Gallery)
Back cover: Waster fragments of Southampton Whiteware (courtesy of Duncan Brown)

CONTENTS

LIST OF FIGURES

List of tables

LIST OF COLOUR PLATES

ACKNOWLEDGEMENTS

The Department of the Environment, latterly English Heritage, provided the initial funding for recording and writing this report, and Southampton City Council also provided financial and organisational support. English Heritage, most recently through the auspices of Sarah Jennings, have also provided comments on the text. The recording of all this pottery was undertaken with the able assistance of Liz Pieksma and Nigel Wilkins and I thank them for their company, good humour and intelligent forbearance. Julia Nurse and Aidan Ackerman also provided help with sorting and recording. I am especially grateful to Simon Griffin, who has produced some excellent drawings; Nick Instone drew catalogue numbers 212, 213, 214, 215 and 370. John Lawrence took the excellent photographs. Thanks also to Ian Brown, computer wizard, who provided the know-how behind the creation of Figure 36. Wendy Barrett typed my first draft into a word processor and Andy Russel, Alan Morton and Karen Wardley were kind enough to offer comments on the text.

Over the years that this book has been in preparation, encouragement and help has come from Gill Andrews, Sarah Jennings, Alan Morton, John Oxley and Karen Wardley. In addition Ken Barton, Bob Burns, Daniel Dufornier, David Gaimster, Remy Guadignin, Alejandra Guttierez, John Hurst, Jaques Le Maho, Frans Verhaeghe, Alan Vince and Tim Wilson were all kind enough to offer their views on the identity of odd bits of pot. Alan Vince undertook analysis of much of the Iberian wares and, with Michael Hughes, of the tin-glazed pottery. Paul Spoerry analysed some of the local wares. Alejandra Gutierrez was kind enough to pursue some references for me. John Hudson provided me with valuable and hilarious potting know-how. Michelle Brown, at the British Library, kindly translated the Saintonge Redware sgraffito inscription for me.

Many people have had to make sacrifices on my behalf during the excruciating development of this work and I thank them all, most especially my wife Kathryn and daughters Matilda and Alys, who in recent weeks have been denied my attentions. All three of them, and my son Dominic, have brightened my mood at crucial times. Most importantly, Bob Thomson gave freely of his own wealth of knowledge, experience, time and understanding, and to me he has been a constant source of support and inspiration, as well as liquid sustenance. This book is dedicated to him with great affection and respect.

Duncan H Brown
December 2001

SUMMARY

This volume presents a catalogue of post-Conquest medieval pottery from nine excavations within the medieval walled town of Southampton. The results of quantification and analysis are also shown, leading to an examination of the assemblage with regard to the themes of chronology, technology, distribution and use. The context of recovery is also elucidated with subsequent interpretations of social, economic and cultural aspects of medieval Southampton.

La céramique dans le Southampton médiéval
Résumé

Ce volume présente un catalogue de céramique médiévale datant d'après la conquête normande, découverte dans neuf fouilles effectuées à l'intérieur de l'enceinte de la ville médiévale de Southampton. Les résultats de la quantification et de l'analyse sont également indiqués, menant à un examen de l'ensemble relativement aux thèmes de la chronologie, de la technologie, de la répartition et de l'utilisation. Les interprétations ultérieures des aspects sociaux, économiques et culturels du Southampton médiéval éclaircissent également le contexte dans lequel elle a été récupérée.

Keramikfunde aus dem mittelalterlichen Southampton
Zusammenfassung

Diese Abhandlung stellt einen Katalog von mittelalterlichen die Keramikfunden zusammen, die der Zeit nach der normannischen Eroberung in 1066 AD zugeschrieben werden. Diese Funde stammen aus neun Ausgrabungen innerhalb der mittelalterlichen Stadtmauern Southamptons. Die Ergebnisse von Quantifizierung und Analyse werden ebenfalls erläutert, und das Keramikinventar wird anhand von Chronologie, Technologie, Fundverteilung und Gebrauchstypus untersucht. Der Kontext der Fundorte wird besonders hervorgehoben und unterstützt die Interpretationen von sozialen, ökonomischen und kulturellen Beziehungen im mittelalterlichen Southampton.

1

INTRODUCTION

The programme of excavations carried out between 1970 and 1980 within the walls of the medieval town of Southampton produced a huge quantity of finds. This study concentrates on pottery recovered from phases of post-conquest medieval activity on those sites, an assemblage numbering 35,940 sherds. The recovery of a relatively compact, coherent group of material from well-stratified deposits has provided the opportunity to undertake a detailed classification and quantification of the pottery of medieval Southampton and the results of that exercise are presented here. It is, however, not enough simply to describe the assemblage, for it represents five centuries of human activity. Interpretations of the technological, commercial and social development of pottery production and use in and around medieval Southampton are presented, and related to the economic and cultural history of the town.

Pottery assemblages from nine excavations are considered here. In Southampton, archaeological sites are identified by unique numbers that have the pre-fix SOU. The site assemblages examined here are from SOU numbers 25, 29, 105, 110, 122, 123, 124, 125 and 128. A summary of the deposits uncovered at each of those sites may be found in Chapter 7, which considers the archaeological context for the pottery types described in earlier chapters. Although more than nine sites were excavated during that period, these are the only assemblages selected for analysis. Included here

are the principal sites excavated within the medieval town by the Southampton Archaeological Research Committee (SARC); SOU numbers 25, 29, 122, 123, 124 and 125; and three that were dug by Southampton Museums; SOU numbers 105, 110 and 128. They were chosen on the basis of their having either useful quantities of finds, or the most coherent surviving site records; usually both. The pottery from certain other sites was excluded either because the bulk of the ceramic assemblage was later in date than the range of this volume, or else because the site archive was of insufficient quality.

The assemblage was sorted and recorded between 1982 and 1986, and a reference series of fabrics and forms was created at the same time. This volume is part of a backlog publication programme, funded jointly by Southampton City Council together with the Department of the Environment (DoE), subsequently the Historic Buildings and Monuments Commission (HBMC) then English Heritage. It is one of an intended series of publications that presents interpretations of the archaeology of Saxon and medieval Southampton. At the time of writing, the archaeology of the medieval town is represented in that series solely by 'Excavations at Southampton Castle' (Oxley 1986) – further volumes, on the medieval tenements and finds such as the metalwork, coins and glass, are planned.

Limits

Material from deposits pre-dating the Norman Conquest has been analysed as part of a different project, and is published elsewhere (Brown 1995). All post-medieval pottery, and all ceramic finds from post-medieval deposits have also been excluded from analysis, principally because of the quantity of material represented and the fact that the stratigraphic information has not been studied. This has, however, been beneficial in limiting the size of the assemblage, thus enabling a programme of detailed classification and analysis.

Quantification and attendant analyses are confined

solely to pottery from stratified medieval deposits, thus lending a greater probability of accuracy to the ceramic sequence here presented. The catalogue is enhanced by illustrations of vessels from less securely provenanced deposits from the same sites. The evidence of other types of finds from these excavations is to be published elsewhere. This particular contribution must therefore be seen as only one component of a more exhaustive study.

'Excavations at Southampton Castle' (Oxley 1986) includes an analysis of the pottery from the sites discussed therein (Brown 1986). It is envisaged that a similar chapter will appear in any forthcoming volume on the archaeology of domestic tenements in medieval Southampton. The particular relevance of ceramics to the dating and interpretation of archaeological deposits rightly belongs within those volumes and such site-specific discussions do not occur here. Instead, the material from these nine sites is presented as one assemblage.

Contained in this volume therefore, is a description, analysis and interpretation of the medieval pottery of Southampton from the Conquest period to the end of the medieval period, based on the evidence of nine excavations within the medieval walled town. As such it is not definitive. As more pottery is excavated from more fully recorded sites the level of understanding of the ceramic evidence will be refined. This work should therefore be seen in its proper context, as a statement of current interpretations and a stepping-stone to improved analysis and theories.

Aims

It is in the same light that one must view the relationship between this work and that of Colin Platt and Richard Coleman-Smith (Platt and Coleman-Smith 1975). They presented a catalogue of the main pottery types present in Southampton from the 10th to the 18th centuries AD. In attempting to progress from their work this analysis considers the local wares in greater detail, characterising different types more distinctly, and employing more exhaustive quantification techniques. The overall sequence of ceramic development is essentially little different from that put forward in 1975, but in accord with current standards, it is, at the very least, now supported by numerical data. The problems of making dull numbers accessible to the reader are outweighed by the benefits which quantification can bring to ceramic interpretation. Relationships, through time and space, between different ceramic types can be explored more sensitively and revealed more explicitly, as also can the relationships between pottery and other forms of evidence, be they depositional, environmental, artefactual or historical.

Quantification provides a database from which further work can go forward, leading to interpretations of the society that inhabited medieval Southampton and the influences that affected its development. The intention here is to make those interpretations comprehensible through the use of a methodology that other archaeologists will recognise.

The progress of research on this assemblage went through three stages; description, analysis and interpretation. A reference system has been created for the classification of fabrics and forms and the principal types are described here in the catalogue, Chapter 2. Analysis is founded on the quantification of each ceramic type and has led to the creation of the chronological sequence presented in Chapter 3. The results of analysis have been interpreted with regard to the broad themes of ceramic technology (Chapter 4), distribution (Chapter 5), use (Chapter 6), context (Chapter 7), consumption (Chapter 8) and identity (Chapter 9). All these themes are drawn together in a concluding chapter (Chapter 10). The order in which these chapters appear is meant to reflect the order in which various events occur in the life of a pot, and also the order in which various questions about a sherd of pottery might be asked. Chronology, manufacture and distribution are therefore considered before function, and all of those before the context of deposition, or descriptions of excavations. All these aspects are drawn together to inform overall interpretations of how pottery studies might provide an insight into the social character of medieval Southampton. This approach, to the author at least, appears logical and also has the effect of putting the stratigraphic evidence in its proper place within the overall scheme of pottery analysis.

Chronological parameters

The chronological focus of this work is the post-Conquest medieval period. It is, however, virtually impossible to date changes in ceramic assemblages to a date as precise as AD 1066 and there is, similarly, no single year in the 16th century which brought an end to the production and use of medieval pottery types. The date range expressed in the title of this work is, therefore, necessarily vague. As will be seen, in discussions of local pottery of the Anglo-Norman period, reference has to be made to pre-Conquest types and there is a corresponding discussion of the major post-medieval products. The period under discussion, however, is easy to identify and characterise by other means. The coming of the Normans still represents an obvious watershed in English history, and in the development of Southampton. On a national level again, the Reformation was a great agent for change in the 16th century and it is tempting to identify the 1530s as the end point for this study. That would appear to be too late, however, because the latest material presented here was probably deposited no later than the first decade of the 16th century. An end date of *c* 1510 is proposed therefore. This lack of precision in dating the end of the medieval ceramic tradition in Southampton is, in part, a result of not studying the post-medieval pottery and this issue needs to be addressed in the future.

There is, also, little absolute chronological evidence from the sites that produced this assemblage and we find ourselves in the familiar conundrum where the pottery is used to date the stratigraphic sequence and yet the stratigraphic sequence is used to date the pottery. As a result, the chronology for the development of pottery use in Southampton is based on the quantification of certain ceramic types through a system discussed in Chapter 3. This has resulted in the identification of three Ceramic Periods that are distinguished by different traditions of pottery manufacture and use. The first of these is the Anglo-Norman period, which roughly extends from the time of the Conquest to *c* 1250. The high medieval period runs from *c* 1250 to *c* 1350 and the late medieval period from *c* 1350 to *c* 1510. Of these, the late medieval period is the most problematic, for neither its beginning nor its end are by any means certain. These periods, however, provide a useful chronological framework for further analysis.

Methodology

Every sherd in this assemblage has been characterised according to fabric and form. Fabric means the clay and its inclusions from which a vessel has been made, form denotes the shape given to a vessel or its individual component parts. A fabric type series and a corpus of form types are the basis for identifying and sorting pottery in Southampton. Both systems are designed for the classification of assemblages from all sites in the city. They have been modified and refined throughout the course of this research, and will continue to change as the methods and requirements of pottery analysis in Southampton develop. What follows is a statement of their condition at the time of writing.

The Southampton fabric type series
Pottery fabrics are classified according to a three-tiered hierarchical system comprising fabric, ware (or Ware Name) and Ceramic Group. Each individual fabric is referred to by a number. Ware Names are given in full, with capital initial letters, and Ceramic Groups are also referred to in full, also with capital initial letters. As an example, Fabric 1123 has the Ware Name 'Southampton Coarseware' and is in the Ceramic Group 'High Medieval Coarseware'. Ceramic Groups are rarely referred to in the text, because they are useful mainly as a tool for classification during analysis, and in ordering the type series, rather than for formal description.

Fabric is the most specific definition. Every pottery fabric is distinguished according to the character and quality of clay and inclusions, following the approach outlined by Peacock (1977) then Orton, Tyers and Vince (1993). A binocular microscope was used to identify each inclusion type and assess shape, size and quantity. Letter codes are used to denote types of clay and inclusion; 'A' stands for earthenware, 'C' for chalk, 'F' for flint, 'Q' for quartz and so on. Each fabric has been given a string of these codes that show the range of the principal inclusions; thus an earthenware with chalk, flint, iron and quartz would be coded 'ACFIQ'. In order to distinguish it from any others that have the same code every fabric is given a unique number in a running sequence that, for the medieval type series, commences at 1000 (in Southampton the Saxon type series starts at 1). The range of inclusions will often give clues as to the origin of a particular fabric, for instance a highly micaceous type will have been produced close to sources of metamorphic or igneous rock. Equally usefully, fabric definition allows particular types to be compared and classified together

This unique numbering system has resulted in a vast array of single types, and in a large assemblage such as this, meaningful analysis is rendered almost impossible. Every fabric, therefore, has also been given a Ware Name. Similar fabrics may share the same Ware Name, which term also confers a character and an identity that will, it is hoped, be more readily understood than a number. Different fabrics may have the same Ware Name, but will never have the same Fabric Number. Ware Names are abbreviated to a code of up to four letters; for example, Southampton Whiteware is coded STWW, Tudor Green TDG and Saintonge Polychrome SOPY. These simple examples also demonstrate how names that are in common currency in

English medieval pottery studies have been adopted, such as Tudor Green. Fabrics that are not so named, or cannot be related to specific production sites, have been given Ware Names that describe any distinguishing characteristic, such as colour or inclusions. Many of the local types, therefore, which are difficult to assign to a specific source have been assigned Ware Names such as ACWX, meaning Anglo-Norman (A) Coarseware (CW) with inclusions of mixed grit (X).

Fabrics and wares have been placed into Ceramic Groups that indicate their date, character and country of origin. These are abbreviated to codes of up to four letters. Fabrics 1007 and 1008, Scratch-marked Gritty (SMKG) and Scratch-marked Sandy (SMKS) are in the Ceramic Group – Anglo-Norman Local Coarseware (ALCW). Fabric 1044, Southampton Whiteware (STWW) is grouped as a High Medieval Local Sandy ware (HLMS), Fabric 1193, Tudor Green ware (TDG) is a Late Medieval Non-local English type (LMNL) and Fabric 1274, Saintonge Polychrome (SOPY) is grouped as High Medieval, French, Saintonge (HFSO). Most English pottery has been classified as either coarseware – unglazed fabrics which mainly take the form of unglazed jars/cooking pots and bowls, or sandy ware – finer fabrics usually made into glazed jugs and bowls. The term coarseware is also applied to certain Continental wares that are similarly distinguishable from finer types, for example Iberian Coarsewares as opposed to Iberian Tin-glazed wares.

Ceramic Group is the broadest term of classification within the system for sorting and recording, but a further category has been created for the purposes of quantification.

Major Wares

Major Ware is a term applied to fabrics or wares that are quantitatively significant and thus important in interpretations of the chronology and culture of ceramic production and use in medieval Southampton. A Major Ware occurs in the assemblage as a minimum of 100 sherds or 1kg in weight and in more than 20 contexts.

The specific fabrics that have been grouped to form Major Wares are described in the Catalogue (Chapter 2). Appendix 2 lists each Major Ware and the specific fabrics they represent. Table 1 lists the Major Wares, giving the character codes used to identify their Ware Codes, total quantities, and the number of contexts in which they occur. A full discussion of Major Wares and their application in establishing a ceramic chronology is set out in Chapter 3.

The Form Corpus

Pottery forms are also classified within a three-tiered hierarchical system, Form Type, Vessel Type and Vessel Group. Form Type identifies vessel components, rim, spout, handle, body, base and foot, which have been distinguished on the basis of shape. Each Form Type is given a unique Form Number with a pre-fix that denotes the relevant component: R for rim, S for spout, H for handle, T for body, B for base and F for foot. Decorative technique and motif are also both classified numerically and pre-fixed D and M respectively.

Vessel Group is a general classification, identified by a code of up to four letters, for example CPOT for cooking pot. Where possible a more specific identification, Vessel Type, is made and also coded using a maximum of four letters. Within the cooking pot group are such Vessel Types as pipkin (PKIN) and tripod pipkin (TPKN). It is difficult to identify the Vessel Group or Type for non-diagnostic body sherds, and many of these are simply coded as miscellaneous (MISC), or unidentifiable (UNID). The use of one particular Vessel Group deserves explanation. Many of the coarsewares described below took the form of rounded or shouldered jars that are often referred to as cooking pots although 'A Guide to the Classification of Medieval Ceramic Forms' (MPRG 1998) suggests that the term jar be universally applied. Sooting on the base suggests that in many, perhaps most, cases, these vessels were indeed used in cooking and the term jar/cooking pot is used as a means of indicating more precisely the type of vessel that is being referred to. The excellent publication: 'A Guide to the Classification of Medieval Pottery Forms' was produced some time after the draft of this work was sent for refereeing and its recommendations are therefore not followed precisely although some attempt has been made to conform to its principles during preparation of the final copy.

At present, this assemblage is the only one in Southampton that has been analysed to this system. The establishment of a Form Corpus and its use in conjunction with the Fabric Type series, is therefore a first step on the way to making possible a more detailed analysis of the local Southampton or Hampshire products. Such an analysis will, it is hoped, incorporate material from this assemblage and those previously and subsequently excavated.

Recording and quantification

A separate pottery record sheet has been completed for every context represented in this assemblage. Context details, such as related feature number and phase are recorded then the pottery is sorted into Fabric and Form Types and decorative technique and motif. These are then recorded and quantified by rim percentage (RP), weight in grams (g), and sherd count (sherds). The RP figure is not used to estimate vessel equivalents in the manner discussed by Orton (1980), it is used simply as another method of quantifying ceramic presence. It has been shown that RP totals will support the quantitative trends shown in sherd weight (Brown 1986, 107) but this is not altogether satisfactory because some fabrics are not represented by any rims at all. Sherd weight and count are therefore utilised most consistently here. Due to the size and nature of the assemblage, vessel counts have not been attempted.

Quantifying every Fabric and Form Type has created a database of enormous variety and unwieldy proportions; hence the grouping of fabrics into Ware Names and Fabric Groups. All this information, together with stratigraphic data, was entered into a computerised database. Quantification indicates those fabrics and forms that occur most often in the assemblage and it is those upon which this study will concentrate. Commonly occurring fabrics have been grouped together as Major Wares.

Pottery quantities for both ceramic periods and settlement phases are given in the form of tables and charts. Sherd weight and count are used here to express relative quantities and are often proportionately different. This contrast may serve to indicate the average sherd size of any ceramic type. For instance, where sherd count is markedly greater than sherd weight one might perceive the sherd size to be small, and vice versa. Dense fabrics will usually occur in thick-walled vessels that are likely to fragment into a few, large, heavy sherds. Fabrics that are light and fine will break into many tiny pieces. Vessel form also has a bearing on the likely weight and number of sherds found. Thickened rims survive in larger pieces than simple types and solid rod handles are less likely to fragment than thin straps. These imbalances arise even before one considers such factors as methods of breakage and disposal, where the time taken for pieces of pottery to reach their final resting place will determine their condition on archaeological rediscovery. Fortunately, the size of this assemblage is such that despite these factors, broad patterns of ceramic occurrence can be clearly perceived.

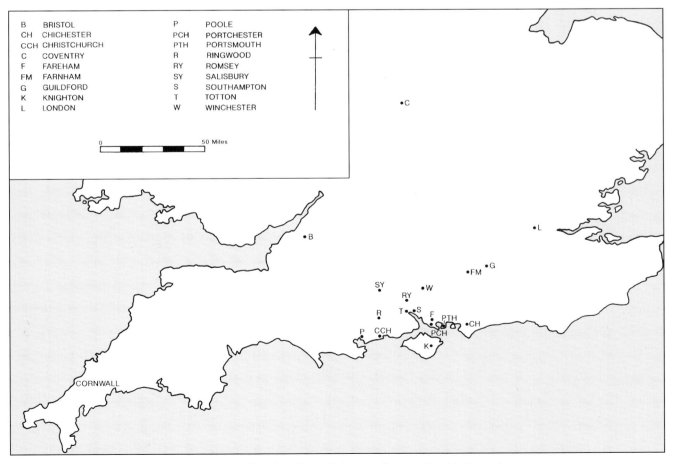

Figure 1. Map of southern England showing sites mentioned in the text

Principles

It is appropriate to present a discussion of the principles governing the analytical process, so that the results of that analysis may be put into perspective. Fabric and form definitions, however hard one tries, will remain somewhat subjective. It is difficult to be consistent in characterising a material that is itself so often affected by the unpredictable vagaries of human action. Kiln stacking and firing will influence fabric colour, for instance, so that there may be variations from red, through brown and grey, to black over the surface of a single vessel. The amounts of inclusions within a group of vessels of the same fabric, made perhaps by a single potter, may also differ. Some fabric definitions, and consequently attributions, will therefore not always be equally sensitive. This has not been seen as a problem. The author has viewed every sherd in this assemblage, and he has decided, taking into account

the opinions of his assistants, how to classify those fragments. At least a consistent approach has been applied to the processes of characterisation and recording.

Determining vessel function, and so assigning a vessel name, can also be subjective. Several types of vessel share similar rim or base forms and some vessel names are thus more general in meaning than others. One must not therefore make the mistake of thinking that this work presents definitions of consistent accuracy. Such can rarely be the result of archaeological classification and it is not necessarily its true purpose. This is an examination of some pottery recovered from nine sites in Southampton, and an interpretation of its meaning with relation to the medieval history of that place.

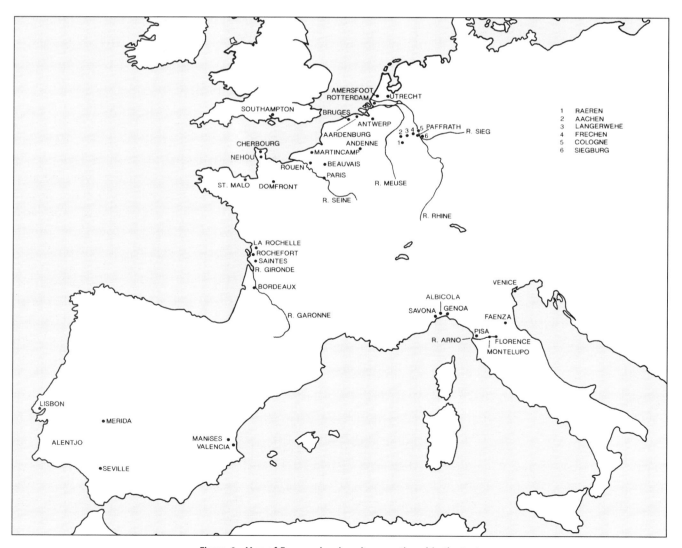

Figure 2. Map of Europe showing sites mentioned in the text

2

CATALOGUE OF FABRICS AND FORMS

The catalogue is based primarily on the system of fabric classification. Pottery types are grouped together by area of origin with English wares described first, followed by those from France, the Low Countries, the Rhineland, the Iberian peninsular and Italy. Within each provenance group, and where appropriate, the different types for each period are discussed in chronological order of Ceramic Period. Items have been selected for illustration either because they show the range of the types of vessels produced in a particular Fabric or Ware Type (eg fig 4), or because they are the most presentable examples of types that are not very well represented (eg illustration numbers 114, 115). All complete vessel profiles have been drawn.

Figures are arranged to show, as far as is possible, all the examples of a particular Fabric or Ware Type grouped together. Each drawn vessel has a catalogue number that is shown in the text in **bold**.

Some fabrics are not described in full in the text. These are mainly undistinguished coarse or sandy wares that are present as a few non-diagnostic sherds. A full description of all fabrics accompanies the Fabric Type Series in the care of Southampton City Council. Where fabrics are described in the text, quantities are given by rim percentage (RP), weight (g) and sherd-count (sherds), they are also cross-referenced to relevant drawing numbers in the illustrated catalogue.

English wares

The English pottery may be divided into four groups, Southampton wares, local wares, non-local wares and other English wares.

Southampton wares were made within, or close to the medieval walled town, and do not appear to have been commonly distributed far from it. Two fabrics have been so identified because they occur in this assemblage in waster form (Fabric 1044, p 13 and Fabric 1230, p 13) while the remainder are called Southampton wares because they occur in high quantities within the town, to the extent that Southampton might be regarded as a sort of 'type-site'.

The region within which 'local' wares were produced is one that represents Southampton's immediate hinterland, namely south Hampshire, east Dorset, south-east Wiltshire, the Isle of Wight, and possibly west Sussex. Local fabrics have characteristics that conform to the pattern of the local drift geology, with sandy iron-rich clays and inclusions of quartz, chalk and flint. They also fit with contemporary local pottery-making traditions in aspects of technique and vessel form. One other important identifier is the fact that local wares occur in large quantities in Southampton assemblages. It seems reasonable to assume that those English products that were most commonly marketed

in Southampton were those made closest to the town. Further confirmation of the local origin of certain types is their distribution among other medieval sites in the area. Some fabrics have been identified as the products of known kilns, Laverstock ware for instance (Fabric 1034, p 15) and this is reflected in the Ware Type name code (LV). Others have been attributed to known traditions or areas of production, for example Dorset Whiteware (Fabric 1156, code DOWW, p 16). There are, however, many types, identified here as local, for which there are no regionally recognised common names. Some of these have Ware Type titles that indicate their area of distribution, for instance South Hampshire Redware (Fabric 1248, code SHR, p 14). Most of them, however, have been given generally descriptive Ware Type names that must serve until their regional distribution and likely source areas have been established. Such Ware Types are specific to fabrics, for example Anglo-Norman Coarseware with Chalk Inclusions (Fabric 1055, code ACWC, p 10); or to groups of fabrics, probably produced at different kilns, that represent a local tradition, such as Late Medieval Well-fired Sandy Redware (code LWFS, p 19).

Non-local wares are those that came into Southampton from production sites situated outside the hinterland. Most of these have been identified because they are well-known types, such as Scarborough-type ware (Fabric 1526, SCRB, p 17) or Tudor Green (Fabric 1193, code TDG, p 20). Others are equally readily identifiable because they have characteristics foreign to this region, for instance Cornish Coarseware is a fabric with igneous inclusions (Fabric 1726, code CRNC, p 13) that show it to be quite different from local products.

There remains a range of fabrics of uncertain origin that cannot be placed in a particular Ware Type and these have been grouped together under the general heading 'Other Wares'. Some may prove to be of local origin, some may be non-local types, but it has not been possible to spend time finding out. Most of these fabrics have no diagnostic characteristics either of fabric or form, occur in this assemblage in very small quantities, and are not described below. Descriptions are given for those types represented in the drawn catalogue.

The pre-Conquest period

Although this work concentrates on pottery of the post-Conquest medieval period, discussion of ceramic traditions cannot usefully take place unless they are placed in context with the Anglo-Saxon products from which they developed.

Middle Saxon pottery is absent from the assemblage discussed here and the material from the middle Saxon town of Hamwic has been published (Timby 1988). Middle Saxon ceramics of local origin were hand-built coarsewares that have been classified according to their inclusions (Timby 1988). The most common identified form is the round-based cooking pot with an everted rim. By the end of the 9th century Hamwic had been abandoned (Morton 1992), and many local pottery types were no longer being made. Flint and shell-tempered fabrics characterise late Hamwic groups.

Late Saxon activity on the Southampton peninsula seems to have been concentrated in the area that became the medieval town. The ceramic assemblage recovered from excavated late Saxon deposits in that area has been published elsewhere (Brown 1995) and is not quantified here. References hereafter to the late Saxon assemblage refer to the pottery examined in that work.

The main components of the late Saxon assemblage are hand-built, locally made flint-tempered and sandy coarsewares in forms related to the middle Saxon tradition (*ibid*). Chalk-tempered ware and the wheel-thrown Michelmersh-type ware are classed as non-local late Saxon products (*ibid*). Sherds of all these types occur as a residual presence in the post-Conquest assemblage. Portchester ware (*ibid*), and glazed wares in the Winchester ware tradition (personal observation) have been found in late Saxon deposits but are not present in this assemblage.

The most common pre-Conquest pottery type, flint-tempered ware, was almost certainly still being made in the late-11th and probably early-12th centuries and occurs in deposits associated with this assemblage. There are two types, Flint-tempered Sandy ware (Fabric 900) and Flint-tempered Gritty ware (Fabric 1000) known collectively as Early Medieval Flint-tempered ware; a name that reflects a lack of certainty around its dating. This Ware Type forms a significant part of the post-Conquest assemblage and is described here. Full descriptions of the other late Saxon wares are given elsewhere (*ibid*).

Anglo-Norman wares (late-11th century to *c* 1250)

There is no evidence to suggest that the common local flint-tempered coarsewares of the late Saxon period went out of production immediately after 1066, nor is there any reason to suppose they should have done. The changes in ceramic production that occurred at this period seem to have been slow, with the use of glaze apparently the only major technological development. However, late Saxon sandy wares, as well as chalk-tempered ware and Michelmersh-type ware pitchers, were apparently no longer being made by the last quarter of the 11th century although they characterise late-10th and early-11th century groups.

Nearly all the English pottery in Southampton at this period can be classified as local coarseware. Inclusions are generally large, and there are few fabrics comparable to the finer sandy types of the late Saxon or high medieval periods. In general, plain coarseware fabrics are different from glazed fabrics, both in character and in form. The character of the plain coarseware fabrics does not appear to alter greatly throughout the 11th and 12th centuries, nor indeed does the fundamental shape of the jar or cooking pot form in which they principally occur. These vessels have the everted rim and rounded base that typifies Saxon forms. Plain bowls and lamps were also produced. A significant variation among coarsewares is the technique of scratch-marking, a scoring of the exterior surface of a vessel with a myriad of random lines. Scratch-marked pottery is the most common English ware of this period and occurs mainly as jars/cooking pots.

The sole Anglo-Norman English glazed form appears to have been a three-footed jug, usually referred to as a tripod pitcher, which often has crude incised or rouletted decoration.

No production sites have been identified for any of these wares. The majority of them were probably produced in or around Southampton and they all contain inclusions that accord with the character of the local drift geology. The few types of more distant origin probably came from the west, most likely Dorset or Wiltshire, the likely source for much of the early medieval glazed pottery.

Coarsewares are described first, then glazed wares.

Local Coarsewares

EMFT Early Medieval Flint-tempered ware

Fabric 900	LSFS 276 RP	3382g	363 sherds
Fabric 1000	LSFG 862	11923	955

EMFT is a Major Ware that includes two flint-tempered fabrics: Fabric 900, Flint-tempered Sandy ware (SLFS), and Fabric 1000, Flint-tempered Gritty ware (SLFG). These are characterised by the relative quantities of flint inclusions. Both fabrics are low-fired, hand-built coarsewares containing abundant flint with chalk, shell and organic matter in an iron-rich sandy clay matrix. Colours range from red-brown to black, even over the surface of a single vessel, while cores are usually grey or black. Flint-tempered ware is the most common pottery in the late Saxon assemblage, accounting for 70% of the total sherd weight (Brown 1995). Both fabrics share the same range of forms. Plain and socketed bowls were made, but jars/cooking pots were by far the most common vessel type. These are round-based with everted rims, in the 'bag-shaped' style (eg Platt and Coleman-Smith 1975, No. 2) typical also of middle Saxon local wares (eg Timby 1988, No. 49, 50, 51). All vessels were hand-built, although some rims may have been finished on a turntable.

Flint-tempered pottery is a late type in Hamwic groups and continuity of traditions in pottery production and use is suggested by its survival into the late Saxon period in a similar range of forms. There would appear to be no further development of these traditions in the 10th and early 11th centuries and the quantities of Early Medieval Flint-tempered ware present in this assemblage suggest that this product was still being made after the Norman Conquest. It is likely, therefore, that this ware was produced in or close to Southampton.

SMK Scratch-marked ware

Fabric 1007	SMKG 2620 RP	52449g	2870 sherds
Fabric 1008	SMKS 510	11374	942

Scratch-marked pottery accounts for 77% of the total sherd weight of all the Anglo-Norman coarsewares. Two fabrics have been distinguished on the basis of the quantity and range of inclusions. Together, these fabrics form the Major Ware SMK.

Fabric 1007, Scratch-marked Gritty ware (SMG) contains abundant chalk, flint and quartz sand in a sandy clay matrix.

Fabric 1008, Scratch-marked Sandy ware (SMS) contains higher quantities of quartz sand and correspondingly less chalk and flint in a similar sandy clay matrix.

Scratch-marked Gritty ware is almost certainly related to the Late Saxon Flint-tempered wares (Fabrics 1000 and 900) in terms of the range of the inclusions and the quality of the clay, and it may be seen as a development out of earlier types. The fabric of Scratch-marked Sandy ware is different, having fewer similarities with earlier pottery types. Even so, it obviously belongs within the same tradition as Scratch-marked Gritty ware. Within these two broad types further fabric divisions could probably be made but this has not yet been attempted.

Jars/cooking pots are the most common vessel, all hand-built and all in the round-based form with everted rim that is typical of Saxon wares. Jars/cooking pots were often further embellished with thumbing on the rim that occurs in a variety of styles, including a very distinctive deep gouging where nail marks can be observed (**8**). Thumbing is common on the largest pots and may have been a way of ensuring a consistent firing of the thicker vessel parts. There is one example of a handled jar/cooking pot (**9**).

In Southampton it appears that Scratch-marked wares were introduced in the post-Conquest period. They flourish throughout the 12th century and cannot yet be dated with any certainty to the late Saxon period. In Southampton therefore the presence of scratch-marked pottery in excavated contexts is seen primarily as an indicator of post-Conquest activity and this ware is quintessentially Anglo-Norman.

Fabric 1007	Jar/Cooking Pot	**1–8**
	Handled Vessel	**9**
Fabric 1008	Jar/Cooking Pot	**10, 11**

ANWX Anglo-Norman Mixed Grit Coarseware

Fabric 1011	112 RP	3004g	153 sherds
Fabric 1014	409	4672	225
Fabric 1095	178	2043	89

These fabrics are all hand-built types, characterised by the presence of mixed inclusions, mainly quartz, flint and chalk with some iron, that give rise to the Ware Name. They are distinguished by differences in the quality of the clay matrix, which is generally sandy, and the quantities of the inclusions. Each of them forms a separate Major Ware.

Fabric 1011 (Major Ware ECWXa) contains abundant ill-sorted quartz inclusions with coarse and medium flint and some chalk. Vessel walls are often relatively thick and pots often seem to have been poorly made and fired. Colours range from red to black. Jars/cooking pots are the only vessels identified in this fabric. These conform to the typical early medieval form, with everted rims and round or sagging bases.

Fabric 1014 (Major Ware ECWXb) has a sandy clay matrix with abundant inclusions of quartz, chalk and flint, occasional organics and some shell. This fabric is possibly related to Scratch-marked Gritty ware. Sherds are usually of an even, moderate thickness and vessels seem to be reasonably well-fired. The range of vessels includes jars/cooking pots of the usual shape, also bowls and simple lamps.

Fabric 1095 (Major Ware ECWXc) has moderate inclusions of medium chalk and flint with sparse shell and organics in a sandy matrix. Colours range from brown to grey and black. This product is comparatively well-made, though often apparently under-fired. Some jars/cooking pots have a ribbed line around the shoulder, perhaps indicating that vessels were turned as they were finished. Jars/cooking pots with everted rims are the most common vessel and there is also a lamp in this fabric.

Fabric 1011	Jar/cooking pot	12
Fabric 1014	Jar/cooking pot	13
	Bowl	14
	Lamp	15
Fabric 1095	Jar/cooking pot	16
	Lamp	17

ACWC Anglo-Norman Chalk-tempered Coarseware

| Fabric 1055 | 88 RP | 2337g | 58 sherds |

This is a hand-built coarseware containing moderately abundant chalk, with flint and some iron. Colours vary from red to black. Vessels seem to be crudely finished. Jars/cooking pots with everted rims are the only forms that have been identified.

| | Jar/cooking pot | 18 |

Non-local Coarsewares

ANLF Anglo-Norman non-local Flint-tempered ware

| Fabric 1013 | 0 RP | 763g | 28 sherds |

This is a hand-built coarseware containing abundant coarse angular flint inclusions and quartz and iron. Surfaces are black in colour, cores grey. All vessels were handbuilt.

There are very few sherds of this fabric in this assemblage, but they include the almost complete profile of a jar/cooking pot. This is quite different from local types in having a sagging, flat base, straight sides and pronounced high shoulders. The form and the fabric both suggest a source perhaps in Dorset but certainly west of the local area.

| Jar/cooking pot | 19 |

ANGT Anglo-Norman Gravel-tempered ware

| Fabric 1073 | 0 RP | 17g | 2 sherds |

A hand-built coarseware characterised by abundant mixed chert inclusions in a hard-fired matrix with red-brown surface colours and a grey core. This is not a local product, nor is it comparable with any Wiltshire types (L Mepham, *pers comm.*). A west Dorset or perhaps Somerset source is considered likely.

No diagnostic sherds are present and none have been illustrated here. A spouted jar or pitcher in this ware has previously been published from Southampton (Platt and Coleman-Smith 1975, No. 182).

ANCW Other Anglo-Norman Coarsewares

| Fabrics | 1009, 1081, 1104, 1141, 1466, 1549, 1563, 1680, 1688, 1725, 1779, 2040, 2041 | | |
| | 174 RP | 3349g | 203 sherds |

Eleven fabrics have been grouped together in a category loosely defined as Anglo-Norman Coarseware, together with two general fabric numbers assigned to sherds in later phases that have not been specifically sorted. These exhibit a range of inclusions, including chalk, flint and quartz sand, which characterise them as southern English products. All of them are hand-built. The few diagnostic sherds are mainly everted rims from jars/cooking pots. Only one example is worth illustrating, a jar/cooking pot with horizontal incised lines that is an unusual form of decoration on local coarsewares of this period. This is in Fabric 1081, a red-firing coarse sandy ware with medium-fine inclusions of quartz, and some chalk and flint. Fabric 1549 is a chalk-tempered type that occurs in the form of a small lamp.

| Fabric 1081 | Jar/cooking pot | 20 |

Local Glazed wares

AWQC Anglo-Norman Wessex Coarseware

| Fabric 1016 | 80 RP | 3195g | 203 sherds |
| Fabric 1065 | 0 | 1510 | 66 |

This is a hand-built coarseware characterised by abundant well-sorted medium quartz inclusions with occasional flint and chalk. The quartz-rich character of the fabric is acknowledged with the insertion of 'Q' into the Ware Type code. Sherds of this fabric are usually thick and relatively crudely formed but well-fired. Colours vary from grey to brown to pink.

Fabric 1016 is an unglazed variety that occurs mainly as body sherds. A few everted rims and rounded base fragments suggest that plain vessels conformed to the typical jar/cooking pot shape for this period, although no examples are shown here. Fabric 1016 is a Major Ware.

Fabric 1065 is similar in composition but is glazed. Vessels in this variety of Anglo-Norman Wessex Coarseware appear to be tripod pitchers. Two are illustrated. The first has a rouletted decoration and a pale green, reduced, lead glaze (**21**), the second has combed decoration under a clear lead glaze (**22**). Fabric 1065 is incorporated into the Major Ware comprised of Early Medieval Glazed wares (EMG see below).

The composition of both these fabrics suggests a source west of Southampton, perhaps around Laverstock or into the New Forest fringes of western Dorset. They are similar to Dorset Sandy ware (ADOS, see below) and may be related. The term Wessex is applied to indicate the broad area of currency this ware may have had. It is relatively common among the sandier coarsewares and glazed products of the Anglo-Norman period and is thus tentatively identified as local to Southampton.

Fabric 1065   Tripod Pitcher   **21, 22**

ADOS   *Anglo-Norman Medieval Dorset Sandy ware*

Fabric 1101	6 RP	308g	15 sherds
Fabric 1102	22	1141	88
Fabric 1103	48	644	62
Fabric 1350	25	783	45

This ware is a hand-built sandy product with abundant ill-sorted quartz inclusions. Colours range from pink to grey, usually with a grey core. Fabric 1102 is a very coarse variant with large inclusions; 1101 has smaller coarse inclusions; 1103 has medium-sized inclusions; 1350 is a finer type. Glazed and unglazed sherds occur in all four fabrics and this ware is identified as a Major Ware. These fabrics compare well, visually, with Poole Type 1 (Jarvis 1992) and with material from Christchurch (Jarvis 1983). It is also similar to later Dorset types (see Fabric 1430). A south and east Dorset source seems likely.

Diagnostic sherds are rare in this ware. One bowl has been identified, but the most common form seems to be the tripod pitcher, identifiable mainly from footed bases. These have an unevenly applied glaze, pale or dark green in colour. Decoration is mainly incised or applied in linear designs. The illustrated example is a tubular spout, another typical feature of tripod pitchers.

Fabric 1350   Tripod Pitcher   **23**

ANG   *Other Anglo-Norman Glazed wares*

Several different fabrics have been grouped together as one Major Ware. These are described below. Fabric 1065, the glazed variety of Anglo-Norman Wessex Coarseware, is also included in this Major Ware. No specific source has been identified for any of these fabrics but they are most probably local, or from the Wessex area.

AGX   *Anglo-Norman Mixed Grit Glazed ware*

Fabric 1099	25 RP	916g	36 sherds

This is a hand-built sandy coarseware with moderate coarse-medium chalk, flint and quartz inclusions. Colours range from brown through red to grey. The lead glaze is dark green. There are few diagnostic sherds in this fabric. There is the complete profile of a jug with a ribbed neck.

Jug   **24**

AGX   *Anglo-Norman Mixed Grit Glazed ware*

Fabric 1663	34 RP	193g	13 sherds

This is a hand-built coarseware with inclusions of chalk, flint, quartz and iron. The fabric is brown or red in colour with a greenish clear lead glaze. No sherds are illustrated.

AGC   *Anglo-Norman Chalk-tempered Glazed ware*

Fabric 1720	0 RP	56g	6 sherds

This is a hand-built coarse fabric with abundant chalk inclusions that have been leached out, leaving vesicles in sherd surfaces. It is brown in colour with a dark green lead glaze. No sherds are illustrated here.

AGCI   *Anglo-Norman Glazed Coarseware with Iron*

Fabric 1084	47 RP	3851g	142 sherds

This is a hand-built coarse fabric with distinctive black iron inclusions, quartz and sparse chalk and flint. Colours range from buff to grey. The lead glaze is clear, pale or dark green. All sherds seem to be from jug-type vessels, of which the most complete examples are tripod pitchers. Two examples are illustrated and both of these vessels probably had rims that were added, or at least finished, on a turntable. Number **25** has a nascent collared rim, while there is a clear thickening at the neck of number **26**. The horizontal incised decoration on number **26** also suggests the use of a turntable. Other examples are decorated with combing and applied pellets.

Tripod Pitcher   **25, 26**

AGS   Anglo-Norman Glazed Sandy ware

Fabric 1063   20 RP   866g   21 sherds

A hand-built sandy ware with abundant fine quartz inclusions and some iron, this fabric is white-brown in colour with a green lead glaze.

A large part of the body of a jug or pitcher is illustrated here. This is decorated with horizontal incised lines and has a ribbed neck. The uneven thickness of the vessel wall indicates that this vessel was hand-built, but it is likely that the decoration was completed while it was being turned.

Pitcher   **27**

AGWW Anglo-Norman Glazed Whiteware

Fabric 1596   0 RP   44g   3 sherds

A hand-built fine sandy ware with moderate fine quartz inclusions and some fine iron, this fabric is relatively soft and white-grey in colour with a grey core. There are only three body sherds in this assemblage, all undecorated but with a pale green lead glaze. None are illustrated.

CWQH Hand-built Quartz-rich Coarseware

Fabric 1731   10 RP   79g   2 sherds

This is a coarse, sandy, hand-built redware with uneven clear glaze on a few non-diagnostic sherds.

High Medieval wares (c 1250 to c 1350)

Locally produced vessels of this period show a marked development in techniques of manufacture, glazing and firing. Use of the throwing wheel became widespread, giving rise to an increase in the variety of forms produced and a considerable advance in the quality of potting. Glazes were used with greater competence and understanding. Pots were better fired too, indicating improvements in kiln construction and firing control. These developments from the Anglo-Norman period were not, naturally, confined to south Hampshire and may be seen throughout England.

Two principal classes of pottery, coarse and sandy wares, have been identified for this period. Coarsewares, although different in many aspects, are clearly related to their Anglo-Norman predecessors, both in fabric and form. The most common high medieval coarseware

vessel is an unglazed jar/cooking pot. The sandy ware group includes most of the glazed vessels in a range of fabrics that is much finer than the preceding tripod pitcher types. Jugs remained the most common vessel type made in these glazed wares, although a far more extensive range of vessels was produced.

Coarsewares

Fifteen different high medieval local coarseware fabrics have been identified. Four of these have been grouped into three Major Wares. None of the remaining eleven occurs in significant quantities and so they have been grouped together as Other High Medieval Coarsewares. There is one other coarseware, Fabric 1726, which has granitic inclusions and is probably from Cornwall. Southampton-type wares are described first, followed by other local types then non-local fabrics. Fabrics are also ordered, within each of these categories, by quantity, with the most common types described first.

STCW Southampton Coarseware

Fabric 1024	630 RP	15295g	1312 sherds
Fabric 1123	3622	67145	4766

Southampton Coarseware represents 92% of the total sherd weight of all the High Medieval coarsewares. These products must have been constantly available in the town, suggesting that they were made within it, or close by. This is reflected in the Ware Name, which puts Southampton forward as a type-site. Two fabrics have been identified. Fabric 1123 is the standard type and Fabric 1024 is a sandy version.

Fabric 1123 is the definitive Southampton Coarseware fabric. It is made in a sandy clay which contains abundant medium chalk and flint inclusions with occasional organics and shell. This is usually well-fired and is red or brown in colour with a grey core. Some examples were fired grey or black. Vessels seem to have been thrown to a consistent, moderate thickness.

The most common form is the jar/cooking pot. These were made in a wide range of sizes but all retain the same basic shape. The rims of these vessels are very distinctive, featuring a bead around the inside edge (eg **28–37**). Jars/cooking pots were occasionally decorated with a horizontal band of thumb-impressions around the shoulder (**38, 39, 40**) while other vessels show vertical thumbing (**41**) or thumbed applied strips (**42**). One small vessel has a pouring lip (**43**), another a single horizontal handle (**44**). These features are the only evidence for the production of saucepans or pipkins in this ware. Bowls are a rare vessel type although one example is shown (**45**). One large jar/cooking pot was made into a lantern by cutting irregular star-shaped holes into the body before firing (**46**). Curfews were also made, and as with some jars/cooking pots, decorated with thumbing and applied strips (**47, 48, 49**).

Fabric 1024 is a finer version of Fabric 1123 and has the Ware Name Southampton Sandy Coarseware (STCS). It has abundant medium fine quartz and some chalk and flint. It is usually a warm red in colour with a pale grey core. The range of forms includes jars/cooking pots with the beaded rim observed in Fabric 1123 (**50, 51**). One example has an opposing pair of handles (**52**). Bowls are a common form and often have an internal clear lead glaze (**53, 54, 55**). Rare forms include a shell-lamp (**56**) and there are fragments of dripping pans (not illustrated). A few sherds have an external glaze but none of those is diagnostic and no Vessel Type can be identified from them. Indeed, it is not always apparent whether the glaze was deliberately applied.

Fabric 1123	Jar/cooking pot	**28–42**
	Pipkin	**43, 44**
	Bowl	**45**
	Lantern	**46**
	Curfew	**47–49**
Fabric 1024	Jar/cooking pot	**50, 51, 52**
	Bowl	**53, 54, 55**
	Lamp	**56**

STHC Southampton High Street Coarseware

| Fabric 1230 | 75 RP | 1979g | 120 sherds |

Fabric 1230 is a wheel-thrown coarseware with abundant medium quartz and moderate ill-sorted chalk and flint. Colours vary from brown to grey with a grey core. Plain jars/cooking pots and glazed jugs (**57**) were made in this fabric. The glaze has a green colour and is often thick and glossy. The form of the illustrated vessel has certain features, combed decoration and a twisted rod handle, which are reminiscent of Anglo-Norman tripod pitchers. Wasters of this type were found at the High Street site SOU 105, hence the Ware Name. Few sherds of this fabric have been recovered from other sites in Southampton, and it is possible that production was short-lived.

| Jug | 57 |

CSX Mixed Grit Coarse Sandy ware

| Fabric 1124 | 132 RP | 1949g | 268 sherds |

This is a wheel-thrown coarse sandy ware with abundant medium-fine quartz and fine chalk and flint with some iron. It is a relatively soft fabric, red or grey in colour with a grey core. No production site for this fabric has been identified, but the nature of the inclusions suggests a local source. Few diagnostic sherds are represented in this assemblage and none are illustrated. The common form is a plain jar/cooking pot and there is also a single sherd from a curfew.

CRNC Cornish Coarseware

| Fabric 1726 | 5 RP | 15g | 1 sherd |

This is a wheel-thrown coarseware with quartz, slate, granite and red iron inclusions in a hard-fired sandy matrix. It is red in colour with patches of grey on the surface. The range of inclusions suggests a Cornish source, although no parallel for the form has been established.

A single rim-sherd is present in this assemblage. This is from a bowl with a plain bevelled rim. It is not illustrated.

HMCW Other High Medieval Coarsewares

Fabrics 1028, 1032, 1033, 1061, 1185, 1503, 1546, 1549, 1592, 1608, 1650

| | 128 RP | 2251g | 140 sherds |

These eleven coarseware fabrics occur in small quantities. All are comparable with the local types described above in the range and quality of inclusions. Diagnostic sherds are rare for these types, thus hindering comparison with local products. Fabric 1061 has the typical inclusions of chalk and flint but is perhaps better characterised by the relatively good quality of the rich lead glaze. This was applied to the inside of the bowls and dripping pans that were made in this fabric.

| Fabric 1061 | Dripping pan | **58, 59, 60** |

Sandy wares

A total of 74 high medieval sandy wares have been identified in this assemblage. Two are Southampton wares, seven are local and five are non-local. Southampton-type fabrics are described first, followed by other local then non-local products. The most common types in each category are described first. The remaining 60 fabrics are of uncertain origin and occur in relatively insignificant quantities; of these, descriptions are given only for those fabrics for which there are illustrated examples.

STWW Southampton Whiteware

| Fabric 1044 | 510 RP | 11484g | 935 sherds |

Southampton Whiteware is a wheel-thrown sandy ware with abundant, well-sorted, fine-medium quartz and occasional fine, black iron. This fabric is well-fired to a buff-white colour. The glaze fits well and has a distinctive bright or dark green colour. This is a Major Ware.

This is the only high medieval sandy fabric that can be attributed to a known Southampton source. Wasters were recovered from the High Street site SOU 105 (Plate 1) and these represent the majority of the sherds present in this assemblage. Finds of this fabric are regularly made on excavations in the medieval town but rarely in very large quantities, evidence perhaps that pottery production on this site was short-lived.

The most common vessel type, among both the wasters and finished vessels found elsewhere, is the jug. These are all apparently similar in overall shape but a variety of rim forms have been identified (see p 120, Table 19). The most common is a ribbed, collared type (**61**, **62**), often with applied vertical strips (**62**). Applied spouts are common and plain strap handles typical, although some are thumbed (**66**). Bases are plain (**63**, **64**, **65**). Decoration most often takes the form of applied pellets that are triangular in cross-section and often occur in panels bounded by horizontal incised lines (**63**, **64**).

Other vessels in this fabric are dripping pans (**67**), small jars/cooking pots and what may be a lid (not illustrated).

Jug	61–66
Dripping pan	67

STS   *Southampton Sandy ware*

Fabric 1105	6 RP	675g	58 sherds
Fabric 1120	263	4524	412
Fabric 1150	764	18728	1701

Southampton Sandy ware is a Major Ware comprised of three related fabrics that have together been identified as varieties of the same Southampton product. This is a wheel-thrown redware made in a sandy clay that has characteristic abundant fine quartz and red iron. Fabric 1150 (STSW) is the standard and most common type. Fabric 1105, Southampton Organic-tempered Sandy ware (STOS) has the same character but also contains moderate organic inclusions. Fabric 1120, Southampton Coarse Sandy ware (STSC) is a coarse variety that contains sparse chalk and flint. Oxidised examples appear red-brown in colour with a bright red core but Fabric 1120 was occasionally reduced to a dark brown or grey.

This ware is identified as a Southampton product because of the quantities in which it occurs in this assemblage and also because the author has not observed the same fabrics at other centres in the region. It is also not of the highest quality – compared to many of the other sandy wares it is pottery poorly made from poor clay. A very local source, providing mainly for the Southampton market, therefore seems likely. This appears to have been a fragile product, often under-fired, and large vessel fragments are rarely recovered. As a result, few examples have been illustrated.

Jars/cooking pots were made in all three fabrics and one example in Fabric 1120 is shown (**68**). One example, not illustrated, has the beaded rim that is characteristic of Southampton coarseware (p 12). Dripping pans were also made (**71**).

Jugs were made in all three fabrics. These take a variety of forms, with sixteen different rim types being identified in a total sample of 45 (see p 120, Table 19). Jugs were often embellished with a pronounced thumbed applied strip around the neck. Bases were usually thumbed, in a variety of styles. Overall jug shapes do not seem to vary extensively, being mainly of the shouldered or rounded variety (**69**, **70**). This is the only Southampton or local ware which was commonly decorated with white slip-painted designs (**70**), usually in linear motifs that do not appear to have been very expertly executed. Other decorative styles include combed and incised lines. A clear lead glaze was usually applied sparingly, this appears brown over the rich red fabric, or takes on a greenish hue in slightly reduced examples.

Jar/cooking pot	68
Jug	69, 70
Dripping pan	71

SHR   *South Hampshire Redware*

Fabric 1066	42 RP	2571g	194 sherds
Fabric 1248	972	28368	1671

South Hampshire Redware is a Major Ware. It is a wheel-thrown sandy ware with abundant coarse or fine quartz and red and black iron. It is usually well-fired to a pink, pink-red or red-brown colour, usually with a grey core, and sometimes reduced to a surface colour of pale grey. A clear lead glaze was commonly used, although copper-green and reduced green colours are also in evidence. Fabric 1248 is the standard type and Fabric 1066 a coarse version, with larger quartz inclusions. A similar range of vessels seems to have been made in both fabrics.

South Hampshire Redware vessels have been observed in assemblages at Portsmouth (Fox and Barton 1986: Fig 31, 1; Fig 35, 1; Fig 37, 1), Romsey (personal observation) and Winchester (Collis 1978, Fig 53, 19–23), hence the name applied to it here. At present, this Ware Name is applied only in Southampton. The location of the kilns is not known, but these products were distributed in large quantities over a wide area and this was obviously a successful and well-established industry.

Jugs are the most common vessel type. Forms include tall balusters (72–75), pear-shaped (76) and tripod (80) jugs and a two-handled pitcher (79). A wide variety of rim, handle and base forms have been distinguished, within a relatively large sample that comprises 36 rims, 39 handles and 40 bases in a total of 1,865 sherds. This is an indication of the extent of production. Decorative styles are mainly confined to incised and applied clay linear motifs but applied designs are also represented (80–85), the most elaborate being anthropomorphic faces (84, 85). Similar designs have been found in this fabric in other Southampton assemblages (Platt and Coleman-Smith, 1975, illustration numbers 462, 497) and at Romsey and Winchester (Collis 1978, Fig 51, 11). Plain rod handles are typical, but straps (77) and stabbed rods (86) are also known.

A wide variety of other vessels was also produced including bowls (none illustrated), pipkins, costrels and dripping pans.

Jug	72–86
Pipkin	87–90
Dripping pan	91–93
Costrel	94

LOPS   Local Pink Sandy ware

Fabric 1087	501 RP	10,368g	686 sherds
Fabric 1107	59 RP	3690	341

This Major Ware is a wheel-thrown sandy ware with abundant fine quartz and moderate red iron, well-fired to a consistent pink colour. Glazes are clear or made dark green through the addition of copper.

Fabric 1087, the most common variety, has medium-sized sand inclusions in contrast to Fabric 1107, which is finer. This ware is comparable to South Hampshire Redware and may be related. It cannot be attributed to any known production site.

A variety of jugs may be identified among the sherds of this ware, including a small jug or mug (95), rounded types (96), and a face jug (100). The variety of forms is reflected in the range of rims, where twelve different types have been identified from a total sample of nineteen. Applied decoration is common and white-painted and iron-rich, dark brown examples are both present. Rod and strap handles are both produced, the latter sometimes having thumbing (97).

Other vessel types include bowls and dripping pans.

There are also jars/cooking pots, some with pulled lips, which may suggest that they were pipkins (102).

Jug	95–100
Bowl	101
Jar/cooking pot	102
Dripping pan	103

LV   Laverstock Wares

Fabric 1034	145 RP	4156g	311 sherds
Fabric 1053	211	2637	196

Kilns at Laverstock, near Salisbury, were excavated in 1968 (Musty *et al* 1969) and provided evidence of an industry which produced jars/cooking pots and plain and highly decorated jugs. Two glazed Laverstock fabrics have been identified after comparison with samples from the kiln site and from excavations in Salisbury (the latter kindly provided by Lorraine Mepham of Wessex Archaeology). No fabrics similar to Laverstock coarsewares have been identified. Both Laverstock fabrics are combined into one Major Ware.

Fabric 1034 is a wheel-thrown sandy ware containing abundant, well-sorted, medium-fine quartz with some iron. This fabric appears evenly fired, usually to a buff or buff-pink colour and glazes are usually translucent or a medium copper-green in colour.

Fabric 1053 is finer, corresponding to Fabric E421 in the Wessex Archaeology fabric series. This is a wheel-thrown, fine sandy fabric with a smooth matrix containing fine quartz and some red iron. The fabric seems softer than other sandy wares and has a consistent orange-red colour. Lead glazes are clear, or range from pale to dark green, through the addition of copper.

The most common vessel is the jug, which is present in a variety of forms. The most frequently occurring diagnostic sherd type is the rim, of which several different types are in evidence. Incised and self-coloured applied decoration occurs most frequently, in an extensive range of linear motifs, with applied clay pellets also common (105, 106). The highly decorated forms seen among the kiln material are largely absent from this assemblage, although a few sherds are adorned with brown applied strips and one example, in Fabric 1034, has a brown floral motif (108). A single pipkin handle (not illustrated) is the only evidence in this assemblage for the use of other vessel types in Fabric 1034. Bowls (not illustrated) and a moneybox (109) also occur in Fabric 1053.

Jug	104–108
Moneybox	109

LOWW Local Whiteware

Fabric 1118   150 RP   3120g   219 sherds

This Major Ware is a wheel-thrown sandy ware with abundant medium to fine quartz, white clay pellets and sparse fine black iron. This is a well-fired fabric, usually white or buff-white in colour. Glazes are usually pale green, perhaps from the addition of copper, or clear. The source of this product is unknown.

Diagnostic sherds, rare overall, are mainly from jugs. There are six rims, two spouts, eight handles and four bases in a total of 219 sherds. Incised lines and pellets were used in decoration and there is one slashed strap handle (**110**). Jug forms include balusters (**111**) rounded (**112**) and tripod jugs. A lamp is also illustrated (**113**). Other forms, not illustrated, include a socketed handle from a saucepan or dripping pan, small bowls, and a rim sherd from a possible lid.

Jug	**110, 111, 112**
Lamp	**113**

LOWF Local Fine Whiteware

Fabric 1215   57 RP   1478g   157 sherds

This is a Major Ware. It is a wheel-thrown sandy ware that contains fine quartz in a soft fine white-firing matrix that is white or buff-white in colour. Glazes are usually pale copper-green. No production site has been identified for this fabric, which is not very well represented in this assemblage.

Most sherds appear to have come from jugs, but there are just five rims, three handles and four bases. Vessels were decorated with incised and applied linear designs. The only illustrated jug sherd is a collared rim similar to Southampton Whiteware types (**114**). A small lamp in this fabric is also shown (**115**).

Jug	**114**
Lamp	**115**

DOQS Dorset Quartz-rich Sandy ware

Fabric 1430	111 RP	1649g	91 sherds
Fabric 1445	21	69	1
Fabric 1729	25	277	40

Dorset Quartz-rich Sandy ware is a Major Ware. All fabrics are wheel-thrown sandy types with abundant rounded quartz inclusions in a clean hard-firing matrix, they all share the same Ware Name. Fabric 1430 is the standard type, while Fabric 1445 is a coarse version with large quartz inclusions, represented only as the complete profile of a small hemispherical bowl (**118**) and Fabric 1729 is a fine variant containing smaller quartz grains. This ware may be related to the Anglo-Norman Dorset Sandy ware described above as they both contain quartz of a similar character, in comparable quantities. Examples of the same fabric have been observed at Poole and identified as Dorset Red-Painted ware and applied-strip ware (Jarvis, 1992, 64). A few red-painted sherds occur in this assemblage, although none has applied-strip decoration. Overall, however, plain sherds are more common. A new Ware Name is suggested here, which reflects its Dorset source. The kiln site may have been located close to the western fringes of the New Forest.

Both jugs and jars/cooking pots occur in this ware, although no complete profiles of either type are present. Jars/cooking pots were made with a characteristic thick, square rim, quite unlike local forms. Jugs have a squared simple rim profile (**116**) and thumbed bases (**117**). Vessels were rarely decorated, although they may exhibit fine striations reminiscent of scratch-marking. These, however, may simply have resulted accidentally from the manufacturing process, where inclusions dragged in the surface of the clay, either during throwing or subsequent surface treatment, such as fettling. The majority of examples are unglazed, and a clear lead glaze is present on only three examples. Four sherds have red-painted decoration in the Dorset tradition recognised not only at Poole but also at Christchurch (Jarvis 1983).

Jug	**116, 117**
Bowl	**118**

DOWW Dorset Whiteware

Fabric 1156   139 RP   3231g   142 sherds

This Major Ware is a distinctive wheel-thrown, well-fired fabric with occasional angular quartz fragments in a clean, smooth clay matrix. Sherds usually have white surfaces with white or pinkish cores. Glazes vary in colour from bright copper-green to clear, with the latter appearing yellow over the white fabric. The smooth clay of this fabric is quite different from the majority of the sandy wares that are presumed to have been made in or close to Southampton. This fabric has been observed at Poole (Jarvis 1992, 64; Fabrics 4 and 5; Barton et al 1992, No. 650, 651) and a Dorset source is suggested.

Jugs are the only Vessel Type identified in Dorset Whiteware in this assemblage. One almost complete example (**121**) is a rounded type with a narrow neck, a wide belly and a thumbed base. It is decorated with dark brown applied-strips and pellets that contrast with the bright yellow appearance of the clear lead glaze. This decorative technique is relatively common on this ware, and can be found on a further 41 sherds out of a total of 78 (**122**), excluding the complete vessel. The remaining examples have green (**119**) or clear glazes. Diagnostic sherds are rare, but both simple (**120**) and collared (**119**) rims occur with rod and strap handles, in which stabbing is common. It is present for instance on all the illustrated examples.

Jug	**119–122**

MIDL *Midlands Ware*

Fabric 1078	30 RP	214g	1 sherd

A wheel-thrown, hard-fired sandy fabric with sparse quartz inclusions. Red-brown in colour with a dark grey core and covered with a rich dark green glaze.

One rim/handle sherd of this fabric is present in this assemblage, from a large, heavily made jug with a complex rim. The handle is a broad thick strap with thumbed ridges. A source in the Midlands, perhaps close to Coventry, has been suggested by R Thomson (*pers comm*) on the basis of the form as well as the fabric.

Jug	**123**

SCRB *Scarborough-type ware*

Fabric 1526	10 RP	494g	18 sherds

A wheel-thrown pink fine sandy fabric covered in a rich dark green glaze.

The development and distribution of this ware is well attested (Farmer and Farmer 1982). There are eighteen sherds in this assemblage including two handles and fragments of a knight jug.

Jug	**124–127**

HAM *Ham Green ware*

Fabric 1778	No stratified sherds.

A wheel-thrown sandy ware with fine quartz and clay inclusions, this fabric is buff-brown in colour with a grey core and has a pale green glaze.

The medieval kilns at Ham Green, near Bristol, and their products have been well-researched (Barton 1963a, 1967). In this assemblage, sherds of a single jug in this fabric have been identified after comparison with kiln material at the British Museum National Reference Collection (courtesy B Nenk). This vessel had a ribbed neck and a handle joined to the body by heavy thumbing. These sherds are unstratified and therefore not included in the quantification analysis discussed below. They are added to this catalogue simply to point up the presence of Bristol products in Southampton.

Jug	**128**

CRNS *Cornish Sandy ware*

Fabric 1761	0 RP	41g	4 sherds

This wheel-thrown sandy ware has abundant white mica, quartz and slate inclusions that suggest a south-western English source and Cornwall is perhaps the most likely region. It is pale brown-red in colour with spots of greenish clear lead glaze. Four body sherds are present in this assemblage, probably from a jug.

HMS *High Medieval Sandy wares*

61 Fabrics	310 RP	10,596g	723 sherds

A wide variety of other high medieval sandy wares have been identified, numbering 60 different fabrics. None of them occurred in quantities comparable with the Major Wares described above, nor can they be attributed to known production sites or areas. Most exhibit the fabric characteristics previously observed in local products, having inclusions of quartz and iron of varying quality and quantity and may very well be of local origin. This cannot be ascertained as diagnostic sherds are few and they have been grouped together here in a miscellaneous category. Those fabrics represented in the drawn catalogue are described below. Three illustrated vessels (**132, 133, 134**) were badly burnt during or after breakage and deposition, rendering the fabric unidentifiable. These are also likely to be of local origin but have been given the general Fabric Number 1740. Those fabrics for which there are illustrated examples are described below.

HMSF *High Medieval Sandy ware with Flint*

Fabric 1209	18 RP	383g	5 sherds

A red-firing sandy ware with ill-sorted quartz inclusions, some iron and sparse moderate angular flint, this fabric occurs as a tubular-handled saucepan of probable mid-13th century date.

Saucepan	**129**

HOS *High Medieval Sandy ware with Organics*

Fabric 1534	0 RP	308g	1 sherd

A buff-coloured sandy ware with fine quartz and iron inclusions and moderate medium and fine organics, this is most likely a local product. The only vessel represented is a lamp.

Lamp	**130**

HSMR *High Medieval Micaceous Sandy Redware*

Fabric 1533	0 RP	306g	12 sherds

This is a sandy redware with fine quartz and iron inclusions and abundant fine white mica visible on the surface. The mica is uncharacteristic of local products, as is the sinuous profile of the decorated jug in this ware and a non-local source, perhaps west of Southampton, is likely.

Jug   131

BRNT   Burnt pottery

Fabric 1740   68 RP   2470g   115 sherds

This group includes pieces that have been so badly burnt that it is impossible to identify the fabric. Because several fabrics and traditions are included in this group it has not been categorised as a Major Ware.

Three vessels in burnt High Medieval Sandy ware are shown here. One (**132**) is a highly decorated jug with a strap handle and applied rods that have zoomorphic rim terminals. The neck and body is decorated with an applied clay design incorporating pellets and linear motifs. There is a pronounced pedestal base with neat, overlapping, thumbing. Another, similar base, from the same deposit is also shown (**133**). In both cases the sandy fabric has been burnt to a bright red. At least one similar vessel, with applied rods and linear decoration, was recovered at Faccombe Netherton, on the north Hampshire border (Fairbrother 1990, vol 2, fig 8.60, 438) and these vessels may well be examples of South Hampshire Redware.

The second burnt vessel illustrated is a small divided bowl in a sandy fabric that is grey throughout (**134**).

Jug   132, 133
Divided Bowl   134

Late medieval wares (c 1350–early 16th century)

Considerable differences can be discerned between the local wares of the late medieval period and those that preceded them. By around 1420 it appears that all the common high medieval products, both coarse and sandy wares, had been replaced by a range of uniformly plain, utilitarian products. The chronology and mechanisms of these changes are hard to establish. In Southampton, archaeological deposits that can be dated with certainty to the late-14th century are rare and tend to be of slight ceramic content (see below). The evidence from Southampton suggests that the production centres of the preceding period went into decline and had finally ceased functioning by the end of the 14th century. The archaeological evidence of the mid- to late-15th century is far more informative, and deposits of this period contain a completely different range of ceramics. It is these new products that are described below.

Southampton and local products of this period can-not be divided into coarse and sandy ware types. A major distinction between the industries of this period and those of the preceding centuries would seem to be that a wide variety of vessel types were produced in the same type of fabric, whereas, previously, jars/cooking pots were made mainly in coarsewares, and jugs in sandy wares. There are two principal wares, Southampton Organic-tempered Sandy, and Late Medieval Well-fired Sandy. Other local sandy fabrics, similar in character but indeterminate in form, are present in this period, but in insufficient quantities to warrant full description here. A similar range of vessels was produced in both wares, although there is greater variety in Late Medieval Well-fired Sandy ware.

The utilitarian character of these local products is emphasised by the refinement of Tudor Green ware, the most common non-local pottery of this period. A related fabric, but far less common in Southampton, is Surrey Whiteware.

These Surrey products are the only late medieval non-local English wares that have been identified in this assemblage.

Local wares

STOS   Southampton Organic-tempered Sandy ware

Fabric 1130   358 RP   7646g   335 sherds
Fabric 1136   419   12609   409

A wheel-thrown quartz-rich sandy redware characterised by the abundant presence of organic inclusions. Sherds are usually red-brown in colour and have a grey core, many examples appear to have been under-fired. Fabric 1130 (STOC: Coarse Southampton Organic-tempered Sandy ware) has relatively coarse inclusions and occasional chalk or flint. Fabric 1136 (STOS) is the standard sandy version and has fine inclusions.

Cooking pots or jars were made in this ware (**135, 136**) but jug or pitcher types appear to be more common. A thin lead glaze, generally greenish-clear, probably as a result of slightly reduced firing conditions, occurs on the inside of bowls or on the neck and belly of jugs and pitchers. The use of galena is evidenced by the survival of lead pellets on the surfaces of some sherds. Decoration is rare, and confined mainly to incised lines around the rims or shoulders of closed vessels (**137**). The typical broad strap handles are frequently stabbed (**137, 139**), or have incised decoration (**140**). Jug and pitcher bases are thumbed, usually in a close, sometimes overlapping style (**140**). One example has applied feet (**142**). There are also dripping pans (**141**).

This fabric is similar to Southampton Sandy ware, which is a high medieval product, suggesting that probably it was made in, or close to the medieval town. It appears not to have been distributed very widely outside the Southampton area and seems to have been a localised industry, unrelated to the types that comprise the bulk of the late medieval assemblage.

Cooking pot/jar	135, 136
Jug	137, 138, 139
Bunghole pitcher	140
Dripping pan	141
Jar/pan	142

LWFS   *Late Medieval Well-fired Sandy wares*

Fabric 1027	106 RP	573g	36 sherds
Fabric 1110	342	3725	111
Fabric 1115	222	5647	206
Fabric 1133	579	11193	294
Fabric 1161	306	4133	136
Fabric 1170	31	424	15
Fabric 1203	148	2209	71
Fabric 1263	157	4151	138
Fabric 1264	332	6144	144
Fabric 1356	116	1970	58
Fabric 1359	21	660	45
Fabric 1365	200	6354	130
Fabric 1381	41	174	15
Fabric 1496	4	228	13
Fabric 1524	0	19	5
Fabric 1574	7	686	21
Fabric 1577	17	77	5
Fabric 1607	160	765	25
Fabric 1633	69	2513	53
Fabric 1643	48	2496	154
Fabric 1648	15	136	14
Fabric 1651	0	18	2
Fabric 1694	5	109	5
Fabric 2018	24	12580	891
Total	**2950**	**66984**	**2587**

Twenty-three fabrics have been grouped together as Late Medieval Well-fired Sandy ware. Despite the variations in the nature of their inclusions these fabrics are all related by aspects of technique and form and are taken to represent a single ceramic industry, although the production centres may not have been closely concentrated. These are wheel-thrown fabrics with a range of inclusions that comprises quartz, flint, chalk, iron and organics, in sandy matrices of varying character. Different fabrics may not contain all of those inclusions and the quality and quantity of them is also variable, but they are all clearly part of the same tradition of pottery making and all have attributes that suggest a local source. They are all redwares, although some vessels were deliberately reduced to a black finish. Overall colours vary from red through brown, to black, but the colour is often consistent on each vessel. Nearly every sherd has a sandwich effect at the core, usually grey in the middle with red at the margins, and the reverse in reduced examples, which may result from the high firing temperature, for these types are characterised by their hardness. They all seem to be fired to a degree not apparent in any of the preceding local fabrics, and the clay is occasionally almost vitrified, although it is doubtful whether the clay could have withstood much higher temperatures.

The range of vessels is extensive and includes cooking pots, jars, pipkins, bowls, jugs or pitchers, bung-hole pitchers and dripping pans. Unusual forms include a lid (Fabric 1027, **162**) a watering pot (Fabric 1607, **163**) and a rectangular-shaped cistern represented by base fragments (**161**). All these vessels share characteristics of form and manufacture. Many vessels were wiped or knife-trimmed after throwing (see wiped wares in Brown 1986). Lead glazes were used sparingly, internally in bowls and pipkins or as a bib on pitchers and are generally clear. On reduced vessels the glaze often has a greenish appearance, while on oxidised pots it has a warm brown colour. Decoration is limited, mainly confined to incised wavy lines on bowls or pitchers (**160**) or thinly painted white slip bands. These wares have little in common with the local products of the High Medieval period and may best be viewed as forerunners of the post-medieval redware industries (Fabrics 1523, 1532 below).

Late Medieval Well-fired Sandy ware fabrics were probably made at a number of centres. Similar fabrics have been observed in Dorset (Jarvis, 1992), Portsmouth (Barton and Fox, 1986) and Sussex (Barton, 1979, 55), while Fabrics 1027 and 1161 have been observed to be comparable to material from the kiln at Knighton on the Isle of Wight (personal observation; Fennelly, L R, 1969). Although several different fabrics have been distinguished in this group, none of them has inclusions that indicate a specific source. In terms of technique and form these wares clearly represent a tradition that prevailed over a wide area of the south.

If these wares were indeed the predecessors of the post-medieval sandy wares then it is likely that some of them were made at the same production centres, such as those around Bishop's Waltham and Fareham. A more detailed study of fabrics and potting techniques might confirm this.

Illustrations are grouped by vessel type rather than in Fabric Number order.

Jar/cooking pot	143–146
Pipkin	147
Skillet	148
Dripping pan	149, 150
Bowl/pan	151–153
Pancheon	154–159
Jug	160
Cistern/jar	161
Lid	162
Watering pot	163

LMS   Other Late Medieval Sandy wares

52 Fabrics   348 RP   8334g   583 sherds

A further 52 fabrics have been identified as local late medieval products. These conform to the pattern of the local drift geology, do not fit with either of the two Ware Types described above and are present in relatively insignificant quantities. None can be attributed to known centres of production. A further Fabric Type in this category has been given to burnt sherds that are clearly of late medieval sandy type but which cannot be identified as any specific fabric.

The few diagnostic sherds present among these fabrics suggest that the range of vessel types and forms is similar to those in Late Medieval Well-fired Sandy ware. No examples are illustrated here.

Non-local wares

SRWW Surrey Whiteware

Fabric 1092   77 RP   818g   69 sherds

A wheel-thrown whiteware with moderate medium-coarse rounded quartz inclusions and red iron. Vessels may have a copper-green lead glaze. This fabric originated from kilns situated around Farnham, on the Hampshire/Surrey border. In London this fabric is known as 'coarse border ware' (Pearce and Vince 1988).

Diagnostic sherds are principally from cooking pots and there is one example of the common form of lid-seated rim (not illustrated, see Pearce and Vince 1988, No. 476). Jugs are represented by one plain rim, a base (164) and a stabbed rod handle. There is also a fragment of candlestick (165). This is a small, hollow, wheel-thrown cylinder with a partial dark green glaze, resembling forms seen in later Surrey Whiteware, or 'Border ware' (Pearce 1992).

Jug	164
Candlestick	165

TDG   Tudor Green ware

Fabric 1193   574 RP   1579g   291 sherds

A wheel-thrown fine whiteware, often thrown very thin and covered in a rich, bright green glaze. This fabric was also made around the Hampshire/Surrey border (Holling 1977) and is a common find in late medieval assemblages all over the south. The extent of the area in which Tudor Green ware was made has previously been the subject of some debate. The Farnham kiln complex is a certain source (Holling 1971) but potteries at Cheam and Kingston were also producing a similar product (Pearce and Vince 1988, Hinton 1980). Farnham is the known source closest to Southampton and perhaps therefore the most likely.

Jugs and cups are the most common forms here. Jugs (166–168) are small and plain. These were possibly used for drinking rather than serving and have been described as drinking jugs (Pearce 1992) although the term mug would be equally accurate. Flared (169), pedestal (170, 171) and waisted (173, 174) cups are all present. There are also lobed cups, some of which have a clear glaze on the inside, giving a yellow colour that contrasts with the green of the outside. Parallels for these forms may be seen in London (Pearce and Vince 1988).

Other forms shown include a cup with a tiny ring-handle (175) and a small tubular spouted vessel (176), perhaps a fragment of a puzzle-jug.

Jug	166, 167, 168
Cup	169–175
Spouted vessel	176

The post-medieval period (after c 1550)

Although it is not the intention here to analyse the ceramics of this period in detail it is worth introducing the principal post-medieval local wares as a means of placing the preceding periods into context.

By the end of the 16th century potteries were producing large quantities of wares in a great variety of forms that were distributed over a very wide area. However, this does not mark the end of the medieval potting tradition in the south. The scale of production and distribution may have increased far beyond the limits of the medieval period but lead-glazed earthenwares were products that remained rooted in the traditions of the preceding centuries. The essence of the medieval earthenware tradition thus survived as long as these wares were produced, and at Verwood production continued into the 20th century (Algar *et al* 1979).

There are two main types of local pottery in this period, redwares, and Verwood-type ware. Both, and especially the sandy wares, may be seen to have developed out of the Well-fired Sandy ware tradition of the late medieval period.

PMR   *Post-medieval Redware*

| Fabric 1523 | 385 RP | 8469g | 326 sherds |
| Fabric 1532 | 295 | 6411 | 337 |

Post-medieval Redware was made from a red-firing sandy clay containing abundant quartz and iron inclusions. Fabric 1523 is an oxidised variety with red-brown surfaces and a bright red core. A thick, clear lead glaze produces a lustrous red-orange finish. Fabric 1532 is reduced and has a grey surface colour that gives the clear lead glaze a greenish colour. Similarities of fabric and form suggest that both types were probably made at the same production sites. Post-medieval Redware represents a widespread post-medieval tradition in the south of England. Local production sites were located in the area around Bishop's Waltham and Fareham in Hampshire and supplied pottery to markets at Winchester and Guildford from the 16th to the 19th centuries. The range of vessel types present here includes jars/cooking pots, pipkins, bowls, pancheons, jugs, pitchers and chafing dishes.

VER   *Verwood-type ware*

| Fabric 1326 | 473 RP | 9995g | 294 sherds |

Verwood is a village near Ringwood, just inside Dorset on the fringes of the New Forest. The industry has medieval origins, but many kilns were established in this area in the post-medieval period and their products are among the most frequent 17th- and 18th-century earthenware finds in Southampton. The most common fabric is a whiteware with well-sorted fine quartz inclusions, usually with an excellent pale greenish-yellow glaze. Redwares and darker green, brown and yellow glazes were also produced.

The pottery is very well-made in what appears to have been superb potting clay. The range of forms is immense, as one might expect from an industry that flourished for over four centuries. Bowls, bushel pans, chamber pots, costrels, jars, jugs and pancheons are all common. Many of these forms clearly developed out of the late medieval local tradition.

French wares

French medieval pottery has been found in rich variety and great quantity in Southampton (Platt and Coleman-Smith 1975) and it is now possible to provenance much of this material with greater certainty. Thirty-six different wares have been identified as French, 22 of which can be attributed to known traditions or production areas. The remaining fourteen fabrics, representing 4% of the total number of French sherds in this assemblage cannot be ascribed any more specific source. There are two main source areas for the French pottery in this assemblage. In the Anglo-Norman and late medieval periods the greater proportion of French wares came from the north, principally the area of the old dukedom of Normandy. In the high medieval period nearly all the French pottery that came to Southampton was made in Saintonge. Pottery from other areas of France has also been identified although it is relatively rare.

The pre-Conquest period

A few residual sherds of 10th- or 11th-century French wares are present in this assemblage, principally red-painted Beauvaisis-type wares and North French white and black wares (Brown 1995). Both these types are considered to be 10th-century imports into Southampton. They are generally quite different in form from their post-Conquest counterparts. Beauvaisis wares mainly take the form of tubular-spouted pitchers. This form is not common in later North French imported wares, although the use of red paint continued. North French white and black wares took the form of jars, with a distinctive lid-seated rim, that seems to have developed out of Gallo-Roman potting traditions and is rarely paralleled in later North French products.

The Anglo-Norman period

In common with the material of the late Saxon period, nearly all the post-Conquest period French pottery in this assemblage has been identified as originating from Normandy. Much of this material, however, especially the highly decorated Rouen-type ware, is quite different from the French pottery coming into 10th-century Southampton. Glaze is used with expert freedom accompanied by such decorative techniques as slip-painted, rouletted, applied clay and incised lines. These techniques are manifested in jugs or pitchers that are quite unlike anything seen in Southampton before. The same is true of the early Saintonge ware that is also described here.

NOG   Normandy Gritty ware

Fabric 1152	6 RP	222g	22 sherds
Fabric 1284	155	4704	311
Fabric 1286	0	90	17
Fabric 1551	0	53	6

Normandy Gritty ware is a wheel-thrown, hard-fired white fabric characterised by frequent coarse angular and sub-angular quartz inclusions. A number of variants have been identified. Normandy Gritty ware has probable pre-Conquest origins, and sherds of similar fabric and form occur in the late Saxon assemblage in Southampton (Brown 1995). Although it may now be seen that varieties of Normandy Gritty ware continued to be produced into the 15th century, and are perhaps related to Normandy Stoneware (see below p 29), the occurrence of these types in Southampton is concentrated in the Anglo-Norman period. Late Medieval types are present in this assemblage, but there appears to be a period, perhaps beginning in the late-13th century, and certainly running through the 14th century, when Normandy Gritty types are as good as absent from Southampton assemblages.

If Normandy Stoneware is descended from Normandy Gritty ware, then a shared source area, around the Cotentin peninsula, seems likely. However, a 10th-century kiln producing material similar to Normandy Gritty ware has been located at Trans, near St Malo, some distance from the Cotentin (Jennings 1981). This demonstrates both the early origins and the geographical extent of the Normandy Gritty ware tradition.

A variety of Fabric Types have been identified in Southampton.

Fabric 1284 is the classic type and the most common fabric in this ware. This is usually buff-white or cream in colour, with a white or grey-white core. It is hard-fired and characterised by the abundant presence of large angular and sub-angular white quartz inclusions. The predominant vessel type is a large, heavily constructed pitcher, with a thick rim, open spout, broad girth and sagging base (eg Platt and Coleman-Smith 1975, Nos 875, 878). A single example in this assemblage, perhaps an early form, has a tubular spout as well as the characteristic square-sectioned rim (177). Handles are wide straps, usually with a thumbed applied strip running vertically down the centre (eg Platt and Coleman-Smith 1975, No. 878). These are big vessels with thick walls and not a great deal of delicacy. Decoration commonly takes the form of vertical thumbed applied strips (178) or a horizontal rouletted band at the shoulder (eg Platt and Coleman-Smith 1975, No. 876).

Fourteen body sherds of Normandy Gritty ware are decorated with red paint.

Fabric 1152, Reduced Normandy Gritty ware (NOGD), is a grey, deliberately reduced version of the classic type, containing the same characteristic coarse quartz grains. It is often finer however, usually found in the form of smaller vessels than the large pitchers described above. Jars/cooking pots appear to be the common form (Platt and Coleman-Smith 1975, No. 871). There are only a few sherds of Reduced Normandy Gritty ware in this assemblage. Fragments of spouts and handles indicate that jugs or pitchers were also made in this fabric.

Fabric 1286, Normandy Smooth ware (NOGS), has an identical clay matrix but fewer of the typical quartz grains. Its presence in this assemblage is confined to a few undiagnostic body sherds. This fabric is worth noting here as a variant of the Normandy Gritty ware tradition, and one which develops significantly in the late medieval period.

Fabric 1551 is an orange-coloured Normandy Gritty ware variant (NOGO). This too is relatively fine in texture but contains the characteristic quartz inclusions and has a comparable smooth clay matrix. The colour may result from under-firing. There are no diagnostic sherds in this assemblage, but body sherds have pronounced throwing rings, a feature of all Normandy Gritty ware vessels.

Fabric 1284	Pitcher		**177, 178**

NFG   North French Glazed wares

Fabric 1128	0 RP	18g	3 sherds
Fabric 1166	44	113	28
Fabric 1200	10	748	71
Fabric 1233	0	103	4
Fabric 1277	0	277	8
Fabric 1278	41	206	43
Fabric 1281	12	53	3
Fabric 1283	2	138	13
Fabric 1288	17	101	6
Fabric 1404	0	45	1
Fabric 1708	4	22	4
Fabric 1759	0	93	2

This is a broad category that includes a variety of fabrics, some of which occur in very small quantities in this assemblage. They are all wheel-thrown, fine whitewares, often with sparse quartz grains and sometimes with red iron. Glazes may be clear or coloured with copper to become bright or dark green.

Diagnostic sherds are few and only five are illustrated here. The common form is a jug, usually with no spout and with a rod handle. Decoration is usually incised (**181, 182**) or applied and rouletted. Comparison with more complete examples from Southampton (Platt and Coleman-Smith 1975, Nos. 943, 991) shows other typical characteristics to be ribbed necks, eared handles (**180**) and bases with cordons (**183**).

These fabrics, vessel forms and decorative styles compare well with types identified as North French elsewhere. In Exeter, Allan distinguished several different types within this class (Allan 1984, 21). The fabrics grouped together here fall broadly within his types ii, iv and vi. Allan describes all these fabrics as glazed fine whitewares, and as such they constitute a recognised North French tradition, known in London as 'North French Monochrome' ware (Vince 1985, 47). In recognition of the tradition they represent, all the different fabrics in this ware have been grouped together with Rouen-type ware into one Major Ware, North French Glazed. A Seine valley source, centred on Rouen, is considered to be most likely, although Dunning suggested a Beauvais provenance for some glazed wares (Dunning 1954).

Fabric 1281	Jug	179
Fabric 1200	Jug	**180, 181, 182**
Fabric 1277	Jug	**183**
Fabric 1404	Jug	**184**

RON Rouen-type ware

| Fabric 1402 | 60 RP | 286g | 50 sherds |

A wheel-thrown fine sandy ware, usually buff-coloured and well fired. Rouen is a type-site rather than the certain site of production for this ware (Barton 1966), although a Seine Valley source is most likely.

Highly decorated jugs are the characteristic vessel. These show some of the elements seen in the 'monochrome' glazed vessels described above including a ribbed neck, an eared rod-handle and a cordon at the vessel base. The decoration usually takes the form of red slipped panels defined by rouletted applied strips and often studded with applied pellets. These decorative features, rather than the unremarkable fabric in which they appear, define this Norman tradition.

Fabric 1402 is in the 'standard' Rouen fabric dated in London to the late-12th to mid-13th centuries (Vince 1985, 43–50). No large sherds of this type are present in this assemblage and none are illustrated here. Fine examples from Southampton have been published before (Platt and Coleman-Smith 1975, Nos. 971, 977). A developed Rouen-type ware, Fabric 1403, has also been identified. This occurs in late-13th century deposits and is described below (p 24).

NFRP North French Red-painted ware

Fabric 1285	0 RP	18g	4 sherds
Fabric 1517	23	63	4
Fabric 1580	0	53	7

These fabrics presumably descended from the long tradition of northern French red slip-painted pottery seen in the pre-Conquest Beauvais wares, and this style is common also in Paris (Nicourt 1989). A Norman source is considered to be most likely for these types however.

They are fine wheel-thrown whitewares with varying quantities of quartz inclusions. Very few sherds occur in this assemblage, and no specific decorative motifs can be discerned. Other sources suggest that vessels in this fabric were jars or cooking pots (*ibid*). No examples are illustrated here.

NFS North French Sandy ware

| Fabric 1413 | 54 RP | 362g | 16 sherds |

This is an unglazed sandy ware, white or grey in colour, with abundant fine quartz contained in a fine sandy clay matrix.

The complete profile of a wheel-thrown cooking pot is present in this assemblage (**185**). A North French source is suggested by the rim form, which is paralleled in jars/cooking pots in Reduced Normandy Gritty ware (Fabric 1152, above). It occurs in a group dated to the mid-13th century, when wheel-thrown jars/cooking pots were not in production locally.

| Jar/Cooking pot | **185** |

SOE Early Saintonge ware

| Fabric 1269 | 0 RP | 82g | 2 sherds |

There are two sherds of a relatively soft, pink, slightly micaceous smooth fabric with occasional fragments of coarse white quartz. Both have a pale green lead glaze. One sherd (**186**) is an applied jug spout from an early to mid-13th century garderobe deposit at the castle (see below Chapter 7). The other (not illustrated) is a body sherd with a thumbed applied strip from the 12th-century castle rampart (site SOU 29). Both the fabric and the form of the spout compare well with later Saintonge products (see below) and the stratigraphic evidence suggests an early date. This fabric is therefore identified as Early Saintonge ware, an unusual find in England but perhaps not unexpected in Southampton, where Saintonge pottery is very common in the high medieval period.

| Jug | **186** |

The high medieval period

In the second half of the 13th century the importation of North French types declined and Saintonge wares became the most common continental import into Southampton. Other high medieval French types identified here include products of Northern France and Brittany. There is also a group of fabrics identified simply as French because they cannot be attributed to any more specific source area.

North French wares

North French wares are relatively rare in the high medieval period. The pottery which characterises earlier groups, especially Normandy Gritty ware, are unusual finds in late-13th- or 14th-century deposits, although glazed North French whitewares occur more frequently. New high medieval types include Developed Rouen-type ware, Seine Valley Whiteware and North French Micaceous Whiteware.

ROND Developed Rouen ware

Fabric 1403	62 RP	320g	48 sherds

The distinction between this type and the Rouen-type ware of the Anglo-Norman period has as much to do with form and vessel construction as fabric. The wheel-thrown fabric is white to buff in colour, with fine quartz sand inclusions and it seems often to have been harder fired than its predecessor.

The common vessel form is a jug. This embodies many of the characteristics of the earlier forms, with eared rod handles, and the use of rouletted applied strips, pellets and paint. The most obvious difference is that developed types have three little feet and are much more finely made, with the decoration and details of form delicately executed. These attributes suggest the 'developed' style that accounts for the Ware Name but it is, in any case, clear from the stratigraphic evidence, that this is a later product than the standard Rouen-type ware. The production area for this ware was not necessarily located in Rouen itself, although the city remains a type-site, but a Seine Valley source is most likely.

Jug	187

NFBI   North French Bichrome

Fabric 1763	14 RP	219g	16 sherds

Similar in fabric to developed Rouen ware, this ware may be from a similar source. It is buff-coloured and well-fired with fine quartz in a clean matrix. Fragments of a single vessel are present but not illustrated. This is a small jug decorated with a red slip under a clear glaze. The slip covers the vessel surface at random, and contrasts gaudily with the yellow colour given by the glaze. Its association with local and Saintonge types indicates a 13th- or 14th-century date. Kenneth Barton previously dubbed this Red and Yellow ware when he observed it in excavations on Jersey (*pers comm*).

SNWW Seine Valley Whiteware

Fabric 1548	15 RP	334g	109 sherds

This is a wheel-thrown whiteware, with well-sorted fine quartz inclusions. Fragments are mainly body sherds from jugs decorated with vertical applied strips of red-firing clay that have a distinctive triangular section. These usually appear brown in colour beneath a clear lead glaze that gives a yellowish-green hue to the undecorated body. On one example the applied clay has fired grey, taking on a dark green colour under the glaze. Remy Guadignin has examined sherds of this fabric and suggested a source in the Seine Valley, perhaps towards Rouen.

Jug	188

SNZO Seine Valley Zoomorphic jugs

Fabric 1407	100 RP	1183g	64 sherds

This is a sandy pink ware with frequent fine quartz inclusions and is represented by two vessels, one of which survives almost complete.

Both vessels are wheel-thrown jugs, decorated with applied clay zoomorphic designs in panels delineated by rouletted applied strips and filled with brown paint. The complete vessel (**189**) shares some of the characteristics of Rouen-type pots. It has a heavily ribbed neck, eared rod handle and a cordon at the shoulder and the base angle. It also has three feet that are very crudely formed and attached. North French traditions are represented in this vessel, but the fabric, and elements of the form, suggest that this product is not exactly comparable with the classic Rouen types. Nicourt has published this as a parallel to known Parisian types (Nicourt 1987), although he hesitates to ascribe a Parisian origin. This view is supported by Remy Guadagnin, who has examined a sample of this fabric and suggests parallels with material excavated at Notre Dame, and thought to originate from St Denys (*pers comm*). Although a Parisian source is not a certainty for this ware, there seems good reason to suggest that it originated from a Seine Valley production site closer to Paris than Rouen.

Jug	189, 190

NFWS   North French Sandy Whiteware

Fabric 1552	0 RP	180g	18 sherds

This wheel-thrown, unglazed whiteware is dated to the high medieval period by its association with other high medieval types. The fabric, which has well-sorted fine quartz inclusions in a sandy clay matrix, is similar to the Anglo-Norman Fabric 1413. A North French source is suggested. Diagnostic sherds are rare, there being just two base sherds. Both are sooted, suggesting that they were from cooking pots. No examples of this fabric are illustrated.

NFPQ   North French Pink ware

Fabric 1291	0 RP	318g	30 sherds

This wheel-thrown, pink, fine fabric contains moderate inclusions of medium-sized, white quartz. Sherds are covered in a bright copper-green or clear lead glaze.

Several sherds from a single vessel are present but cannot be fitted together in any coherent fashion and they are not illustrated. The vessel is decorated with applied clay in an undecipherable anthropomorphic or zoomorphic motif. The fabric and the form of the decoration suggest a similarity with other North French wares, perhaps Seine Valley Zoomorphic jugs.

NFMW North French Micaceous Whiteware

Fabric 1711	0 RP	275g	17 sherds

This fabric is a wheel-thrown, fine whiteware with very abundant fine white mica. There are several body and handle sherds from a single jug and a handle fragment from another. This is covered in an external speckled copper-green lead glaze and is decorated all over with overlapping applied pellets (**191**). One of the two jug handles illustrated (**192**) was recovered from the same context and may be from this vessel. One other jug handle is also illustrated. Jacques Le Maho has suggested a source close to Rouen (*pers comm.*).

Jug		191, 192, 193

Breton wares

Two sherds, representing two fabrics, have been identified as originating in Brittany.

CONC Céramique Onctueuse

Fabric 1458	0 RP	13g	1 sherd

This is a dark red, highly micaceous coarseware, distinguished by inclusions of talc and chlorite, that produce a soft, smooth texture with a very soapy feel. A single, small, probably hand-built, body sherd is present in this assemblage. Common forms are jar/cooking pots, dishes and jugs (Giot et Morzadec

1996) and it is most likely that this sherd, thick-walled and unglazed, came from such a jar.

The peculiarity of the inclusions has suggested a source in western Brittany, away from the Armorican massif, near Ty-Lan, west of Quimper (*ibid*).

BTCW Breton Coarseware

Fabric 1753	0 RP	54g	1 sherd

A single base-sherd, not illustrated, perhaps from a cooking pot, in a wheel-thrown brown fabric with abundant coarse mica and igneous inclusions has been attributed to Brittany although Cornwall is a possible alternative source.

Miscellaneous French wares

There are five fabrics that have been identified as high medieval in date and French in origin, but which cannot be located to a specific source area. These are described in Fabric Number order.

ZWQI   French Whiteware with quartz and iron

Fabric 1191	13 RP	141g	14 sherds

A wheel-thrown, slightly micaceous sandy white fabric with distinctive medium sized red and clear quartz and red iron inclusions. Some sherds have a clear lead glaze that appears dull yellow in colour. No diagnostic sherds are present and none is illustrated. A North French source seems most probable.

ZCMM French Micaceous Coarseware

Fabric 1279	11 RP	141g	3 sherds

A wheel-thrown white fabric characterised by very abundant coarse mica inclusions. There are just three sherds, a rim, a body and a base, each recovered from different sites – none is illustrated. All three are fragments of mortars, decorated with vertical applied brown clay strips. The micaceous nature of this fabric suggests Brittany as a likely source.

ZPQ   French Pink ware

Fabric 1290	10 RP	86g	10 sherds

This is a wheel-thrown, fine pink fabric. Sherds usually have a clear lead glaze. A single rim sherd and nine body sherds are present in this assemblage and none are illustrated. The rim is a plain upright form, probably from a jug.

ZFWW French Whiteware

Fabric 1781	100 RP	815g	40 sherds

A single complete jug profile survives in this fabric, which is a fine whiteware with some quartz inclusions.

The fabric is less remarkable than the vessel, which has both northern and south-western French characteristics. It is covered in a dull, dark green glaze and decorated with alternately straight and wavy horizontal combed lines, a form of decoration that may be seen on north French green-glazed wares. The handle however, is a wheel-thrown strap of a type commonly found on Saintonge vessels. Typologically this vessel could have either northern or south-western French origins and a Loire Valley source might therefore represent a suitable compromise.

Jug   194

Saintonge wares

The pottery of the Saintonge is well-known in England and has been well-researched here and in France (Barton 1963b, Chapelot 1983, David and Gabet 1972, Platt and Coleman-Smith 1975, Watkins 1987). Dunning related its presence in this country to the trade in Gascon wine (Dunning 1968) and it must be for that reason that such large quantities of Saintonge pottery are found in Southampton. Assemblages dating from the 13th and 14th centuries in the medieval town are noted for the quantity and variety of their Saintonge wares. The material presented here is no exception, and provides an opportunity to describe and quantify the wide range of Saintonge types found in Southampton.

All types are wheel-thrown and the most common types typically all have a fine, slightly micaceous fabric with occasional fragments of white quartz. This is the case with Fabrics 1267, 1272, 1274, 1500 and 1758, and these have been grouped together as the Major Ware, High Medieval Saintonge (HSO). More rare types here include Gritty, Pink and Redwares (Fabrics 1464, 1249 and 1273 respectively). Saintonge Sgraffito ware is not present here but is known from other Southampton assemblages (Platt and Coleman-Smith 1975, No. 1020, Thomson & Brown 1991).

The location of kiln sites in the Saintonge has been well-researched (Barton 1963b, Chapelot 1983). Centres of production have been identified near Rochefort, at Breuil-Magne and Saint Symphoren, around Saintes at Archingeay, La Chapelle-des-Pots and Les Ouillieres, and further south near the River Gironde at Bussax, Montendre and Montguyon. Given the longevity of the industry and the tremendous variety of fabrics and forms it is certain that many more kiln sites existed. The precise attribution of each type to specific kiln sites cannot yet be achieved. Merchants operating from the ports of Bordeaux, Rochefort and La Rochelle distributed Saintonge pottery throughout Western Europe and it has been found as far south as Lisbon (personal observation) and as far north as Trondheim (Reed 1990, 41). It may be that different Saintonge kilns provided each of the three ports of exit and further work on the exact origins of the Saintonge wares found in Southampton might therefore elucidate the relationship between this port and its French counterparts, but this is dependant on a reciprocal analysis of Saintonge kiln material.

SOWW Saintonge Whiteware

| Fabric 1272 | 1134 RP | 18266g | 1825 sherds |

This is the standard white Saintonge fabric. It is fine, slightly micaceous, with occasional inclusions of rounded clear or white quartz and rare flecks of red iron. There are three main vessel forms, jugs, pégaux and pitchers, but others, such as costrels are also present. The standard green-glazed jug is the most common and it appears in a variety of shapes and sizes. These have not been classified here as they were at Hull (Watkins 1987) and sufficient examples are illustrated here and elsewhere (Platt and Coleman-Smith 1975) to show the range of forms. The copper and lead glaze is usually thickly applied and appears as a dull mottled green. It usually covers most of the exterior surface, although on later examples it may be confined to an area beneath the spout. Under-fired examples usually have a pink fabric and a matt olive-coloured glaze.

The classic features of the typical Saintonge jug of this period are embodied in this form and these comprise a collared rim, a parrot-beak bridge spout, a wheel-thrown strap handle, thin body walls and a splayed base. Decoration on green-glazed jugs is usually limited to vertical thumbed applied strips, although horizontal straight or wavy combed lines also occur. Stamped medallions (**201**) seem to have been a less frequently used decorative device.

Pégaux are large, three-handled pots with big parrot-beak spouts that have a cut-away bridge. Decoration is usually confined to thumbed applied strips running diagonally across the body to meet beneath the spout. A thin green or greenish clear glaze was usually applied over the same area. This is a relatively common form in this assemblage, although only one example is illustrated. Good examples from Southampton have been published already (Platt and Coleman-Smith 1975, Nos 1014, 1049, 1050, 1053, 1054). These vessels were often thrown very thin for their size, and are likely to have fragmented into small pieces, although base fragments are often thicker than those of jugs. This fragmentation is perhaps one reason for the lack of illustratable examples. For a type that numbers 396 sherds the average sherd weight is 10 grams. Spout, handle and base sherds survive best.

The third type of vessel is a smaller one-handled pitcher with high shoulders and a parrot-beak spout. These were undecorated and unglazed. No examples are illustrated here (but see *ibid*, Nos 1005, 1006).

Base sherds of a barrel costrel, covered with a thin green glaze are also present (**208**). Costrels are notoriously difficult to identify without the mouth or convex base sherds and excavated examples are rare. A more complete example has been recovered from the site of a wreck at St Peterport, Guernsey (Thomson and Brown 1991).

Merchant marks, symbols scratched onto the surface of a pot after firing, seem to occur more frequently on Saintonge wares than any other contemporary pottery. All the examples in this assemblage are illustrated here.

Pégau	195
Jug	196–207
Costrel	208
Merchant Marks	203–207

SOBG *Saintonge Bright Green-glazed ware*

Fabric 1500	270 RP	1704g	193 sherds

This is a fine, hard-fired, whiteware, similar to the standard type Fabric 1272 but without the distinctive quartz or iron inclusions. The most notable characteristic of this product is the bright, shiny green glaze, much more consistent in colour than other green-glazed types. The lower quarter of these vessels may often remain unglazed, although at Hull this type is called all-over green-glazed ware (Watkins 1987).

The common form is a jug in the typical Saintonge style, although usually smaller than the standard and polychrome forms. A cup in this fabric was found at excavations at the Brooks in Winchester (Morris *et al* 1988) but similar forms have not been identified here.

Jug	209, 210, 211

SOPY *Saintonge Polychrome ware*

Fabric 1274	327 RP	3210g	219 sherds

This well-known Saintonge type has a fine, smooth, white fabric, simlar to Fabric 1500, but is characterised by its painted decoration. Designs are outlined in brown, presumably an iron oxide, and filled with geen and yellow.

The range of motifs includes heraldic devices (**212**) vine-leaves (**213**) and birds (**214**), sometimes in combination. A single sherd has a geometric motif of the type better exemplified at Hull (Watkins 1987, No.

291). Moulded faces, also painted, are sometimes applied at the rim (**212, 213, 214**). Other distinctive decorative elements include a green stripe down the centre of the handle, running into a trefoil on the body. Two green stripes also run horizontally, enclosing the principal design. The upper stripe runs on or just beneath the rim, looping under the spout, the lower one is above the base; both are usually combined with dark brown lines.

The vessel form is exclusively a jug. Overall shapes range from round-bellied (eg Platt and Coleman-Smith 1975, No. 1047) to tall with a pedestal type base (eg **214**). The collared rim, parrot-beak spout and wheel-thrown strap handle are typical of the Saintonge style noted in the green-glazed jugs described above. The lead glaze is thin and often has a dull, matt finish, some vessels have an internal green glaze similar to that seen on Saintonge Bright Green-glazed ware (Fabric 1500).

Jug	212–214

SORP *Saintonge Red-painted Whiteware*

Fabric 1267	0 RP	130g	16 sherds

Although this is a relatively well-known Saintonge type (David and Gabet 1972; Thomson and Brown 1991) finds of Red-painted Saintonge ware are rare in Southampton. This type was made in the common white fine fabric and painted with a red slip, usually in vertical lines, beneath a lustrous, clear lead glaze. When reduced, the firing affected the painted slip, giving it a greenish appearance beneath the glaze. The main vessel form would appear to be a jug in the usual style, with a parrot-beak spout and strap handle, but diagnostic sherds are rare here, and none has been illustrated.

SOHD *Saintonge Highly Decorated Whiteware*

Fabric 1758	0 RP	8g	1 sherd

This is a rare type with a bright green glaze and applied vertical strips of red clay. A single sherd is present here and is not illustrated.

SOGT *Saintonge Gritty ware*

Fabric 1464	215 RP	5813g	38 sherds

This type appears to be the common Saintonge white fabric deliberately coarsened by the addition of large fragments of crushed quartz. The quartz is opaque white and similar to that which occasionally occurs in the finer white fabrics. The purpose of its addition is to provide a rough grinding surface on the interior of mortars, the principal vessel form. These are thick-walled forms, and the addition of coarse inclusions will also have ensured a more even firing. In some examples coarse inclusions were added to the interior surface only, while finer white clay is used for the external surface, making the outside suitable for decoration.

The mortars are flat-based and straight-sided with a flanged rim and, usually, three short strap handles. Every component – rim, handle, walls and base – was made very thick. Bases are partially pierced to ensure a consistent firing. One example (**215**) has a ring of large holes in the base, under the body wall, which was presumably the thickest part of the vessel, while another (**216**) has holes all over the base. All examples are partially covered in a poorly fitting dull green glaze. These vessels were often decorated with thumb-impressed applied strips (**216**). Applied moulded faces are also relatively common and were present on both illustrated examples. The most complete example had three such faces, only one of which survives, placed between each of the three handles (**215**). On the second illustrated example (**216**), which was badly burnt, the faces are missing. Other examples of mortars with applied faces are known from elsewhere, and some vessels were also painted with red slip (Thomson and Brown 1991).

Another, even more unusual form is a large flat lid with a tall, upright tubular handle. The diameter of this piece is the same as mortar **215** and it is probable that such lids were made for use with mortars.

| Mortar | 215, 216 |
| Lid | 217 |

SORD   Saintonge Redware

Fabric 1273   87 RP   3742g   37 sherds

This is similar to the white fabric in being fine, slightly micaceous with rare fragments of white quartz. It is dull red in colour, with thick sherds often having a grey core.

In this assemblage there are two pégaux and a few miscellaneous body sherds. The rim of an ornate mortar is also published here but it is an unstratified find. One pégau has a lead glaze that appears green in colour, although it is unclear whether this is due to the addition of copper or a slightly reduced firing. It is decorated with vertical applied strips with thumbed terminals (**219**). A similar vessel was excavated at Nottingham (Thomson and Brown, 1991 No. 23).

The other pégau is a quite different piece (**218**). It is an enormous vessel with a clear lead glaze that gives a rich brown colour. It is decorated in white slip with a heraldic motif that appears four times. The top of each shield bears a sgraffito inscription that reads S. gairant, shown in larger scale in Figure 3, presumably

the name of a saint, in a Gothic textualis script that accords with a mid-13th century date (Michelle Brown *pers comm*).

There seems never to have been a Saint Gairant and it seems unlikely that Saint Gerent, or Geraint, the patron saint of Cornwall, should appear on a Saintonge pot. A more likely candidate might perhaps be Saint Gereon, or Geron. He was one of fifty martyrs, be-headed by Roman soldiers at Cologne in the 4th century, whose legend was revived in the 13th century (Farmer D, 1992, 200) and because he was beheaded he was often invoked against headaches. Such a saint would seem to be an appropriate person to figure on a pot with a capacity approaching three gallons (13.5 litres).

Sgraffito decoration is also present on the rim sherd of what must have been a spectacular mortar (**220**). The top of the rim is painted with a white slip through which has been scratched a vine leaf motif similar to that seen on the polychrome jugs (**213**). This has been further embellished with the partial use of green glaze. In section the rim has two wide external flanges and between these was a row of applied moulded faces, of which two can be seen on the surviving fragment.

These vessels establish Saintonge Redware among the most exotic of the Saintonge types. The use of sgraffito and moulded faces accords with the best decorative traditions of the Saintonge, as seen on the Polychrome jugs and the Gritty ware mortars.

| Pégau | 218, 219 |
| Mortar | 220 |

The late medieval period

In common with ceramic traditions in England the transition from the high to late medieval periods in France is characterised by technological and stylistic change. The production of stoneware in northern France is one obvious technological development. North French wares include developed Normandy Gritty ware types, Normandy Stoneware, Beauvais fine earthenwares and stonewares, and Martincamp wares. Saintonge products were imported, but not in the same quantities as the preceding period. New Saintonge types include tubular-spouted pitchers and chafing dishes. The proportion of French material in comparison with imports from other countries is lower in the late medieval than in both the preceding periods (see below p 94, Table 5).

North French wares

Developed Normandy Gritty ware types reappear in Southampton in late medieval assemblages. Most of the North French wares of this date are completely new types however. These include Normandy Stoneware, the final development of the Gritty ware tradition. Bright green and yellow glazed Beauvais earthenware mugs are a colourful addition to the North French assemblage, better still the exquisite sgraffito ware. Martincamp flasks or bottles represent a new ceramic form.

NOGL Developed Normandy Gritty ware

Fabric 1754	22 RP	133g	14 sherds

This is a hard, well-fired fabric. Colours vary from buff-white to grey. The sub-angular quartz inclusions that characterise Normandy Gritty ware are present, albeit smaller in size and quantity. A similar area of production is probable. Forms include jugs, often with hollow rod handles (**225**) and jars or cooking pots. This product seems to be a direct descendant of Normandy Gritty ware and therefore was probably made in the same production area. It is much harder fired, almost semi-vitrified in some instances and may therefore also be seen as an intermediate phase between Normandy Gritty ware and Normandy Stoneware.

Jar	**221**
Jug	**222**

NSTP Proto-Normandy Stoneware

Fabric 1347	0 RP	12g	1 sherd

This fabric is rare in Southampton but significant, as it represents what may be the transition between the earthenware Developed Normandy Gritty wares and Normandy Stoneware. It is a pale grey, semi-vitrified fabric with quartz inclusions. A single body sherd is present in this assemblage. Barton and Thomson (Barton *et al* 1992, 122) coined the term Proto-Normandy Stoneware to signify a type that is a direct predecessor of true Normandy Stoneware.

NST Normandy Stoneware

Fabric 1349	224 RP	4071g	205 sherds

This is the most common French product in the late medieval assemblage. Two main production areas for Normandy Stoneware have been suggested (Dufornier 1990, Burns 1991). It is considered that the earliest stonewares were made around Domfront, south of the Cotentin peninsula. Domfront wares have a pimply feel and are purple-grey in colour. More common in Southampton are the products of the Bessin potteries, particularly those on the Contentin around Nehou. These are smooth in texture, brown-purple in colour and have occasional coarse fragments of quartz.

A wide variety of vessel forms was produced (Burns 1991) but in Southampton jugs, jars and flasks or upright costrels are the main types. There is also a small lid. One notable characteristic of Normandy Stoneware is the hollow rod handle (**228**), common on jugs and a feature also of Developed Normandy Gritty ware and proto-Normandy Stoneware. None of the Southampton vessels are decorated.

Costrel	**223**
Jug	**224–228**
Lid	**229**

MCP Martincamp ware

Fabric 1296	0 RP	74g	8 sherds
Fabric 1363	109	1615	116
Fabric 1583	106	704	80
Fabric 1751	115	2613	235

Martincamp is a village in eastern Normandy that has been cast as the type-site for a particular vessel type, a rounded flask, or bottle, which has a wide distribution. Recent work has shown that the area of production extends beyond Martincamp (Ickowicz 1993) and that this attribution needs to be reconsidered. This is not the place to suggest an alternative name and Martincamp is adopted, as it is a clearly understood term that remains in currency. Hurst first defined the source area for Martincamp wares (Hurst 1977) although no kilns have yet been excavated in the area. Martincamp is in the north of the pottery-producing

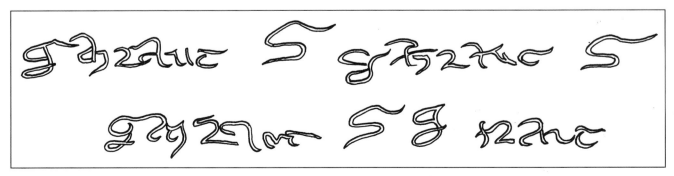

Figure 3. Transcript of sgraffito lettering on Saintonge Redware pégau, **218**.

area around Beauvais, in the Pas-de-Bray. There are certain similarities between the Martincamp wares and the Beauvais products that reflect the location of the production area. The fabrics of both white earthenwares are almost identical and the vitrified Martincamp types are equally similar to Beauvais Stoneware.

Four Martincamp fabrics have been identified. They have been distinguished primarily on the basis of colour, as in every case the clay is smooth and free of inclusions. Fabric 1296 is orange-pink in colour; Fabric 1363 is white; Fabric 1583 is brown-pink; Fabric 1751 is vitrified and brown-grey in colour. No differences in form can be discerned among these fabrics and it is likely that fabric 1296 is an underfired version of 1363, while 1583 is an under-fired type of the stoneware fabric 1751.

The only vessels represented are globular flasks or bottles with long, narrow, tapering necks. Hurst identified three form types, which he placed into a chronological sequence. Type I has a flattened profile and occurs in the white earthenware fabric in the late-15th and early-16th centuries. The stoneware fabric appears as Type II flasks – more rounded – and these are considered to be mainly 16th-century in date. Type III is 17th-century, globular, and made in a dark red earthenware that is not present in this assemblage (*ibid*). Both flattened (**232**) and rounded (**230**) flasks occur here, together with some examples that are in-between the two (**231, 233**). The rounded example is in Fabric 1583, the flattened type in the stoneware, Fabric 1751, and one of the others is in the white earthenware, 1363. This suggests a need to revisit Hurst's typology although this evidence may confirm his chronology.

These vessels were used as bottles, and were delivered covered in wicker, which presumably protected the thin walls of the vessel. A complete example with the wicker preserved was recovered from the wreck of the *Mary Rose* (personal observation). They seem to have been made mainly for export, as these vessels are rarely found in France (Ickowicz 1993).

Fabric 1363	Bottle	**231**
Fabric 1583	Bottle	**230**
Fabric 1751	Bottle	**232, 233, 234**

BVMO *Beauvais monochrome glazed earthenwares*

| Fabric 1195 | 99 RP | 922g | 82 sherds |
| Fabric 1436 | 194 | 751 | 74 |

Beauvais earthenware is a smooth, fine white fabric with some fine quartz grains. Vessels have a rich lustrous lead glaze. Fabric 1195 has a clear glaze that appears bright yellow in colour. Fabric 1436 has a copper glaze that is a vibrant green. Mugs and bowls are most common. The mugs are similar in size and form to contemporary Rhenish stoneware types (see below) with a globular body and narrow handles. These may be decorated with applied medallions (**235**) and two examples bear the English Royal escutcheon, presumed to signify Henry VII (**236, 237**). Bowls have a broad rim, and may be decorated with incised wavy lines (**244**). There is also the base of a jug (not illustrated), the rim of a chafing dish (**245**) and a fragment of what was either a dripping pan or fish dish (**241**).

These fabrics have been combined with the Beauvais Sgraffito types described below, to form a Major Ware.

Fabric 1195	Mug	235–237
	Bowl	238–240
	Dripping pan	241
Fabric 1436	Mug	242
	Bowl	243, 244
	Chafing dish	245

BVSG *Beauvais Sgraffito*

| Fabric 1316 | 15 RP | 202g | 19 sherds |
| Fabric 1319 | 14 | 163 | 9 |

There are two types of Beauvais Sgraffito ware. Both have a very smooth white fabric comparable to that of Beauvais Monochrome Glazed ware.

Fabric 1319 is known as Single-slipped Beauvais Sgraffito. Here, the white body was covered in a red slip through which decorative motifs were incised. The rich, clear, lead glaze that covers these vessels appears yellow over the exposed white clay and brown over the applied slip. Floral (**246**) and geometric designs were produced, often accompanied by lettering. The common form is a bowl, slipped and glazed on the inside only.

Fabric 1316 is Double-slipped Sgraffito. This is exquisite pottery, produced with great care and obvious effort. The white body was covered with a red slip, then a second covering of white slip was applied and this was scratched through to reveal the red below. Floral (**247**) and geometric motifs are common. A polychrome effect is achieved through the skilful use of blue, green and clear lead glazes. Fragments of bowls and jars are present. Fine examples from Southampton have been published before (Platt *et al* 1975, Nos 1073, 1095). Fragments of a chafing dish are also present.

Fabric 1319	Bowl	246
Fabric 1316	Bowl	247
	Chafing dish	248

BVST *Beauvais Stoneware*

| Fabric 1744 | 70 RP | 44g | 4 sherds |

Beauvais Stoneware is fine and pale grey, often with a

brown firing bloom. Vessels are usually delicately made, thin-walled and finely proportioned. Small bowls and mugs are represented, but no fragments are large enough to be illustrated. The range of vessels is similar to Siegburg Stoneware (see below) but unlike those Rhenish products, they do not have clubbed bases. The bowls usually have an inverted conical profile and were probably used for drinking.

NOPG Normandy Pink-greyware

Fabric 1749   0 RP   15g   2 sherds

This is a hard-fired sandy ware with well-sorted fine quartz inclusions. The name derives from its external colour, which is a patchy combination of pink and grey. The most characteristic feature is that the internal surface is usually fully reduced to a dark grey or black. The origins of this ware are unclear. It occurs at Guernsey (Barton, K J, 1984) and Poole (Barton *et al* 1992, No. 888), both places where late medieval North French earthenwares occur with greater frequency than at Southampton. Barton coined the term pink-grey and in the absence of any better title it has been adopted here.

Saintonge wares

In comparison with the high medieval period, Saintonge pottery is rare in 15th-century Southampton. The same fine, white, slightly micaceous fabric remained consistent throughout the medieval period but the later forms are different. Two types are described below. These have been grouped together as the Major Ware, Late Medieval Saintonge wares (LSO).

SOLW Late Saintonge Whiteware

Fabric 1454   291 RP   8798g   246 sherds

This is similar to the standard white fabric described above, but tends to be harder fired and sometimes slightly reduced.

Jugs have the same characteristics as their high medieval predecessors, with collared rims, parrot-beak spouts and wheel-thrown strap handles. Bases are different however, being straight rather than splayed. All these elements often appear more neatly made, and spouts, especially, are smaller. The use of glaze is confined to a 'bib' beneath the spout. The overall effect is of an altogether more modest type of vessel in comparison with the large brightly glazed types of the 13th century.

By the 15th century the pégau had developed into the tubular-spouted pitcher (**249**). These were equally large vessels but the rim diameter is smaller and a tubular spout had replaced the parrot-beak form. Strap handles were pulled rather than wheel-thrown. As with the pégau, glaze was applied on the belly beneath the spout, an area usually decorated with rouletted applied strips. The glaze could be clear, appearing yellow in colour, or coloured green with the addition of copper. A form of pitcher with a basket handle, crossing over the rim, was also made (**250, 251, 252**). Merchant's marks are occasionally seen on these vessels (**253**).

Another new form is the chafing dish, which is typically decorated with applied faces on the crown. A clear lead glaze, that appears yellow, and copper-green glaze was used alternately over each face to create a striped effect (**255, 256, 257**).

The neck and handle of a costrel show that this form was still in production in the 15th century (**254**). This is slightly under-fired to a pink colour that gives the clear lead glaze an orange hue.

There are also three fragments of a figurine, in the form of a woman, with a yellow skirt, holding a basin or dish (**258**). The back of this figure is flattened and undecorated, implying that perhaps it was designed for fixing to a wall. It is suggested that this might have been a holy water stoup used in a church or chapel. This piece was not made to the highest standards, but it must have been quite striking when complete.

Pitcher	249–252
Merchant mark	253
Costrel	254
Chafing dish	255, 256, 257
Figurine	258

SOPL Late Medieval Saintonge Polychrome

Fabric 1770   50 RP   510g   17 sherds

The polychrome jug of the high medieval period seems to have been a short-lived product but this colourful tradition was reintroduced in the late medieval period. The fabric is the typical white fine type and the range of decorative colours is the same, with green and yellow bordered by brown lines. The forms are different, however, as bowls or dishes have replaced jugs.

Examples of a late medieval polychrome dish have been previously published from Southampton (Platt 1975, No. 1098) and another example is shown here. This has green and yellow bands around a vegetable or fruit, possibly an onion, garlic bulb or pomegranate.

Dish	259

Low Countries wares

The term 'Low Countries' is used here to mean the modern states of Belgium and Holland. In the Middle Ages these were the states of Flanders, Holland, Brabant and Zeeland. Most of the Low Countries pottery present in Southampton is imported in the late medieval period, a time when the ports of Antwerp and Bruges were achieving increased status in European trade. Flemish Greyware (Verhaege *pers comm.*) is present in the late Saxon assemblage from Southampton, but is not among the material presented here. This section therefore begins with the Anglo-Norman period.

The Anglo-Norman period

There is only one type of pottery from the Anglo-Norman phase that can be provenanced to the Low Countries.

ANN   *Andenne-type ware*

Fabric 1390	0 RP	132g	18 sherds

Andenne is situated in the Meuse Valley and was the centre of an industry which produced pottery from the 11th to the 15th centuries (Borremans and Warginaire 1966). The term Andenne-type ware is used here to indicate that this fabric belongs within that tradition and is not definitely an Andenne product. It is wheel-thrown, with a few fine quartz inclusions in a fine clay matrix , white or pink in colour with a characteristic amber-coloured clear lead glaze.

Usually dated in England to the 12th or early-13th centuries (Vince 1985, 39–43), Andenne-type ware is perhaps the most common early medieval Low Countries pottery in England. Even so it occurs only in small quantities, and Southampton proves to be no exception. The only diagnostic sherd is a tubular spout, decorated with annular stamps and applied scales. Two other sherds are decorated in a dark red slip, although no motif can be discerned. An example of a slip-decorated Andenne-type vessel has been previously published from Southampton (Platt 1975, No. 1117). Although definitive sherd types are rare it seems most probable that the typical imported vessel forms were jugs or pitchers.

Pitcher	260

The high medieval period

Only one Low Countries fabric has been identified for the high medieval period and this is represented by a single vessel.

LCHR   *Low Countries Highly Decorated Redware*

Fabric 1494	45 RP	752g	12 sherds

At least from the mid-13th century onwards, redware was the most common type of pottery produced in the Low Countries. The section on Low Countries redwares of the late medieval period describes the wide extent of this tradition, and many of the production sites identified there were surely making pottery in the 13th century. At that time the most widely distributed vessel type was the jug, often decorated with white slip and applied or rouletted decoration under a rich green glaze (Verhaege 1983). This type was, in this country, formerly named Aardenburg ware, after a known production site, becoming Aardenburg-type ware once the variety of possible manufactories became understood. It is now more politic, and indeed more accurate, to refer to this type as a representative of a tradition and to avoid any attribution to Aardenburg unless that town is demonstrably the source of a particular vessel.

The sole example in this assemblage has not been related to any specific source but clearly belongs within the Low Countries Highly Decorated Redware tradition (Verhaeghe *pers comm*). The fabric is a wheel-thrown sandy redware with abundant quartz and iron inclusions, very similar to Late Medieval Low Countries Redware. It is present in the form of the complete profile of a jug that has a bright green glaze over a partial white slip. Close horizontal rouletting adorns the neck and body. This vessel is associated with classic Saintonge types and local high medieval glazed wares.

Jug	261

The late medieval period

In the 15th century, and quite possibly in the last quarter of the 14th, a much greater quantity of Low Countries pottery was coming into Southampton. The range of fabrics represented here is not extensive however. Low Countries Redware is the most common type, and is present in a variety of forms, and as a slip-decorated variety. Low Countries Greyware is extremely rare in Southampton and does not occur in this assemblage. Tin-glazed wares are present and these all appear to be South Netherlands Maiolica types.

LCRD   *Low Countries Redware*

Fabric 1297	LCRD	2418 RP	30332g	1294 sherds
Fabric 1300	LCRB	181	1092	49
Fabric 1610	LCBG	25	302	21

Fabric 1775 LCSG   0   26   2

This is a fabric very similar to Low Countries Highly Decorated Redware. It is commonly an iron-rich, orange-red sandy fabric, its colour enhanced by the application of a rich, clear lead-glaze. Many redware production centres are known, primarily from waster evidence, throughout Belgium and Holland, including Aardenburg, Amersfoort, Amsterdam, Bergen-op-Zoom, Breda, Delft, Dordrecht, Haarlem, Leiden, Middleburg, Maastricht, (Jansenn 1983; Bart 1994), although actual kilns are rare. None of the types found in Southampton have been attributed to specific production centres, although close examination of these products has revealed slight differences in fabric composition.

The four Fabric Numbers listed above represent different styles. Fabric 1297 is the standard plain type, commonly in the form of cooking pots and jugs. Fabric 1300 has a white slip decoration beneath a clear lead-glaze. Fabric 1610 has a green-glaze over a white slip. Fabric 1775 has a white slip, green glaze and sgraffito decoration. Fabric 1297 and the slipped redwares form two separate Major Wares.

Fabric 1297 (LCRD, Low Countries Redware) occurs in a wide variety of vessel forms, including cooking pots, frying pans, dripping pans, bowls and jugs. Unusual forms include lids, colanders and a candlestick (not illustrated). Cooking pots are the most common form. Typically these have three feet, two opposing handles and cordons or rilling around the shoulder (eg 265). The rim is usually lid-seated, but lids are rare in this assemblage. Glaze may cover the entire interior surface while the outside is usually partially glazed down to the shoulder or waist. Splashes or spots of glaze are usually found on the outer surface of the belly and base. Small single-handled cooking pots (271) and pipkins (272, 273) were also produced.

Bowls commonly have three or four feet, often in the form of broad pinched flanges that have pronounced finger-marks (277). Bowls also often have small rod handles applied horizontally.

Several frying pans are represented in this assemblage. These have a pouring lip at right angles to the flat strap handle and a flat base (279, 280, 281).

The profiles of two very different colanders are shown. One is a more familiar type, deep and frequently pierced (282). The other is relatively shallow and has fewer holes (283) and was perhaps used in some other way or served some other function.

Dripping pans usually have a reduced green glaze on the inner surface. They are large vessels, with a thick flat handle on one side and ornate flanged rims at each end (284, 285).

Jugs are rare in this assemblage and are recognised mainly in rim and handle sherds. Rims are usually distinctively collared, although one illustrated example, a large jug or pitcher, has a horizontal thumbed applied strip around the neck (286). Handles are usually thick rods. Jugs occasionally have three or four pulled 'feet' or a foot-ring (287).

The range of forms in Fabric 1300 (LCRB, Low Countries Slipped Redware) is similar, primarily cooking pots and bowls, although an albarello is also present. Slip decoration on cooking pots is usually confined to linear motifs, often spirals and swags painted on the shoulder and belly (271), while rims may also have lines dabbed across them. Bowls have slip-painted linear patterns on the inside, usually swags (289), or are completely covered with slip (288), with rims treated in the same way as cooking pots. In every case the slip is white, which appears yellow beneath the clear lead-glaze. Lids are slightly convex, with stubby knobs surrounded by slip-painted swags (290, 291). No undecorated lids have been identified.

Bowls also occur in Fabric 1610 (LCBG, Low Countries Green-glazed Slipped Redware) (292). These are identical in form to those occurring in Fabrics 1297 and 1300, but they have a bright copper-green glaze over an internal white slip. One unusual form is an albarello, which has an all-over external white slip and a partial green glaze around the rim and neck, the glaze being clear over the rest of the vessel (293).

The only two sherds in Fabric 1775 (LCSG, Low Countries Sgraffito) are from bowls.

Fabric 1297	Cooking pot	262–269
	Pipkin	272, 273
	Bowl	274–278
	Frying pan	279, 280, 281
	Colander	282, 283
	Dripping pan	284, 285
	Jug	286, 287
Fabric 1300	Cooking pot	270, 271
	Bowl	288, 289
	Lid	290, 291
Fabric 1610	Bowl	292
	Albarello	293

LCTG South Netherlands Tin-glazed ware

Fabric 1422   181 RP   429g   84 sherds

In this assemblage, tin-glazed wares that can positively be identified as originating in the Low Countries all appear to be in what is known as South Netherlands Maiolica (Hurst 1986, 117–119), although it is preferred here to apply the term 'maiolica' solely to Italian products. The fabric has few distinctive characteristics, being soft, fine and white. The most common form here seems to be the ring-handled vase, painted with blue or polychrome floral or 'IHS' motifs (**294**). There is also a pedestal base from a small jar (**295**) and a few fragments of an albarello (not illustrated).

No kiln sites are known for the production of South Netherlands Maiolica, although Antwerp is a recognised production centre, as Italian maiolica-makers are known to have been working there by 1513 (Wilson, T, 1999). The contexts that produced these few finds are dated slightly earlier, to *c* 1500, and such a date is not out of the question for South Netherlands Tin-glazed ware. Indeed, the comparative rarity of this ware in relation to North Italian Maiolica suggests that the former type was not very widely distributed, perhaps because it was the product of a newly-established industry.

Ring-handled vase	294
Jar	295

LCML   Low Countries Malling-type Tin-glazed ware

Fabric 1426	10 RP	87g	5 sherds

There is a single mug that has been identified as a Malling-type vessel, initially on the basis of the mottled purple glaze. It was once thought that Malling-type vessels were made in Kent, but it has since been shown that this is a Low Countries product (Hurst *et al*, 1986, 126). A probable Antwerp source has been confirmed for this piece by ICPS analysis (Vince and Brown 2002, 468). In form, this vessel is similar, but not identical to, the style of mug based on stoneware products, that typify Malling-type ware (Hurst *et al*, 1986, nos 174, 175). True Malling-type vessels are thought to date from *c* 1550, but this example occurs with a group that is comprised mainly of late-15th-century pottery and an earlier date may be possible, for this vessel is slightly different to the established forms. A date fifty years earlier seems unlikely, given the present state of knowledge, and this may be an intrusive piece. Even so, the origins and chronology of Malling-type Tin-glazed ware require reconsideration.

Mug	296

Rhenish wares

The term Rhenish is applied to pottery made in the area of the lower Rhine, around Cologne and the modern German-Belgian border. Most of this material is late-medieval stoneware, Rhenish wares of the early and high medieval periods being very rare. Late Saxon Rhenish wares are known in Southampton, and include Badorf and Pingsdorf types, but these are not present in this assemblage.

The Anglo-Norman period
Only one type of Rhenish pottery has been found in 12th- and 13th-century deposits in Southampton.

BLAG   Blaugrau ware

Fabric 1385	119 RP	415g	35 sherds

Blaugrau, Blue-Grey, or Paffrath ware is a semi-vitrified earthenware characterised by its colour and its hard, pimply texture. The form most usually found in England is a globular, one-handled vessel commonly referred to as a ladle. The example illustrated here is typical and has parallels on earlier Southampton sites (Platt and Coleman-Smith 1975, No. 1118), and at Exeter (Allan 1983, Nos 649,838) and London (Vince 1985, Fig 8.1). Paffrath, east of Cologne, is a recognised source but similar fabrics may have been produced at other centres (Janssen 1983).

Ladle/pipkin	297

The high medieval period
Rhenish wares of this period are extremely rare in Southampton.

RSTP   Rhenish Proto-stoneware

Fabric 1599	0 RP	41g	5 sherds

Five small body sherds in this assemblage have been tentatively attributed to this group. These are wheel-thrown, almost vitrified proto-stonewares, dark brown in colour and unglazed. They are dated to this period by their association with known 13th- and 14th-century local and imported types. Such a date places these wares firmly into a recognised Rhenish proto-stoneware tradition (Stephan 1983). No vessel types can be discerned but the common form is a mug or jug.

A number of centres in the Rhineland were producing proto-stonewares during this period, most especially Siegburg (*ibid*). No specific provenance has been identified for this material.

The late medieval period

It was not until the 15th century that significant quantities of Rhenish pottery began to come into Southampton. The production of true stonewares in the Rhineland was achieved in the 14th century at Siegburg and Langerwehe (Beckmann 1974) but these types are rare here. It is Raeren-type ware, especially in the frilled-based mugs, which is the most common stoneware in late medieval Southampton. These forms date from the late-15th century (Hurst 1986, 194). Cologne-type mugs and Frechen products are also known.

The main problem in dealing with stoneware is the difficulty in confidently identifying a specific source. Production sites were concentrated in the area of the Rhineland at the modern border between Belgium and Germany. Cologne and Frechen are in the Rhine Valley, Siegburg is on the River Sieg, a tributary of the Rhine and Langerwehe and Raeren are in the Valley of the Meuse, which flows into the Rhine Delta. Each production site is said to have its 'classic type'; the fine light grey Siegburg, the coarse, purplish Langerwehe, the brown-grey Raeren, the barbotine-decorated Cologne, the brown, pimply-glazed Frechen; but there is a great degree of overlap between these types. The earlier wares, especially Langerwehe products, remain fairly distinctive, but stonewares of the mid-15th century onwards are less easy to characterise. Factories at Aachen, Cologne, Frechen and Raeren were all producing wares more or less identical in fabric, if not in form. Undiagnostic body sherds are consequently difficult to provenance, and a general fabric group for Rhenish Stonewares (Fabric 1346 – RSTN) has been created for those pieces which cannot confidently be identified more specifically. The quantities for this category are: 64 RP, 960 grams, 67 sherds.

SIG   Siegburg Stoneware

Fabric 1246	137 RP	502g	27 sherds
Fabric 1710	15	13	2
Fabric 1774	0	123	5

Siegburg Stoneware is a delightful light-grey in colour and has a delicate appearance which is enhanced by the thinness of vessel walls. It commonly has ash-glazed orange patches on its exterior surface. It is finely potted, for stoneware, into a range of bowls, cups and mugs. Diagnostic sherds are rare in this assemblage, but it seems that mugs were more common than bowls. These are tall and slender in shape, in contrast to later Raeren types, and have a clubbed foot-ring. No decorated examples are known in this assemblage. A cup or beaker with a clubbed base is also present (**301**). This type

of Siegburg may be identified as an early type, dating perhaps from the 14th century. It certainly pre-dates Fabric 1774 and also perhaps the Raeren mugs.

Fabric 1710 is a green lead-glazed version of Fabric 1246. The glaze was added in a second firing at Low Countries potteries, and redware kilns at Bruges, Utrecht and Aardenburg have all yielded green-glazed stoneware (Gaimster 1997, 60).

Fabric 1774 is Late Siegburg Stoneware (SIGL). This is also pale grey and has a salt glaze. The single example in this assemblage is a tall straight-sided mug or *Schnelle* that has a complex moulded panel showing an allegorical scene in relief (**318**). These vessels are dated from *c* 1550, but the example shown here is from a context that contains large quantities of late-15th-century pottery. This piece may have been misidentified, it may be an intrusive find, or else the date range of these vessels requires reconsideration.

Fabric 1246	Mug	**298, 299, 300**
	Cup	**301**
Fabric 1774	Schnelle	**318**

LANG   Langerwehe Stoneware

Fabric 1257	0 RP	521g	17 sherds

Langerwehe Stoneware is quite different from Siegburg, although it may be more or less contemporary, with production beginning in the first half of the 14th century (Hurst *et al* 1986, 184). It is cruder in both fabric and form than Siegburg, and the fabric is darker and fired a dark brown to purple colour with the addition of an iron wash. Firing is often inconsistent, and under-fired or over-fired examples are not uncommon. In Southampton mugs are the common form, although cups are known. These are not well made and bases are often very poorly finished. No sherds are illustrated here.

RARN   Raeren-type Stoneware

Fabric 1245	2007 RP	18198g	682 sherds

Raeren is the most common late medieval stoneware found in Southampton. It has a dark-grey fabric and is salt-glazed to give a bright finish over an external colour that ranges from dark brown to grey. The fabric, macroscopically, is almost identical to vessels produced at Aachen, Cologne and Frechen (D Gaimster *pers comm*). Many non-diagnostic body sherds of this fabric have therefore been attributed to Raeren when in fact they may not be. The use of the term Raeren-type for this material may therefore be more appropriate.

The most common form is the mug. This is characterised by a frilled foot-ring, a narrow concave-sectioned handle, a cordon at the shoulder and a groove around the upright rim. Face mugs, as illustrated in the Van Beuningen Collection (Hurst 1986) are not present in this assemblage but are known from other sites in Southampton. One vessel has a moulded decoration showing a human figure holding an orb and sceptre (**314**). This is probably a straight-sided mug or tankard in the Pinte tradition (Hurst 1986, Fig 95). A third form is a narrow-necked jug or bottle (**313**).

Mug	**302–312**
Jug	**313**
Pinte	**314**

CLGN   Cologne Stoneware

Fabric 1378	29 RP	648g	40 sherds

The fabric of Cologne Stoneware is indistinguishable in hand specimen from that of Raeren. The only distinctive features are found in the form, where vessels have flat, rather than frilled, bases, and in the decoration. The classic Cologne mug has sprigged oak leaf and acorn motifs. The examples shown here include a mug with a sprigged panel of human heads around the neck (**319**) and a face-mug (**320**). There is also a larger jug-sized vessel (**321**). It is difficult to identify any of the plain stoneware body sherds as Cologne and that has not been attempted here.

Mug	**315, 316**
Jug	**317**

FRCN   Frechen Stoneware

Fabric 1375	126 RP	691g	23 sherds
Fabric 1750	15	90	9
Fabric 1757	100	625	4

Fabric 1375 is the typical brown, salt-glazed stoneware similar to Cologne and Raeren types. In form, the early plain mugs are also similar to Cologne types, which is perhaps not surprising, as in 1500 some potters moved from Frechen to Cologne (Hurst *et al* 1986, 214). Later Frechen wares have a characteristic mottled brown salt glaze and the surface texture of orange peel but this does not help in the attribution of earlier forms, and again, many sherds currently ascribed to Raeren may in fact be from Frechen. Bellarmine or Bartmann-type jugs are present in this assemblage, and although they post-date the late medieval period they are at least recognisably Frechen products. Other diagnostic pieces are rare, and consequently very few late medieval sherds have been identified as Frechen types. None is illustrated here.

Fabric 1750 is a blue-glazed variant of the grey Frechen Stoneware. Late medieval blue-glazed Frechen products are known (Hurst *pers comm*) and are represented in this assemblage by a single rim sherd and eight body sherds which have a dark grey fabric with an overall blue-glazed outer surface. This vessel is associated with late medieval pottery of local, French, Low Countries, Rhenish and Spanish origin and a date around 1500 is inferred.

Fabric 1757 is White Frechen Stoneware, attributed on the basis of form, and it is represented here by the rim, handle and upper body of a large salt-glazed jug (**319**). A late medieval date for this piece, which appears post-medieval in character, is suggested by its association with quantities of late-15th- or early-16th-century English, Low Countries and Italian pottery.

Fabric 1757	Jug	**319**

Iberian wares

The term Iberian has been adopted here as a more accurate reflection of the current state of knowledge concerning the origins of some of the products described below. The red micaceous wares, for example, are as likely to have originated from Portugal as Spain. Iberian pottery is, at least, easily recognised in Southampton assemblages, and has been divided into coarse and fine wares. The former group includes oil-jar fabrics and redwares. The finewares include tin-glazed and lustrewares.

Most of the Iberian pottery in this assemblage is from late medieval deposits. Coarsewares and redwares do occur in high medieval contexts, and were almost certainly brought into Southampton in the 13th and early-14th centuries, but they are not significantly different from later types. They are therefore all described in the late medieval section. Two types of fineware have been identified as high medieval products.

High medieval wares

ANDL   Andalusian Lustreware

Fabric 1067	10 RP	124g	17 sherds

Andalusian Lustreware was imported into England in the 13th and 14th centuries and examples are known from elsewhere in Hampshire, for instance at Faccombe Netherton (Fairbrother 1990, 315). It is an unusual find in Southampton, the best examples being two vessels excavated at Cuckoo Lane (Platt and Coleman-Smith 1975, Nos 1277, 1278). Shown here is a handle from a jug or jar that was burnt in situ and is very fragmentary, although a gutter spout also survives. This may be viewed as a relatively exotic type of pottery in the high medieval period, quite unlike anything else available at the time.

Jug 342

SVGB Seville Green and Brown

| Fabric 1298 | 0 RP | 24g | 1 sherd |

A single base sherd from a bowl or dish (**343**) occurs in a white fabric with characteristic calcareous inclusions. The inner surface is painted with a motif outlined in brown and filled with green. A clear lead glaze is present on both interior and exterior surfaces.

The calcareous nature of the clay, and the Moorish character of the decoration suggest a Spanish source and Seville has been suggested by Neutron Activation Analysis (conducted by Michael Hughes at the British Museum Research Laboratory, results analysed by Alan Vince, see Gutierrez 2000, 143). This sherd occurs in a feature containing typical high medieval local and imported wares, including Saintonge Whiteware, and a high medieval date seems likely.

Bowl 343

Late medieval wares

There are four main types of Iberian ware, coarsewares, mainly from the Seville area, red micaceous wares, Valencian lustreware and Morisco tin-glazed wares. These have been placed into three Major Wares. Iberian Coarseware (IBCW) consists of Seville-type and other coarsewares. Iberian Micaceous Redwares (IBMR) comprise a single Ware Type. Spanish Tin-glazed wares (SPTG), include Valencian Lustre and Morisco wares.

Coarsewares

IBCW Iberian Coarsewares

Fabric 1308	210 RP	7756g	164 sherds
Fabric 1311	0	48	3
Fabric 1327	53	3394	91
Fabric 1405	0	417	14
Fabric 1428	0	60	2
Fabric 1437	0	202	18
Fabric 1457	0	19	2
Fabric 1505	40	1475	184
Fabric 1507	0	8	1
Fabric 1654	0	157	4
Fabric 1766	10	89	2
Fabric 1769	0	125	1
Fabric 1773	19	446	4
Fabric 1777	0	17	3
Fabric 2026	0	87	10

Several different Iberian coarseware fabrics have been identified in this assemblage, together with one other general fabric number, 2026 and they have all been grouped together to comprise a single Major Ware. This group of fabrics commonly occurs in the form of oil jars and most of them may be attributed to the Seville area. Body sherds are usually thick and white or buff coloured. Eight of these fabrics occur solely as body sherds in quantities of nineteen fragments or less and are not described or illustrated here. The remaining five fabrics are described more fully and illustrated. All these coarsewares have similarities of fabric and form. They were all wheel-thrown, usually pink or buff-pink in colour often with a pale cream or buff throwing slip on the outside. Coarse quartz is a common inclusion, and mica is also present. Fabrics may be soft but they are usually well-fired.

Body sherds are thick, and often large, denoting their origin from oil jars. The basic elements of this vessel seem to have developed out of the Roman amphora tradition. Late medieval types in Southampton appear to be smaller than their Roman predecessors, but the thickness of the body, the rolled rim form and the rounded or pointed base all hark back to classical forms. That these vessels had barely changed since the Roman period is hardly surprising, for they were still made for the same purpose. The fact that the medieval vessels are smaller perhaps serves to emphasise the greater scale of the demand for, and traffic in, olive oil in the Roman period. One significant difference between the earlier and later medieval forms is the use of an internal glaze, although this is not very common in Southampton examples. The glaze is usually thin, and a pale green-yellow in hue, although richer brown-coloured glazes appear at a later date.

Other forms include glazed albarelli, jugs or jars and large bowls.

The number of different oil jar fabrics indicates a wide variety of sources but the identification of manufacturing sites and the corresponding attribution of the specific fabrics in this group is beyond the scope of this work. The manufacture of olive jars is thought to have concentrated in the area around Seville. This is based on the presence there of a Roman amphora-making industry, and the importance of the port as an embarkation point for the Americas, where Spanish coarsewares are found in quantity (Goggin 1960, Hurst 1977, 1986). These vessels were in use all over the Iberian Peninsula however, and olive oil was also produced over a wide area. Hurst, for instance, has recognised that olive jars were made in Portugal in Merida-type ware (Hurst 1986). Although the bulk of the Iberian coarsewares identified here are of the type commonly recognised as coming from Seville (Fabrics 1308 and 1505), the presence of vessels from other production centres, brought here from other ports such as Lisbon, seems likely.

Fabric 1308 is a hard-fired smooth pink ware with quartz and characteristic white inclusions. The exterior surface typically has a buff-white throwing slip. Body sherds usually have pronounced throwing rings. A complete oil jar in this fabric has a thick, rolled rim and no handles. This is a typical Seville type.

Oil jar	320, 321

Fabric 1327 is a sandy ware with medium-fine quartz inclusions. It is relatively hard-fired, usually off-white in colour with a pale pink core. Oil jar forms include those of 'poppy-neck' form (326). The most complete oil jar bears a merchant's mark, inscribed after firing. Some oil jars have a pale green internal glaze. A variety of vessels is indicated by the variable thickness of body sherds. A jug or jar base has also been identified. This is also most probably a Seville product.

Oil jar	322, 323
Jug	324

Fabric 1505 is a smooth pink fabric with few inclusions. Sherds commonly have a buff coloured 'slip', typical of Seville coarsewares. All sherds are identified as oil jar fragments.

Oil jar	325

Fabric 1773 is a soft smooth pink fabric. The common form is a large, wide bowl or lebrillo, with a dark green glaze on the inside. The rim is exceptionally thick and has cord-impressed decoration. Lebrillos are usually identified as Seville products and these pieces are likely to fall into that category.

Lebrillo	326

Fabric 1766 is a pink fabric. Two albarelli with a honey-coloured glaze are illustrated. The calcareous inclusions and soft fabric suggest a Seville source.

Albarello	327, 328

Fabric 1778 is a soft buff-white coloured fabric with fine quartz inclusions. It occurs as an unstratified albarello with a dark green glaze that is not quantified in this assemblage.

Albarello	329

ANDC Andalusian Coarseware

Fabric 1439	25 RP	3087g	120 sherds

This is a dense red fabric with distinctive inclusions of red mica schist that are characteristic of Andalusian pottery types (thanks to Alan Vince for identifying this type). A large two-handled jar, with stamped roundels that may be a potter's or a consignment mark, represents most of the sherds present here. Other fragments of this fabric have been recovered from high medieval deposits, which suggests that this type was first brought into Southampton in the 14th century, or earlier.

Jar	330

IBMR Iberian Micaceous Redwares

Fabric 1305	0 RP	25g	5 sherds
Fabric 1355	100	466	28
Fabric 1371	8	2270	165
Fabric 1470	37	76	8
Fabric 1476	6	277	22
Fabric 1484	7	229	27
Fabric 1536	15	135	14
Fabric 1617	0	10	1
Fabric 1776	28	275	17
Fabric 2028	10	24	5

Several different fabrics have been distinguished according to the range and quantity of inclusions and the nature of the matrix. In English assemblages these types are often grouped together under the common name 'Merida-type ware'. This is thought to originate in the area of Alentjo, Portugal (Hurst 1986), presumably coming to Southampton via the ports of Lisbon and Oporto. Redwares are a common Iberian ceramic type, as much today as in the 15th century, and the different types in this group could have come from many of the pottery-producing areas of Spain or Portugal. Those located nearest to coastal trading centres are of course the most likely. One point which arises from the distinction here of several types of Iberian Micaceous Redware is that more attention must be given to the precise definition of 'Merida-type ware'. It is not certain which of these redware fabrics are Spanish in origin and which Portugese and the term Iberian Micaceous Redware is preferred. All these fabrics represent variations of the same broad class and have been grouped together as a Major Ware.

The range of vessel types includes unglazed oil jars, bowls, and flasks or costrels. Glazed vessels include albarelli and cooking pots. Another form is a small, thick-walled vessel in a smooth red fabric with quartz inclusions. This has a dark green external glaze. Such vessels have been identified as mercury jars.

The most common fabrics, and those represented by illustrated examples, are described below.

Fabric 1307 is a fine, slightly micaceous pink-red type with quartz inclusions. A small flask handle is the only diagnostic sherd present.

| Flask | 338 |

Fabric 1355 is a smooth micaceous redware with moderate fine white mica and red iron. The outer surfaces often appear to have been burnished or smoothed. This fabric is usually a warm orange-red in colour. The common form is a small, plain bowl.

| Bowl | 331, 332, 333 |

Fabric 1371 is the most common of the redware fabrics. It has a granular feel, with abundant, ill-sorted, sub-angular, clear and grey quartz inclusions and moderate ill-sorted white mica. This ware is usually hard-fired and sometimes has a reduced surface. Colours range from red to dark brown. Forms include two-handled flasks, plain bowls, jugs and oil jars but diagnostic sherds are rare and only one oil jar handle is illustrated here. Previously excavated Southampton examples have been published (Platt and Coleman-Smith 1975, Nos 1280, 1283, 1287).

| Oil jar | 339 |

Fabric 1470 is a soft, smooth ware with very fine white mica and abundant powdery white inclusions. It is usually pale red in colour. This is rare in this assemblage, occurring principally in flask form. A rim and base are shown.

| Flask | 334, 335 |

Fabric 1471 is a fine red fabric with moderate, clear quartz inclusions. Few sherds of this fabric are present, but they include the rim and base of a small flask, not illustrated here.

Fabric 1476 is a fine sandy red micaceous ware. The matrix has abundant very fine quartz and white mica with sparse medium-sized clear quartz inclusions. There are occasional coarse fragments of metamorphic rock. A few thick body sherds with an internal greenish-coloured glaze may have come from oil jars. The only diagnostic sherds are from flasks and consist of a handle and a base which was perforated after firing. No sherds are illustrated here.

Fabric 1536 is a sandy micaceous redware with abundant fine white quartz, white powdery inclusions and white mica. Sherds are thin and hard fired with an internal clear lead glaze that is a rich dark brown in colour. The rim, handle and base of a small jug or handled jar are the only diagnostic sherds.

| Jug | 336 |

Fabric 1543 is a soft redware with sparse mica inclusions. This occurs as the base of a small, thick-walled, globular jar. This type of vessel has been identified as a mercury jar (R G Thomson, *pers comm*). Its size and thickness make it a likely container for such a valuable and liquid substance.

| Mercury jar | 341 |

Fabric 1776 is a fine sandy micaceous redware with abundant fine white mica. Outer surfaces are red, inner surfaces have a clear lead glaze that is dark red in colour. A single vessel, a two-handled jar or cooking pot, is represented in this assemblage.

| Jar/Cooking Pot | 337 |

Tin-glazed wares

Three categories of Iberian tin-glazed ware have been identified, based on source area. They are those from Valencia, Seville and Aragon (Muel). The first group is composed entirely of Valencian Lustreware. Morisco tin-glazed wares were produced around Seville. The system of nomenclature based on material recovered from New Mexico (Goggin 1968) does not acknowledge this, and has therefore not been followed here as it is considered more accurate to name them as Seville types. These types have, however, been sub-divided according to the style of decoration. Bowls, dishes, jars and albarelli all occur in this group of wares in a similar fine white or pinkish fabric with no distinctive inclusions. One example of Muel Blue has been identified.

A fourth group is comprised of sherds that can only be identified as Iberian, these have been given the general Fabric Number 1348 and occur in quantities of 10rp, 76g and 7 sherds.

VALL   *Valencian Lustreware*

| Fabric 1070 | 224 RP | 1666g | 33 sherds |

Valencian Lustreware is a relatively well-known 15th-century Iberian import (Hurst 1986, 40–53). Vessels include bowls and dishes decorated solely with lustre (**344, 345, 346, 347**) or with lustre and paint (**348**). Bowls vary in form from flange-rim types (**348**) to handled, 'bleeding-bowl' types (**345**) and small finger-bowl types (**344**). It is not uncommon to find fragments that have a blackened glaze that obscures the pattern of the decoration. One example is a dish that has no lustre surviving, but the pattern is visible in relief (**347**). On the body sherd of a large albarello (**349**) the lustre has faded, leaving the blue painted decoration behind.

| Bowl/dish | 344, 345, 346, 347, 348 |
| Albarello | 349 |

SVBP   Seville Blue and Purple

| Fabric 1421 | 6 RP | 56g | 3 sherds |

Classified by Goggin as Isabela polychrome (Goggin 1968), this type has blue and purple painted decoration, often in the form of concentric circles. Only two vessels are present in this assemblage. Both are open forms, probably dishes. A rim sherd is illustrated here.

| Dish | 350 |

SVB   Seville Blue

| Fabric 1448 | 39 RP | 228g | 18 sherds |

Classified by Goggin as Yayal blue (Goggin 1968), this type has a monochrome blue-painted decoration, similar in motif to the polychrome forms. Dishes, bowls, including 'bleeding bowl' types (**356**) and albarelli are all present.

| Dish | 351 |

SVGW   Seville Green and White

| Fabric 1765 | 111 RP | 793g | 15 sherds |

This type is produced by dipping a plain white vessel into a green glaze solution to achieve a half-green, half-white effect.

Plates, in the same form seen in other Seville products, with a plain rim and indented base, are common vessels. There are also fragments of two ring-handled cups, both illustrated here.

| Dish | 353 |
| Cup | 354, 355 |

SVPW   Seville Plain White

| Fabric 1472 | 30 RP | 727g | 22 sherds |

Classified by Goggin as Columbia plain (Goggin 1968), this type has no painted decoration. Bowls, dishes and albarelli are all present in this assemblage as small sherds. A large bowl is shown here.

| Bowl | 356 |

MULB   Muel Blue Tin-glazed

| Fabric 1449 | 20 RP | 59g | 1 sherd |

A single small bowl with a flat lugged handle has been identified elsewhere as Muel Blue (Gutierrez 2000, 155), presumably on the basis of the decoration. This vessel was originally identified as probably Seville Blue but that attribution must be reconsidered and the style of the decoration certainly seems to match Muel, or other Aragonese types such as Calatayud, as shown by Gutierrez (*ibid*, 73). Such a find is very unusual for Southampton, where the emphasis is firmly placed on Seville and Valencia.

| Bowl | 352 |

Italian wares

All the Italian wares in this assemblage are late medieval in date. The most common types are tin-glazed wares. North Italian Sgraffito and a range of plain lead-glazed earthenwares also occur.

Tin-glazed wares

Several traditions of Italian maiolica may be distinguished in this assemblage. Apart from the red Pisan wares, Italian maiolicas have a similar fine white fabric which does not obviously vary between separate production centres.

Different types have therefore been identified on the basis of form and decorative motif. However, the exact provenance of each of these separate types is not so easily established. All of them are likely to be North Italian in origin, and the Arno region, between Pisa and Florence, is the most probable source for most of them. Faenza types are apparently rare. Different types are considered here under separate headings but all

these wares have been grouped together as a Major Ware, Italian Maiolica (ITMA).

MONT   Montelupo Maiolica

| Fabric 1446 | 176 RP | 996g | 33 sherds |

It is difficult to distinguish Montelupo products from those made in nearby Florence. A complete small bowl (**357**) with a concentric design in blue and yellow has Montelupo character and other vessels include a bowl base with a blue and yellow floral design (**358**) and two dish bases with geometric decoration (**359, 360**). One of these has a chequer pattern (**360**) paralleled in the Van Beuningen collection (Hurst 1986, Plate 1).

One jug (**361**) is decorated in an overall blue and purple floral style surrounding a blue and yellow armorial motif. It has a turquoise handle with a manganese-painted signature below. Alejandra Gutierrez kindly sought a parallel for this mark and matched it to a version of the letter R in Cora's Group XVID (Cora

1973), which is attributed to Montelupo and dated to the end of the fifteenth century. A parallel to the decoration, however, on a jar provenanced to the Florence district, can be seen at the British Museum (Wilson 1987, No. 24) and there are further parallels in a group from the hospital of Santa Fina at San Gimignano (Vannini 1981).

Bowl	357, 358
Dish	359, 360
Jug	361

FLOM Florentine Maiolica

Fabric 1767	75 RP	1699g	31 sherds

This is a ware group that includes all Italian tin-glazed wares thought to originate from Tuscany but not attributable to particular production centres. Illustrated here is a jug with a blue-painted floral design in-filled with pink and turquoise (362) and a bowl (363) painted with a floral motif in green and brown.

Jug	362
Bowl	363

FNZA Faenza Maiolica

Fabric 1450	255 RP	2539g	134 sherds

Jugs painted with blue ladder-medallions are considered to have been made in Faenza. The centre of the medallions shown here are filled with geometric (365), floral (364) or piscine zoomorphic (366) designs. Ladder-medallions are characteristic of South Netherlands Maiolica jugs also but it is interesting to note that those vessels have medallions on the side (Allan 1984, No. 2756; Hurst 1986, No. 167), while on all the examples shown here they are situated on the front. A small jug very similar to 364, but with a central 'YHS motif' from Askett, Buckinghamshire, has been identified as Tuscan, however (Blake 1999). This calls into question the attribution of all the Faenza types identified here, and it might be preferable to identify them all simply as north Italian. This illustrates the difficulties, for those of us relatively inexperienced in the practice, of differentiating various types of Italian maiolica.

Jug	364–367

NITM North Italian Maiolica

Fabric 1467	192 RP	1209g	74 sherds
Fabric 1468	60	300	20

Fabric numbers 1467 and 1468 have been applied to a group of sherds that are considered to be of North Italian origin but cannot be attributed to any known production centre. Included in Fabric 1467 are several featureless fragments of maiolica, but more specifically this ware name includes three ring-handled vases, which are somewhat enigmatic. These three were all recovered from the same feature, a garderobe that it is thought was filled in *c* 1490/1500 (see Chapter 7).

One vase, the only vessel represented in Fabric 1468, is all-over white with a brown 'YHS' monogramme on both sides of the body, between two horizontal yellow lines (368). Two others, in Fabric 1467, have floral motifs, one entirely in blue (369) the other in blue and orange (370). These vessels were originally identified as Low Countries types, mainly on the basis of form, although the white piece (368) was rejected by Dutch and Belgian specialists (J Baart, B Hillewaert, *pers comm*) and Tuscan origins were also denied (M Milanese, *pers comm*). All three have since been subjected to Inductively-coupled Plasma Spectroscopy (ICPS) and an Italian source for the clay has been confirmed (Vince and Brown 2002, 466). Comparison with Neutron Activation Analysis (NAA) data may suggest the Arno Valley as a likely provenance for the all-over white example, although this is by no means certain, and in fact this sample was originally matched with Iberian data (*ibid*). There is a white Venetian glass ring-handled vase with the same decoration in the collections of the Victoria and Albert Museum, and a Venetian source should not be ruled out (R Thomson, *pers comm*), especially as no Venetian samples have been included in the programme of analysis. The tall necks of the two blue-painted vessels differentiate them from Low Countries types (eg Hurst *et al* 1986, 316) and a North Italian source seems likely.

A number of points are raised by the problems of provenancing these vessels. ICPS and NAA analysis may characterise the clay, but only within previously established parameters. There also remains the possibility that raw materials were moved around, between production centres. It is therefore important to examine aspects of form and style for further clues. It is also useful to show that ring-handled vases found in England need not all originate from the Low Countries and there is clear need for deeper research into the origins and development of this vessel type.

Ring-handled vase	368, 369, 370

LIGF Ligurian Faience

Fabric 1772	14 RP	16g	2 sherds

There are two sherds from a plate in a blue-on-blue floral style that belongs in the Ligurian tradition. The exact source is unknown, although historically Genoa has most associations with Southampton. Ligurian

Faience is a very rare find in late medieval England (Hurst 1986, 26).

Dish	371

APM   Archaic Pisan Maiolica

Fabric 1241	106 RP	753g	47 sherds

This is a very distinctive dense, red fabric. Open forms usually have a tin-glazed interior with a lead-glazed exterior, the reverse being true on closed forms. The tin-glaze may be applied directly to the red clay, thus appearing pink in colour, or onto a painted white slip. Sherds of Archaic Pisan Maiolica are rare in this assemblage but further examples are known in Southampton (Thomson and Brown 1992). Bowls often have a monogrammatic motif painted on the inside and jugs and jars are often painted in green and brown on the outside. Shown here are the complete profile of a plain bowl, a bowl rim and the base of a small jug.

Bowl	372, 373
Jug	374

Lead-glazed earthenwares

A wide range of lead-glazed wares, considered to be from northern Italy, complement the maiolica assemblage. A similar variety of forms is represented.

ITSG   North Italian Sgraffito

Fabric 1760	146 RP	1276g	37 sherds

The complete profiles of two North Italian Sgraffito ware vessels occur in this assemblage. Both are bowls made of relatively soft, fine, red earthenware. The interior surface is covered with a white interior slip, that was scratched through to reveal the red body, and by a clear lead glaze. On both vessels the decoration takes the form of a floral motif. Hurst suggests that the most widely traded Italian sgraffito products were made at Pisa (Hurst 1986, 30) and there is no reason to dispute such an attribution for the two vessels shown here.

Bowl	375, 376

NITR   North Italian Red Earthenware

Fabric 1768	177 RP	934g	62 sherds

This is a hard-fired fine redware with no distinctive inclusions. Vessels are usually covered in a white slip and a clear lead glaze. Similarities between these fabrics and the red-firing Archaic Pisan Maiolica and Sgraffito wares suggests Pisa as a likely source.

Vessel types include bowls, albarelli and costrels. Two bowls are illustrated. One of these has bands of white slip around the outside (377). The glaze on the inside has a different character from that on the outside which has decayed and may have been made to a different recipe. The rim and base forms of this vessel are paralleled in Archaic Pisan Maiolica vessels (Thomson and Brown 1992). The other bowl is completely covered in a white slip (378). One albarello has an overall white slip and brown painted stripes on the rim (381), another has a green lead glaze and no slip (379). Plain white-slipped albarelli (380) are more common and other Southampton examples have been published (ibid). The base of a flask or costrel in a similar fabric also with a rich clear lead glaze is also shown (382).

Bowl	377, 378
Albarello	379, 380, 381
Costrel	382

Miscellaneous imported wares

A small quantity of sherds have not been related to known source areas, although they have been identified as imported from mainland Europe and can be categorised as high medieval or late medieval. High medieval types amount to 6 RP, 103g and 14 sherds, while late medieval examples total 21 RP, 655g and 78 sherds.

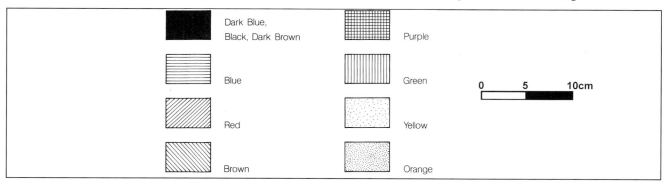

Figure 4. Conventions for pottery drawings

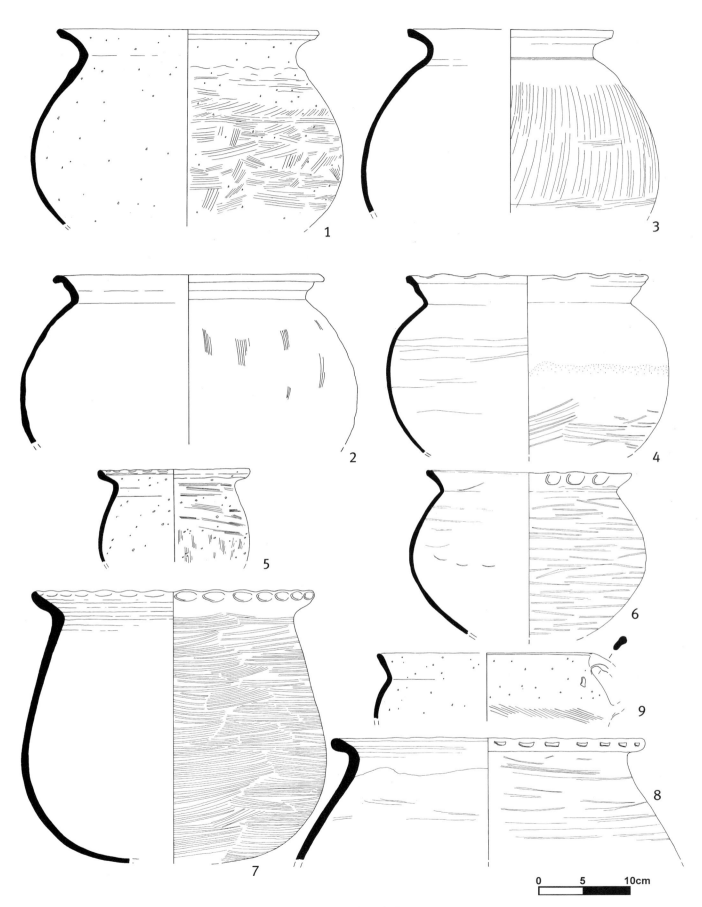

Figure 5. Scratch-marked ware

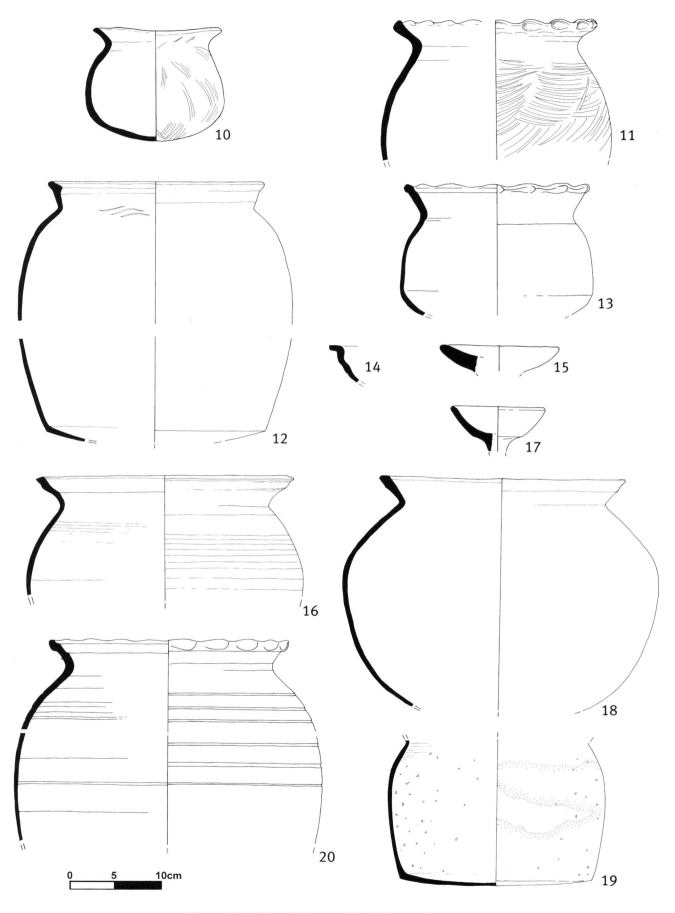

Figure 6. Scratch-marked ware and Anglo-Norman Coarsewares

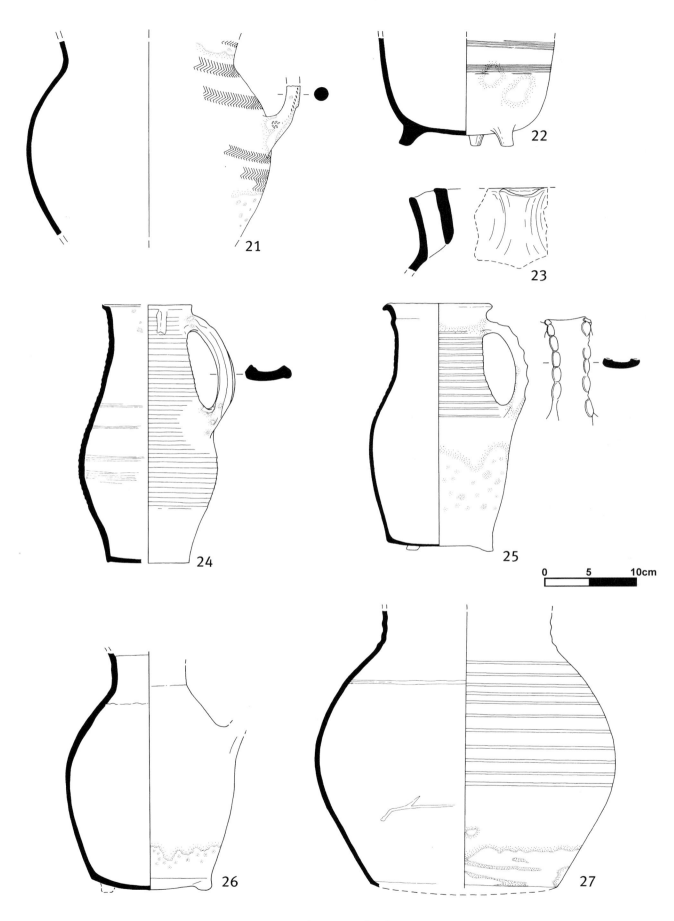

Figure 7. Anglo-Norman Glazed wares

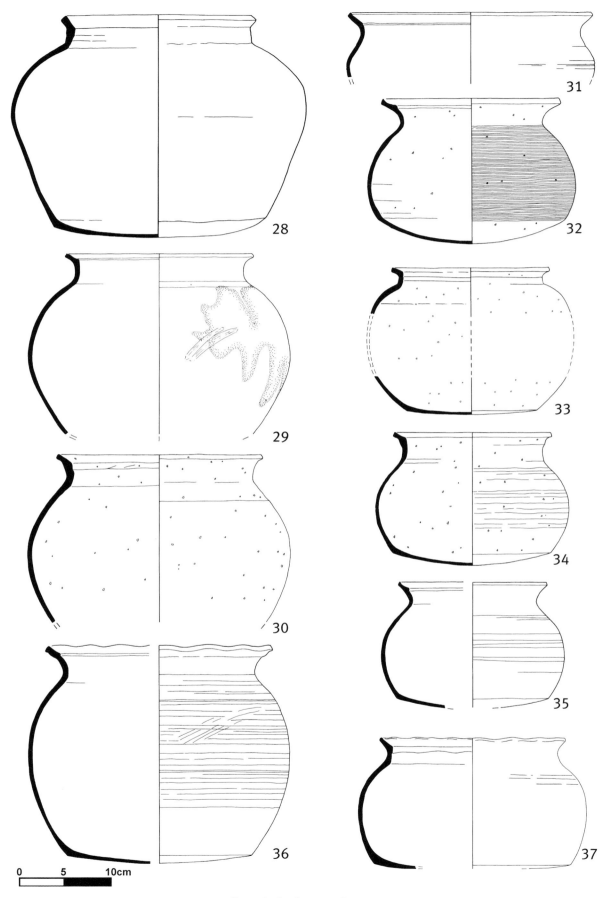

0 5 10cm

Figure 8. Southampton Coarseware

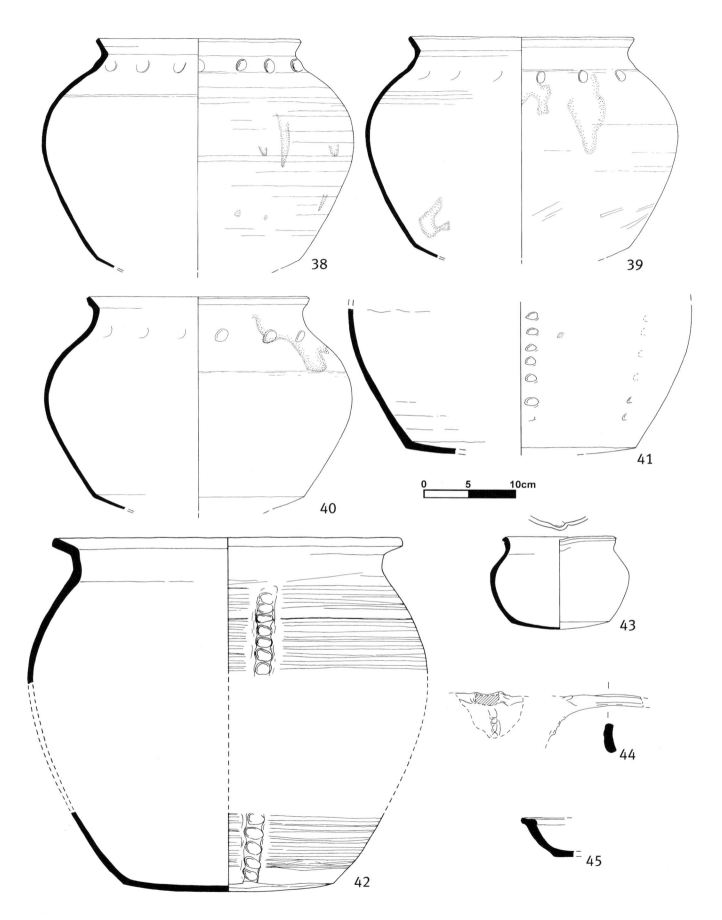

Figure 9. Southampton Coarseware

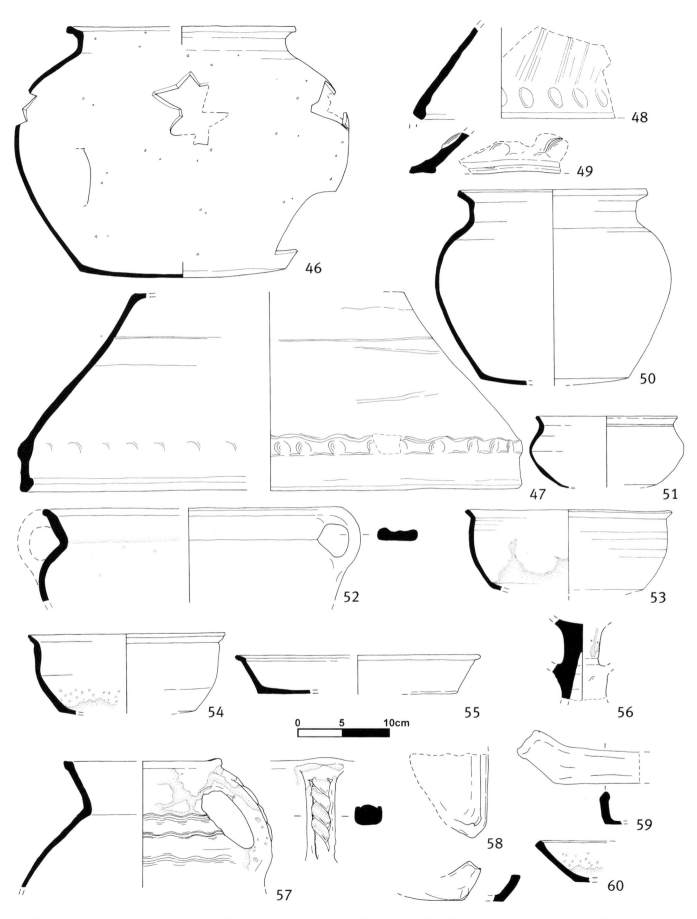

Figure 10. Southampton Coarseware, Southampton Sandy Coarseware, Southampton High Street Coarseware, High Medieval Coarsewares

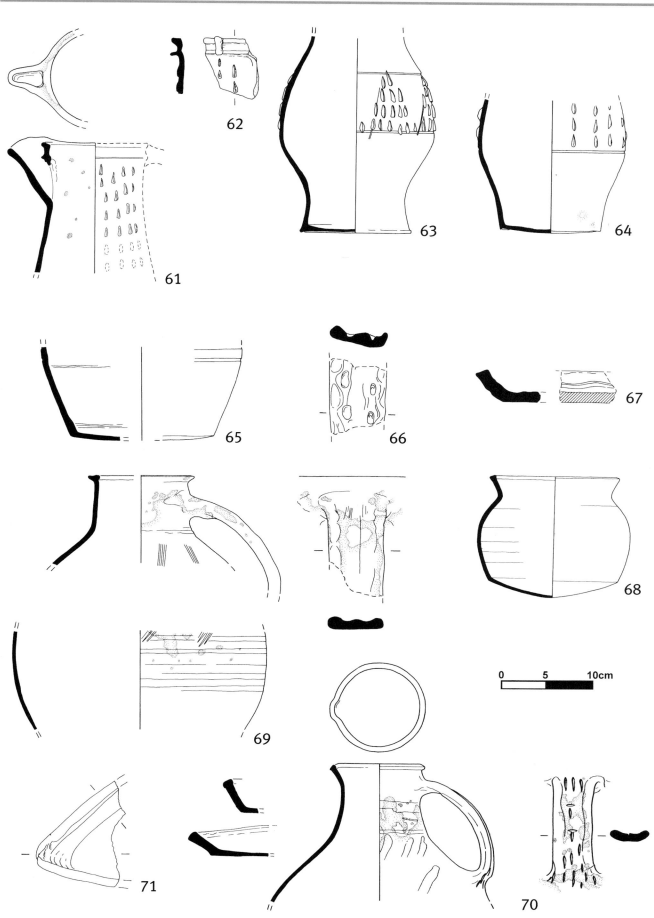

Figure 11. Southampton Whiteware, Southampton Sandy ware

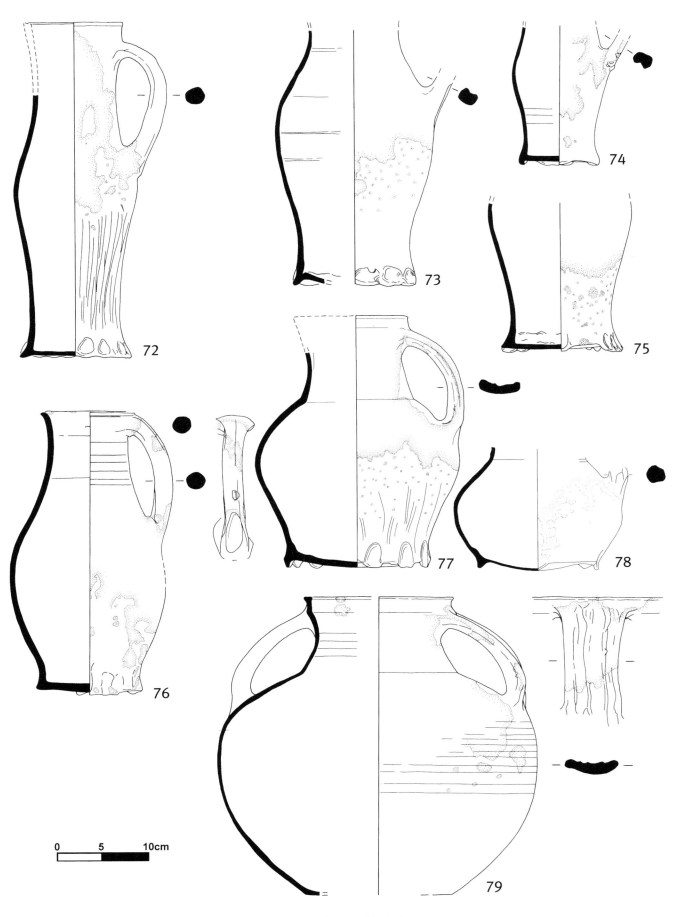

Figure 12. South Hampshire Redware

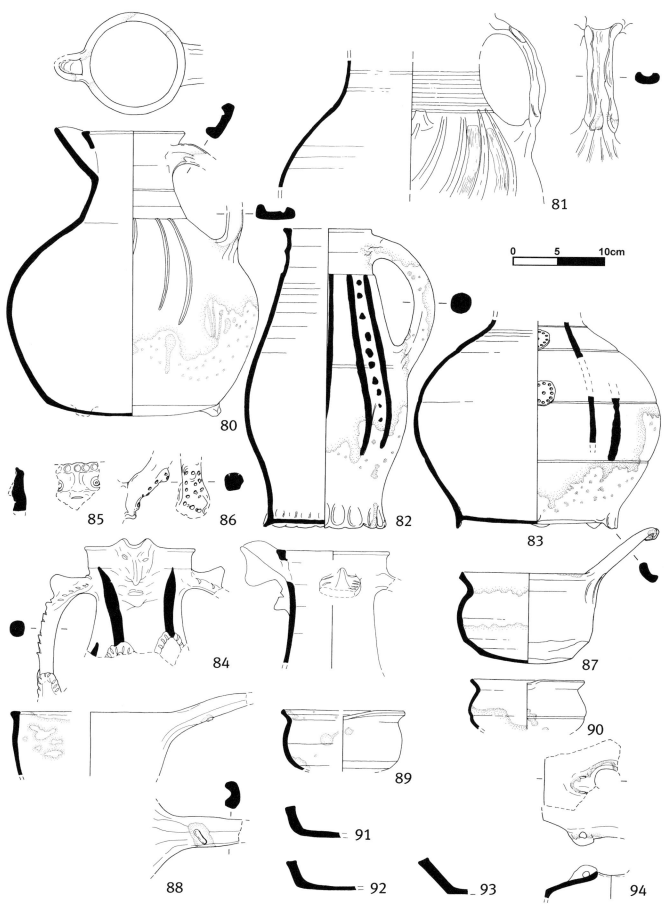

Figure 13. South Hampshire Redware

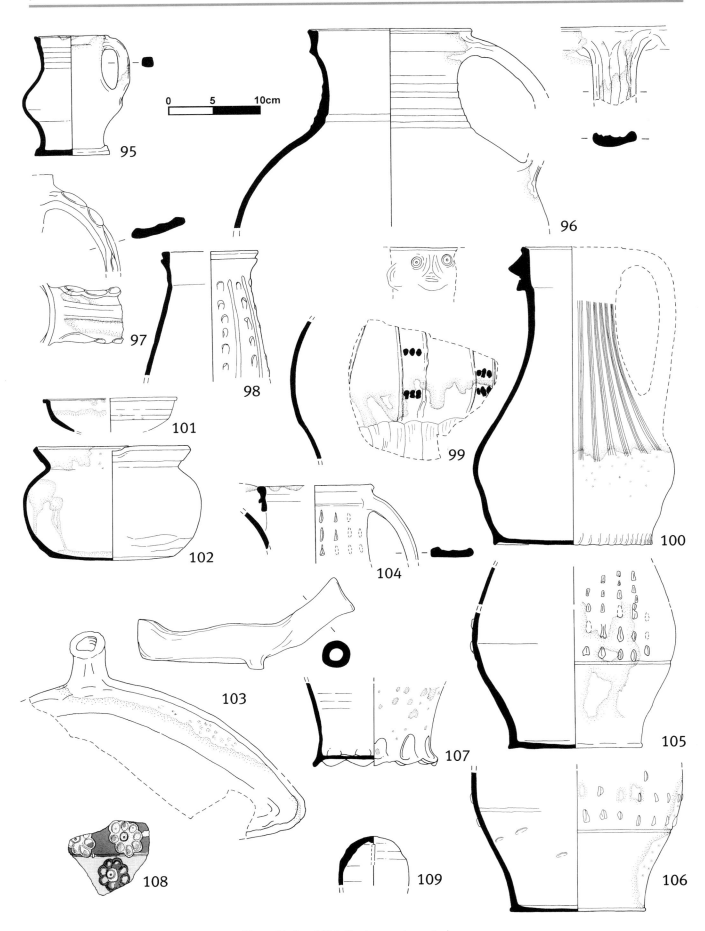

Figure 14. Local Pink Sandy ware, Laverstock ware

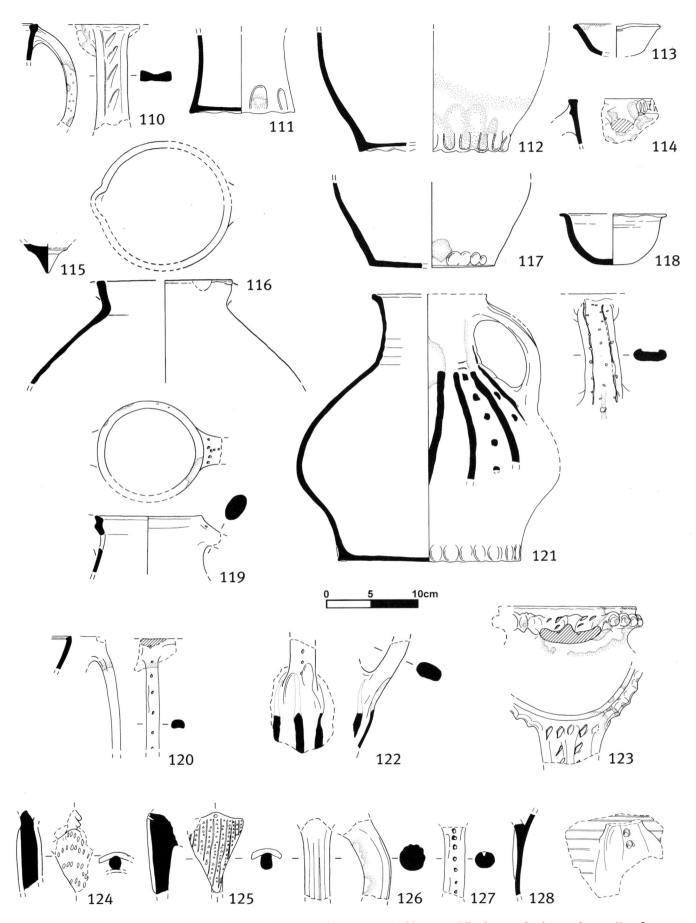

Figure 15. Local Whiteware, Local Fine White Sandy ware, Dorset Sandy ware, Dorset Whiteware, Midlands ware, Scarbourough ware, Ham Green ware

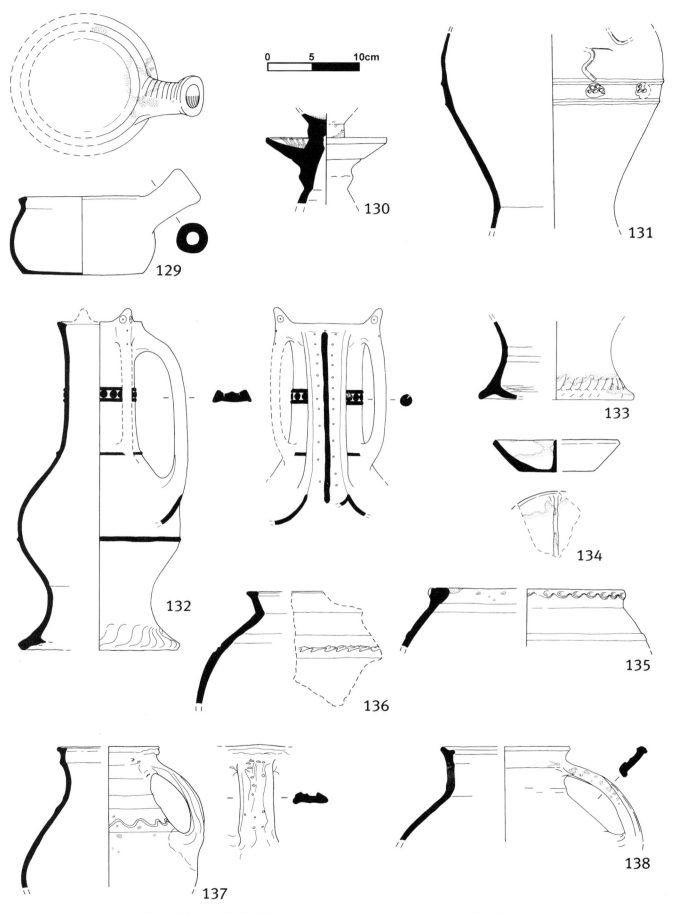

Figure 16. High Medieval Sandy wares, Southampton Organic-tempered Sandy ware

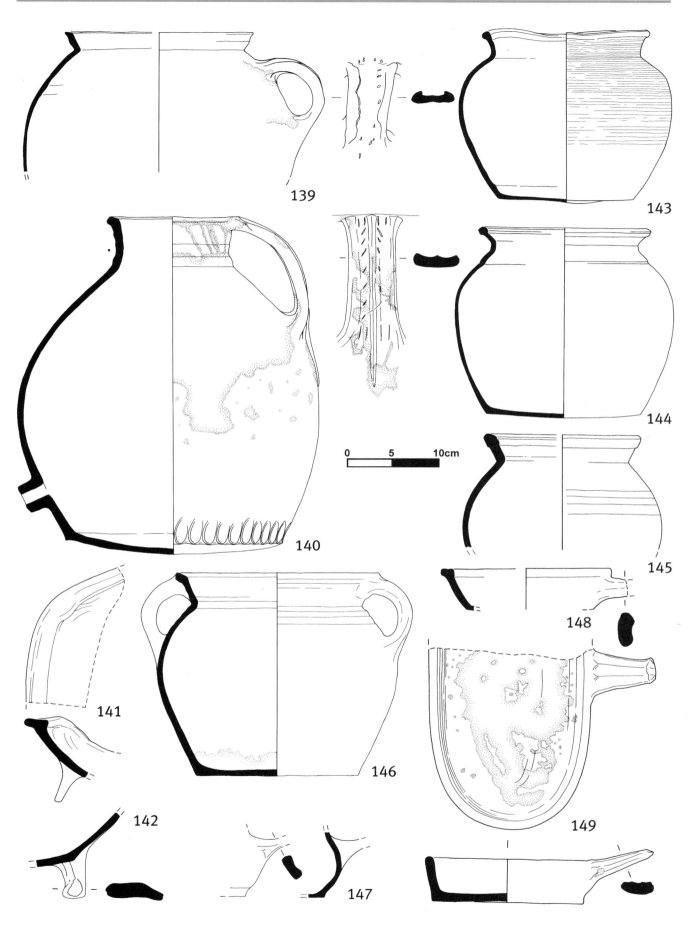

Figure 17. Southampton Organic-tempered Sandy ware, Late Medieval Well-fired Sandy ware

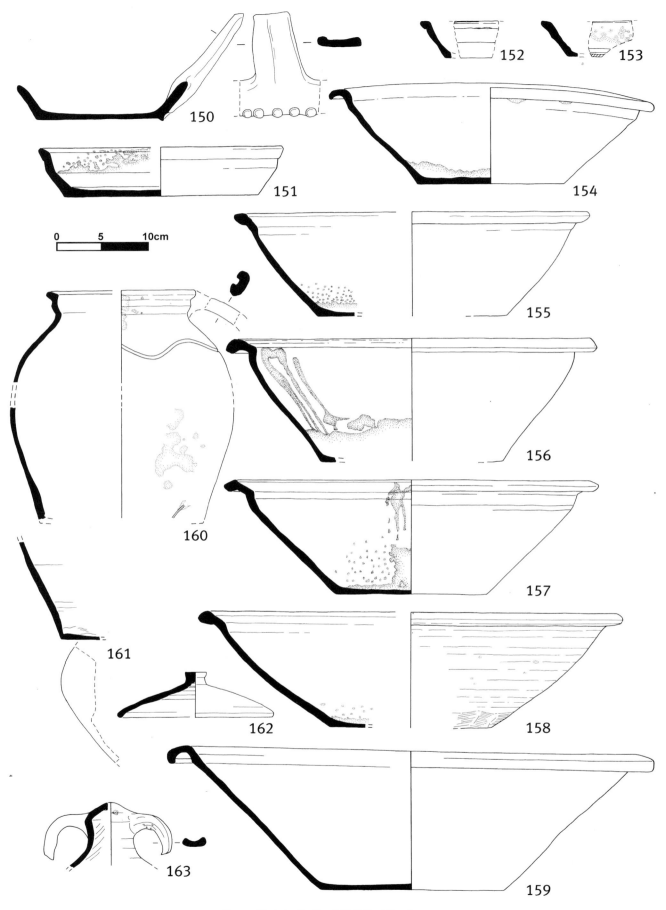

Figure 18. Late Medieval Well-fired Sandy ware

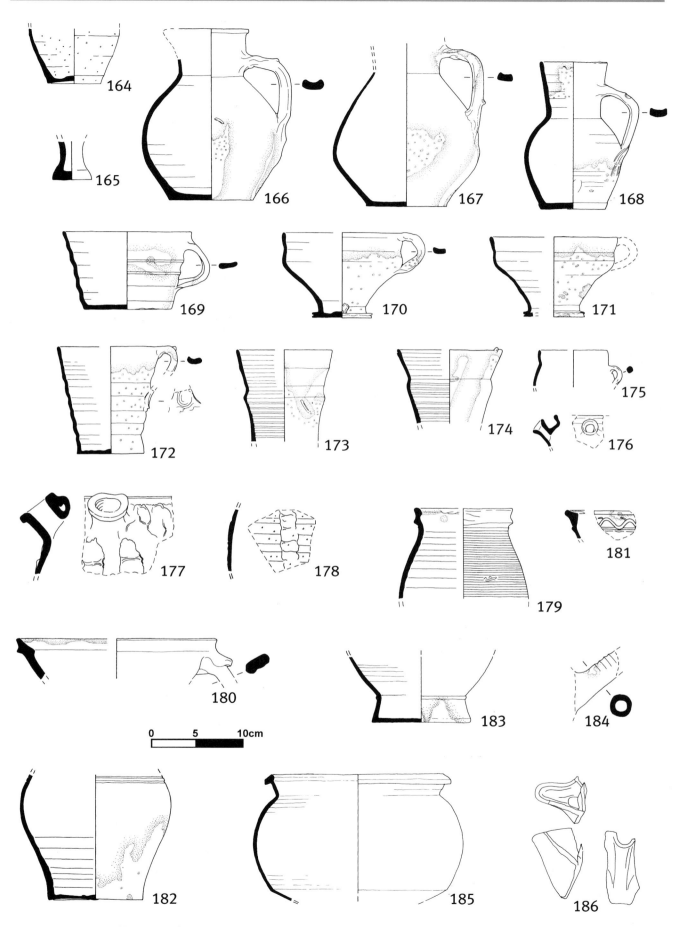

Figure 19. Surrey Whiteware, Tudor Green, Normandy Gritty, North French Glazed wares, North French Sandy ware, Early Saintonge ware

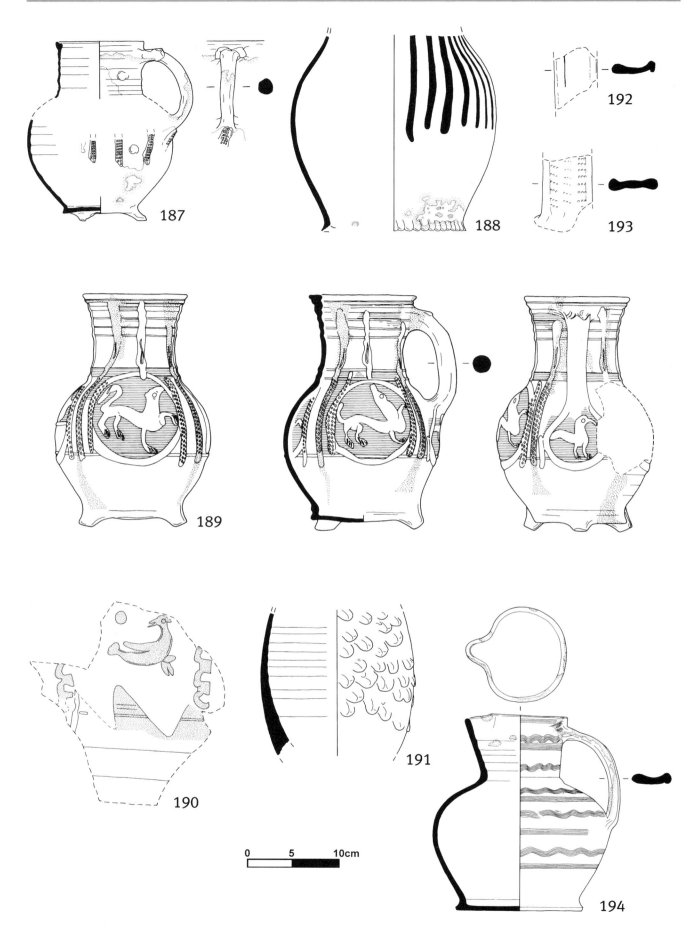

Figure 20. Developed Rouen-type ware, Seine Valley Whiteware, North French Micaceous Whiteware, Seine Valley Zoomorphic, North French Pink ware

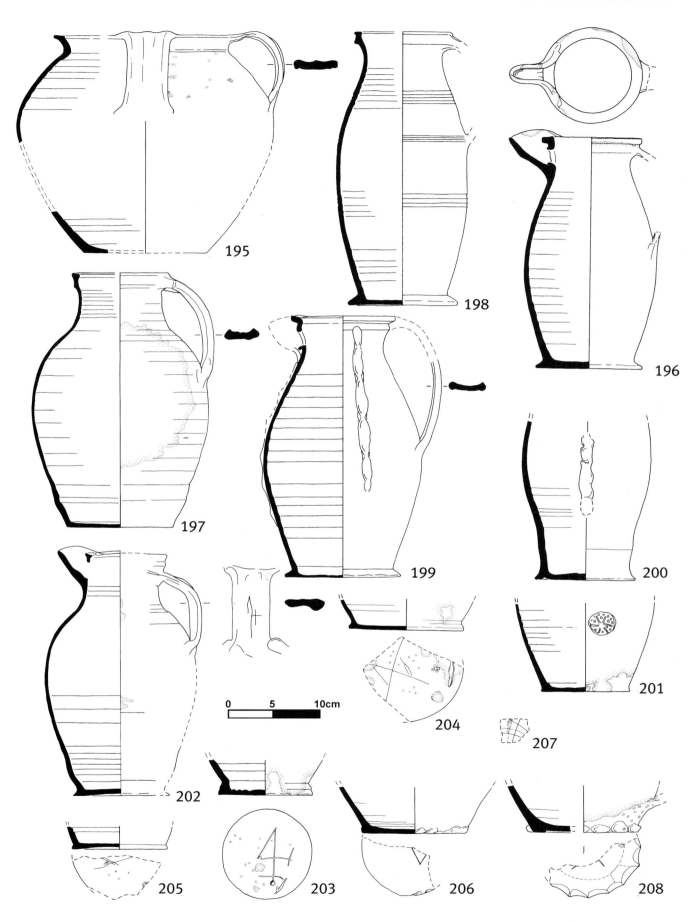

Figure 21. Saintonge Whiteware

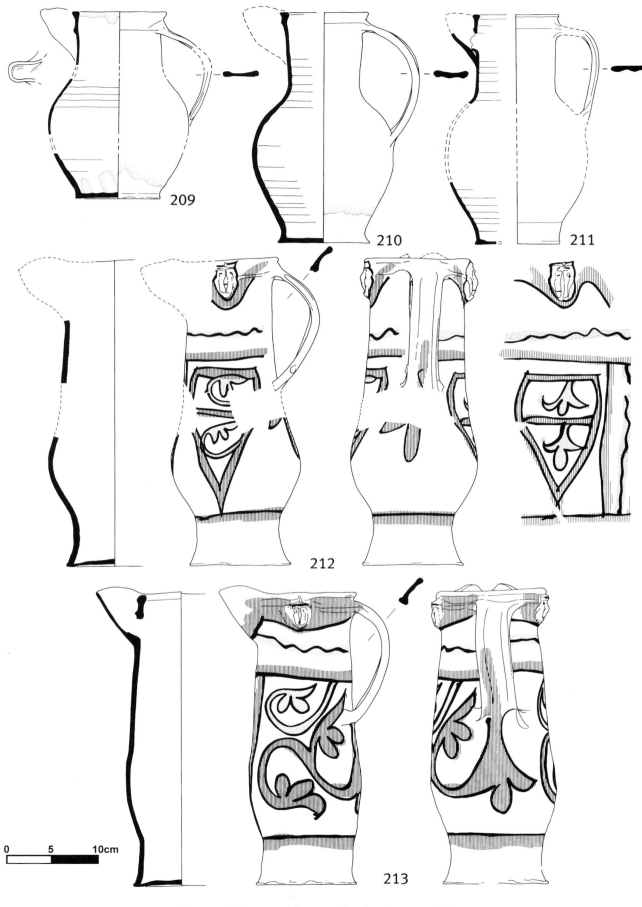

Figure 22. Saintonge Bright Green-glazed, Saintonge Polychrome

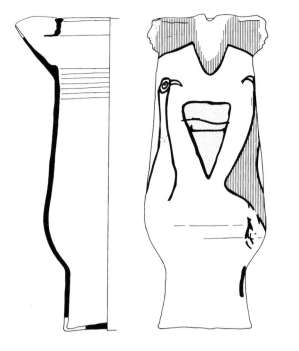
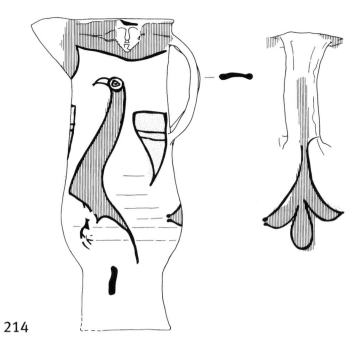

214

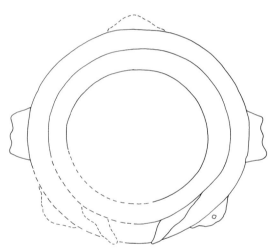

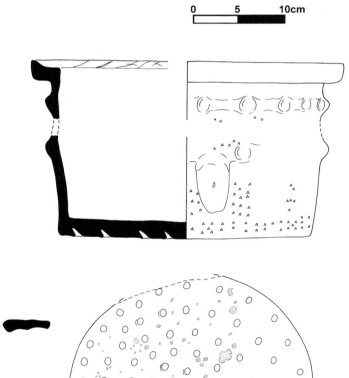

215

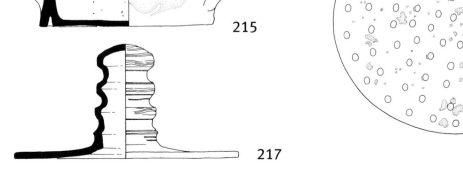

216

217

Figure 23. Saintonge Polychrome, Saintonge Gritty ware

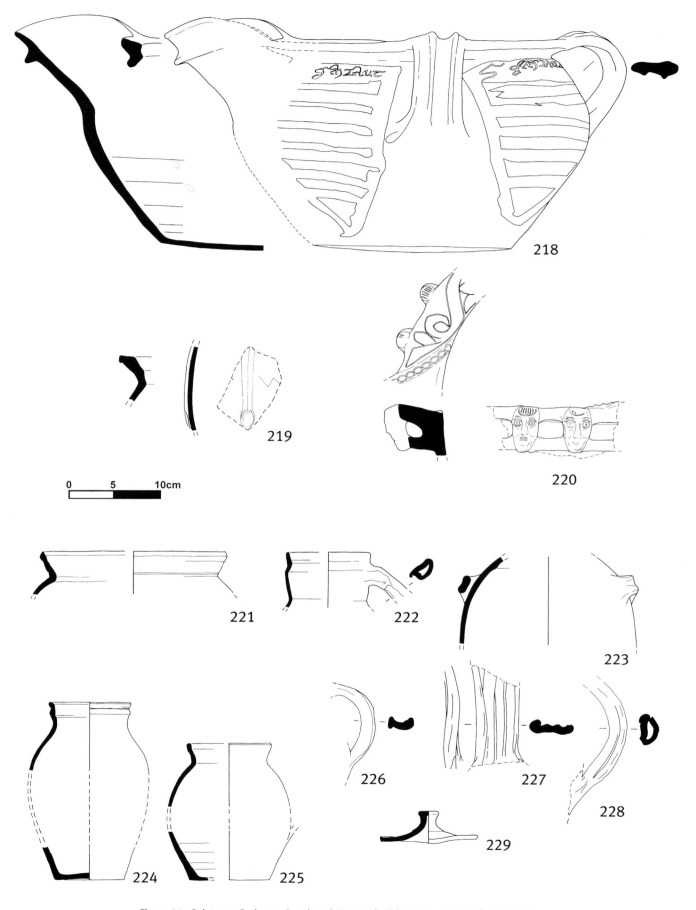

Figure 24. Saintonge Redware, Developed Normandy Gritty ware, Normandy Stoneware

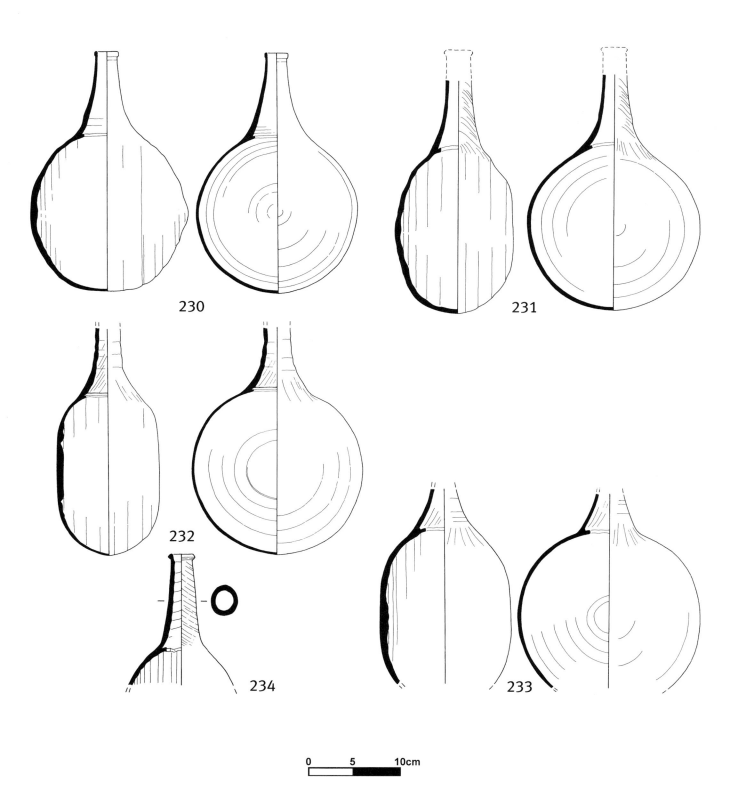

230   231

232

234   233

0   5   10cm

Figure 25. Martincamp-type ware

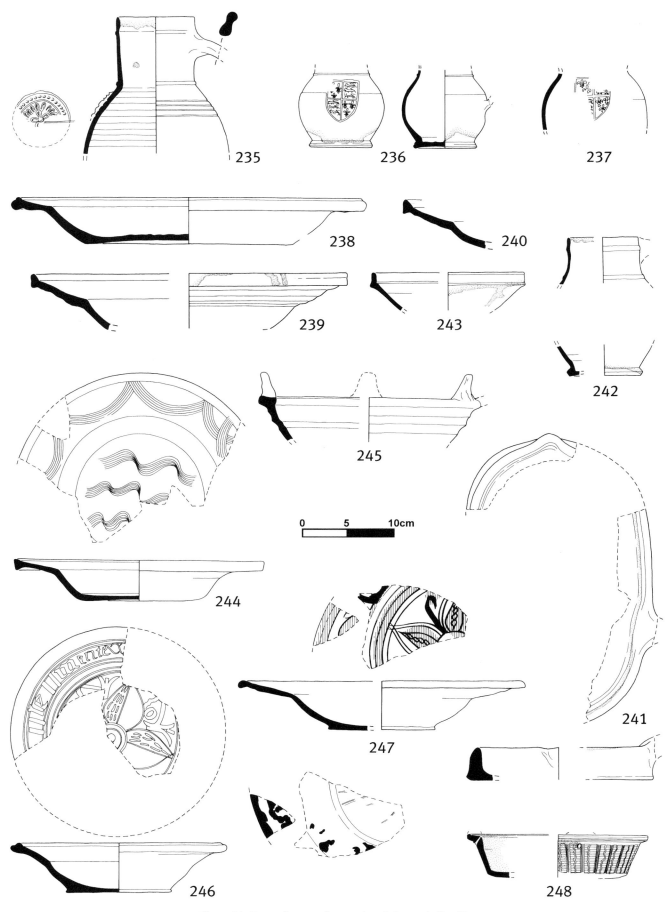

Figure 26. Beauvais monochrome glazed, Beauvais Sgraffito

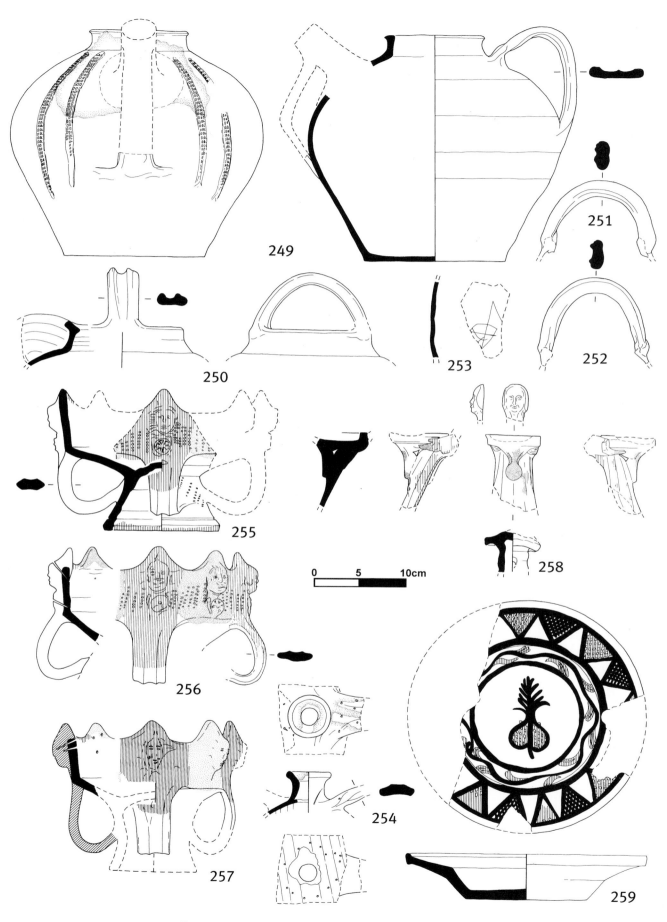

Figure 27. Late Saintonge Whiteware, Late Saintonge Polychrome

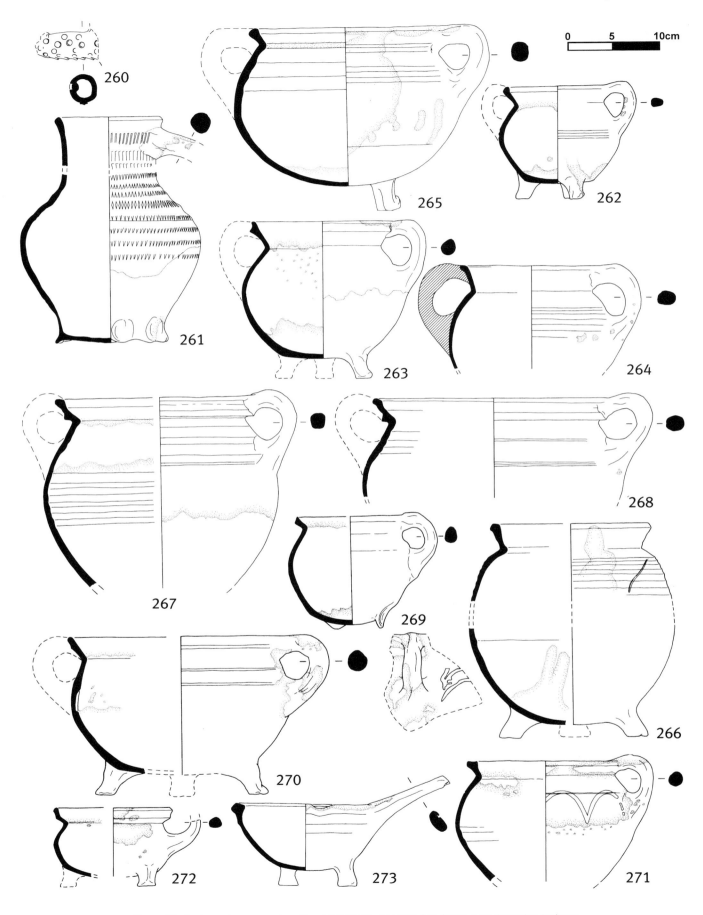

Figure 28. Andenne-type ware, Low Countries Highly Decorated Redware, Low Countries Redware

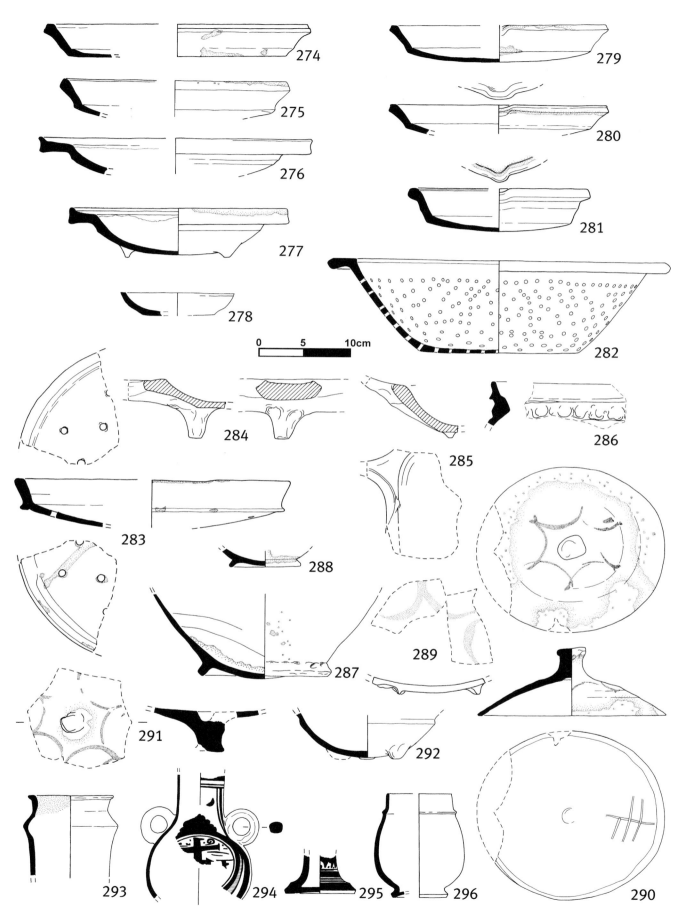

Figure 29. Low Countries Redwares, South Netherlands Tin-glazed, Malling-type Tin-glazed

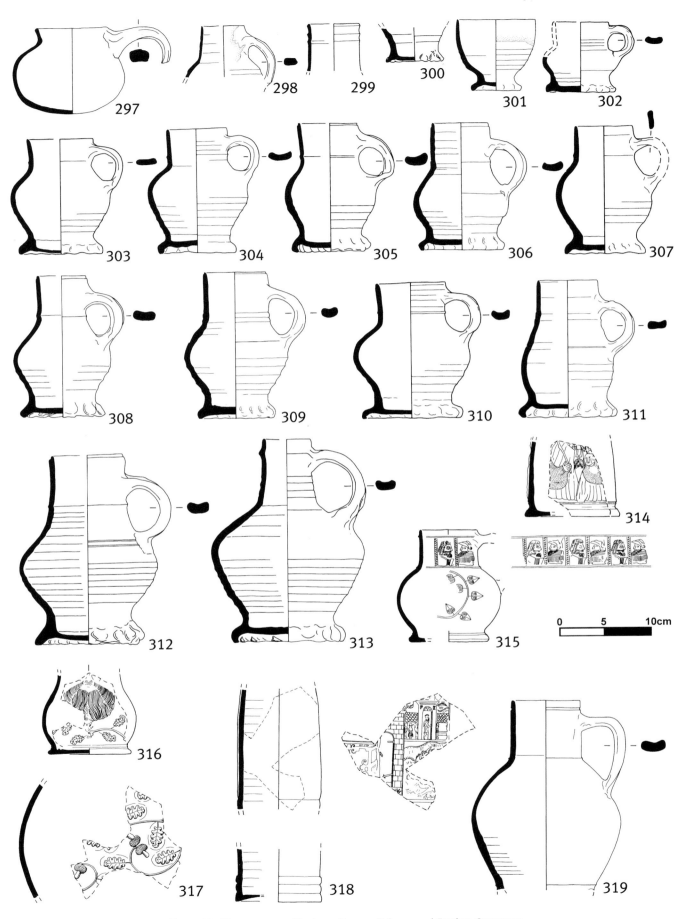

Figure 30. Blaugrau ware, Siegburg, Raeren, Cologne and Frechen Stoneware

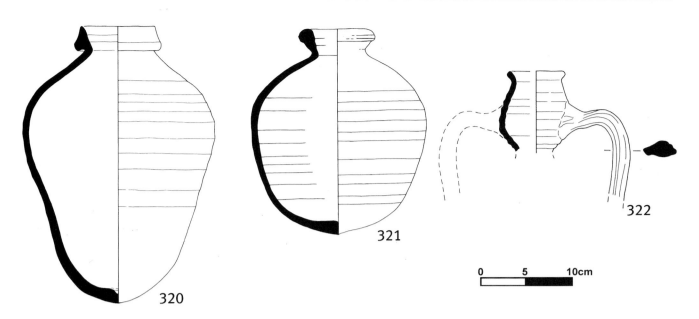
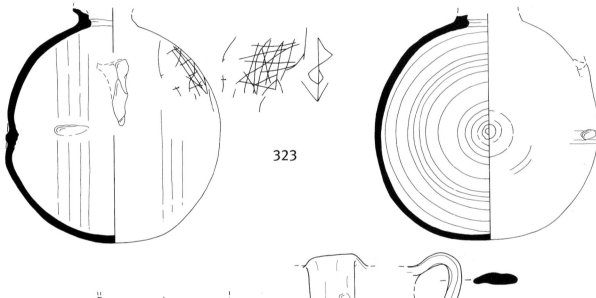
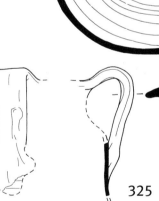

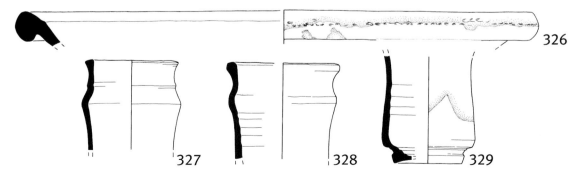

Figure 31. Seville-type Coarseware

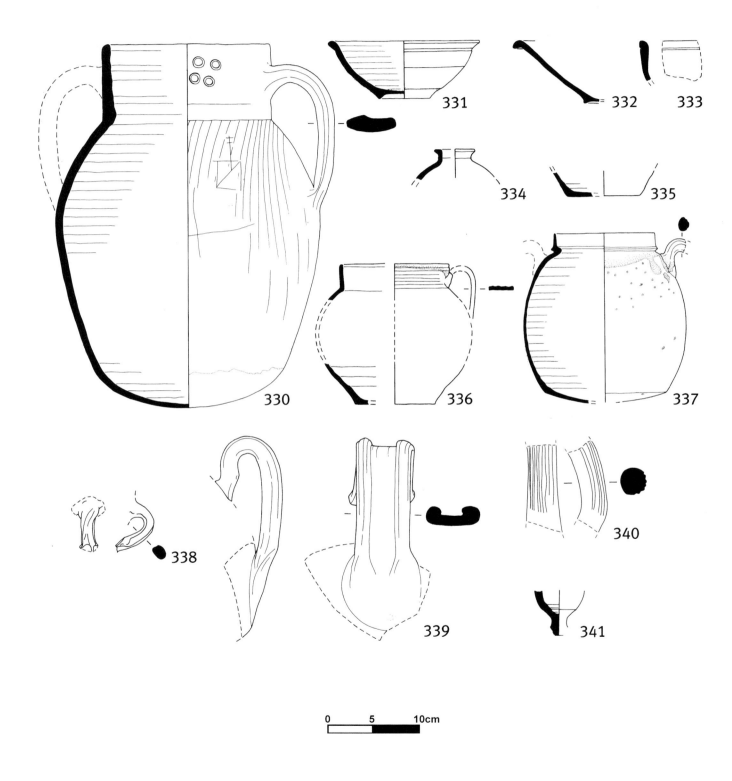

Figure 32. Andalusian Coarseware, Iberian Red Micaceous ware

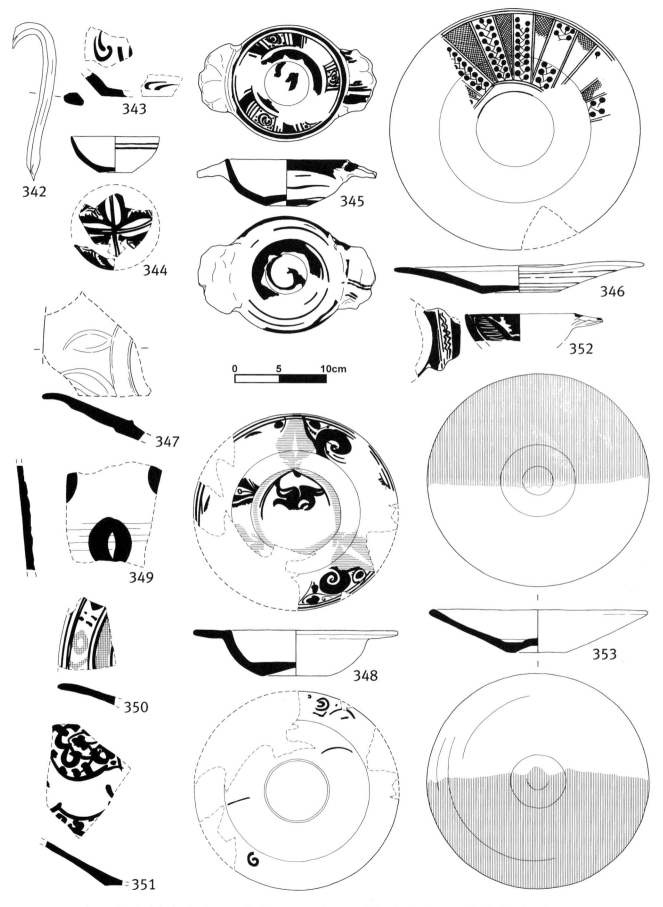

0   5   10cm

Figure 33. Andalusian Lustreware, Iberian Green and Brown, Valencian Lustreware, Seville Tin-glazed ware

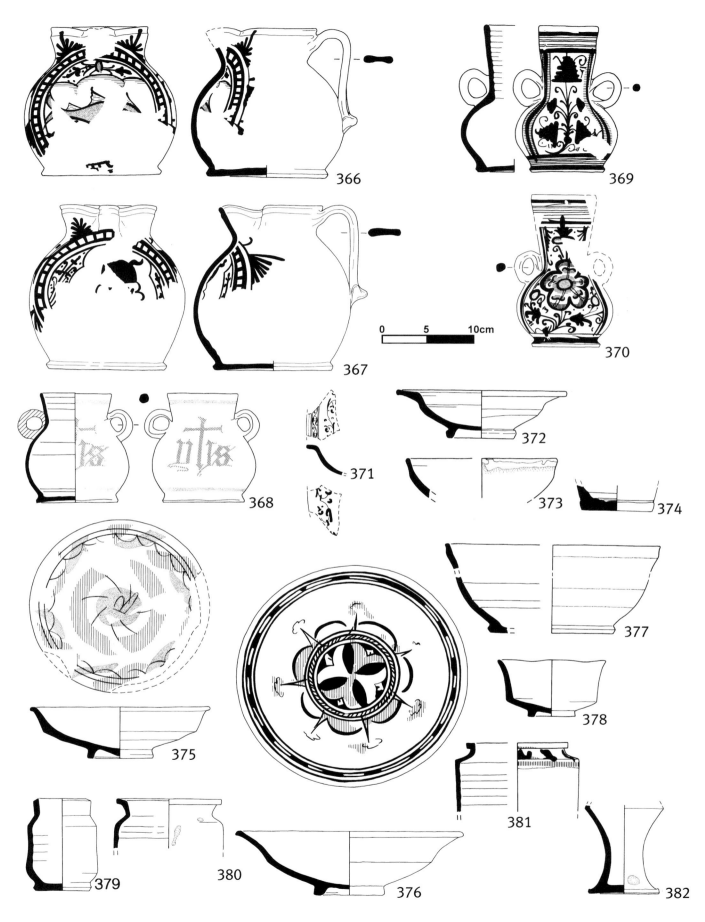

Figure 34. Seville Green and White, Montelupo Maiolica, Florentine Maiolica, Faenza-type Maiolica

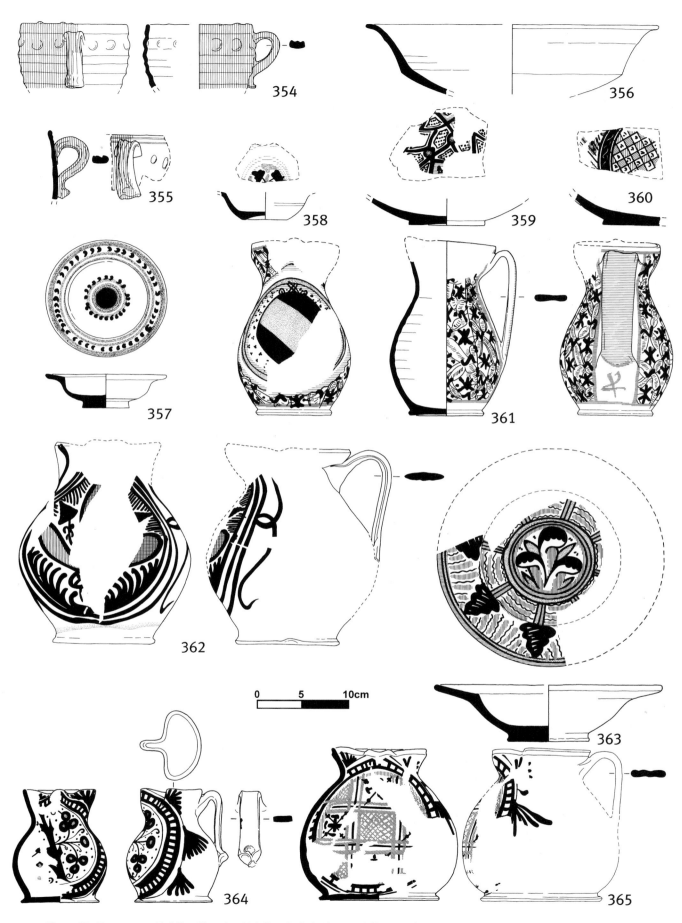

Figure 35. Faenza-type Maiolica, Venetian Maiolica, Archaic Pisan Maiolica, North Italian Sgraffito, North Italian Red Earthenware

Annexe to Chapter 2

Descriptions of illustrated vessels in illustration number order. Date ranges are given that usually reflect the relevant ceramic period, some more specific dates are based on current understanding of particular types, or on the contextual evidence.

Figure 5

1   Fabric 1007 Scratch-marked Gritty ware.
    Jar/Cooking pot.
    Anglo-Norman *c* 1070–1250
    SOU 122 B61

2   Fabric 1007 Scratch-marked Gritty ware.
    Jar/Cooking pot.
    Anglo-Norman *c* 1070–1250
    SOU 125 719

3   Fabric 1007 Scratch-marked Gritty ware.
    Jar/Cooking pot.
    Anglo-Norman *c* 1070–1250
    SOU 124 94

4   Fabric 1007 Scratch-marked Gritty ware.
    Jar/Cooking pot with lightly thumbed rim.
    Anglo-Norman *c* 1220–1250
    SOU 123 A294/297

5   Fabric 1007 Scratch-marked Gritty ware.
    Small jar/cooking pot with delicate thumbing at the rim.
    Anglo-Norman *c* 1070–1250
    SOU 124 91

6   Fabric 1007 Scratch-marked Gritty ware.
    Jar/Cooking pot with thumb-impressed rim.
    Anglo-Norman *c* 1220–1250
    SOU 123 A294

7   Fabric 1007 Scratch-marked Gritty ware.
    Large jar/cooking pot with thumb-impressed rim.
    Anglo-Norman *c* 1220–1250
    SOU 123 A294

8   Fabric 1007 Scratch-marked Gritty ware.
    Large jar/cooking pot with deep thumbing at the rim.
    Anglo-Norman *c* 1220–1250
    SOU 123 A293/294

9   Fabric 1007 Scratch-marked Gritty ware.
    Handled jar/cooking pot or jar.
    Anglo-Norman *c* 1070–1250
    SOU 25 5011

Figure 6

10 Fabric 1008 Scratch-marked Sandy ware.
    Small jar/cooking pot.
    Anglo-Norman *c* 1070–1250
    SOU 122 B227

11 Fabric 1008 Scratch-marked Sandy ware.
    Jar/Cooking pot with thumb-impressed rim.
    Anglo-Norman *c* 1070–1250
    SOU 124 46

12 Fabric 1011 Mixed Grit Coarseware.
    Jar/Cooking pot.
    Anglo-Norman *c* 1220–1250
    SOU 123 A294

13 Fabric 1014 Mixed Grit Coarseware.
    Jar/Cooking pot with thumbed rim.
    Anglo-Norman *c* 1070–1250
    SOU 25 1208

14 Fabric 1014 Mixed Grit Coarseware.
    Bowl.
    Anglo-Norman *c* 1070–1250
    SOU 125 536

15 Fabric 1014 Mixed Grit Coarseware.
    Lamp.
    Anglo-Norman *c* 1070–1250
    SOU 125 612

16 Fabric 1095 Mixed Grit Coarseware.
    Jar/Cooking pot.
    Anglo-Norman *c* 1220–1250
    SOU 123 A294

17 Fabric 1095 Mixed Grit Coarseware.
    Lamp.
    Anglo-Norman *c* 1070–1250
    SOU 125 664

18 Fabric 1055 Chalk-tempered Coarseware.
    Jar/Cooking pot.
    Anglo-Norman *c* 1220–1250
    SOU 123 A293

19 Fabric 1013 Non-local Flint-tempered ware.
    Jar/Cooking pot with thumbed rim and rilling on the body.
    Anglo-Norman *c* 1220–1250
    SOU 123 A296

20 Fabric 1081 Anglo-Norman coarseware.
    Flat-based jar/cooking pot.
    Anglo-Norman *c* 1220–1250
    SOU 123 A296

Figure 7

21 Fabric 1065 Anglo-Norman Dorset Sandy ware.
    Tripod pitcher with rouletted chevron decoration and thin green lead glaze.
    Anglo-Norman *c* 1220–1250
    SOU 123 A294

22 Fabric 1065 Anglo-Norman Dorset Sandy ware.
    Base of tripod pitcher with combed decoration and clear lead glaze

Anglo-Norman *c* 1220–1250
SOU 123 A294

23 Fabric 1101 Anglo-Norman Dorset Sandy ware.
Spout of tripod pitcher with clear lead glaze.
Anglo-Norman *c* 1070–1250
SOU 122 unstratified

24 Fabric 1099 Anglo-Norman Glazed Coarse Sandy ware.
Handbuilt jug with rilled body and greenish-clear lead glaze.
Anglo-Norman *c* 1070–1250
SOU 25 1021

25 Fabric 1084 Anglo-Norman Glazed Coarseware.
Tripod pitcher with rilled neck and greenish-clear lead glaze.
Anglo-Norman *c* 1220–1250
SOU 123 A293

26 Fabric 1084 Anglo-Norman Glazed Coarseware.
Tripod pitcher with green glaze. Evidence of use of turntable to add rim.
Anglo-Norman *c* 1070–1250
SOU 110 73A

27 Fabric 1063 Anglo-Norman Glazed Sandy ware.
Body of large pitcher with green lead glaze with incised or ribbed decoration.
Anglo-Norman *c* 1220–1250
SOU 123 A294

Figure 8

28 Fabric 1123 Southampton Coarseware.
Jar/cooking pot.
High medieval *c* 1250–1350
SOU 125 13

29 Fabric 1123 Southampton Coarseware.
Jar/cooking pot with pitch on outer surface.
High medieval *c* 1270–1350
SOU 29 980

30 Fabric 1123 Southampton Coarseware.
Jar/cooking pot.
High medieval *c* 1250–1350
SOU 25 1285

31 Fabric 1123 Southampton Coarseware.
Jar/cooking pot.
High medieval *c* 1250–1350
SOU 25 1285

32 Fabric 1123 Southampton Coarseware.
Jar/cooking pot with close throwing rings or fettling marks.
High medieval *c* 1250–1350
SOU 125 332

33 Fabric 1123 Southampton Coarseware.
Jar/cooking pot.
High medieval *c* 1250–1350
SOU 123 C170

34 Fabric 1123 Southampton Coarseware.
Jar/cooking pot.
High medieval *c* 1250–1350
SOU 25 1021

35 Fabric 1123 Southampton Coarseware.
Jar/cooking pot.
High medieval *c* 1250–1350
SOU 25 1193

36 Fabric 1123 Southampton Coarseware.
Jar/cooking pot.
High medieval *c* 1250–1350
SOU 123 B265

37 Fabric 1123 Southampton Coarseware.
Jar/cooking pot.

High medieval *c* 1250–1350
SOU 25 1211

Figure 9

38 Fabric 1123 Southampton Coarseware.
Jar/cooking pot with thumbing at shoulder and external pitch residue.
High medieval *c* 1270–1350
SOU 29 980

39 Fabric 1123 Southampton Coarseware.
Jar/cooking pot with thumbing at shoulder and external pitch residue.
High medieval *c* 1270–1350
SOU 29 980

40 Fabric 1123 Southampton Coarseware.
Jar/cooking pot with thumbing at shoulder and external pitch residue.
High medieval *c* 1270–1350
SOU 29 949

41 Fabric 1123 Southampton Coarseware.
Large jar/cooking pot with finger-impressed vertical line.
High medieval *c* 1250–1350
SOU 25 1286

42 Fabric 1123 Southampton Coarseware.
Large jar/cooking pot with thumb-impressed applied strip.
High medieval *c* 1250–1350
SOU 125 334

43 Fabric 1123 Southampton Coarseware.
Small jar/cooking pot or pipkin with pouring lip.
High medieval *c* 1250–1350
SOU 25 1246

44 Fabric 1123 Southampton Coarseware.
Handle of pipkin.
High medieval *c* 1250–1350
SOU 25 1285

45 Fabric 1123 Southampton Coarseware.
Bowl.
High medieval *c* 1250–1350
SOU 105 98

Figure 10

46 Fabric 1123 Southampton Coarseware.
Lantern made by cutting holes in a jar before firing.
High medieval *c* 1250–1350
SOU 25 1260

47 Fabric 1123 Southampton Coarseware.
Curfew with horizontal thumbed applied strip.
High medieval *c* 1250–1350
SOU 25 1285

48 Fabric 1123 Southampton Coarseware.
Curfew with thumbing at the rim.
High medieval *c* 1250–1350
SOU 25 1281

49 Fabric 1123 Southampton Coarseware.
Curfew with thumbing at the rim.
High medieval *c* 1250–1350
SOU 25 1211

50 Fabric 1024 Southampton Sandy Coarseware.
Jar/cooking pot.
High medieval *c* 1250–1350
SOU 25 1285

51 Fabric 1024 Southampton Sandy Coarseware.
Small jar/cooking pot.
High medieval *c* 1250–1350

SOU 122 A655

52 Fabric 1024 Southampton Sandy Coarseware.
Handled cooking pot.
High medieval *c* 1250–1350
SOU 125 536

53 Fabric 1024 Southampton Sandy Coarseware.
Bowl with internal greenish-clear lead glaze.
High medieval *c* 1250–1350
SOU 123 B255

54 Fabric 1024 Southampton Sandy Coarseware.
Bowl with internal greenish-clear lead glaze.
High medieval *c* 1250–1350
SOU 123 B255

55 Fabric 1024 Southampton Sandy Coarseware.
Bowl or dish.
High medieval *c* 1250–1350
SOU 123 C125

56 Fabric 1024 Southampton Sandy Coarseware.
Lamp.
High medieval *c* 1250–1350
SOU 110 72

57 Fabric 1230 Southampton High Street Coarseware
Jug with combed decoration and twisted inlay rod handle
and external greenish-clear lead glaze.
High medieval *c* 1270–1300, dated on likely period of
production.
SOU 105 145

58 Fabric 1061 High Medieval Sandy Coarseware.
Dripping pan with internal greenish-clear lead glaze.
High medieval *c* 1250–1350
SOU 123 B275

59 Fabric 1061 High Medieval Sandy Coarseware.
Dripping pan with internal greenish-clear lead glaze.
High medieval *c* 1250–1350
SOU 124 574

60 Fabric 1061 High Medieval Sandy Coarseware.
Dripping pan with internal greenish-clear lead glaze.
High medieval *c* 1250–1350
SOU 125 160

Figure 11

61 Fabric 1044 Southampton Whiteware.
Jug rim and spout, with applied pellets, green-glazed.
High medieval *c* 1270–1300, dated on likely period of
production.
SOU 124 unstratified

62 Fabric 1044 Southampton Whiteware.
Jug rim, ribbed form, with applied strips and pellets,
green-glazed.
High medieval *c* 1270–1300, dated on likely period of
production.
SOU 123 A269

63 Fabric 1044 Southampton Whiteware.
Jug with triangular panels of applied pellets between incosed
lines, green-glazed.
High medieval *c* 1270–1300, dated on likely period of
production.
SOU 25 1239

64 Fabric 1044 Southampton Whiteware.
Jug with vertical lines of applied pellets, green-glazed.
High medieval *c* 1270–1300, dated on likely period of
production.
SOU 25 1021

65 Fabric 1044 Southampton Whiteware.

Plain jug base with bright green glaze.
High medieval *c* 1270–1300, dated on likely period of
production.
SOU 25 1021

66 Fabric 1044 Southampton Whiteware.
Strap handle with bright green glaze.
High medieval *c* 1270–1300, dated on likely period of
production.
SOU 124 581

67 Fabric 1044 Southampton Whiteware.
Dripping pan with internal green glaze.
High medieval *c* 1270–1300, dated on likely period of
production.
SOU 123 C194

68 Fabric 1120 Coarse Southampton Sandy ware.
Plain cooking pot.
High medieval *c* 1250–1350
SOU 123 A296

69 Fabric 1150 Southampton Sandy ware.
Jug with external clear lead glaze.
High medieval *c* 1250–1350
SOU 123 C11

70 Fabric 1150 Southampton Sandy ware.
Jug with external painted white slip decoration under a clear
lead glaze, stabbed handle.
High medieval *c* 1250–1350
SOU 123 C118

71 Fabric 1150 Southampton Sandy ware.
Dripping pan with internal clear lead glaze.
High medieval *c* 1250–1350
SOU 123 A291

Figure 12

72
Fabric 1248 South Hampshire Redware.
Baluster jug with partial clear lead glaze.
High medieval *c* 1250–1350
SOU 25 1291

73 Fabric 1248 South Hampshire Redware.
Baluster jug with partial clear lead glaze.
High medieval *c* 1250–1350
SOU 25 1246

74 Fabric 1248 South Hampshire Redware.
Small baluster jug with partial clear lead glaze.
High medieval *c* 1250–1350
SOU 123 B333

75 Fabric 1248 South Hampshire Redware.
Base of baluster jug with partial clear lead glaze.
High medieval *c* 1250–1350
SOU 25 2166

76 Fabric 1248 South Hampshire Redware.
Pear-shaped jug with partial dull green lead glaze.
High medieval *c* 1250–1350
SOU 123 C203

77 Fabric 1248 South Hampshire Redware.
Rounded jug with partial dull green lead glaze.
High medieval *c* 1250–1350
SOU 123 unstratified

78 Fabric 1248 South Hampshire Redware.
Small rounded jug with partial green lead glaze.
High medieval *c* 1250–1350
SOU 25 1246

79 Fabric 1248 South Hampshire Redware.

Rounded two-handled pitcher with partial dull green lead glaze.
High medieval *c* 1250–1350
SOU 25 1120

Figure 13

80 Fabric 1248 South Hampshire Redware.
Reduced to a grey colour.
Tripod jug with self-coloured applied clay strips and a partial greenish-clear glaze.
High medieval *c* 1250–1350
SOU 25 1124

81 Fabric 1248 South Hampshire Redware.
Jug with white slip decoration and partial clear lead glaze.
High medieval *c* 1250–1350
SOU 124 573

82 Fabric 1248 South Hampshire Redware.
Jug with iron-rich applied clay strip and pellet decoration, partial clear lead glaze.
High medieval *c* 1250–1350
SOU 25 1246

83 Fabric 1248 South Hampshire Redware.
Rounded jug with roundels and iron-rich applied strips.
High medieval *c* 1250–1350
SOU 25 1246

84 Fabric 1248 South Hampshire Redware.
Elaborate face-jug with applied clay on handles and neck.
High medieval *c* 1250–1350
SOU 122 unstratified

85 Fabric 1248 South Hampshire Redware.
Rim of a face-jug.
High medieval *c* 1250–1350
SOU 105 91B

86 Fabric 1248 South Hampshire Redware.
Stabbed handle of a small jug, green glaze.
High medieval *c* 1250–1350
SOU 124 654

87 Fabric 1248 South Hampshire Redware.
Pipkin with internal greenish-clear lead glaze.
High medieval *c* 1250–1350
SOU 25 1285

88 Fabric 1248 South Hampshire Redware.
Pipkin with internal greenish-clear lead glaze.
High medieval *c* 1250–1350
SOU 122 A668

89 Fabric 1248 South Hampshire Redware.
Pipkin or small cooking pot with pouring lip and patches of internal greenish-clear lead glaze.
High medieval *c* 1250–1350
SOU 123 C194

90 Fabric 1248 South Hampshire Redware.
Pipkin or small cooking pot with pouring lip and partial internal greenish-clear lead glaze.
High medieval *c* 1250–1350
SOU 25 1285

91 Fabric 1248 South Hampshire Redware.
Dripping pan with internal lead glaze.
High medieval *c* 1250–1350
SOU 122 C288

92 Fabric 1248 South Hampshire Redware.
Dripping pan with internal lead glaze.
High medieval *c* 1250–1350
SOU 122 A624

93 Fabric 1248 South Hampshire Redware.
Dripping pan with internal lead glaze.
High medieval *c* 1250–1350
SOU 25 1184

94 Fabric 1248 South Hampshire Redware.
Costrel base and mouth with external green glaze.
High medieval *c* 1250–1350
SOU 122 unstratified

Figure 14

95 Fabric 1087 Local Pink Sandy ware.
Small jug with bright green glaze.
High medieval *c* 1250–1350
SOU 25 1295

96 Fabric 1087 Local Pink Sandy ware.
Large jug with greenish-clear lead glaze.
High medieval *c* 1250–1350
SOU 123 B103

97 Fabric 1087 Local Pink Sandy ware.
Strap handle of jug with green glaze.
High medieval *c* 1250, based on the date of the deposit
SOU 123 A293

98 Fabric 1087 Local Pink Sandy ware.
Jug with white clay strips and pellets under a greenish-clear glaze.
High medieval *c* 1250–1350
SOU 122 B308

99 Fabric 1087 Local Pink Sandy ware.
Body of jug with applied clay and iron-rich pellets under a greenish-clear lead glaze.
High medieval *c* 1250–1350
SOU 123 C172

100 Fabric 1087 Local Pink Sandy ware.
Face-jug with combed decoration, clear lead glaze.
High medieval *c* 1250–1350
SOU 122 A682

101 Fabric 1087 Local Pink Sandy ware.
Bowl with internal lead glaze.
High medieval *c* 1250–1350
SOU 124 526

102 Fabric 1087 Local Pink Sandy ware.
Pipkin or cooking pot with pouring lip and internal lead glaze.
High medieval *c* 1250–1350
SOU 25 1227

103 Fabric 1087 Local Pink Sandy ware.
Dripping pan with tubular handle and internal greenish-clear lead glaze.
High medieval *c* 1250–1350
SOU 25 1211

104 Fabric 1053 Laverstock ware.
Jug rim with applied pellet decoration, green lead glaze.
High medieval *c* 1250–1350
SOU 122 unstratified

105 Fabric 1034 Laverstock ware.
Jug with applied pellet decoration, green lead glaze.
High medieval *c* 1250–1350
SOU 123 B265

106 Fabric 1034 Laverstock ware.
Jug base with applied pellet decoration, green lead glaze.
High medieval *c* 1250–1350
SOU 123 B265

107 Fabric 1034 Laverstock ware.
Thumbed jug base, patches of greenish-clear lead glaze.
High medieval *c* 1250–1350

SOU 25 1245

108   Fabric 1034 Laverstock ware.
       Body sherd of jug with applied rosettes and brown slip decoration, clear lead glaze.
       High medieval *c* 1250–1350
       SOU 124 532

109   Fabric 1053 Laverstock ware.
       Money box with green glaze.
       High medieval *c* 1250–1350
       SOU 105 141
       Figure 15

110   Fabric 1118 Local Whiteware.
       Jug-handle with slashed decoration, green glaze.
       High medieval *c* 1250–1350
       SOU 25 1239

111   Fabric 1118 Local Whiteware.
       Thumbed jug base with partial green glaze.
       High medieval *c* 1250–1350
       SOU 123 A296

112   Fabric 1118 Local Whiteware.
       Thumbed jug base with green glaze.
       High medieval *c* 1250–1350
       SOU 123 A294

113   Fabric 1118 Local Whiteware.
       Lamp patchy greenish-clear glaze.
       High medieval *c* 1250–1350
       SOU 25 1239

114   Fabric 1215 Local Fine Sandy Whiteware.
       Rim and handle of jug with impressed clay pads at rim, green glaze.
       High medieval *c* 1250–1350
       SOU 122 C136

115   Fabric 1215 Local Fine Sandy Whiteware.
       Base of pricket lamp, unglazed.
       High medieval *c* 1250–1350
       SOU 105 65

116   Fabric 1430 Dorset Sandy ware.
       Rim and shoulder of jug, unglazed.
       High medieval *c* 1250–1350
       SOU 122 A657

117   Fabric 1430 Dorset Sandy ware.
       Jug base with thumbing, patch of clear glaze.
       High medieval *c* 1250–1350
       SOU 123 unstratified

118   Fabric 1445 Dorset Sandy ware.
       Small round bowl, unglazed.
       High medieval *c* 1250–1350
       SOU 29 59

119   Fabric 1156 Dorset Whiteware.
       Rim and stabbed handle of jug, green lead glaze.
       High medieval *c* 1250–1350
       SOU 124 574

120   Fabric 1156 Dorset Whiteware.
       Thin handle or strut from a highly decorated jug, clear lead glaze.
       High medieval *c* 1250–1350
       SOU 125 40

121   Fabric 1156 Dorset Whiteware.
       Large rounded jug with iron-rich strips and pellets, stabbed handle, clear lead glaze appears bright yellow over white clay.
       High medieval *c* 1250–1350
       SOU 122 C286

122   Fabric 1156 Dorset Whiteware.

Jug painted with iron-rich slip beneath lustrous clear lead glaze.
       High medieval *c* 1250–1350
       SOU 124 603

123   Fabric 1078 Midlands ware.
       Elaborate jug rim and handle rich, green glaze.
       High medieval *c* 1250–1350
       SOU 123 B338

124   Fabric 1526 Scarborough ware.
       Figure and shield from a knight jug; thick, dark green lead glaze.
       High medieval *c* 1250–1350
       SOU 122 C136

125   Fabric 1526 Scarborough ware.
       Shield, dark green glaze; possibly from the same vessel as 124.
       High medieval *c* 1250–1350
       SOU 122 C136

126   Fabric 1526 Scarborough ware.
       Grooved handle, dark green glaze; possibly from the same vessel as 124 and 125.
       High medieval *c* 1250–1350
       SOU 122 C136

127   Fabric 1526 Scarborough ware.
       Small stabbed jug handle or strut; rich, dark green lead glaze.
       High medieval *c* 1250–1350
       SOU 105 93

128   Fabric 1778 Ham Green ware.
       Handle and body sherd of jug, dull green lead glaze.
       High medieval *c* 1250–1350
       SOU 122 unstratified

Figure 16

129   Fabric 1209 High Medieval Sandy ware.
       Saucepan with tubular handle and internal greenish-clear lead glaze.
       High medieval *c* 1250, based on date of deposit
       SOU 123 A293

130   Fabric 1534 High Medieval Sandy ware.
       Lamp, patches and runs of greenish-clear glaze.
       High medieval *c* 1250–1350
       SOU 125 536

131   Fabric 1533 High Medieval Sandy ware.
       Jug with complex applied clay decoration, green glaze.
       High medieval *c* 1250–1350
       SOU 125 182

132   Fabric 1740 Burnt. High Medieval Sandy ware.
       Highly decorated jug with iron-rich applied clay and struts.
       High medieval *c* 1338 based on possible date of house destruction
       SOU 125 40

133   Fabric 1740 Burnt. High Medieval Sandy ware.
       Base of jug with overlapping thumbing.
       High medieval *c* 1338 based on possible date of house destruction
       SOU 125 40

134   Fabric 1740 Burnt. High Medieval Sandy ware.
       Divided dish, internal greenish-clear lead glaze.
       High medieval *c* 1250–1350
       SOU 125 151

135   Fabric 1130 Coarse Southampton Organic-tempered Sandy ware.
       Jar rim with impressed decoration.

Late medieval *c* 1350–1450
SOU 29 3004

136   Fabric 1136 Fine Southampton Organic-tempered Sandy
ware.
Jar rim with impressed decoration at the shoulder, splashes
of greenish clear glaze.
Late medieval *c* 1350–1450
SOU 29 83

137   Fabric 1136 Fine Southampton Organic-tempered Sandy
ware.
Jug with incised wavy line, patches of greenish-clear glaze.
Late medieval *c* 1350–1450
SOU 29 428

138   Fabric 1130 Coarse Southampton Organic-tempered Sandy
ware.
Jug, partial greenish-clear glaze.
Late medieval *c* 1350–1450
SOU 125 191

Figure 17

139   Fabric 1136 Fine Southampton Organic-tempered Sandy
ware.
Pitcher with short strap handle, partial greenish-clear glaze.
Late medieval *c* 1350–1450
SOU 29 62

140   Fabric 1136 Fine Southampton Organic-tempered Sandy
ware.
Bunghole pitcher, red fabric with partial greenish-clear lead
glaze.
Late medieval *c* 1350–1450
SOU 29 62

141   Fabric 1136 Fine Southampton Organic-tempered Sandy
ware.
Dripping pan, internal greenish-clear lead glaze.
Late medieval *c* 1350–1450
SOU 123 B455

142   Fabric 1130 Coarse Southampton Organic-tempered Sandy
ware.
Base fragment of large dripping pan or footed cooking pot.
Late medieval *c* 1350–1450
SOU 123 C136

143   Fabric 1356 Late Medieval Well-fired Sandy ware.
Cooking pot, plain, reduced grey surfaces.
Late medieval *c* 1420–1510
SOU 125 191

144   Fabric 1365 Late Medieval Well-fired Sandy ware.
Cooking pot, plain, reduced grey surfaces.
Late medieval *c* 1420–1510
SOU 124 214

145   Fabric 1264 Late Medieval Well-fired Sandy ware.
Rim of cooking pot in red unglazed fabric.
Late medieval *c* 1420–1510
SOU 125 181

146   Fabric 1633 Late Medieval Well-fired Sandy ware.
Two handled jar or cooking pot, red fabric with internal
clear lead glaze.
Late medieval *c* 1490–1510
SOU 128 76

147   Fabric 1115 Late Medieval Well-fired Sandy ware.
Base and handled of pipkin, black fabric, patches of
greenish-clear glaze.
Late medieval *c* 1420–1510
SOU 29 63

148   Fabric 1161 Late Medieval Well-fired Sandy ware.

Skillet, red-grey fabric.
Late medieval *c* 1490–1510
SOU 128 43

149   Fabric 1203 Late Medieval Well-fired Sandy ware.
Dripping pan, red fabric with internal greenish-clear lead
glaze.
Late medieval *c* 1490–1510
SOU 128 58

Figure 18

150   Fabric 1115 Late Medieval Well-fired Sandy ware.
Dripping pan, red fabric with internal clear lead glaze.
Late medieval *c* 1490–1510
SOU 128 58

151   Fabric 1133 Late Medieval Well-fired Sandy ware.
Bowl, red fabric with internal clear lead glaze.
Late medieval *c* 1490–1510
SOU 128 56B

152   Fabric 1263 Late Medieval Well-fired Sandy ware.
Bowl in red-grey fabric.
Late medieval *c* 1420–1510
SOU 29 51

153   Fabric 1176 Late Medieval Well-fired Sandy ware.
Dripping pan with internal, greenish-clear lead glaze.
Late medieval *c* 1420–1510
SOU 110 107

154   Fabric 1203 Late Medieval Well-fired Sandy ware.
Pancheon, dark grey fabric, internal greenish-clear lead glaze.
Late medieval *c* 1490–1510
SOU 122 B308

155   Fabric 1110 Late Medieval Well-fired Sandy ware.
Pancheon, red fabric, internal clear lead glaze.
Late medieval *c* 1490–1510
SOU 128 59

156   Fabric 1161 Late Medieval Well-fired Sandy ware.
Pancheon, red fabric, internal clear lead glaze.
Late medieval *c* 1490–1510
SOU 124 220

157   Fabric 1133 Late Medieval Well-fired Sandy ware.
Pancheon, red fabric, internal clear lead glaze.
Late medieval *c* 1490–1510
SOU 124 479

158   Fabric 1133 Late Medieval Well-fired Sandy ware.
Pancheon, red fabric, internal clear lead glaze.
Late medieval *c* 1490–1510
SOU 128 58

159   Fabric 1365 Late Medieval Well-fired Sandy ware.
Pancheon, grey fabric, internal greenish-clear lead glaze.
Late medieval *c* 1490–1510
SOU 124 205

160   Fabric 1115 Late Medieval Well-fired Sandy ware.
Pitcher, grey fabric, incised wavy line decoration, patchy
greenish-clear
lead glaze.
Late medieval *c* 1420–1510
SOU 124 1

161   Fabric 1574 Late Medieval Well-fired Sandy ware.
Base sherd of oval or rectangular shaped vessel, possibly a
cistern.
Late medieval *c* 1490–1510
SOU 128 56B

162   Fabric 1110 Late Medieval Well-fired Sandy ware.
Lid, red fabric.
Late medieval *c* 1420–1510

SOU 122 B414

163   Fabric 1607 Late Medieval Well-fired Sandy ware.
Neck of watering pot, dark red-grey fabric, splashes of clear glaze.
Late medieval c 1420–1510
SOU 105 39

Figure 19

164   Fabric 1092 Surrey Whiteware.
Jug or jar base, unglazed.
Late medieval c 1420–1510
SOU 29 428

165   Fabric 1092 Surrey Whiteware.
Base of lamp or candle-stick, splash of green glaze.
Late medieval c 1420–1510
SOU 29 112

166   Fabric 1193 Tudor Green ware.
Jug, bright green external glaze.
Late medieval c 1450–1510
SOU 124 salvage

167   Fabric 1193 Tudor Green ware.
Jug, bright green glaze.
Late medieval c 1450–1510
SOU 124 salvage

168   Fabric 1193 Tudor Green ware.
Jug, bright green glaze.
Late medieval c 1490–1510
SOU 128 100

169   Fabric 1193 Tudor Green ware.
Cup, internal and external green glaze.
Late medieval c 1490–1510
SOU 124 491

170   Fabric 1193 Tudor Green ware.
Pedestal cup, internal and external green glaze.
Late medieval c 1450–1510
SOU 124 salvage

171   Fabric 1193 Tudor Green ware.
Pedestal cup, internal and external green glaze.
Late medieval c 1450–1510
SOU 124 salvage

172   Fabric 1193 Tudor Green ware.
Flared cup, internal and external green glaze.
Late medieval c 1450–1510
SOU 124 salvage

173   Fabric 1193 Tudor Green ware.
Waisted cup or beaker, internal and external green glaze.
Late medieval c 1450–1510
SOU 124 salvage

174   Fabric 1193 Tudor Green ware.
Waisted cup or beaker, internal and external green glaze.
Late medieval c 1450–1510
SOU 124 salvage

175   Fabric 1193 Tudor Green ware.
Small ring-handled cup, internal and external green glaze.
Late medieval c 1450–1510
SOU 105 10

176   Fabric 1193 Tudor Green ware.
Small tubular spout, external green glaze.
Late medieval c 1450–1510
SOU 124 127

177   Fabric 1284 Normandy Gritty ware.
Tubular-spouted pitcher, unglazed.
Anglo-Norman c 1070–1250
SOU 25 2025

178   Fabric 1284 Normandy Gritty ware.
Body sherd showing typical applied strip decoration.
Anglo-Norman c 1070–1250
SOU 110 33D

179   Fabric 1281 North French Glazed ware.
Jug rim, pinkish fine fabric with green lead glaze, rilled neck and shoulder.
Anglo-Norman c 1100–1250
SOU 123 B348

180   Fabric 1200 North French Glazed ware.
Rim of a large jug in a buff fabric with bright green lead glaze.
Anglo-Norman c 1100–1250
SOU 122 unstratified

181   Fabric 1200 North French Glazed ware.
Jug rim, whiteware, with bright green glaze and incised decoration.
Anglo-Norman c 1100–1250
SOU 110 107

182   Fabric 1200 North French Glazed ware.
Jug base, whiteware, with green lead glaze.
Anglo-Norman c 1100–1250
SOU 25 1208

183   Fabric 1277 North French Glazed ware.
Jug base with cordon, whiteware, with bright green lead glaze.
Anglo-Norman c 1100–1250
SOU 124 574

184   Fabric 1404 North French Glazed ware.
Tubular spout, whiteware, with bright green lead glaze.
Anglo-Norman c 1100–1250
SOU 125 445

185   Fabric 1413 North French Sandy ware.
Cooking pot, unglazed, white-grey sandy fabric.
Anglo-Norman c 1100–1250
SOU 123 A294

186   Fabric 1269 Early Saintonge ware.
Parrot-beak spout, pink-buff fabric with thick apple green lead glaze
Anglo-Norman c 1200–1250
SOU 123 A294

Figure 20

187   Fabric 1403 Developed Rouen ware.
Three-footed jug with rouletted applied strip, clear glaze.
High Medieval c 1250–1350
SOU 25 1211

188   Fabric 1548 Seine Valley Whiteware.
Jug base with red slip vertical lines beneath greenish-clear glaze.
High Medieval c 1250–1350
SOU 125 332

189   Fabric 1407 Seine Valley Zoomorphic.
Jug with applied clay zoomorphic motif, red slip and green-glazed rouletted applied strips.
High Medieval c 1250–1350
SOU 110 6/18

190   Fabric 1407 Seine Valley Zoomorphic.
Body sherd of jug with white applied clay zoomorphic motif and brown slip, clear glaze.
High Medieval c 1250–1350
SOU 125 719

191   Fabric 1711 North French Micaceous Whiteware.
Jug body with applied scales and green lead glaze.

High Medieval *c* 1250–1350
SOU 110 33D

192 Fabric 1711 North French Micaceous Whiteware.
Jug handle with green lead glaze.
High Medieval *c* 1250–1350
SOU 110, 33D

193 Fabric 1711 North French Micaceous Whiteware.
Jug handle, green glaze; probably from 193.
High Medieval *c* 1250–1350
SOU 110 78

194 Fabric 2054 French Whiteware.
Jug with thrown strap handle, combed lines and dark green glaze.
High Medieval *c* 1250–1350
SOU 25 1246

Figure 21

195 Fabric 1266 Saintonge Whiteware.
Three-handled pitcher or pégau, it probably had a large applied spout, external splashes of green glaze.
High medieval, *c* 1250–1350
SOU 25 1189

196 Fabric 1272 Saintonge Whiteware.
Plain jug with applied 'parrot-beak' spout and green lead glaze.
High medieval, *c* 1250–1350
SOU 25 1184

197 Fabric 1272 Saintonge Whiteware.
Jug, green lead glaze at front, possibly a pulled handle. This may be a late Saintonge type, although it was recovered from a high medieval context.
High medieval, *c* 1250–1350, probably closer to 1350
SOU 25 1291

198 Fabric 1272 Saintonge Whiteware.
Jug, combed decoration, green lead glaze.
High medieval, *c* 1250–1350
SOU 25 1021

199 Fabric 1272 Saintonge Whiteware.
Jug with applied spout, thrown strap handle, typical splayed base, vertical thumbed applied strip, green lead glaze.
High medieval, *c* 1250–1350
SOU 25 1124

200 Fabric 1272 Saintonge Whiteware.
Jug base, vertical thumbed applied strip, green lead glaze.
High medieval, *c* 1250–1350
SOU 25 1227

201 Fabric 1272 Saintonge Whiteware.
Jug base, stamped applied roundel, green lead glaze.
High medieval, *c* 1250–1350
SOU 125 22

202 Fabric 1272 Saintonge Whiteware.
Jug, partial green glaze, with merchant's mark on handle.
High medieval, *c* 1250–1350
SOU 125 40

203 Fabric 1272 Saintonge Whiteware.
Jug base with merchant's mark.
High medieval, *c* 1250–1350
SOU 122 A655

204 Fabric 1272 Saintonge Whiteware.
Jug base with merchant's mark.
High medieval, *c* 1250–1350
SOU 124 563

205 Fabric 1272 Saintonge Whiteware.
Jug base with merchant's mark.

High medieval, *c* 1250–1350
SOU 122 A449

206 Fabric 1272 Saintonge Whiteware.
Jug base with merchant's mark.
High medieval, *c* 1250–1350
SOU 122 unstratified

207 Fabric 1272 Saintonge Whiteware.
Jug base with merchant's mark.
High medieval, *c* 1250–1350
SOU 105 193

208 Fabric 1272 Saintonge Whiteware.
Costrel with faceted base, green glaze, and suggestion of a merchant's mark.
High medieval, *c* 1250–1350
SOU 125 329

Figure 22

209 Fabric 1500 Saintonge Bright Green-glazed ware.
Jug with all over bright green glaze.
High medieval, *c* 1250–1350
SOU 125 544

210 Fabric 1500 Saintonge Bright Green-glazed ware.
Jug with all over bright green glaze.
High medieval, *c* 1250–1350
SOU 25 1292

211 Fabric 1500 Saintonge Bright Green-glazed ware.
Jug with all over bright green glaze.
High medieval, *c* 1250–1350
SOU 125 544

212 Fabric 1274 Saintonge Polychrome.
Jug with painted heraldic motif and applied human faces at rim.
High medieval, *c* 1250–1300
SOU 122 B380

213 Fabric 1274 Saintonge Polychrome.
Jug with painted vine leaf motif and applied human faces at rim.
High medieval, *c* 1250–1300
SOU 122 B380

Figure 23

214 Fabric 1274 Saintonge Polychrome.
Jug with painted bird and shield motif and applied human faces at rim.
High medieval, *c* 1250–1300
SOU 122 B380

215 Fabric 1464 Saintonge Gritty ware.
Mortar with applied human faces, external olive green lead glaze, applied human faces, partially pierced base.
High medieval, *c* 1250–1350
SOU 25 1292

216 Fabric 1464 Saintonge Gritty ware.
Mortar with stabbed base, applied faces.
High medieval, *c* 1250–1350
Burnt. SOU 122 B388

217 Fabric 1464 Saintonge Gritty ware.
Lid with long, hollow handle, dark green lead glaze.
High medieval, *c* 1250–1350
SOU 25 2122

Figure 24

218 Fabric 1273 Saintonge Redware.

Pégau with white slip shield and sgraffito inscription 'Saint gerant' (see Fig 2)
High medieval, *c* 1250–1350
SOU 25 1292

219   Fabric 1273 Saintonge Redware.
Body sherd of pégau, applied clay strip with thumbed terminal.
High medieval, *c* 1250–1350
SOU 122 C114

220   Fabric 1273 Saintonge Redware.
Mortar rim with white slip, sgraffito and human face decoration.
High medieval, *c* 1250–1350
SOU 124 unstratified

221   Fabric 1754 Developed Normandy Gritty ware.
Jar or pitcher rim.
Late medieval *c* 1450–1510
SOU 124 unstratified

222   Fabric 1754 Developed Normandy Gritty ware.
Jug with hollow handle.
Late medieval *c* 1450–1510
SOU 124 unstratified

223   Fabric 1349 Normandy Stoneware.
Costrel with horizontal loop handles.
Late medieval *c* 1450–1510
SOU 122 B230

224   Fabric 1349 Normandy Stoneware.
Jug.
Late medieval *c* 1490–1510
SOU 124 479

225   Fabric 1349 Normandy Stoneware.
Jug.
Late medieval *c* 1490–1510
SOU 124 479

226   Fabric 1349 Normandy Stoneware.
Jug handle.
Late medieval *c* 1490–1510
SOU 128 59

227   Fabric 1349 Normandy Stoneware.
Jug handle.
Late medieval *c* 1450–1510
SOU 105 93

228   Fabric 1349 Normandy Stoneware.
Hollow jug handle.
Late medieval *c* 1450–1510
SOU 105 60

229   Fabric 1349 Normandy Stoneware.
Lid.
Late medieval *c* 1450–1510
SOU 105 39

Figure 25

230   Fabric 1583 Martincamp under-fired stoneware.
Bottle.
Late medieval *c* 1490–1510
SOU 128 58

231   Fabric 1363 Martincamp whiteware.
Bottle.
Late medieval *c* 1490–1510
SOU 128 58

232   Fabric 1751 Martincamp stoneware.
Bottle.
Late medieval *c* 1490–1510
SOU 128 58

233   Fabric 1751 Martincamp stoneware.
Bottle.
Late medieval *c* 1490–1510
SOU 128 58

234   Fabric 1751 Martincamp stoneware.
Bottle neck.
Late medieval *c* 1490–1510
SOU 128 58

Figure 26

235   Fabric 1195 Beauvais Monochrome Yellow.
Mug or jug with stamped applied medallion, yellow glaze.
Late medieval *c* 1490–1510
SOU 128 76

236   Fabric 1195 Beauvais Monochrome Yellow.
Mug with English Royal heraldic device, probably that of Henry Tudor, yellow glaze.
Late medieval *c* 1490–1509
SOU 128 67

237   Fabric 1195 Beauvais Monochrome Yellow.
Mug with English Royal heraldic device, probably that of Henry Tudor, yellow glaze.
Late medieval *c* 1490–1509
SOU 124 205

238   Fabric 1195 Beauvais Monochrome Yellow.
Bowl, yellow glaze.
Late medieval *c* 1490–1510
SOU 122 unstratified

239   Fabric 1195 Beauvais Monochrome Yellow.
Bowl, yellow glaze.
Late medieval *c* 1490–1510
SOU 128 76

240   Fabric 1195 Beauvais Monochrome Yellow.
Bowl, yellow glaze.
Late medieval *c* 1490–1510
SOU 128 76

241   Fabric 1195 Beauvais Monochrome Yellow.
Dripping pan, yellow glaze.
Late medieval *c* 1490–1510
SOU 122 unstratified

242   Fabric 1436 Beauvais Monochrome Green.
Mug, green glaze.
Late medieval *c* 1490–1510
SOU 128 59

243   Fabric 1436 Beauvais Monochrome Green.
Bowl, green glaze.
Late medieval *c* 1490–1510
SOU 128 58

244   Fabric 1436 Beauvais Monochrome Green.
Green-glazed bowl with combed decoration.
Late medieval *c* 1490–1510
SOU 128 56

245   Fabric 1436 Beauvais Monochrome Green.
Chafing dish rim with green glaze.
Late medieval *c* 1490–1510
SOU 128 59

246   Fabric 1319 Beauvais Sgraffito.
Bowl with red slip and sgraffito floral decoration and lettering.
Late medieval *c* 1500
SOU 122 unstratified

247   Fabric 1316 Beauvais Double-slipped Sgraffito.
Dish, red and white slip sgraffito, green and clear glaze.
Late medieval *c* 1490–1510

SOU 128 56

248   Fabric 1319 Beauvais Sgraffito.
      Chafing dish, red slip sgraffito, green and clear glaze, internal
         green glaze.
      Late medieval *c* 1500
      SOU 105 61

Figure 27

249   Fabric 1454 Late Saintonge Whiteware.
      Tubular-spouted pitcher with rouletted applied strip and
         greenish-clear bib-glaze.
      Late medieval *c* 1490–1510
      SOU 128 49

250   Fabric 1454 Late Saintonge Whiteware.
      Pitcher spout and basket handle, unglazed.
      Late medieval *c* 1450–1510
      SOU 122 unstratified

251   Fabric 1454 Late Saintonge Whiteware.
      Basket pitcher-handle, unglazed.
      Late medieval *c* 1490–1510
      SOU 128 59

252   Fabric 1454 Late Saintonge Whiteware.
      Basket pitcher-handle, unglazed.
      Late medieval *c* 1450–1510
      SOU 122 unstratified

253   Fabric 1454 Late Saintonge Whiteware.
      Body sherd of pitcher with merchant's mark.
      Late medieval *c* 1450–1510
      SOU 122 unstratified

254   Fabric 1454 Late Saintonge Whiteware.
      Costrel neck and handle, yellow lead glaze.
      Late medieval *c* 1450–1510
      SOU 122 E511

255   Fabric 1454 Late Saintonge Whiteware.
      Chafing dish with faces, medallions and green and clear
         glaze.
      Late medieval *c* 1490–1510
      SOU 128 76

256   Fabric 1454 Late Saintonge Whiteware.
      Chafing dish with faces and roundels and green and yellow
         glaze.
      Late medieval *c* 1490–1510
      SOU 128 56

257   Fabric 1454 Late Saintonge Whiteware.
      Chafing dish with applied faces and green and yellow glaze.
      Late medieval *c* 1500
      SOU 122 B264

258   Fabric 1454 Late Saintonge Whiteware.
      Figurine or salt with yellow lead glaze.
      Late medieval *c* 1490–1510
      SOU 128 67

259   Fabric 1770 Late Saintonge Polychrome.
      Plate with green and brown painted decoration.
      Late medieval *c* 1490–1510
      SOU 128 100

Figure 28

260   Fabric 1390 Andenne-type ware.
      Spout with ring-stamped decoration, yellow glaze.
      Anglo-Norman *c* 1150–1250
      SOU 110 33D

261   Fabric 1494 Low Countries Highly Decorated Redware
         ware.

Jug with partial white slip and green glaze, rouletted
   decoration, thumbed base.
High Medieval *c* 1250–1350
SOU 25 1246

262   Fabric 1297 Low Countries Redware.
      Tripod two-handled cooking pot with partial internal and
         external clear glaze.
      Late medieval *c* 1490–1510
      SOU 128 56B

263   Fabric 1297 Low Countries Redware.
      Two-handled tripod cooking pot with partial internal and
         external clear glaze.
      Late medieval *c* 1490–1510
      SOU 122 B318

264   Fabric 1297 Low Countries Redware.
      Two-handled cooking pot with partial internal and external
         clear glaze.
      Late Medieval *c* 1490–1510
      SOU 124 501

265   Fabric 1297 Low Countries Redware.
      Tripod two-handled cooking pot with partial internal and
         external clear glaze.
      Late Medieval *c* 1400–1510
      SOU 122 308

266   Fabric 1297 Low Countries Redware.
      Tripod cooking pot with partial internal and external clear
      glaze.
      Late Medieval *c* 1490–1510
      SOU 124 501

267   Fabric 1297 Low Countries Redware.
      Two-handled cooking pot with partial internal and external
         clear glaze.
      Late Medieval *c* 1490–1510
      SOU 124 479

268   Fabric 1297 Low Countries Redware.
      Two-handled cooking pot with partial internal and external
         clear glaze.
      Late Medieval *c* 1490–1510
      SOU 124 205/214

269   Fabric 1300 Slipped Low Countries Redware.
      Handled cooking pot with white slip decoration and partial
         internal and external clear glaze.
      Late Medieval *c* 1490–1510
      SOU 128 56

270   Fabric 1300 Slipped Low Countries Redware.
      Two-handled tripod cooking pot with white slip decoration
         and partial internal and external clear glaze.
      Late Medieval *c* 1400–1510
      SOU 29 108

271   Fabric 1297 Low Countries Redware.
      Handled tripod cooking pot with pulled rather than applied
         feet and partial internal and external clear glaze.
      Late Medieval *c* 1490–1510
      SOU 128 58

272   Fabric 1297 Low Countries Redware.
      Tripod pipkin with partial internal and external clear glaze.
      Late Medieval *c* 1490–1510
      SOU 128 33

273   Fabric 1297 Low Countries Redware.
      Tripod pipkin with pouring lip and partial internal and
         external clear glaze.
      Late Medieval *c* 1400–1510
      SOU 110 49

Figure 29

274 Fabric 1297 Low Countries Redware.
Frying pan or dish with clear lead glaze.
Late Medieval *c* 1490–1510
SOU 128 58

275 Fabric 1297 Low Countries Redware.
Frying pan or dish with clear lead glaze.
Late Medieval *c* 1490–1510
SOU 128 58

276 Fabric 1297 Low Countries Redware.
Dish with clear lead glaze.
Late Medieval *c* 1490–1510
SOU 128 76

277 Fabric 1297 Low Countries Redware.
Bowl with three pulled feet and clear lead glaze.
Late Medieval *c* 1490–1510
SOU 128 67

278 Fabric 1297 Low Countries Redware.
Shallow bowl with clear lead glaze.
Late Medieval *c* 1450–1510
SOU 123 C136

279 Fabric 1297 Low Countries Redware.
Frying pan with clear lead glaze.
Late Medieval *c* 1490–1510
SOU 128 56B

280 Fabric 1297 Low Countries Redware.
Frying pan with clear lead glaze.
Late Medieval *c* 1490–1510
SOU 128 56B

281 Fabric 1297 Low Countries Redware.
Frying pan with clear lead glaze.
Late Medieval *c* 1490–1510
SOU 128 58

282 Fabric 1297 Low Countries Redware.
Strainer with internal and external clear lead glaze.
Late Medieval *c* 1490–1510
SOU 128 58

283 Fabric 1297 Low Countries Redware.
Colander with internal and external clear lead glaze.
Late Medieval *c* 1490–1510
SOU 128 34

284 Fabric 1297 Low Countries Redware.
Dripping Pan with green-coloured lead glaze
Late Medieval *c* 1490–1510
SOU 124 471

285 Fabric 1297 Low Countries Redware.
Dripping pan with internal clear lead glaze.
Late Medieval *c* 1400–1510
SOU 125 323

286 Fabric 1297 Low Countries Redware.
Jug or cooking pot rim.
Late Medieval *c* 1490–1510
SOU 124 405

287 Fabric 1297 Low Countries Redware.
Base of jug or pitcher, internal clear lead glaze and external splashing.
Late Medieval *c* 1490–1510
SOU 124 479

288 Fabric 1297 Low Countries Redware.
Bowl base with internal overall white slip and clear glaze.
Late Medieval *c* 1450–1510
SOU 122 E511

289 Fabric 1300 Low Countries Slipped Redware.
Three-footed bowl base with internal white slip swags and clear glaze.
Late Medieval *c* 1490–1510
SOU 124 215/220

290 Fabric 1300 Low Countries Slipped Redware.
Lid with external white slip swags.
Late Medieval *c* 1400–1510
SOU 122 B313

291 Fabric 1300 Low Countries Slipped Redware.
Lid with external white slip swags, slightly reduced or overfired.
Late Medieval *c* 1490–1510
SOU 124 426

292 Fabric 1610 Green-glazed Low Countries Redware.
Three-footed bowl base with internal green glaze over white slip.
Late Medieval *c* 1450–1510
SOU 105 60

293 Fabric 1300 Low Countries Slipped Redware.
Albarello with internal clear glaze, external green glaze over white slip.
Late Medieval *c* 1490–1510
SOU 124 479

294 Fabric 1422 South Netherlands Maiolica.
Ring-handled vase with blue painted decoration.
Late medieval *c* 1490–1510
SOU 128 58

295 Fabric 1422 South Netherlands Maiolica.
Flask base with blue painted decoration.
Late Medieval *c* 1500
SOU 125 329

296 Fabric 1426 Malling-type Tin-glazed ware.
Cup with mottled (sponged) purple paint overall.
Late Medieval? *c* 1510 or Post-medieval *c* 1550
SOU 124 225

Figure 30

297 Fabric 1385 Blaugrau ware.
Ladle or pipkin.
Anglo-Norman *c* 1100–1250
SOU 123 A296

298 Fabric 1246 Siegburg Stoneware.
Mug.
Late medieval *c* 1400
SOU 124 491

299 Fabric 1246 Siegburg Stoneware.
Mug rim.
Late medieval *c* 1400
SOU 128 56C

300 Fabric 1246 Siegburg Stoneware.
Mug base.
Late medieval *c* 1400
SOU 123 B217

301 Fabric 1246 Siegburg Stoneware.
Cup.
Late medieval *c* 1450–1500
SOU 122 B318

302 Fabric 1245 Raeren Stoneware.
Mug.
Late medieval *c* 1490–1510
SOU 128 58

303 Fabric 1245 Raeren Stoneware.
Mug.
Late medieval *c* 1490–1510

SOU 128 58

304 Fabric 1245 Raeren Stoneware.
Mug.
Late medieval *c* 1490–1510
SOU 128 33

305 Fabric 1245 Raeren Stoneware.
Mug.
Late medieval *c* 1490–1510
SOU 124 225

306 Fabric 1245 Raeren Stoneware.
Mug.
Late medieval *c* 1475–1510
SOU 122 B230

307 Fabric 1245 Raeren Stoneware.
Mug.
Late medieval *c* 1490–1510
SOU 128 58

308 Fabric 1245 Raeren Stoneware.
Mug.
Late medieval *c* 1490–1510
SOU 124 214

309 Fabric 1245 Raeren Stoneware.
Mug.
Late medieval *c* 1490–1510
SOU 128 49

310 Fabric 1245 Raeren Stoneware.
Mug.
Late medieval *c* 1490–1510
SOU 128 56

311 Fabric 1245 Raeren Stoneware.
Mug.
Late medieval *c* 1490–1510
SOU 128 99

312 Fabric 1245 Raeren Stoneware.
Mug.
Late medieval *c* 1490–1510
SOU 124 215

313 Fabric 1245 Raeren Stoneware.
Jug.
Late medieval *c* 1490–1510
SOU 124 214

314 Fabric 1245 Raeren Stoneware.
Tankard decorated with a figure holding a sceptre and orb.
Late medieval *c* 1510 or later
SOU 122 E511

315 Fabric 1378 Cologne Stoneware.
Mug with moulded panel of human profiles on the neck, sprigged leaves.
Late medieval *c* 1490–1510
SOU 128 56

316 Fabric 1378 Cologne Stoneware.
Mug with bearded face and sprigged oak-leaves.
Late medieval *c* 1490–1510
SOU 128 45

317 Fabric 1378 Cologne Stoneware.
Body of large mug or jug decorated with sprigged oak-leaves and acorns
Late medieval *c* 1490–1510
SOU 128 58

318 Fabric 1774 Late Siegburg Stoneware.
Tall mug or Schnelle with moulded decoration.
Early post-medieval *c* 1550
SOU 128 35

319 Fabric 1757 Frechen White Stoneware.
Large mug or jug.

Late medieval *c* 1500 or later
SOU 124 475

Figure 31

320 Fabric 1308 Seville-type Coarseware.
Olive jar of elongated type.
Late medieval *c* 1400–1510
SOU 124 salvage

321 Fabric 1308 Seville-type Coarseware.
Rounded olive jar.
Late medieval *c* 1490–1510
SOU 124 414

322 Fabric 1327 Seville-type Coarseware.
Poppy-neck of olive jar.
Late medieval *c* 1490–1510
SOU 122 B308

323 Fabric 1327 Seville-type Coarseware.
Handled olive jar, probably a poppy-necked type, with merchant's marks.
Late medieval *c* 1490–1510
SOU 122 B308

324 Fabric 1327 Seville-type Coarseware.
Jug or jar base.
Late medieval *c* 1490–1510
SOU 128 56D

325 Fabric 1505 Seville-type Coarseware.
Handle of jar or olive jar.
Late medieval *c* 1475–1510
SOU 110 109

326 Fabric 1773 Seville-type Coarseware.
Lebrillo with impressed band at rim and internal green glaze.
Late medieval *c* 1490–1510
SOU 128 58

327 Fabric 1766 Seville-type Coarseware.
Albarello with amber-coloured glaze.
Late medieval *c* 1450–1510
SOU 105 117B

328 Fabric 1766 Seville-type Coarseware.
Albarello with amber-coloured glaze.
Late medieval *c* 1490–1510
SOU 128 58

329 Fabric 1773 Seville-type Coarseware.
Albarello with partial dark green glaze.
Late medieval *c* 1450–1510
SOU 122 unstratified

Figure 32

330 Fabric 1439 Iberian Micaceous Redware.
Two-handled jar with stamped roundels and scratched merchant's mark.
Late medieval *c* 1490–1510
SOU 128 45

331 Fabric 1355 Iberian Micaceous Redware.
Bowl.
Late medieval *c* 1490–1510
SOU 124 414

332 Fabric 1355 Iberian Micaceous Redware.
Bowl.
Late medieval *c* 1490–1510
SOU 128 34

333 Fabric 1355 Iberian Micaceous Redware.
Bowl rim.
Late medieval *c* 1450–1510
SOU 124 423

334   Fabric 1470 Iberian Micaceous Redware.
      Flask neck.
      Late medieval *c* 1450–1510
      SOU 123 A251

335   Fabric 1470 Iberian Micaceous Redware.
      Flask base.
      Late medieval *c* 1450–1510
      SOU 123 A251

336   Fabric 1536 Iberian Micaceous Redware.
      Cooking pot or jug with rich brown internal glaze.
      Late medieval *c* 1490–1510
      SOU 124 501

337   Fabric 1776 Iberian Micaceous Redware.
      Cooking pot with rich brown internal glaze.
      Late medieval *c* 1490–1510
      SOU 128 100

338   Fabric 1307 Iberian Micaceous Redware.
      Flask handle.
      Late medieval *c* 1450–1510
      SOU 105 84

339   Fabric 1371 Iberian Micaceous Redware.
      Olive jar handle.
      Late medieval *c* 1490–1510
      SOU 128 76

340   Fabric 2026 Iberian Micaceous Redware.
      Olive jar handle.
      Late medieval *c* 1450–1510
      SOU 122 unstratified

341   Fabric 1543 Iberian Micaceous Redware.
      Base of small mercury jar with green glaze.
      Late medieval *c* 1450–1510
      SOU 124 unstratified

Figure 33

342   Fabric 1067 Andalusian Lustreware.
      Jug handle, burnt.
      High medieval *c* 1270–1350
      SOU 125 544

343   Fabric 1298 Iberian Green and Brown ware.
      Dish with internal green and brown painted decoration and
          clear lead glaze.
      High medieval *c* 1270–1350
      SOU 122 C286

344   Fabric 1070 Valencian Lustreware.
      Small bowl with internal copper-lustre decoration.
      Late medieval *c* 1490–1510
      SOU 122 B318

345   Fabric 1070 Valencian Lustreware.
      Handled bowl with internal copper-lustre decoration.
      Late medieval *c* 1490–1510
      SOU 128 58

346   Fabric 1070 Valencian Lustreware.
      Dish with copper-lustre decoration that has faded during in
          deposition.
      Late medieval *c* 1490–1510
      SOU 128 100

347   Fabric 1070 Valencian Lustreware.
      Dish with impressions showing the outline of copper-lustre
          decoration.
      Late medieval *c* 1490–1510
      SOU 128 68

348   Fabric 1070 Valencian Lustreware.
      Bowl with copper-lustre and blue paint decoration.
      Late medieval *c* 1490–1510

      SOU 128 560

349   Fabric 1070 Valencian Lustreware.
      Albarello, the lustre has faded, blue paint remains (shown
          as black).
      Late medieval *c* 1490–1510
      SOU 128 83

350   Fabric 1421 Seville Blue and Purple.
      Dish with blue and purple painted decoration.
      Late medieval *c* 1490–1510
      SOU 128 58

351   Fabric 1448 Seville Blue.
      Dish with blue painted decoration.
      Late medieval *c* 1490–1510
      SOU 128 59

352   Fabric 1448 Muel Blue.
      Handled bowl with blue painted decoration.
      Late medieval *c* 1490–1510
      SOU 124 176

353   Fabric 1765 Seville Green and White.
      Dish, half green, half white.
      Late medieval *c* 1490–1510
      SOU 122 B313

Figure 34

354   Fabric 1765 Seville Green and White.
      Cup, half green, half white.
      Late medieval *c* 1490–1510
      SOU 128 58

355   Fabric 1765 Seville Green and White.
      Cup, half green, half white.
      Late medieval *c* 1490–1510
      SOU 122 E632

356   Fabric 1472 Seville Plain White.
      Bowl, plain white.
      Late medieval *c* 1490–1510
      SOU 128 unstratified

357   Fabric 1446 Montelupo Maiolica.
      Bowl with yellow and blue painted decoration.
      Late medieval *c* 1490–1510
      SOU 124 205

358   Fabric 1446 Montelupo Maiolica.
      Bowl with yellow and blue painted decoration.
      Late medieval *c* 1490–1510
      SOU 123 A200

359   Fabric 1446 Montelupo Maiolica.
      Bowl or dish with yellow, blue and red painted decoration.
      Late medieval *c* 1490–1510
      SOU 128 67

360   Fabric 1446 Montelupo Maiolica.
      Bowl or dish with yellow, blue and red painted decoration.
      Late medieval *c* 1490–1510
      SOU 128 58

361   Fabric 1767 Florentine Maiolica, 'Santa Fina' style.
      Jug with blue and yellow heraldic medallion, blue, yellow
          and purple body and turquoise handle. The monogram
          below the handle is in purple.
      Late medieval *c* 1490–1510
      SOU 124 220

362   Fabric 1767 Florentine Maiolica.
      Jug with blue, turquoise and pink floral motif.
      Late medieval *c* 1490–1510
      SOU 122 B313

363   Fabric 1767 Florentine Maiolica.
      Bowl or dish with green and brown painted floral motif.

Late medieval *c* 1490–1510
SOU 124 501

364   Fabric 1450 Faenza Maiolica.
Small jug with blue and yellow floral motif.
Late medieval *c* 1490–1510
SOU 128 100

365   Fabric 1450 Faenza Maiolica.
Jug with blue and brown/yellow geometric motif.
Late medieval *c* 1490–1510
SOU 124 205

Figure 35

366   Fabric 1450 Faenza Maiolica.
Jug with blue and orange piscine motif.
Late medieval *c* 1490–1510
SOU 124 176

367   Fabric 1450 Faenza Maiolica.
Jug with blue and orange painted decoration.
Late medieval *c* 1490–1510
SOU 128 43

368   Fabric 1468 Venetian Maiolica.
Ring-handled vase, white with yellow bands and brown 'YHS' motif.
Late medieval *c* 1490–1510
SOU 124 225

369   Fabric 1422 North Italian Maiolica.
Ring-handled vase with blue painted decoration.
Late medieval *c* 1490–1510
SOU 124 214

370   Fabric 1422 North Italian Maiolica.
Ring-handled vase with blue and orange painted decoration.
Late medieval *c* 1490–1510
SOU 124 214

371   Fabric 1772 Ligurian Faience.
Dish with dark blue on light blue floral motif.
Late medieval *c* 1490–1510
SOU 128 58

372   Fabric 1241 Archaic Pisan Maiolica.
Bowl, external clear glaze, internal pinkish tin-glaze.
Late medieval *c* 1490–1510
SOU 122 B318

373   Fabric 1241 Archaic Pisan Maiolica.

Bowl rim, external clear lead glaze, internal pinkish tin-glaze.
Late medieval *c* 1490–1510
SOU 122 B318

374   Fabric 1241 Archaic Pisan Maiolica.
Base, jar or albarello?
Late medieval *c* 1490–1510
SOU 123 A312

375   Fabric 1760 North Italian Sgraffito.
Bowl or dish with white slip and sgraffito, green and clear glaze.
Late medieval *c* 1490–1510
SOU 122 B230

376   Fabric 1760 North Italian Sgraffito.
Dish, white slip and sgraffito, green and clear glaze.
Late medieval *c* 1490–1510
SOU 122 B313

377   Fabric 1768 North Italian Red Earthenware.
Bowl, external white slip glazed bands, internal lead glaze.
Late medieval *c* 1490–1510
SOU 128 76

378   Fabric 1768 North Italian Red Earthenware.
Bowl, overall white slip and lead glaze.
Late medieval *c* 1490–1510
SOU 128 58

379   Fabric 1768 North Italian Red Earthenware.
Albarello, exterior and interior green-coloured lead glaze.
Late medieval *c* 1490–1510
SOU 128 49

380   Fabric 1768 North Italian Red Earthenware.
Albarello, clear glaze over external white slip.
Late medieval *c* 1490–1510
SOU 124 491

381   Fabric 1768 North Italian Red Earthenware.
Albarello, external white slip, dark brown stripes, lead glaze.
Late medieval *c* 1490–1510
SOU 128 43

382   Fabric 1768 North Italian Red Earthenware.
Flask or flagon base, external clear lead glaze.
Late medieval *c* 1490–1510
SOU 128 33

3

QUANTIFICATION AND CHRONOLOGY

The purpose of quantification is to identify those types of pottery that occur together most often, or are most common in certain deposits or phases of activity. This will lead to an understanding of the development of pottery production and use through time and perhaps identify areas of specific activity. Analysing the relative proportions of ceramic types, whether fabrics or forms, may also illuminate the social, economic and cultural position of certain households or communities. Above all, pottery is often relied upon to provide a dated sequence for stratigraphic phases. If this is not always easy it is certainly true that before other areas of ceramic interpretation can be fully explored a dated framework needs to be established.

Methodology

Two techniques have been utilised to establish a comprehensive and accessible framework for quantitative and chronological analysis. The first method is based on examining the pattern of occurrence of principal pottery types, or Major Wares, with every other. This has resulted in the identification of the three ceramic periods, Anglo-Norman, high medieval and late medieval, which framed the catalogue in Chapter 2.

The second method of chronological analysis is related to the stratigraphic sequence. The problem of coordinating the stratigraphy and ceramic finds of sites excavated by different methods over a period of ten years, has been addressed by placing each stratigraphic phase into one of four general settlement phases, each of which represents a different period of activity within Southampton.

Major Wares

The classification and quantification of every fabric type has led to the identification of Major Wares. These may be specific fabrics, as identified by Fabric Numbers, or groups of fabrics that share the same Ware Name. Fabrics are combined to form a Major Ware if individually they occur in small quantities but they are recognised components of a single tradition. For instance, all the Iberian Micaceous Redware fabrics have been grouped together as a Major Ware. Individually they may occur in statistically insignificant amounts, yet they assume greater meaning when quantified as a single type. Major Wares are those that occur in the assemblage as a minimum of 100 sherds or 1kg in weight and in more than twenty contexts.

The specific fabrics that have been grouped to form Major Wares have been described above (Chapter 2). Appendix 2 lists each Major Ware and the specific fabric types they represent. Table 1 lists the Major Wares, giving their Ware Names, Codes, total quantities, and the number of contexts in which they occur.

Ceramic periods

A sequence for the consumption of pottery in medieval Southampton has been constructed by plotting the occurrence of each Major Ware with every other, using those of known date to provide a framework.

Figure 36, dubbed a Pottery Matrix, shows the incidence of every Major Ware with every other. This has been calculated by plotting the percentage of the total sherd weight that occurs in any context with every other Major Ware. The total amount of every Major Ware is known, as are the contexts it occurs in. It is therefore possible to establish what percentage of that total was found in contexts that also contained any other Major Ware. This is why the number of contexts is one of the criteria for selecting a Major Ware. A ware might be represented by a few vessels, which weigh more than a kilogram but occur in a few contexts.

In such cases the chronological pattern of this ware, as represented in Figure 36, may be misleading.

As one might expect in a large urban assemblage, where residuality and intrusion are constant complicating factors, small amounts of each Major Ware occur with practically every other. In order to clarify the picture this analysis can give, only occurrences greater than 50% are depicted in Figure 36.

The Pottery Matrix is read in the following manner. It may be seen from reading along the y-axis for STWW, Southampton Whiteware, that over 80% of the total sherd weight or number of this type occurs with Scratch-marked ware (SMK), South Hampshire Redware (SHRW), Southampton Coarseware (STCW) and High Medieval Saintonge wares (HSO). Reading down the x-axis for the same fabric will establish how

much of each Major Ware occurs with Southampton Whiteware. This shows that various high medieval sandy wares, LOPS, SHRW and LV, all occur in significant quantities with Southampton Whiteware, suggesting their contemporaneity.

By plotting the quantitative relationship of each Major Ware with every other, a chronological sequence has been developed. In Figure 36 Major Wares are arranged in an order that best illustrates that sequence, and is therefore chronological. Each of the three ceramic periods, Anglo-Norman, high and late medieval, emerges clearly from this pattern. On the y-axis Anglo-Norman wares are grouped to the left, high medieval wares in the middle and late medieval wares on the right. On the x-axis Anglo-Norman wares are at the top, high medieval wares in the middle and late me-

Table 1. List of Major Ware codes with quantities and number of contexts from which they were recovered

Ware Code	Ware Name	RP	Weight	Sherds	No. of Contexts
EMFT	Early Medieval Flint-tempered	1138	15305	1318	277
ACCW	Anglo-Norman Chalk-tempered Coarseware	88	2337	58	21
AXCWa	Anglo-Norman Mixed Grit Coarseware (1011)	112	3004	153	46
AXCWb	Anglo-Norman Mixed Grit Coarseware (1014)	409	4672	225	93
SMK	Scratch-marked	3130	63823	3812	365
ACWX	Anglo-Norman Wessex Coarseware	180	4705	269	79
NOG	Normandy Gritty	161	5069	356	146
ANG	Anglo-Norman Glazed	136	6005	223	61
ADOQ	Anglo-Norman Dorset Sandy	101	2876	210	91
AXCWc	Early Medieval Mixed Grit (1095)	178	2043	89	50
ANFG	Anglo-Norman North French Glazed	178	2150	233	116
STWW	Southampton Whiteware	510	11484	935	162
STHC	Southampton High Street Coarseware	98	2484	145	45
LOWW	Local Whiteware	150	3120	219	99
LOWF	Local Fine White Sandy	57	1478	157	69
LV	Laverstock	356	6793	507	141
STCS	Southampton Sandy Coarseware	630	15295	1312	223
STCW	Southampton Coarseware	3622	67145	4766	371
SHRD	South Hampshire Redware	1014	30939	1865	239
LOPS	Local Pink Sandy	560	14058	1027	190
HSO	High Medieval Saintonge	1731	23035	2248	303
DOWW	Dorset Whiteware	139	3231	142	38
STS	Southampton Sandy	1033	23927	2171	256
HCSX	High Medieval Mixed Grit Sandy Coarseware	132	1949	268	78
HDOQ	High Medieval Dorset Sandy	157	1995	132	45
STO	Southampton Organic-tempered Sandy	777	20255	744	189
LWFS	Late Medieval Well-fired Sandy	2950	66984	2587	221
IBR	Iberian Redwares	223	3787	292	97
IBCW	Iberian Coarseware	332	14300	503	113
TDG	Tudor Green	574	1579	291	90
LCRD	Low Countries Redwares	2624	31726	1364	147
RARN	Raeren Stoneware	2007	18198	682	92
LSO	Late Medieval Saintonge	341	9591	269	53
SPTG	Spanish Tin-glazed wares	440	3605	99	36
NST	Normandy Stoneware	224	4071	205	36
ITMA	Italian Maiolica	878	7512	341	45
ITEW	North Italian Lead-glazed Earthenware	323	2210	99	26
BV	Beauvais wares	392	2082	188	39
MCP	Martincamp	330	5006	439	27

	EMFT	ACCW	AXCWa	AXCWb	SMK	ACWX	NOG	ANG	ADOQ	AXCWc	ANFG	STWW	STHC	LOWW	LOWF	LV	STCS	STCW	SHRD	LOPS	HSO	DOWW	STS	HCSX	HDOQ	STO	LWFS	IBR	IBCW	TDG	LCRD	RARN	LSO	SPTG	NST	ITMA	ITEW	BV	MCP
EMFT	\			79																																			
ACCW	72	\		93	95		67		51				65								81		82	51															
AXCWa			\	74																																			
AXCWb	53		74	\										66	74	52					69																		
SMK	60				\	59	66	54	A			B									56					C													
ACWX				86		\								57	64						81			65															
NOG	60			77			\																																
ANG	53		63	82	73	76		\				62			56		53	53	61		68	89																	
ADOQ	51		51	85					\								52	60			63																		
AXCWc				88	50		75			\					51		58	57	55		68																		
ANFG	51			77							\							60			69																		
STWW	75		64	87	65	67	66	68	54	75		\	68	76	72	85	78	90	91	83	90		80				70	76	55	60	53								
STHC	69		54	73	56	56	53	56		57	53		\	62	59	59	86	88	63	62	81	71	76	51			80	55		52									
LOWW				76									63	\			57	51			65		58																
LOWF				66									51	55	\		64	62	89	74	65	82		56			54												
LV				51	59								65			\	58	76	67	64	69		65				55	55											
STCS																	\	86	55	62	60		55																
STCW				54													72	\	65	60	59																		
SHRD				58									56				55	54	\	87		76	81		66														
LOPS				53									57			57	56	87	76	\		89		73			51											F	
HSO	D			53									53				60	79	73	55	\		59																
DOWW			76	77		73							82	70			82	88	97	86	93	\	90					71					69						
STS				50													63	77	62	61	77		\																
HCSX			62					E									68	78	59	59	69		67	\		63	60												
HDOQ																	77	79	62	72	57				\														
STO																	67		60	51			68			\	76	56		65									
LWFS																											\	53	73		89	83	64		64	66		65	66
IBR																										80		\	69	60	73	66	65		54				56
IBCW																										70	55		\			64	59	54		I			
TDG																										67				\		59	57						
LCRD																										87		63			\		74	50		50			
RARN																										82		63			90	\		57	56	68	53	58	55
LSO			G																		58					87	68	79	54	87	89		\	51	65	64		64	72
SPTG																										56	62		51	73	66	57	\		75	53		
NST				51									50			56							65	52		56	93	61	61	61	97	74	67	\	60	61	63	
ITMA																										75			89	79		60			\		52	
ITEW																										50			96		71	78			\		
BV																										95	68	86		98	91	85		79	77	56	\	78
MCP																			61	72		67		64		100	74	98	76	99	97	94	79	87	90	81	88	\

Figure 36. 'Matrix' showing percentage occurrence by weight of each Major Ware with every other Major Ware (see Table 1 for key to Ware Codes)

dieval wares at the bottom. Each Major Ware is arranged in the same order on both the x- and y-axes. The central diagonal line indicates the 100% occurrence of each Major Ware with itself. Ideally, the squares showing the highest percentages would cluster around that line, and percentages would diminish with distance from it. This cannot be achieved as some Major Wares are present in greater quantities than others, and they were produced over different lengths of time, and therefore occur with a wider variety of types than do certain others. There are however three distinct clusters of high percentage occurrences that show the principal components of each ceramic period. Each period has been highlighted in Figure 36 by the addition of horizontal and vertical lines, which divide the diagram into nine different areas, labelled A to I. The pottery of the Anglo-Norman period is represented in area A, the high medieval in area E and the late medieval in

area I. Table 2 shows the quantities of each ceramic period present in the whole assemblage. Tables 3, 4 and 5 give the total quantities of each Major Ware, and the other types described in the catalogue, for each of the three ceramic periods.

Table 2. Quantities of each Ceramic Period in the total assemblage

Period	Weight	Sherds	% Total Weight	% Total Sherds
Prehistoric	3	1	<1	<1
Roman	119	15	<1	<1
Late Saxon	9532	955	2	3
Anglo-Norman	117296	7268	20	20
High medieval	235434	17281	39	48
Late medieval	208675	9255	35	26
Misc. medieval	505	58	<1	<1
Post-medieval	27116	1085	4	3
Early Modern	481	28	<1	<1
Total	598878	35940		

The Anglo-Norman period

Table 2 shows that Anglo-Norman wares comprise 20% of the total assemblage by weight and sherd count. The relative quantities of the Anglo-Norman pottery types described in the catalogue are shown in Table 3.

Coarsewares are generally dominant, and of these Scratch-marked wares are the most common. English glazed wares comprise five percent by weight, and three percent by count, of all the English wares. Continental wares amount to seven percent of the total weight and nine percent of the sherd count. North French wares comprise over 90% of all the imported types.

As Figure 36 shows, every Anglo-Norman Major Ware occurs with Scratch-marked ware in proportions higher than 70%. The Anglo-Norman date of Scratch-marked ware itself is shown by its significant correspondence with Early Medieval Flint-tempered, Normandy Gritty and Wessex Coarseware and Anglo-Norman Glazed wares. Most Anglo-Norman wares occur in large quantities with Early Medieval Flint-tempered ware, confirming the probability that this ware, although originating in the late Saxon period, was still being produced in the late-11th and 12th centuries. The correspondence of the early and high medieval traditions is shown by the fact that most Anglo-Norman Major Wares occur in significant quantities with those of the high medieval period, most particularly Southampton Coarseware, and Saintonge wares. A relatively high proportion of these two wares occur with Scratch-marked ware, reinforcing the notion that at one time, perhaps only briefly, all these types were being produced and used together. It is notable that there is no significant occurrence of Anglo-Norman Major Wares with those of the late medieval period.

Table 3. Quantities of early medieval wares

Fabric Number	Ware Name	Weight	Sherds	% Weight	% Sherds
	Early Medieval Flint-tempered	15305	1318	14	20
	Scratch-marked	63823	3812	59	58
1011	Mixed Grit Coarseware	3004	153	3	2
1014	Mixed Grit Coarseware	4672	225	4	3
1095	Mixed Grit Coarseware	2043	89	2	1
1055	Chalk-tempered Coarseware	2337	58	2	1
1016	Wessex Coarseware	4705	269	4	4
1013	Non-local Flint-tempered	763	28	1	<1
1073	Non-local Gravel-tempered	17	2	<1	<1
	Other Plain Coarsewares	3349	203	3	3
	Dorset Sandy ware	2876	210	3	3
	Glazed wares	6005	223	5	3
	Total English	108899	6590		
	Total English % all Anglo-Norman	93	91		
	Normandy Gritty	5069	356	61	53
	North French Glazed	1917	186	21	27
1402	Rouen-type	286	50	3	7
1413	North French Sandy	362	16	4	2
	North French Red-painted	134	15	2	2
1269	Early Saintonge	82	2	1	<1
1390	Andenne-type	132	18	2	3
1385	Blaugrau	415	35	5	5
	Total Continental	8397	678		
	Total Continental % all Anglo-Norman	7	9		
	Total	117296	7268		

The high medieval period

Table 2 shows that the high medieval period is the best represented in this assemblage; material of this date represents 39% of the total pottery weight and 48% of the total count. Table 4 shows that, in contrast to the Anglo-Norman period, glazed or sandy wares represent a greater proportion of the English pottery than coarsewares. Southampton Coarseware is the most common single type, while Southampton Sandy ware and South Hampshire Redware dominate the glazed wares. Non-local English wares comprise a very small

Table 4. Quantities of high medieval wares

Fabric Number	Ware Name	Weight	Sherds	% Weight	% Sherds
1123	Southampton Coarseware	67145	4766	75	72
1024	Southampton Sandy Coarseware	15295	1312	17	20
1230	Southampton High Street Coarseware	2484	145	3	2
1124	Mixed Grit Sandy Coarseware	1949	268	2	4
1726	Cornish Coarseware	15	1	<1	<1
	Other Coarsewares	2180	139	2	2
	Total Coarsewares	89068	6631		
	Total Coarseware % of English	45	46		
1044	Southampton Whiteware	11484	935	11	12
	Southampton Sandy	23927	2171	22	27
1248	South Hampshire Redware	30939	1865	29	24
1087	Local Pink Sandy ware	14058	1027	13	13
	Laverstock	6793	507	6	6
1118	Local Whiteware	3120	219	3	3
1215	Local Fine White Sandy ware	1478	157	1	2
	Dorset Sandy ware	1995	132	2	2
1156	Dorset Whiteware	3231	142	3	2
1078	Midlands ware	214	1	<1	<1
1526	Scarborough-type ware	494	18	<1	<1
1761	Cornish Sandy ware	41	4	<1	<1
	Other Sandy wares	10596	723	10	9
	Total Sandy wares	108370	7901		
	Total Sandy ware % of English	55	54		
	Total English	197438	14532		
	Total English % all HMed	84	84		
1403	Developed Rouen ware	320	48	1	2
1763	North French Bichrome	219	16	1	1
1548	Seine Valley Whiteware	334	109	1	4
1552	North French Sandy Whiteware	180	18	<1	<1
1291	North French Pink ware	318	30	1	1
1711	North French Micaceous Whiteware	275	17	1	1
1407	Seine Valley Zoomorphic	1183	64	3	2
1458	Ceramique Onctueuse	13	1	<1	<1
1753	Breton Coarseware	54	1	<1	<1
1272	Saintonge Whiteware	18266	1825	49	67
1500	Saintonge Bright Green-glazed ware	1704	193	5	7
1274	Saintonge Polychrome	3210	219	9	8
1267	Saintonge Red-painted Whiteware	130	16	<1	1
1758	Saintonge Highly Decorated	8	1	<1	<1
1464	Saintonge Gritty ware	5813	38	16	1
1273	Saintonge Redware	3742	37	10	1
	Other French wares	1183	67	3	3
	Total French wares	36952	2700		
	Total French Ware % of Continental	97	98		
1494	Low Countries Highly Decorated Redware	752	12		
1599	Rhenish Proto-stoneware	41	5		
1067	Andalusian Lustreware	124	17		
1298	Iberian Green and Brown	24	1		
	Miscellaneous Continental	103	14		
	Total Non-French Continental	1044	49		
	Total Non-French % of Continental	3	2		
	Total Continental	37996	2749		
	Total Continental % all HMed	16	16		
	Total	235434	17281		

proportion of the high medieval group, although a wide spread of sources, including the Midlands, Scarborough and Cornwall is represented.

French pottery remains the most common Continental import in the high medieval period, although a significant shift in source, from the north to the south-west, is shown by the dominance of Saintonge wares. As was the case for the Anglo-Norman period, pottery from the Low Countries and the Rhineland is represented in very small quantities, while Iberian types occur for the first time in the high medieval period.

This pattern is reflected in Figure 36, where it is seen that many Major Wares occur in high percentages with the three principal types, Southampton Coarseware, South Hampshire Redware and Saintonge wares. The concentration of high percentages in Sector E demonstrates the validity of the high medieval group and its chronological cohesion. Exceptions to this are the two High Street fabrics, Southampton Whiteware and Southampton High Street Coarseware. Both occur in significant quantities with early and late medieval types. This is probably because they are represented mainly by wasters, recovered from contexts that produced a mixed range of ceramics. By reading down the x-axis for each of these wares one can see that few early or late types occur with them in correspondingly high amounts. It is therefore shown to be unlikely that the High Street kiln was in production from the 12th to the 15th centuries, although a date that corresponds with the transition from the Anglo-Norman to high medieval periods is suggested. The longevity of that transitional period may be understood by the way in which many high medieval types occur significantly with Scratch-marked ware, as shown in Sector D. This may, however, also reflect residuality among Scratch-marked wares as they themselves do not occur significantly with any high medieval types.

Some high medieval Major Wares also occur with Late Medieval Well-fired Sandy ware, as shown in Sector F. This is likely to reflect an intrusive element rather than contemporaneity as Late Medieval Well-fired Sandy ware itself does not occur significantly with any early or high medieval types.

The late medieval period

For the late medieval period, as Table 5 shows, there is no division of coarse and sandy glazed wares. English pottery forms a smaller proportion of this period group in comparison with the quantities shown for the Anglo-Norman and high medieval periods. Non-local English wares are no more significant than they were among the high medieval pottery. What is important, however, is that a single source area is represented, the Hampshire/Surrey border. This implies a regular traffic in these products. There is a considerable increase in the quantity and the range of Continental wares. The products of France, the Low Countries, the Rhineland and the Iberian peninsula occur in roughly equal proportions. Italian wares also figure for the first time, although in smaller amounts than the pottery of other countries.

Figure 36 shows that the most significant late medieval Major Wares are the local Late Medieval Well-fired Sandy wares, and Low Countries Redware. High percentages of almost every other late medieval Major Ware occur with these two types. A number of late medieval wares occur with high medieval types, as shown in Sector H. The production of Southampton Organic Sandy ware may have overlapped with the end of the high medieval tradition, as the same pattern can be seen in Sector F. However, it is unlikely that Normandy Stoneware and Martincamp wares were imported in the 13th and 14th centuries, and an element of residuality is suggested.

Residuality and intrusion

Figure 36 is useful also as an indicator of the pattern of residuality and intrusion throughout this assemblage.

The factors of residuality and intrusion are a common problem in the study of finds from archaeological excavations. In an urban environment, where the depth of deposits and the intensity of ancient activity are profound, it is rare to find groups of pottery untainted by the presence of earlier or later wares. The means by which contaminating material might be introduced into any context are many and various. Residuality is perhaps easier to explain because at least sherds of earlier material were already in existence at the time that the deposit from which they were recovered was laid down. The digging of pits or foundation trenches will disturb earlier material, thus bringing it back into circulation before finally burying it. Intrusion may be

Table 5. Quantities of late medieval wares

Fabric Number	Fabric Name	Weight	Sherds	% Weight	% Sherds
1130	Southampton Organic-tempered Sandy	7646	335	8	8
1136	Southampton Organic-tempered Fine Sandy	12609	409	13	9
	Late Medieval Well-fired Sandy	66984	2587	68	61
	Other Local Late Medieval Sandy	8334	583	8	14
1092	Surrey Whiteware	818	69	1	2
1193	Tudor Green	1579	291	2	7
	Total English wares	97970	4274		
	Total English % LMed	47	46		
1754	Developed Normandy Gritty	133	14	1	2
1347	Proto-Normandy Stoneware	12	1	<1	<1
1349	Normandy Stoneware	4071	205	19	18
	Martincamp types	5006	439	24	39
	Beauvais Monochrome	1673	156	8	14
1319	Beauvais Sgraffito	163	9	1	1
1316	Beauvais Double-slipped Sgraffito	202	19	1	2
1744	Beauvais Stoneware	44	4	<1	<1
1749	North French Pink-grey	15	2	<1	<1
1454	Late Saintonge Whiteware	8798	246	43	22
1770	Late Saintonge Polychrome	510	17	2	1
	Total French wares	20627	1112		
	French wares % of Continental	19	22		
1297	Low Countries Redware	30332	1294	92	88
1300	Slipped Low Countries Redware	1092	49	3	3
1610	Green-glazed Low Countries Redware	302	21	1	1
1775	Low Countries Sgraffito	26	2		
1422	South Netherlands	429	14	4	7
1426	Malling-type Tin-glazed	87	5		
	Total Low Countries wares	32268	1455		
	Low Countries % of Continental	29	29		
	Siegburg Stoneware	638	34	2	3
1257	Langewehe Stoneware	521	17	2	2
1245	Raeren-type Stoneware	18198	682	81	78
1378	Cologne Stoneware	648	40	3	5
	Frechen Stonewares	1406	36	6	4
1346	Miscellaneous Rhenish Stoneware	960	67	4	8
	Total Rhenish wares	22371	876		
	Rhenish % of Continental	20	18		
	Seville-type Coarsewares	14300	503	58	50
1439	Andalusian Coarseware	3087	120		
	Iberian Micaceous Redwares	3787	292	28	41
1070	Valencian Lustreware	1666	33	7	3
	Morisco and other Tin-glazed wares	1939	66	8	6
	Total Iberian wares	24779	1014		
	Iberian % of Continental	22	20		
1446	Montelupo Maiolica	996	33	5	5
1767	Florentine Maiolica	1699	31	24	8
1450	Faenza Maiolica	2539	134	28	33
1241	Archaic Pisan Maiolica	753	47	8	12
	North Italian Maiolica	1509	94	6	13
1772	Ligurian Faience	16	2	<1	<1
1760	North Italian Sgraffito	1276	37	14	9
1768	North Italian Red Earthenware	934	62	10	15
	Total Italian wares	9722	440		
	Italian % of Continental	9	9		
	Unidentified LMed Continental	655	78		
	Unidentified % of Continental	1	2		
	Total Continental	110422	4975		
	Continental % of Total	53	53		
	Total	208392	9249		

a more worrying factor, leading to doubts about the integrity of ceramic groups and even the quality of their excavation. Single, small sherds of later material are to be expected, and may happily be explained away as the results of soil movement. The presence of numerous later sherds in a context is a problem not so easily answered. Although no explanations are offered here, there follows an examination of the pattern of residuality and intrusion in this assemblage as a means of exploring its own internal integrity.

In Figure 36 the occurrence of ware types in relation to the central diagonal line demonstrated the contemporaneity of the Major Wares identified as Anglo-Norman, high or late medieval. The three sectors through which the diagonal line passes show a distinct grouping of wares in each of the three ceramic periods. However, for the purposes of this discussion, the remaining six sectors B, C, D, F, G and H are of greater interest.

Sectors B and D illustrate the relationship between early and high medieval wares. Sector B shows that large percentages of most Anglo-Norman wares occur with common high medieval types, especially Southampton Coarseware and Saintonge types. This may be seen to reflect primarily the intrusive element of the high medieval wares because of the quantities indicated. Southampton Coarseware and the Saintonge wares are the largest components of the high medieval ware assemblage and it is therefore not surprising to find that these are a common intrusive presence in Anglo-Norman deposits. Even so, the quantity of this intrusion is not expressed in Figure 36. For instance, it may be that a single high medieval sherd is intrusive in a context containing a large quantity of Anglo-Norman wares. Sector D clarifies this by showing that over 50% of all the Saintonge material occurs with Scratch-marked wares but less than that amount with any other Anglo-Norman types. This demonstrates not only the longevity of the scratch-marked tradition, but also that the pattern visible in sector B reflects

residuality among the other Anglo-Norman types. This is confirmed in sector D by the fact that large quantities of other high medieval types occur with those of the Anglo-Norman period. The low occurrence of Anglo-Norman wares with high medieval types indicated in sector B, confirms this residuality rather than suggesting complete contemporaneity. Both areas must therefore be looked at together for a clear understanding of the relationship between the early and high medieval period groups.

The same process can be applied to sectors C and G, to demonstrate the relationship between Anglo-Norman wares and those of the late medieval period. Sector C shows that late medieval wares are a rare intrusive element in contexts with high quantities of Anglo-Norman pottery. Sector G indicates that although Anglo-Norman pottery does occur with late medieval wares, this is less frequent than with high medieval material.

Similarly sectors F and H show how high and late medieval wares relate. Area F shows late medieval wares occurring with some frequency amongst high medieval types. Sector H illustrates the residuality of high medieval material amongst the late medieval pottery.

Throughout, it is those fabrics that are most common by quantity that persist as residual elements, or are represented as intrusive. The very fact that they are common to some extent explains this. Their quantities may, alternatively, reflect popularity and a longer period of use, implying that they are not entirely residual but were contemporary with wares that are later introductions.

The pattern expressed in Figure 36 is a broad one, giving only relative quantities, and cannot be related to actual deposits and it does not illuminate any discussion of the processes that give rise to the phenomena of residuality and intrusion. Figure 36 has, however, established the coherence of the Anglo-Norman, high and late medieval ceramic periods, providing a sound chronological basis for subsequent interpretation.

Settlement phases

Having identified three periods of ceramic production and consumption in Southampton, through an analysis of the relationships between certain ceramic types, the next step must be to relate this sequence to a chronology based on the excavated stratigraphic evidence. The purpose here is to relate the three ceramic periods introduced above, to phases of human activity. This will also help to achieve an understanding of some of

the differences between those ceramic periods.

Stratigraphically, each excavation is a separate entity, comprised of different features and deposits, each of which plays a different part in the quest for an overall understanding of the structure of medieval Southampton. It is not the purpose here, however, to become involved in a detailed stratigraphic analysis of each site assemblage. In order to combine the evidence of several excavations, each stratigraphic phase, as identified by the excavators, has been placed in one of four broad overall phases, each of which relates to recognisable periods in the development of Southampton between the 11th and 16th centuries. These four phases are:

Phase 1   c 1066–1250
Phase 2   c 1250–1350
Phase 3   c 1350–1430
Phase 4   c 1430–1510

Each phase has its own ceramic character, determined by quantifying the types of pottery present. Where types occur most abundantly they are assumed to have been in use during that phase. Certain ceramic types will of course continue in use through more than one phase but the occurrence of types with known dates of production, here mainly imported wares, will help to confirm the accuracy of this phasing. This section quantifies and discusses ceramic distribution through all four phases.

It is not possible to phase every deposit from the nine sites considered here. The variable nature of the records from certain excavations and the confused stratigraphy of parts of others render certain deposits unphaseable. Only those that can, with certainty, be related to identified periods of activity are included.

It is important that deposits, rather than features, are accurately phased. Pottery is not recovered from a feature but from the fills introduced into it. It is therefore these fills, rather than the features themselves, which give the pottery its stratigraphic and chronological context. The fills of a pit may date to several phases, all much later than the cutting of the feature itself. It should also be remembered that it is the sequence of pottery use that is being examined by this method rather than the development of the stratigraphic deposits from which the assemblage was recovered.

Excluded from this phasing is the whole of the assemblage from the High Street site SOU 105, where no stratigraphic sequence has been determined. Pottery from the fills of the castle ditch, partially sectioned at the Upper Bugle Street sites SOU 123 and SOU 124, is also not included amongst the phased material. That material dates from the 12th to the 17th centuries (Brown 1986) and comes from a variety of half-sections that nowhere amount to a full investigation of the ditch fills. Phasing the ditch itself is a relatively simple matter, but phasing its fills is much more problematic, as processes of partial cleaning and the probability of secondary dumping confuse the stratigraphic sequence.

It is safer simply to exclude this material, as doing so has little effect on the final interpretation of the pottery that has been phased. Other unphased deposits are those that are stratigraphically isolated. These come mainly from SOU 25, but there are others from SOU 122, SOU 123 and SOU 124. All the contexts from sites SOU 29, 110 and 125 have been phased.

A total of 921 contexts have been phased as described. The total quantities of pottery present in each phase are shown in Table 6. Phases 2 and 4 produced the greatest amounts of material. These two phases equate with the period of production and consumption for the high and late medieval ceramic periods respectively. It is no surprise, given that these two ceramic periods are the best represented in the assemblage, to find that these two settlement phases should be the most productive. It is noteworthy that the percentage of the total sherd number represented by unphased deposits is markedly greater than the unphased sherd weight. This suggests a below-average sherd size for the unphased material, thus giving a clue to the reasons for the difficulty in phasing those contexts.

Tables 7, 10, 12 and 13 list the quantities of each Major Ware in each of the four settlement phases. Other pottery types are also shown, grouped together in general categories such as high medieval sandy wares. These tables form the basis for the discussion of the ceramic character of each phase, which is further illustrated through the description of specific ceramic groups. The ceramic composition of these groups is presented in tabular form, and they are also illustrated in Plates 2–6. The relative occurrence in each phase of the pottery types described in Chapter 2, and quantified in Tables 3–5, is shown in Tables 15–17. These conclude this chapter by bringing together both types of chronological evidence, ceramic and stratigraphic. The broad pattern they show is illustrated more accessibly in the pie charts of Figures 37–39.

The activities that characterised each of these phases are described and discussed in Chapter 8 but a short introduction to each of them is included here.

Table 6. Quantities of pottery in each phase

Phase	RP	Weight (g)	Sherd No.	% Weight	% Sherd No.
1	4609	94170	5587	16	16
2	8141	169933	9828	28	27
3	2644	51381	3195	9	9
4	12039	188983	7951	32	22
Unphased	5566	94411	9379	16	26
Total	32919	598878	35940		

Phase 1 (*c* 1050–1250)

Phase 1 broadly coincides with the Anglo-Norman ceramic period described above. This was a time of change and consolidation in Southampton, following the Norman Conquest. William I established the town as his premier south coast port and founded the castle as his royal warehouse. Previously established links with northern France were reinforced and Southampton soon became home to an increasingly successful mercantile community that expressed its wealth through the construction of stone houses and cellars.

Table 7 shows that Anglo-Norman wares comprise over 70% of the total quantity, by weight and sherd number, for Phase 1. Local coarse and glazed wares are the most common types, as they are for the Anglo-Norman pottery as a whole. North French types such as Normandy Gritty ware and the Monochrome and Rouen-type glazed wares represent the bulk of the Continental imports. Others include Andenne-type and Blaugrau wares. High medieval wares represent 17% of the total sherd weight. The most common of these are the two Southampton types, Southampton Whiteware and Southampton Sandy wares. All the high medieval Major Wares are represented however, indicating perhaps a transitional period when both early and high medieval pottery types were being produced and consumed. Late medieval types are a far less significant presence, although Southampton Organic Sandy wares are well represented. There may be some grounds here for questioning the precision of the phasing for some of these deposits, but that exercise has not, as yet, been undertaken. At least the information shown in Table 7 most obviously supports the identification of Anglo-Norman pottery types.

The end of Phase 1 has been identified as a period of transition, when high medieval wares were being introduced. This is further emphasised by the fact that two ceramic groups have been presented as illustrative of this period. The first group represents the early part of Phase 1; the second can be dated to the end of it.

Group 1: three pits, SOU 124

A typical group of pottery from the early part of this phase is exemplified in a series of three pits, features 46, 91 and 94 from Upper Bugle Street 3, SOU 124. These pits were cut into the natural sub-soil and were truncated by a stone cellar built in the 13th century. The upper fills of all three features were removed by this building, but they produced a group of pottery comparatively large for this period, and securely dated by the later cellar.

Table 7. Quantities of pottery types in Phase 1

Fabric Number	Major Wares and Others	Weight (g)	Sherd No.
	Residual Pre-Conquest	4658	541
	Residual % of Total	5	10
	Early Medieval Flint-tempered ware	6885	714
	Scratch-marked wares	41948	2439
1011	Mixed Grit	1134	35
1014	Mixed Grit	1135	64
1095	Mixed Grit	871	26
1055	Chalk-tempered ware	2139	42
1016	Early Wessex Coarseware	2450	90
	Early Dorset Sandy ware	1320	84
	Other Early Medieval Coarsewares	2354	113
	Early Medieval Glazed wares	3986	108
	Normandy Gritty wares	2473	179
	North French Glazed wares	637	49
	Other EMed Continental wares	883	50
	Total Anglo-Norman wares	68215	3993
	Anglo-Norman % of Total	72	71
1123	Southampton Coarseware	7323	285
1024	Sandy Southampton Coarseware	1016	40
1230	Southampton High Street Coarseware	189	9
1124	Mixed Grit Coarse Sandy	152	15
	Other HMed Coarsewares	432	19
1044	Southampton Whiteware	124	18
	Southampton Sandy ware	887	59
1248	South Hampshire Redware	555	46
1087	Local Pink Sandy ware	489	28
	Laverstock wares	725	37
1118	Local Whiteware	995	35
1215	Local Fine White Sandy ware	155	13
1156	Dorset Whiteware	21	2
	Dorset Sandy ware	59	5
	Other HMed Sandy wares	1676	109
	HMed French wares	745	39
	HMed Saintonge wares	769	89
	Other HMed Continental wares	42	4
	Total high medieval wares	16354	852
	High medieval % of Total	17	15
	Southampton Organic Sandy wares	1751	52
	Late Medieval Well-fired Sandy wares	472	37
	Other LMed Sandy wares	197	15
1092	Surrey Whiteware	59	3
1193	Tudor Green ware	13	5
	Beauvais wares	60	3
1349	Normandy Stoneware	39	2
	Martincamp wares	22	2
	Other LMed North French wares	16	3
	Late Medieval Saintonge wares	129	2
	Low Countries Redwares	792	14
	Other Rhenish Stonewares	33	3
	Seville-type Coarsewares	148	10
	Iberian Micaceous Redwares	34	5
	Spanish Tin-glazed wares	64	2
	Italian Maiolicas	18	1
	Other LMed Continental wares	1	1
	Total late medieval wares	3848	160
	Late medieval % of Total	4	3
	Post-medieval wares	1095	41
	Post-medieval % of Total	1	1
	Total	94170	5587

Table 8 shows the quantities of each ceramic type present. Pottery types that were present in the late Saxon period, mainly the flint-tempered wares but also sandy wares, account for 25% of the total sherd number. This suggests that these products continued in use after the Norman Conquest. Scratch-marked wares comprise the largest proportion of this group however. These are mainly jar/cooking pots of a consistent size, with a rim diameter of about eleven centimetres. Amongst the Anglo-Norman coarsewares just one rim sherd is from a bowl. Anglo-Norman glazed wares comprise seven percent of the Anglo-Norman sherd number and these sherds, of which two have rouletted decoration, are all probably from tripod pitchers. Continental wares represent five percent of the Anglo-Norman sherd number but a good range of types is included. Normandy Gritty ware, including a reduced type, is the most common import, while green-glazed North French Whiteware jugs and fragments of a Rouen-type jug are also present. Low Countries Andenne and Blaugrau types and three hard-fired white and grey sherds, probably of Rhenish origin, complete the range of imports. There are eleven sherds of high medieval pottery, and one fragment of Late Medieval Well-fired Sandy ware, all of which are probably the products of intrusion. The high medieval types may be associated with the 13th-century construction of the cellar that removed the tops of these features, while the Late Medieval pottery can be associated with subsequent disturbances of the cellar floor. Plate 2 illustrates how fragmentary much of this material is.

On ceramic grounds alone this group is most probably 12th century in date. The date of the construction of the cellar gives a useful *terminus ante quem*. As the composition of this group includes most of the types recognised as Anglo-Norman, useful evidence for the period of their use has been established. The fact that this is one of the largest groups of this period, yet small in comparison to those from later periods, indicates the ephemeral nature of the Phase 1 deposits.

Group 2: garderobe, SOU 123

The end of Phase 1 and the beginning of Phase 2 has been placed in the middle of the 13th century. This

Table 8. Quantities of all wares in SOU 124 pit group

Fabric Number	Fabric Name	Weight	Sherds	% Weight	% Sherds
	Late Saxon	157	30		
	Late Saxon % of Total	2	5		
	Early Medieval Flint-tempered	865	112	12	23
	Scratch-marked	6236	356	84	73
1011	Mixed Grit	7	1	<1	<1
1014	Mixed Grit	43	4	1	1
1095	Mixed Grit	95	3	1	1
1016	Wessex Coarseware	176	10	2	2
	Dorset Sandy ware	24	2	<1	<1
	Anglo-Norman glazed	6	1	<1	<1
	Total English	7452	489		
	Total English % all Anglo-Norman	98	95		
	Normandy Gritty wares	155	13	82	54
	North French Glazed wares	8	3	4	12
1402	Rouen-type ware	7	3	4	12
1390	Andenne-type	16	4	8	17
1385	Blaugrau	3	1	2	4
	Total Continental	189	24		
	Total Continental % all Anglo-Norman	2	5		
	Total Anglo-Norman	7641	513		
	Total A-Norm % of Total	97	93		
1053	Laverstock	1	1		
1272	Saintonge Whiteware	87	6		
	Total High medieval	88	7		
	Total HMed % of Total	1	1		
	LMed Well-fired Sandy ware	4	1		
	Total LMed % of Total	<1	<1		
	Total	7890	551		

Table 9. Quantities of all wares in castle garderobe

Fabric Number	Fabric Name	Weight	Sherds	% Weight	% Sherds
	Scratch-marked	10000	239	55	59
1011	Mixed Grit	840	24	5	6
1095	Mixed Grit	583	4	3	1
1055	Chalk-tempered	2046	38	11	9
1013	Non-local Flint-tempered	704	19	4	5
	Other Plain Coarsewares	684	9	4	2
1016	Wessex Coarseware	1767	35	10	9
	Anglo-Norman Glazed	1688	36	9	9
	Total Anglo-Norman English	18312	404		
	Anglo-Norman English % of EMed	95	95		
	Normandy Gritty ware	38	2	4	9
	North French Glazed	249	2	27	9
1413	North French Sandy	296	10	33	44
1269	Early Saintonge	60	1	7	4
1385	Blaugrau	263	8	29	35
	Total Anglo-Norman Continental	906	23		
	A-Norm Continental % of EMed	5	5		
	Total Anglo-Norman	19218	427		
	Anglo-Norman % of Total	90	88		
	High Medieval Coarsewares	219	13	10	23
	High Medieval Local Sandy	1812	39	86	70
	Saintonge Whiteware	71	4	3	7
	Total high medieval	2102	56		
	High medieval % of Total	10	12		
	Post-medieval Redware	44	1		
	Post-medieval % of Total	1	1		
	Total	21364	484		

division is obviously a convenient construct that is by no means chronologically concise, either in terms of changes in pottery types or in the make-up of the stratigraphy. Periods of change are always difficult to date. The second group discussed here is later than that described above and may have been deposited during the period of the Phase 1/Phase 2 transition. It comes from a stone-lined garderobe excavated at the castle on the Upper Bugle Street site SOU 123. This was apparently filled in *c* 1250 (Oxley 1986).

Table 9 shows the ceramic composition of this group. The pottery is mainly Anglo-Norman in date with Scratch-marked jar/cooking pots typically dominant. A range of sizes is represented, including some very large vessels (Plate 2). Several rims, including those of the largest vessels, exhibit deep thumbed impressions that seem to be a feature of later Scratch-marked forms (8). Complete profiles of plain hand-built cooking pots in other local coarseware fabrics also occur. This is a fine array of cooking pots, and it includes an example in a heavily flint-tempered fabric from Dorset (19) and a North French type (185). No bowls have been identified. Anglo-Norman glazed wares are a significant presence and include the complete profile of a tripod

pitcher (25), the bases of two others (22) and large body sherds of a third (21). Imported continental products are comparatively rare. There is no Normandy Gritty ware, and just two sherds of North French green-glazed ware. An almost complete Blaugrau-type ladle/cooking pot (297) was recovered from the lowest level, and this may be associated with the use of the garderobe, rather than the time of its closure. Pottery from the high medieval period may not represent a large proportion of the group's total weight or sherd number, but is present in significant fragments. These include the complete thumbed base of a wheel-thrown jug (111) in Local Whiteware and the rim and handle of another. There is also the profile of a small wheel-thrown jar/cooking pot in Southampton Sandy ware (68) and a rare tubular-handled saucepan (129). The handle of a Saintonge Green-glazed jug is the only fragment of high medieval imported pottery. Early Saintonge ware is present in the form of a parrot-beak spout (186).

A series of cross-fits between the contexts that filled the garderobe suggests that the feature was closed in a single, rapid operation rather than by a gradual build-up (Brown 1986). It is possible that the pottery found in these deposits was previously incorporated in another dump used as the source for the filling of the garderobe. The combined presence of early and high medieval ceramics need not lead to the conclusion that any earlier source was the result of many years of dumping. The extent of the cross-fits and the good condition of the sherds gives this group an internal integrity, which suggests that the high medieval material need not be intrusive. It is mixed into every layer and was presumably introduced into the garderobe at the same time as all the other finds. A mid-13th century date for the closure of the garderobe is suggested by other structural changes at the castle (Oxley 1986). There is no reason why the hand-built wares, both coarse and glazed, should not have been in production at this period. Similarly, the appearance of new types is quite likely at this date. This group contains the expected elements of any Anglo-Norman deposit, but the presence in a well-sealed context of high medieval material provides useful evidence for the transitional relationship between the two ceramic periods, and indicates a date at the end of the Anglo-Norman period.

Phase 2 (c 1250–1350)

Phase 2 coincides with the high medieval period. Trade links with Normandy were interrupted and mercantile attentions became focused on Gascony. The trade in Gascon wines was huge and doubtless accounts for the fact that Saintonge wares became the most common imported pottery. This was also a time of technological change, as wheel-thrown local products replaced the hand-built wares that characterise Phase 1. The high medieval period was also a time of enormous creativity, throughout western Europe, and the quantity and range of the ceramics reflects this.

Table 10 shows that high medieval wares represent 80% of the total Phase 2 pottery weight, and 78% of the sherd count. It is of interest that Anglo-Norman wares are present in approximately the same proportion as high medieval wares occur in Phase 1. A certain element of residuality may be assumed, but the emphasis on coarsewares, and especially scratch-marked types, is further evidence that they were still being made in the late-13th century. The full range of high medieval local coarsewares, glazed sandy wares and

Table 10. Quantities of pottery types in Phase 2

Fabric Number	Major Wares and Others	Weight (g)	Sherd No.
	Residual pre-Conquest	1557	172
	Residual % of Total	1	2
	Early Medieval Flint-tempered ware	2229	199
	Scratch-marked wares	13376	800
1011	Mixed Grit	221	15
1014	Mixed Grit	2558	93
1095	Mixed Grit	653	30
1055	Chalk-tempered ware	151	11
1016	Early Wessex Coarseware	1195	72
	Early Dorset Sandy ware	986	73
	Other Early Medieval Coarsewares	927	44
	Early Medieval Glazed wares	1590	72
	Normandy Gritty wares	1498	78
	North French Glazed wares	786	78
	Other A-Norm Continental wares	104	14
	Total Anglo-Norman wares	26274	1579
	Anglo-Norman % of Total	15	16
1123	Southampton Coarseware	39633	2491
1024	Sandy Southampton Coarseware	6973	538
1230	Southampton High Street Coarseware	619	31
1124	Mixed Grit Coarse Sandy	662	81
	Other HMed Coarsewares	895	59
1044	Southampton Whiteware	3125	173
	Southampton Sandy ware	12562	859
1248	South Hampshire Redware	22723	1013
1087	Local Pink Sandy ware	9479	512
1034	Laverstock	2130	135
1118	Local Whiteware	811	63
1215	Local Fine White Sandy ware	614	50
1156	Dorset Whiteware	2579	97

Fabric Number	Major Wares and Others	Weight (g)	Sherd No.
	Dorset Sandy ware	765	26
	Other HMed Sandy wares	3877	233
	HMed French wares	2981	281
	HMed Saintonge wares	25066	1044
	Other HMed Continental wares	860	23
	Total high medieval wares	136354	7709
	High medieval % of Total	80	78
	Southampton Organic Sandy wares	1626	96
	Late Medieval Well-fired Sandy wares	1026	55
	Other LMed Sandy wares	896	83
1092	Surrey Whiteware	47	6
1193	Tudor Green	36	8
	Beauvais wares	4	1
1349	Normandy Stoneware	20	1
	Late Medieval Saintonge	14	1
	Low Countries Redwares	184	10
1245	Raeren Stoneware	12	2
	Other Rhenish Stonewares	80	6
	Iberian Coarsewares	540	16
	Iberian Micaceous Redwares	345	19
	Spanish Tin-glazed wares	23	3
	Italian Maiolicas	15	1
	Italian Lead-glazed Earthenwares	32	2
	Other LMed Continental wares	129	8
	Total late medieval wares	5029	318
	Late medieval % of Total	3	3
	Post-medieval wares	719	50
	Post-medieval % of Total	<1	<1
	Total	169933	9828

Table 11. Quantities of all wares in SOU 25 pit group

Fabric No.	Fabric Name	Weight	Sherds	% Weight	% Sherds
	Late Saxon wares	37	4		
	Late Saxon % of Total	1	1		
	Early Medieval Flint-tempered	148	13		
	Scratch-marked wares	1299	62		
1011	Mixed Grit	33	3		
1014	Mixed Grit	678	19		
1095	Mixed Grit	57	3		
1016	Wessex Coarseware	211	11		
	Dorset Sandy ware	72	4		
	Other Plain Coarsewares	65	2		
	Other Glazed wares	785	21		
	Normandy Gritty wares	203	18		
	North French Glazed wares	106	12		
	Total Anglo-Norman	3657	168		
	Total Anglo-Norman % of Total	7	7		
1123	Southampton Coarseware	12315	556	84	78
1024	Southampton Sandy Coarseware	1727	120	12	17
1230	Southampton High Street Coarseware	45	6	<1	1
1124	Mixed Grit Coarse Sandy	132	5	1	1
	Other Coarsewares	477	25	3	3
	Total HMed Coarsewares	14696	712		
	Total Coarseware % of Hmed English	43	47		
1044	Southampton Whiteware	1909	76	10	9
	Southampton Sandy ware	1656	137	8	17
1248	South Hampshire Redware	11832	392	61	49
1087	Local Pink Sandy ware	1749	71	9	9
	Laverstock	1083	55	6	7
1118	Local Whiteware	455	27	2	3
1215	Local Fine White Sandy ware	219	17	1	2
	Dorset Sandy ware	20	2	<1	<1
1156	Dorset Whiteware	6	2	<1	<1
	Other Sandy wares	491	24	2	3
	Total HMed Sandy wares	19420	803		
	Total Sandy ware % of Hmed English	57	53		
	Total HMed English	34116	1515		
	Total English % all HMed	69	73		
1403	Developed Rouen	283	30	2	6
1548	Seine Valley Whiteware	32	4	<1	1
1552	North French Sandy Whiteware	76	5	<1	1
1291	North French Pink ware	17	1	<1	<1
1458	Ceramique Onctueuse	13	1	<1	<1
1272	Saintonge Whiteware	7215	357	48	66
1500	Saintonge Bright Green-glazed ware	692	62	5	11
1274	Saintonge Polychrome	10	2	<1	<1
1464	Saintonge Gritty ware	1915	11	13	2
1273	Saintonge Redware	3392	22	23	4
	Other French wares	862	44	6	8
	Total Hmed French wares	14507	539		
	Total French Ware % of Hmed Continental	95	98		
1494	Low Countries Highly Decorated Redware	749	11	99	85
	Miscellaneous Continental	6	2	1	5
	Total Non-French Continental	755	13		
	Total Non-French % of Continental	5	2		
	Total HMed Continental	15262	552		
	Continental % of HMed	31	27		
	Total high medieval	49378	2067		
	HMed % of Total	91	89		
	Southampton Organic-tempererd Sandy	312	23		
	Late Medieval Well-fired Sandy	178	19		
	Other Late Medieval Sandy wares	195	20		
	Surrey Whiteware	8	1		
	Tudor Green	17	5		
	Beauvais Monochrome	4	1		
	Siegburg Stoneware	10	1		
1257	Langerwehe stoneware	29	1		
1346	Miscellaneous Rhenish Stoneware	9	1		
	Iberian Coarsewares	40	2		
	Iberian Micaceous Redwares	324	14		
1448	Morisco Tin-glazed wares	13	1		
1467	North Italian Maiolica	15	1		
	Unidentified Tin-glazed wares	8	1		
	Total late medieval wares	1162	91		
	LMed % of Total	2	4		
	Total	54197	2326		

Continental types occurs in larger quantities than any of the other phases. The small quantities of late and post-medieval pottery are presumed to be the products of intrusion, although once again, Southampton Organic Sandy wares are the most common of these. Some of the late medieval Continental material, particularly the Seville-type Coarsewares and Iberian Micaceous Redwares, must have come into the town in the late 13th and early 14th centuries. It is notable that these are the most common types of late medieval Continental wares and some of these finds could probably be characterised as high medieval.

Amongst the high medieval pottery local coarsewares and glazed sandy wares occur in almost equal proportions. All together, local products comprise over 70% of the Phase 2 high medieval pottery. All the Major Wares of the high medieval period are represented, with Southampton Coarseware and South Hampshire

Redware dominant. English wares brought in from further afield are poorly represented, as they are in the assemblage as a whole. Phase 2 has the widest range of non-local pottery types however, including Scarborough ware, material from Cornwall and the Midlands, and Dorset types. Continental products comprise 20% of all the high medieval pottery. French pottery accounts for 97% of the imports and Saintonge material 88% of the French wares. In Phase 1 North French wares accounted for 93% of the total weight of Anglo-Norman imports, in Phase 2 they represent just 6% of the total weight of high medieval imports. The significance of Southampton's interests in the south-west of France, and the corresponding decline in contact with Normandy is thus clearly demonstrated. Aardenburg-type ware and a few sherds of Rhenish Proto-stoneware are the only high medieval imports that were not made in France.

Group 3: pits and garderobe, SOU 25

One group of pottery has been selected to illustrate this phase. A series of twelve features excavated at Westgate Street, SOU 25 were stratified in the same phase of activity (Westgate Street Phase 2B, Blackman). Their contemporaneity is further evidenced by a number of ceramic cross-fits between these features. There are six inter-cutting pits, the stratigraphy of which suggests that they were cut over a short period of time, and the date-range of the pottery supports this interpretation, for seven vessels cross-fit between these features. There are four more pits, two irregularly shaped and two square-cut cesspits, also a stone-lined garderobe and a hearth set into a shallow depression. Each of these features is linked by a ceramic cross-fit with at least one other. It is beyond the scope of this work to discuss in greater detail the stratigraphic and other site-related aspects of this group of features and its ceramics.

Table 11 quantifies the range of pottery types present and Plate 3 is a representation of the more complete vessel types. Table 11 shows that the overall proportions of Anglo-Norman, high, late and post-medieval pottery are similar to those demonstrated for Phase 2 as a whole. High medieval wares dominate, comprising *c* 90% of the total sherd weight and number. There is a good range of coarseware cooking pots, mainly in Southampton Coarseware. An unusual vessel in this fabric is a lantern made by cutting holes into a typical cooking pot (**46**). Quantities of Scratch-marked ware evidence the survival of this tradition into the last half

of the 13th century. There are also fragments of Southampton Coarseware curfews, sandy ware bowls, dripping pans and a pipkin.

There is a wide range of jugs, with a varied selection of local forms represented, mainly in South Hampshire Redware and including some decorated examples (for example **80**, **82**). Saintonge wares account for 24% of the total weight of high medieval pottery in this group. These occur mainly in the form of standard green-glazed whiteware jugs, of which several survive in complete profile (see Plate 4). There is a complete Saintonge Bright Green-glazed ware jug (**210**) but only one sherd of Polychrome ware. North French wares are represented by a Developed Rouen ware jug (**187**). The only Low Countries highly decorated type vessel (**261**) in this assemblage also came from this group. These are all serving vessels but there are also larger jugs or pitchers, perhaps best suited to the storage or mixing of liquids. Local types include a two-handled pitcher (**79**). Saintonge pégaux are represented mainly in the common whiteware fabric, but most astonishing is the large Redware example with a slipped heraldic decoration and sgraffito inscription (**218**). Other rare Saintonge types include a Gritty ware mortar, decorated with applied faces (**215**) and a lid (**217**). Fragments of three other Saintonge mortars were also recovered.

Much of the Anglo-Norman material, and all of the late Saxon pottery, is considered to be residual. The disturbance of earlier deposits is inevitable during a period of such intense activity. Whether any of the features represented in this group were of earlier date cannot be established through artefactual or stratigraphic study. The constant digging of pits in the same area also provides an explanation for the pattern of pottery cross-fits in this group. The only isolated feature is the stone-lined garderobe, feature 1260, which has a cross-fit with the hearth, feature 1328. The garderobe produced 49 sherds of late medieval pottery, 56% of the total number of late medieval sherds in the group as a whole, which represent later fills in this structure. The remaining late and post-medieval material is distributed fairly evenly among the other features in this group. Late medieval and later pottery represents four percent of the total sherd number, an acceptable level of intrusion in such a concentrated sequence of features.

The range of fabrics and forms in this group splendidly illustrates the ceramic character of Phase 2, while the quantity and range of material reflects the prosperity of the occupants of the tenement associated with these features.

Phase 3 (*c* 1350–1420)

Phase 3 represents the period of transition between the ceramics of the high and late medieval periods. That transition must have been enforced partly through the effects of the recession that followed the Hundred Years War and the Black Death. The resultant decline in trade, together with the expense of constructing the town wall, (a measure necessitated by the sacking of the town in 1338) was bankrupting the community and Southampton was in the doldrums. The ceramic traditions that characterised the happier times of the late 13th and early 14th centuries were gone, to be replaced by pottery of less flamboyant, more utilitarian, aspect. The exact chronology of this process is unclear, but there is no doubt that by the beginning of Phase 4, in the middle part of the 15th century, the wares of the high medieval period were no longer being produced. There is a marked paucity of productive archaeological deposits in Phase 3 and this must have been a period of relatively little activity. One effect of this is that it has been impossible to identify a group of material that satisfactorily illustrates the ceramic character of Phase 3.

Just as stratigraphy of this date is hard to find, the amount of finds recovered is relatively slight. Table 6 shows that pottery from Phase 3 deposits comprises just nine percent of the whole assemblage and this is one reason why the mechanics of the transition from the ceramic types of the high medieval period to those of the late medieval are so elusive. Table 12 shows that high medieval and late medieval types are present in roughly the same amounts by weight. There is however a greater number of high medieval sherds. This may be because most of this material was deposited in site layers, where vessels will break into smaller fragments than those buried in pits. The evidence suggests, however, that local pottery of the high medieval tradition was still being produced at this period. There is a notably low quantity of high medieval continental wares in comparison with Phase 2, where imports represent 20% of the high medieval ceramic weight. In Phase 3 they represent eight percent. Most of these are Saintonge wares, but there is clear evidence here of a decline in commercial contact with the Continent. This quantification suggests that by the end of Phase 3 late medieval pottery types had replaced earlier traditions.

Phase 4 (*c* 1420–1550)

Phase 4 represents a period of recovery for Southampton, stimulated largely by the arrival of Italian

Table 12. Quantities of pottery types in Phase 3

Fabric Number	Major Wares and Others	Weight (g)	Sherd No.
	Residual Pre-Conquest	989	81
	Residual % of Total	2	2
	Early Medieval Flint-tempered ware	1853	126
	Scratch-marked wares	2010	114
1011	Mixed Grit	319	19
1014	Mixed Grit	555	25
1095	Mixed Grit	68	5
1055	Chalk-tempered ware	5	1
1016	Wessex Coarseware	228	25
	Early Dorset Sandy ware	244	17
	Other Anglo-Norman Coarsewares	95	11
	Anglo-Norman Glazed	38	6
	Normandy Gritty wares	430	30
	North French Glazed wares	173	27
	Other Anglo-Norman Continental wares	64	10
	Total Anglo-Norman wares	6082	416
	Anglo-Norman % of Total	12	13
1123	Southampton Coarseware	6439	456
1024	Sandy Southampton Coarseware	1775	130
1230	Southampton High Street Coarseware	358	33
1124	Mixed Grit Coarse Sandy	140	21
	Other HMed Coarsewares	215	13
1044	Southampton Whiteware	527	43
	Southampton Sandy ware	2721	234
1248	South Hampshire Redware	1098	98
1087	Local Pink Sandy ware	720	77
1034	Laverstock	645	37
1118	Local Whiteware	319	24
1215	Local Fine White Sandy ware	65	5
1156	Dorset Whiteware	133	11
	Dorset Sandy ware	438	38
	Other HMed Sandy wares	2557	141
	HMed French wares	133	15
	HMed Saintonge wares	1908	232
	Other HMed Continental wares	136	20
	Total high medieval wares	20327	1628
	High medieval % of Total	40	51
	Southampton Organic-tempered Sandy	2897	127
	Late Medieval Well-fired Sandy wares	5145	180
	Other LMed Sandy wares	1441	77
1092	Surrey Whiteware	157	7
1193	Tudor Green	256	56
	Beauvais wares	6	3
	Normandy Stoneware	206	13
	Martincamp wares	61	8
	Late Medieval Saintonge	186	5
	Low Countries Redwares	2375	132
	Low Countries Tin-glazed wares	4	1
1245	Raeren stoneware	1052	33
	Other Rhenish stonewares	339	19
	Iberian Coarsewares	3918	174
	Iberian Micaceous Redwares	774	45
	Spanish Tin-glazed wares	58	5
	Italian Maiolicas	128	5
	Italian Red Earthenwares	136	11
	Other LMed Continental wares	176	12
	Total late medieval wares	19315	913
	Late Medieval % of Total	38	29
	Post-medieval wares	4668	157
	Post-medieval % of Total	9	5
	Total	51381	3195

Table 13. Quantities of pottery types in Phase 4

Fabric Number	Major Wares and Others	Weight (g)	Sherd No.
	Residual pre-Conquest	1854	137
	Residual % of Total	1	2
	Early Medieval Flint-tempered ware	476	40
	Scratch-marked wares	2147	132
1011	Mixed Grit	12	1
1014	Mixed Grit	53	7
1095	Mixed Grit	19	1
1016	Wessex Coarseware	21	2
	Dorset Sandy ware	27	2
	Other Anglo-Norman Coarsewares	138	16
	Anglo-Norman Glazed wares	14	1
	Normandy Gritty wares	236	19
	North French Glazed wares	233	10
	Other EMed Continental wares	23	2
	Total Anglo-Norman wares	3399	233
	Anglo-Norman % of Total	2	3
1123	Southampton Coarseware	495	42
1024	Sandy Southampton Coarseware	328	23
1230	Southampton High Street Coarseware	42	3
1124	Mixed Grit Coarse Sandy	214	26
	Other HMed Coarsewares	222	14
1044	Southampton Whiteware	267	21
	Southampton Sandy ware	381	28
1248	South Hampshire Redware	141	17
1087	Local Pink Sandy ware	622	33
	Laverstock	455	25
1118	Local Whiteware	341	12
1215	Local Fine White Sandy ware	75	8
1156	Dorset Whiteware	9	2
	Dorset Sandy ware	130	5
	Other HMed Sandy wares	1120	84
	HMed French wares	33	4
	HMed Saintonge wares	456	71
	Total high medieval wares	5331	418
	High medieval % of Total	3	5
	Southampton Organic-tempered Sandy	11130	312
	Late Medieval Well-fired Sandy wares	56535	2030
	Other LMed Sandy wares	3554	247
1092	Surrey Whiteware	226	15
1193	Tudor Green	997	119
	Beauvais wares	1827	166
	Normandy Stoneware	1912	80
	Martincamp wares	4909	425
	Other LMed North French wares	160	17
	Late Medieval Saintonge wares	8286	234
	Low Countries Redwares	26201	1051
	Low Countries Tin-glazed wares	479	80
1245	Raeren Stoneware	16096	569
	Other Rhenish Stonewares	3507	149
	Iberian Coarsewares	7699	238
	Iberian Micaceous Redwares	4569	220
	Spanish Tin-glazed wares	3424	82
	Italian Maiolicas	7246	321
	Italian Lead-glazed earthenwares	2038	84
	Other LMed Continental wares	295	46
	Total late medieval wares	161090	6473
	Late medieval % of Total	85	81
	Post-medieval wares	17326	684
	Post-medieval % of Total	9	9
	Total	188983	7951

merchants. Genoese concerns established offices in the town, while Venetian merchant fleets arrived annually, bringing quantities of exotic items from the Mediterranean. The rise of Antwerp, Bruges and Ghent also stimulated local shipping and the existing customs accounts, or port books, detail the range and intensity of mercantile activity. The resultant increase in domestic activity is reflected in the quantities of both ceramics and archaeological deposits.

The pottery of this period is overwhelmingly late medieval in character. Table 13 shows that over 80% of the total quantity is comprised of late medieval wares. Anglo-Norman and High Medieval types represent just five percent of the total Phase 4 pottery weight. The fact that they also comprise eight percent of the total sherd number implies a small sherd size, suggesting that their occurrence is residual. All the late medieval Major Wares are well represented, including the full range of Continental types. The relative proportion of these wares compares well with those shown for each ceramic period (see Table 5).

Group 4: garderobe and associated feature, SOU 124
Italian pottery figures impressively in the ceramic group chosen to represent this phase. It came from Upper Bugle Street Site 3, SOU 124. Here, two features, a stone lined garderobe, and a short tunnel-like feature connecting two cellars, were filled in at the same time. The contemporaneity of the two deposits is evidenced by the character of the pottery, and the recovery from each feature of fragments of the same Venetian glass vessel. The presence in both features of many fragments of Venetian glass, as well as exceptionally fine ceramics is evidence of a prosperous household. The reason for the in-filling of these features seems to be the combination of two houses to form a single property.

The ceramic character of this group is shown in Table 14 and Plate 6. A residual element of earlier types inevitably exists, along with a large amount of intrusive post-medieval pottery, but late medieval wares dominate. The local pottery types are mainly in the Well-fired Sandy ware tradition with jars, pitchers, bung-hole pitchers and pancheons all represented. As Plate 6 shows, several almost complete vessels were recovered including a cooking pot (**143**) and a large pancheon (**159**). Non-local English pottery is exclusively represented by Tudor Green and Surrey Whiteware, and as is the case with the whole assemblage, these do not comprise a high percentage of the group. The quantity of French pottery is relatively low, yet of a wide variety. There are fragments of a Beauvais

Table 14. Quantities of all wares in SOU 124 garderobe

Fabric No.	Fabric Name	Weight	Sherds	% Weight	% Sherds
	Scratch-marked wares	40	2		
1016	Wessex Coarseware	13	1		
	Normandy Gritty wares	4	1		
	Total Anglo-Norman	57	4		
	Total Anglo-Norman % of Total	1	1		
1123	Southampton Coarseware	73	9		
1024	Southampton Sandy Coarseware	77	4		
	Other Coarsewares	9	1		
1044	Southampton Whiteware	17	1		
	Southampton Sandy ware	5	1		
1087	Local Pink Sandy ware	95	1		
1118	Local Whiteware	174	1		
1215	Local Fine White Sandy ware	12	1		
	Other Sandy wares	65	7		
	Total high medieval	527	26		
	HMed % of Total	2	4		
1130	Southampton Organic-tempered Sandy	63	1	<1	<1
	Late Medieval Well-fired Sandy	10448	157	94	91
	Other Local Late Medieval Sandy	332	6	3	3
1193	Tudor Green	244	9	2	5
	Total English wares	11087	173		
	Total English % LMed	46	33		
1349	Normandy Stoneware	800	22	70	48
	Martincamp types	203	10	18	22
	Beauvais Monochrome	92	9	8	20
1319	Beauvais Sgraffito	9	1	1	2
1744	Beauvais Stoneware	44	4	4	9
	Total French wares	1148	46		
	Total French % of Continental	8	13		
1297	Low Countries Redware	3713	89	74	66
1300	Slipped Low Countries Redware	308	12	7	10
1422	South Netherlands Maiolica	89	6	19	24
	Total Low Countries wares	4110	107		
	Total Low Countries % of Continental	30	29		

Fabric No.	Fabric Name	Weight	Sherds	% Weight	% Sherds
	Siegburg Stoneware	3	1	<1	<1
1245	Raeren-type Stoneware	3444	65	82	87
	Frechen Stonewares	660	6	16	8
1346	Miscellaneous Rhenish Stoneware	98	3	2	4
	Total Rhenish wares	4205	75		
	Total Rhenish % of Continental	31	20		
	Seville-type Coarsewares	260	4	43	16
	Iberian Micaceous Redwares	240	16	40	64
	Valencian Lustreware	28	1	5	4
	Morisco Tin-glazed wares	78	4	13	16
	Total Iberian wares	606	25		
	Total Iberian % of Continental	4	7		
1446	Montelupo Maiolica	690	13	17	10
1767	Florentine Maiolica	634	3	16	2
1450	Faenza Maiolica	1502	59	38	44
	North Italian Maiolica	1021	46	25	19
1768	North Italian Red Earthenware	158	12	4	9
	Total Italian wares	4005	133		
	Total Italian % of Continental	30	33		
1420	Unidentified Tin-glazed	6	2		
	Unidentified Tin-glazed % of Continental	1	1		
	Total late medieval Continental	13484	366		
	LMed Continental % of LMed	54	67		
	Total late medieval	25167	549		
	Total LMed % of Total	83	82		
	Post-medieval and Early Modern	4389	94		
	PMed and EMod % of Total	15	14		
	Total	30140	673		

yellow-glazed mug decorated with the armorial escutcheon of the king of England (237) and fragments of Martincamp flasks and Normandy and Beauvais Stoneware. A few sherds of late Saintonge pitchers are also present. Pottery from the Netherlands includes Redware cooking pots and a frying pan. There are Slipped Redware bowls and a White-slipped, Green-glazed albarello (293). Rhenish wares are well-represented with three almost complete Raeren-type vessels amongst fragments of many others. One is a standard mug (308), the other a larger version of the same form (312) and the third is a bottle (313). Siegburg and

Frechen types are also present. Spanish wares are not numerous but are present in a wide variety, which includes fragments of olive jars, a Micaceous Redware bowl (331) and flask, a Valencian Lustreware bowl, a Seville Blue bowl (352) and a Seville Plain White Maiolica dish.

The Italian tin-glazed pottery is of superb quality, further enhanced when one considers that it was found with some exceptional glass. Montelupo and Florentine Maiolica is represented by a Santa Fina style jug, painted with a blue and yellow armorial device (361) and a bowl with a green and brown floral design (363).

There is also a small Montelupo bowl with a blue and yellow concentric pattern (**357**). A white ring-handled vase with an 'IHS' motif may be Venetian (**368**) while two other vases, one painted in blue, the other blue and yellow, are also attributed to northern Italy (**369, 370**). Four Faenza-style jugs are represented (only three illustrated **365, 366, 367**) and fragments of a blue-painted albarello are also perhaps Faenza Maiolica.

Overall, an astonishing range of Continental wares is represented here, with some vessels of very high quality and this amply illustrates the up-turn in Southampton's fortunes represented by Phase 4.

All this material, and also the glass, may be dated to the end of the 15th century but there is a disturbingly large post-medieval element that requires explanation. Post-medieval pottery represents fifteen percent of the total weight and is scattered throughout the sequence of fills in this group. The character of the group is overwhelmingly late medieval but some disturbance, either in antiquity or during excavation is suggested. The post-medieval pottery is all late-17th- or 18th-century in date, comprising mainly Verwood type wares and local late redwares that form a category of material

quite distinct from the medieval types. The presence of two groups of material separated by a substantial time-period might indicate that the later finds were introduced accidentally during excavation, a not unlikely possibility by all accounts, as the features were dug in something of a hurry (R Thomson *pers comm*). Included in this group is one vessel of a type that is usually considered to be post-medieval in date, but not 18th-century. This is a Malling-type Tin-glazed cup, with mottled purple paint (**296**). It is now thought that Malling-type ware mugs were made in Antwerp, and they are usually dated to the mid-16th century (Hughes and Gaimster 1999, 61), but that date is somewhat later than the general character of this group. This particular vessel included does not conform to the typical Malling-type mug form – it is probably not a handled vessel, but it does have a purple mottled tin-glaze. This vessel may perhaps be viewed as an early type.

The evidence of the archaeology points to alteration of the houses at this site taking place in the late medieval period, and a 1490–1500 date seems to be the likeliest conclusion.

Summary

The relative quantities in each phase of the pottery types of each ceramic period, as described in Chapter 2, are shown in Tables 15–17. These bring together the ceramic periods and the settlement phases, and

support the chronological sequence suggested in Chapter 2.

Table 15 lists the Anglo-Norman wares. A few wares occur in Phase 2 in greater quantities than Phase 1.

Table 15. Percentage occurrence of early medieval wares in each stratigraphic phase (upper line shows percentage of total sherd weight for each ware, lower line shows percentage of total sherd number)

Fabric No.	Fabric Name	Phase 1	Phase 2	Phase 3	Phase 4	Un-phased
	Early Medieval Flint-tempered	45	15	12	3	25
		54	15	10	3	18
	Scratch-marked	65	21	3	3	7
		64	21	3	3	9
1011	Mixed Grit	37	7	11	1	44
		23	10	12	1	54
1014	Mixed Grit	24	55	12	1	8
		28	41	11	3	16
1095	Mixed Grit	40	33	4	1	22
		27	35	6	1	31
1055	Chalk-tempered	91	6	1	0	2
		72	19	2	0	7
1016	Wessex Coarseware	52	25	5	1	17
		33	27	9	1	30
1013	Non-local Flint-tempered	98	2	0	0	1
		89	7	0	0	4
1073	Non-local Gravel-tempered	100	0	0	0	0
		100	0	0	0	0
	Other Plain Coarsewares	49	28	3	4	16
		43	21	5	8	23

Fabric No.	Fabric Name	Phase 1	Phase 2	Phase 3	Phase 4	Un-phased
	Dorset Sandy ware	46	34	9	1	10
		40	35	8	1	16
	Glazed wares	66	26	1	1	6
		48	32	3	1	16
	Normandy Gritty wares	48	30	9	5	8
		51	22	9	5	13
	North French Glazed wares	30	40	7	11	11
		20	37	12	5	26
1402	Rouen-type ware	10	34	10	0	46
		18	26	10	0	46
1413	North French Sandy	82	11	2	0	5
		63	25	6	0	6
	North French Red-painted	58	7	31	0	4
		40	13	40	0	7
1269	Early Saintonge	100	0	0	0	0
		100	0	0	0	0
1390	Andenne-type	55	0	10	16	19
		39	0	6	11	44
1385	Blaugrau	84	14	2	0	0
		71	23	6	0	0

Table 16. Percentage occurrence of high medieval wares in each stratigraphic phase (upper line shows percentage of total sherd weight for each ware, lower line shows percentage of total sherd number)

Fabric No.	Fabric Name	Phase 1	Phase 2	Phase 3	Phase 4	Un-phased
1123	Southampton Coarseware	11	59	10	1	18
		6	52	10	1	31
1024	Southampton Sandy Coarseware	7	46	12	2	34
		3	41	10	2	44
1230	Southampton High Street Coarseware	8	25	14	2	51
		9	31	33	3	69
1124	Mixed Grit Coarse Sandy	8	34	7	11	40
		6	30	8	10	47
1726	Cornish Coarseware	0	100	0	0	0
		0	100	0	0	0
	Other Coarsewares	19	38	9	12	21
		14	41	9	11	25
1044	Southampton Whiteware	1	27	5	2	66
		2	18	5	2	73
	Southampton Sandy ware	4	52	11	2	31
		3	40	11	1	46
1248	South Hampshire Redware	2	73	3	1	1
		3	54	5	1	37
1087	Local Pink Sandy ware	4	67	5	4	20
		3	50	7	3	7
	Laverstock	11	31	9	7	42
		7	27	7	5	54
1118	Local Whiteware	32	26	10	11	21
		16	29	11	5	39
1215	Local Fine White Sandy ware	11	42	4	5	38
		8	32	3	5	52
	Dorset Sandy ware	3	40	23	3	31
		4	20	29	3	44
1156	Dorset Whiteware	1	80	4	1	15
		1	68	8	1	21
1078	Midlands ware	0	100	0	0	0
		0	100	0	0	0
1526	Scarborough-type ware	0	61	24	3	12
		0	61	17	6	17
1761	Cornish Sandy ware	0	100	0	0	0
		0	100	0	0	0
	Other Sandy wares	16	29	23	11	21
		36	22	14	9	19
1403	Developed Rouen ware	0	93	0	1	7
		0	75	0	2	23

Fabric No.	Fabric Name	Phase 1	Phase 2	Phase 3	Phase 4	Un-phased
1763	North French Bichrome	0	100	0	0	0
		0	100	0	0	0
1548	Seine Valley Whiteware	1	47	1	0	51
		1	48	1	0	51
1552	North French Sandy Whiteware	42	55	0	0	3
		42	50	0	0	8
1291	North French Pink ware	43	17	20	0	20
		40	10	27	0	23
1711	North French Micaceous Whiteware	62	21	2	4	11
		41	29	6	6	18
1407	Parisian Highly Decorated	22	77	0	0	1
		7	88	0	0	5
1458	Breton wares	0	100	0	0	0
		0	100	0	0	0
1753	Saintonge Whiteware	4	62	10	2	22
		4	40	12	4	39
1272	Saintonge Bright Green-glazed ware	3	85	2	1	10
		6	63	2	1	29
1500	Saintonge Polychrome	0	88	1	0	12
		0	52	1	0	47
1274	Saintonge Red-painted Whiteware	0	35	25	10	29
		0	56	12	12	19
1267	Saintonge Highly Decorated	0	100	0	0	0
		0	100	0	0	0
1758	Saintonge Gritty ware	1	99	0	1	0
		3	94	0	3	0
1464	Saintonge Redware	0	99	0	0	1
		0	92	0	0	8
1273	Other French wares	8	81	5	2	4
		12	68	7	3	10
1454	Low Countries Highly Decorated Redware	0	99	1	0	0
		0	92	8	0	0
1494	Rhenish Proto-stoneware	0	100	0	0	0
		0	100	0	0	0
1599	Andalusian Lustreware	0	0	100	0	0
		0	0	100	0	0
1067	Iberian Green and Brown	0	100	0	0	0
		0	100	0	0	0
1298	Miscellaneous Continental	41	45	9	0	6
		29	43	14	0	14

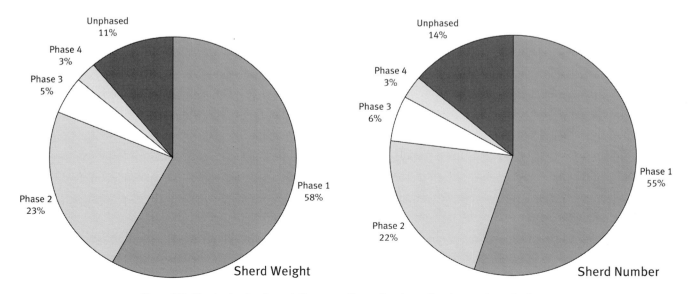

Figure 37. Pie charts showing relative proportions of early medieval wares in each phase

Table 17. Percentage occurrence of late medieval wares in each stratigraphic phase (upper line shows percentage of total sherd weight for each ware, lower line shows percentage of total sherd number)

Fabric No.	Fabric Name	Phase 1	Phase 2	Phase 3	Phase 4	Un-phased
1130	Southampton Organic-temp Sandy ware	19	12	22	22	24
		10	13	23	21	32
1136	Southampton Organic-temp Fine Sandy	2	6	9	75	8
		4	12	12	59	12
	Late Medieval Well-fired Sandy	1	1	8	84	6
		1	2	7	79	11
	Other Local Late Medieval Sandy	2	11	17	43	27
		3	14	13	42	28
1092	Surrey Whiteware	7	6	19	28	40
		4	9	10	22	55
1193	Tudor Green	1	2	16	63	18
		2	3	19	41	35
1754	Developed Normandy Gritty ware	0	0	0	100	0
		0	0	0	100	0
1349	Normandy Stoneware	1	1	5	47	46
		1	1	6	39	53
	Martincamp types	1	0	1	98	1
		1	0	2	97	1
	Beauvais wares	3	1	1	88	9
		2	1	2	88	8
1749	North French Pink-grey	0	0	0	100	0
		0	0	0	100	0
1454	Late Saintonge Whiteware	1	1	2	86	11
		1	1	2	86	11
1770	Late Saintonge Polychrome	0	0	0	100	0
		0	0	0	100	0
1297	Low Countries Redware	2	1	8	82	7
		1	1	10	77	12
1422	South Netherlands Maiolica	0	0	1	97	3
		0	0	1	92	7

Fabric No.	Fabric Name	Phase 1	Phase 2	Phase 3	Phase 4	Un-phased
	Siegburg Stonewares	0	7	11	68	14
		0	10	21	52	17
1257	Langewehe Stoneware	0	6	19	59	16
		0	6	18	29	47
1245	Raeren-type Stoneware	0	1	6	88	6
		0	1	5	83	11
1378	Cologne Stoneware	0	0	2	98	0
		0	0	2	98	0
	Frechen Stonewares	0	0	5	95	0
		0	0	8	92	0
1346	Miscellaneous Rhenish Stoneware	3	1	10	80	6
		4	3	9	78	6
	Iberian Coarsewares	1	4	28	54	14
		2	3	35	47	12
	Iberian Micaceous Redwares	1	5	11	67	16
		1	5	11	54	30
	Valencian Lustreware	2	0	0	98	0
		3	0	0	97	0
	Morisco Tin-glazed wares	2	2	3	92	1
		1	6	8	76	9
	Italian Maiolica	1	1	3	95	2
		1	1	3	89	7
1760	North Italian Sgraffito	0	0	0	100	0
		0	0	0	100	0
1768	North Italian Lead-glazed Earthenware	0	0	7	93	1
		0	0	16	79	5
	Unidentified LMed Continental	1	15	35	41	8
		1	7	26	54	12

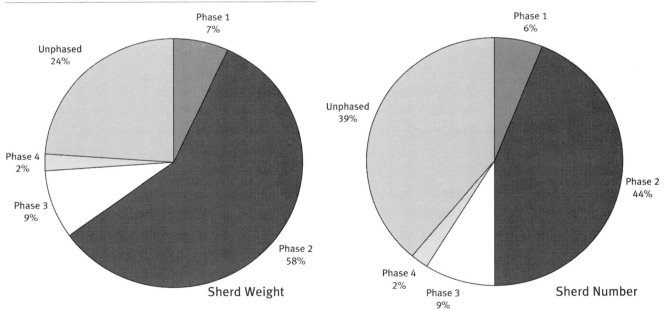

Figure 38. Pie charts showing relative proportions of high medieval wares in each phase

The Mixed Grit ware, Fabric 1014, is the only local pottery for which this is true. This is considered to be similar to Scratch-marked ware, and it is possible that it may have been introduced towards the end of Phase

1. North French glazed wares and Rouen-type wares also occur in Phase 2 in larger proportions than in Phase 1 and these may also have been current towards the middle of the 13th rather than the 12th century.

PLATE 1. Waster fragments of Southampton Whiteware.

(NB Drawings of each plate are displayed with the catalogue numbers of illustrated vessels marked. Pieces that are not illustrated elsewhere are marked with letters.)

PLATE 2. Anglo-Norman pit group from SOU 124:

A Rim of scratch-marked gritty ware cooking pot; B Rim of scratch-marked ware cooking pot; C Profile of scratch-marked ware cooking pot; D–G Fragments of Normandy Gritty ware; H Fragment of Anglo-Norman Glazed ware; I Fragment of Rouen ware; J Fragment of Andenne-type ware; K Fragment of Andenne-type ware; L Fragment of North French Glazed ware; M Fragment of North French Glazed ware; N Fragment of Andenne-type ware.

PLATE 3. Anglo-Norman group from castle garderobe.

PLATE 4. High medieval local wares from SOU 25 pit group.
A/B Southampton Coarseware cooking pot.

PLATE 5. High medieval imported wares from SOU 25 pit group.

PLATE 6. Late medieval pottery from SOU 124 garderobe.
A Low Countries Redware cooking pot rim and handle;
B Normandy Stoneware base.

PLATE 7. Illumination from Book of Hours. (courtesy of Southampton Archaeology Collections)

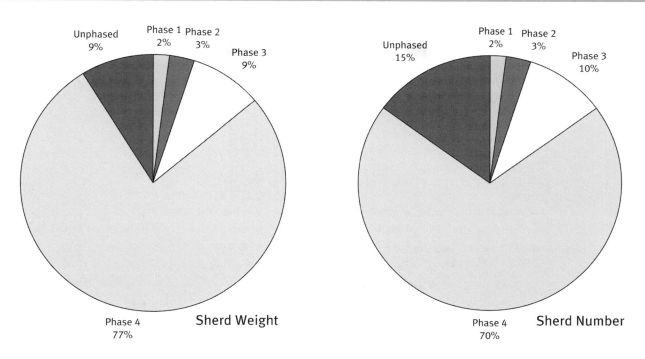

Figure 39. Pie charts showing relative proportions of late medieval wares in each phase

Overall, however, Figure 37 shows that the Anglo-Norman origins of the fabrics listed in Table 15 seem to be confirmed.

Table 16 shows all the high medieval wares. Local Whiteware (Fabric 1118) is the only type that occurs in greater quantities outside Phase 2. By weight, 32% of it was recovered from Phase 1 deposits. This represents the material from the castle garderobe fill described above, which has been dated to the mid-13th century. Figure 38, based on Table 16, demonstrates that most of the pottery identified as high medieval in origin occurs in Phase 2, thus confirming the date assigned to this material.

The picture is equally clear for the late medieval wares listed in Table 17. The largest quantities of nearly all of these occur in Phase 4 deposits. Southampton Organic Sandy ware is present in equal proportions in Phases 3 and 4. It is probable that these were being produced before the Well-fired Sandy wares and they therefore superseded it. Southampton Organic Sandy ware may therefore represent an interim production, filling the gap between the disappearance of the high medieval wares and the later local products. Seville-type

Coarsewares and Iberian Micaceous Redwares are also present in Phase 3 in significant proportions. This confirms the suggestion that they were brought into Southampton at an early date. This is also true of Siegburg Stoneware. Other types of Continental wares identified as late medieval occur almost exclusively in Phase 4, confirming their late-15th-century date. The overall pattern is illustrated more simply in Figure 39, which shows that over 70% of all late medieval pottery occurs in Phase 4.

Several methods have been utilised to establish and confirm the suggested sequence for the introduction and decline of particular pottery types in medieval Southampton. Three ceramic periods have been established and for each of these the typical ware types have been described. This has shown how each ceramic period has a distinctive character. The distribution of those wares throughout the stratigraphic sequence has also been plotted, both in a ceramic-specific way, and over four separate phases of activity within the town. Quantification has been an essential tool in building this chronology but it has also provided the data from which further interpretations can be made.

4

TECHNOLOGY, TECHNIQUE, TRADITION

Studying the ways in which a pot was made may reveal something of the technological status of a production site, the technical preferences and ability of a potter and the cultural conditions within which a potter worked. Comparing the results of such a study between different periods will allow an understanding of the development of pottery-making through time. It is possible to appreciate something of the technological background of almost every sherd of pottery, usually whether it was hand-built or wheel-thrown and how well it was fired. Overall vessel forms, and the component parts thereof, for example rims, spouts, handles, bases and decorative method and style, will provide an insight into a potter's technique (eg Pearce 1984), and may also be interpreted as indicators of ceramic tradition or cultural expression. Such information helps to identify the technical and cultural origins of certain types of pottery, enabling us to relate them to particular production centres and periods.

Form definition

A form corpus has been established, which allows each sherd to be characterised on the basis of its shape. Every different form, of rim, spout, handle etc is identified by a number with a letter pre-fix that denotes its type; R for rim, S for spout, H for handle, T for body, B for base, F for foot, D for decorative technique and M for decorative motif. A string of these codes will describe the form details of any sherd or sherds from the same vessel. An example is T10D2M100, which identifies a convex body-sherd with incised decoration in the form of a vertical line; R500T10D2 M100 describes a simple upright rim and a body sherd as above, both from the same vessel. Every different form type has been drawn on Form Corpus Record Sheets and stored in sherd type order. Every form variant can therefore be identified and recorded, either singly or in combination, and its appearance recalled by relating the numeric code to the drawing.

A drawing of every form type is not included in this publication nor is there a list of all form numbers. The system has been described to show the extent of analysis of this assemblage and the approach that has led to the discussion of form types presented in this chapter. There are, for example, at present over 260 different rim forms, and it seems extravagant to publish them all. The significance of some differences remains totally obscure and may be due entirely to the whim of the potter, or perhaps the ceramicist — for medieval pottery-making was an individualistic process and form description can be just as subjective.

In this chapter the pottery-producing technology of the ware types described in Chapter 2 are examined. This discussion is presented chronologically, with pottery of English and Continental origin considered together for each of the three ceramic periods. At the same time, aspects of technique are touched upon, but this is discussed more specifically in the second part of this chapter, in a detailed form study of two classes of vessel, jar/cooking pots and jugs. In conclusion the broad theme of tradition is considered as a means of placing the pottery of medieval Southampton into a wider framework.

Technology

In this section aspects of pottery-making technology are discussed by period, beginning with the late Saxon. This includes a consideration of methods of manufacture, techniques of finishing and decoration and the relative quality of the finished product.

The late Saxon period
All the pottery likely to have been made in or around Southampton at this period was hand-built, almost certainly by the coil-building method. There is some evidence for vessels having been turned during the

addition of the rim, in the form of a pronounced 'furrow' at the neck and particularly in Early Medieval Flint-tempered ware jar/cooking pots. No pots were decorated, or burnished, as some middle Saxon types were (Timby 1988). Thumbing of rims apparently was the only embellishment. Vessels were fired at low temperatures, almost certainly in clamps or bonfires.

Among the non-local products, chalk-tempered ware vessels were also hand-built, crudely finished and low-fired. Decoration takes the form of stamps, usually around the rim and shoulder, and thumbed applied strips. Michelmersh-type ware is exceptional in being wheel-thrown, neatly made and well fired. Vessels were decorated with stamps and applied strips.

Continental wares represent a potting tradition quite different from that expressed in the typical local products. Both Beauvais and North French Whitewares were wheel-thrown products. Vessels were well made and comparatively thin-walled, achievable through expert throwing and confident firing. Beauvais wares were painted with red slip designs, a form of decoration not evident among the local material of this period. North French Whiteware jars were undecorated.

The Anglo-Norman period

There seems to have been few obvious technological developments in local pottery-making at this period. All local coarsewares were hand-built and probably fired in clamps. Scratch-marked wares represent a different technique in vessel finishing, but this is more likely to have served a practical rather than decorative role. Decorated coarsewares are rare, although thumbed rims are common and some jar/cooking pots were ornamented with horizontal incised lines (**20**). Non-local coarsewares such as Non-local Flint-tempered ware exhibit the same technological characteristics. Anglo-Norman coarsewares do seem to show some technical superiority over their late Saxon counterparts and the appearance, towards the mid-13th century, of much larger vessels (eg 7 and 8), suggests advances in potting technique and perhaps improved firing control.

The most significant local technological change coincided with the appearance of a new range of vessels. The use of glaze, a technique rarely seen on pre-Conquest types, became more widespread but was confined solely to jug forms, principally tripod pitchers, which were all hand-built and often round-based (**22**), placing them firmly within existing local traditions of pottery-making. Glaze was probably seen as an adornment and seems to have been used relatively inexpertly, although this may be the effect of uneven firing, and tripod

pitchers were also decorated with combed or rouletted lines. There are a wide variety of vessel shapes, rim and handle forms, so that apparently no two vessels appear to be exactly alike and this may be a reflection, perhaps, of the developmental nature of this product. These vessels were not very well-fired, although the use of glaze might suggest a primitive flued kiln rather than a clamp. Splashes of glaze on a few sherds of scratch-marked ware jar/cooking pots indicate that both coarse and glazed wares were occasionally fired together.

There are profound technical differences between Anglo-Norman local pottery and that imported from the Continent. Nearly all the Continental types were superior in terms of vessel construction, decorative technique, the use of glaze and the quality of firing. The use of the fast, or throwing wheel, hereafter simply wheel, may be viewed as an important technological difference, as is the working of flued kiln structures. Both of these factors will influence all aspects of pottery-making because they allow the use of finer clays and the results of that are evident among the glazed wares in the comparatively neat aspects of rim and handle forms, the use of complex roulettes, other decorative details such as cordons and pellets and more consistent glaze. The clamp-based firing technology used locally demanded the addition of coarser tempering agents, resulting in thick-walled, often crudely finished pots. Normandy Gritty ware exhibits fewer of these characteristics, yet pitchers in that ware are usually much bigger than the glazed jugs, and therefore were not created with as much finesse. The most crudely formed Continental pottery of this period is Blaugrau ware, where the ladle form is hand-built and relatively unsophisticated, yet this ware is semi-vitrified, thus representing early steps towards a level of kiln technology way beyond the capabilities of contemporary local English producers.

The high medieval period

It was not until the high medieval period that the wheel was universally adopted by local potters and by *c* 1300 at the latest, nearly every common form was wheel-thrown. This significant technological development led also to some technical improvements along the lines of those suggested above for the Anglo-Norman North French glazed wares. The use of temper declined, although a clear distinction can be drawn between coarsewares and glazed sandy wares.

Coarsewares remained largely unglazed, except for open forms such as bowls and dripping pans, which are relatively rare. The most common vessel is the unglazed jar/cooking pot, typical of Southampton Coarseware. Here, a mixed temper continued to be used, consisting mainly of quartz sand, chalk and flint with occasional shell and organics; ingredients common in Anglo-Norman coarsewares. However, the size of the temper used in Southampton Coarseware is finer and this may be attributed to the use of the wheel, for coarse inclusions would drag against the rotation, cutting into the potter's hands and scoring the vessel surface.

More obvious progress in local pottery-making can be discerned among the sandy wares. Jugs remain the most common glazed vessel type, but these are far superior to the earlier tripod pitchers. They exhibit a higher standard of potting and glazing, and an exuberant decorative style that reflects the general use of the wheel, finer clays and more controlled firing. The extended variety of vessel shapes and sizes must stem, at least partially, from the creative confidence discovered with the wheel. This confidence is further expressed in a range of decorative techniques that includes the use of roulettes, applied clay, combing, stabbing and coloured slips and it is possible to relate particular techniques to individual products (see below pp 116–123). The overall health of the local ceramic industry is demonstrated not only by technological and technical improvements, but also by the quantity and variety of the vessels produced.

Few technological differences can be discerned between high medieval local ceramics and those with non-local or Continental origins. The products in Low Countries Highly Decorated Redware, and those from Brittany, certainly do not look superior to local products in any sense. Modern observers may perceive such products as Scarborough-type ware, or the pottery of the Saintonge, to be technically superior, but this may be related to the quality of local resources, and aspects of organisation, rather than technological advances. The occurrence of Saintonge ware in large quantities in Southampton allows a more detailed examination of the technical background to their production as a means of demonstrating this point.

Saintonge pottery has an elegant style that alone is sufficient testament to the skill of its creators. These potters were helped by the availability of a superb potting clay and its quality is evidenced by the thin walls of many of the vessels described here, particularly the jugs. The physical lightness of these products is enhanced by the delicacy of touch that characterises their manufacture. Amidst this variety of forms, however, are examples that appear somewhat awkward. The

pégaux often have huge, ungainly spouts, and indeed some of the jugs are similarly ill-proportioned. Although Saintonge pottery was thrown with great skill many vessels were poorly finished. Stray pieces of clay were often not removed from the walls of vessels before firing, and may be seen still attached, especially to bases. Pouring holes may be untidily cut, with pieces of waste clay left in place. Elements such as handles and spouts were applied with little care, so that ugly smears of clay may be seen at joins. Spouts and handles are also often disproportionate to the size and shape of the vessel. Handles especially are inconsistent in length, so that some describe a right angle, others a flattish curve. This carelessness is apparent on all types, including the polychrome jugs, which might be regarded as being of the highest quality.

Such features may be clues to the organisation of the Saintonge potteries. The evidence suggests that pots were produced rapidly and it is even possible that different people performed each task, including forming the body, attaching spouts and handles and applying decoration and glaze. The consistency of the slip-painted motifs on polychrome jugs suggests that they were the product of the same hand. The application of handles made from thrown cylinders is of interest here. The technique of pulling handles from the leather-hard pot demands more expertise than the application of handles made from thrown cylinders (J Hudson *pers comm*). The almost exclusive use of thrown handles may be evidence for hierarchical organisation among the Saintonge industries, where people of varying degrees of skill performed individual tasks. The large parrot-beak spouts were also formed from thrown strips and the quality of finishing on these two components may suggest the use of less skilled labour, perhaps apprentices, in vessel production. What is certain is that the industry at the Saintonge produced an enormous quantity of pottery, and this is reflected in the evidence for rapid manufacture. The long history of pottery-making in the Saintonge, and the sheer quantity of the material produced there, suggests a well-organised industry where the establishment of some form of production hierarchy does not seem unnatural.

Decorative techniques include the use of painted oxides, sgraffito, applied clay and incised lines. Moulded faces were also a popular decorative style. Although highly decorated vessels are a feature of the high medieval Saintonge tradition, the standard jugs and pégaux were essentially plain vessels and the applied clay or incised decoration that appears on these also shows signs of having been rapidly executed.

Furthermore, the polychrome decoration is in an extremely fluid style. The birds were formed by two strokes of a brush with the further addition of an eye, a beak and feet. The shields were similarly composed, and their curving form suggests quick work. The vine leaves are formed of continuous lines, suggesting the vessel was on a turntable at the time. These vessels were not very neatly coloured, and the green and yellow are often inconsistent in their coverage. The colours were thin oxide washes, with copper used for green and perhaps antimony for yellow. The brown outline was created with an iron slip. The overall clear glaze is lead-based.

The quality and use of glaze varies widely on Saintonge vessels. The best-glazed vessels are the Bright Green-glazed types. These, and the Saintonge Whiteware standard green-glazed jugs, were probably dipped in a glaze solution, while pégaux were probably brushed or dusted, as these were partially glazed on the front. Polychrome vessels often have a very thin lead glaze, perhaps to ensure that the colours did not run. Gritty ware mortars had a dull matt green glaze that apparently did not fit very well, for flaking is common, although in some instances this may have been caused by the presence of large inclusions in the clay (J Hudson *pers comm*). The red-slip painted wares have a lustrous clear lead glaze that contrasts with the polychrome vessels. One Saintonge Redware vessel has a greenish-coloured lead glaze but the others have a relatively good clear glaze that has a slightly matt finish.

Amongst the local glazed sandy wares there is little evidence for production on such a large, well-organised scale. Local industries, such as those at Laverstock, were probably based around a few kilns established to service a relatively small market area. Their output, although locally significant, was not intended to achieve the levels of the Saintonge and this is reflected in the fact that a greater variety of jug forms were produced locally, while imported Saintonge types seem to have conformed to a standard style, at least in the formation of component parts. The skill of the Saintonge potters has been discussed at some length, and their methods related to the organisation of their industry. The potters of the Saintonge were able to produce vessels that were thin-walled, brightly coloured and vibrantly decorated and their apparent technical superiority may be related to the long history of pottery-making in the Saintonge, where it had become a regional speciality. The character of the local industries was quite different and because of this their products, which embody a similar set of technical and decorative values, even if they are not expressed quite so fluently, should not be looked upon as inferior.

The late medieval period

The three English Major Wares of this period each exemplify different technical standards, while the increased range of Continental wares include types that represent quite different technologies.

Southampton Organic Sandy ware typically was poorly made and fired – vessels often appearing ill-proportioned or asymmetrical. Decorated sherds are rare, and decorative techniques are mainly incised, stabbed or slashed lines on or around the handle, and thus may have as much to do with ensuring that handles were properly fixed and thoroughly fired. The typical thumbed base is reminiscent of high medieval forms, suggesting that the makers of this ware were influenced by earlier traditions. A low firing temperature is suggested by flaking sherd breaks, and also the deliberate use of organic temper, which served to conduct heat more efficiently during firing. All these attributes suggest that this ware was a sort of interim, very localised product, perhaps filling a gap in supply between the decline of the high medieval producers and the rise of their late medieval successors.

Late Medieval Well-fired Sandy wares appear to be of much higher quality. Vessels were better fired and much more cleanly produced and finished, although they were rarely decorated and present themselves as a dour, utilitarian product. This quality is present in all the fabrics included in this ware, which has the singular characteristic of combining an increased variety of vessel forms with a greater standardisation of their appearance. The variety of rim forms, for instance, is much more limited than among the jar/cooking pot wares of the Anglo-Norman or high medieval periods (see below p 117) and this is perhaps more than simply a technical development. If, however, the techniques of this period are to be compared to those of preceding centuries then this standardisation is a notable development that may perhaps be seen as a sign of increased production towards industrial levels. A more obvious sign of progress is perhaps in the quality of firing, which indicates advances in kiln construction and control.

Tudor Green ware is technically quite different from the local pottery discussed above. The fine nature of the clay, the delicacy of the potting and the expert use of glaze are qualities beyond the reach, or aspirations, of local producers at this time. In technique and in vessel form, Tudor Green has more in common with

Continental pottery, especially Beauvais types, than local products, a similarity not observed in earlier periods within this assemblage.

The level of technical ability shown in the late medieval North French products is evidence of a healthy industry. The production of stoneware demonstrates considerable advances in kiln technology. The Beauvaisis types, especially the Sgraffito wares, show a level of technical expertise quite beyond the experience of contemporary local English potters. The pottery from the Saintonge shows a continuation of the high medieval traditions, including the use of polychrome decoration. These vessels, however, do not seem to have the same delicacy or vibrancy that is evident in much of the high medieval material, for although vessels may be more neatly produced, they are also more modest. No decline in technical standards is necessarily indicated and a change in social or economic circumstances may be a more likely explanation. The reappearance of slip-painted wares, and the production of colourful chafing dishes suggests that the industry began to regain its vigour in the 15th century, a development that found fruition in the elaborate Palissey types of the post-medieval period (Hurst *et al* 1986).

Late medieval Low Countries Redwares exhibit a relatively coarse quality that may also be observed in the high medieval version. Tripod cooking-pots, the most common form, show a competent but scarcely refined technique, for instance feet and handles were added securely but not finished with care. Bowls, too, have pinched feet that again seem to have been competently rather than carefully formed. On most of these vessels glaze was not consistently employed, its coverage being uneven in both extent and thickness. Jar/cooking pots were embellished with rilling and cordons and occasionally swags of white slip. Some vessels were produced with greater care – slipped bowls, for instance, have a more consistent covering of glaze on the inside. Dripping pans were apparently press-moulded and knife-trimmed, their flanged rims cut to form a variety of decorative, sometimes complex, shapes. All these vessels have a robust, vigorous quality that surely indicates a healthy industry organised for mass-production.

The successful introduction of tin-glazed pottery manufacture into the Netherlands in the later 15th or early 16th century represents an important technological development, but one that took some time to take effect. By 1513 Italian potters had been moved to the Low Countries to stimulate the tin-glazed industry there (Wilson 1999, 7) and their products, together with the tin-glazed wares from Spain and Italy, must have been far beyond the capabilities of pottery-makers local to Southampton. The technology of making tin-glazed pottery is discussed below (pp 115).

Rhenish Stoneware also represents a technology far removed from the experience of local English manufacturers. Progress towards the production of true stoneware in the Rhineland can be seen throughout the medieval period and was finally achieved in the 14th century. One prerequisite for salt-glazed stoneware production is clay that will not melt at temperatures higher than c 1150°C, where salt-glazing may be successfully performed. Another is a kiln that can generate sufficiently high temperatures. The proto-stoneware industries of the 13th century had used iron washes to colour vessels (Stephan 1983) and this technique was suitable for true stoneware, although salt-glazing rapidly became preferred. In the late medieval period decoration seems to be less bold or detailed than it was to become in the late-16th and 17th centuries, however, the use of sprigged and moulded decoration on Cologne and Raeren types, together with the production of white and blue-glazed vessels indicates a development of decorative techniques and values. Stoneware products are superior to earthenwares in durability and impermeability and thus were in great demand throughout late medieval Europe. This seems to have led to the creation of a genuine mass-production industry that turned out the same basic forms over and over again. Thousands of Raeren mugs must have come into Southampton, each of them with the same basic design and shape. This aspect of uniformity may be seen as the most definitive quality of the stoneware industry.

A number of ceramic technologies and techniques are evident in Iberian pottery types. All the coarseware vessels were wheel-thrown, and olive jars are distinctive in having accentuated throwing lines. Although the clay matrix is usually fine, and presumably excellent for pottery making, the size of the vessels and the thickness of vessel walls must have made throwing these pots a demanding task and this may be reflected in the depth of the throwing lines. These vessels are all expertly made, as one might expect in a tradition that had survived for over sixteen centuries, and are well-balanced and symmetrical in appearance. Large coarseware bowls may also have been hard work to throw. The interiors of these vessels were covered with a lead glaze, as is the case with some oil jars. Iberian Micaceous Redwares are similarly well-made, showing a greater variation in the quality of firing, but most fabrics are consistent in colour. The larger vessels are somewhat crudely made, but the small flasks and bowls are very neatly executed. Similarities in technique between the oil jar fabrics and Micaceous Redware may suggest that in some cases both types originated from the same area.

At this period tin-glazed pottery was produced in Spain with great skill. Although the range of colours appears limited in comparison with the vibrant palette employed by the potters of Renaissance Italy, the use of coloured oxides is equally impressive in terms of execution as well as design, while the utilisation of copper-lustre is perhaps the most obvious technical difference.

The process of tin-glazing originated in the Eastern Mediterranean and spread west along the North African coast. In Italy, the first maiolicas were being made probably in the 13th century (Blake 1987, 15) but it was in the Renaissance period that the art of making painted pottery flourished. The method of making tin-glazed pottery was comprehensively described in the mid-16th century by Cipriano Piccolpasso (Piccolpasso 1980). Wares were biscuit-fired at *c* 1000°C before the glaze was applied. The glaze was lead-based, with tin oxide added as an opacifier to turn the glaze white, and once dry, the decoration was painted onto the resultant smooth surface. The range of colours is extensive in Italian pottery and all are based on mineral pigments. Manganese was used for brown and purple, cobalt for blue, copper for green, antimony for yellow and antimony mixed with iron for orange. The painted product was then given a ghost-firing before being covered with a clear glaze mixture before its final firing at around 950°C. Kilns are shown to be permanent structures. Piccolpasso indicates a specialisation in manufacture, with throwing, painting and firing all being performed by different people.

Italian Maiolica, perhaps due to the influence of the Renaissance, is far ahead of Iberian and Dutch types in the use of colour and the expression of artistic inspiration. In the late-16th and 17th centuries it developed into an art form, while the quality of Spanish Maiolicas was declining and the Dutch began copying Oriental forms. Even before then, in Piccolpasso's time, painting on pottery was regarded as a skilled craft. Painted ceramics represent a typically vital product of the Italian Renaissance. In Southampton these wares stand out as coming from a culture that had a completely different set of values in terms of the production, decoration and use of fine ceramics.

The technique of sgraffito was common in the north of Italy throughout the medieval period, apparently inspired by Eastern Mediterranean influences (Hurst 1986). The floral pattern is a common motif in this tradition. In North Italy sgraffito would never compete with tin-glazed products in colour or style and it is perhaps for this reason that these vessels are of comparatively poor quality. Certainly they do not compare well with contemporary Beauvais sgraffito products, where the execution of the decoration and the use of colour were far more precise. Sgraffito wares may be perceived as the finest products of late medieval Beauvais, whereas those of northern Italy were overshadowed by tin-glazed wares. The other Italian Red earthenwares demonstrate equally skilled if less obviously remarkable potting techniques.

Summary

The development of local pottery making is well-illustrated through a consideration of the coarsewares. It is noteworthy that the size of inclusions in local coarsewares diminishes through time. Early medieval flint-tempered ware, and scratch-marked ware especially, contain large fragments, of flint, chalk and quartz, sometimes also shell, that were probably added to improve firing in clamp kilns and perhaps to strengthen vessel walls during handbuilding. The makers of Southampton Coarseware maintained the tradition of adding similar materials, but these are smaller inclusions, which perhaps reflect the use of the wheel and improved kilns. Large inclusions would have dragged during throwing, both within the clay and against the hands, while the use of flued kilns should have improved firing consistency. Both these factors led to a reduction in the size of inclusions. Indeed, the manufacture of sandy wares during this period shows that it was not necessary to employ any tempering agents, and the continuation of this practice may be related as much to culture as technology. At this time there is a stark division between coarseware kitchen pots and glazed, sandy ware serving vessels that is surely cultural. One possible practical explanation might be that cooking pots conducted heat more efficiently, and thus lasted longer, with the addition of tempering agents, but sandy ware cooking pots were in exclusive use in many other places at this time. Southampton Organic-tempered Sandy ware represents a departure from the tradition of adding rock fragments in favour of chopped grass or straw. This suggests that firing methods were unreliable, and perhaps more rudimentary, which reinforces the view that this might be a short-lived, local, interim product that answered a need during a period of change enforced by plague and depression. Late Medieval Well-fired Sandy ware is virtually free of large inclusions and there is no evidence for the use of tempering agents. This probably reflects improvements in pottery-making technology, as it is apparent that this product was far superior to its predecessor. High firing temperatures, also the deliberate reduction of certain vessels, are indicative of advanced kiln structures and firing control.

A broad interpretation of the development of ceramic technology might be that local English potters were somewhat adrift of their Continental counterparts. In the late Saxon period virtually all local pottery was handbuilt and fired in clamps, while in France, from where most of the imported pottery was derived, vessels were wheel-thrown and fired in more controlled conditions. Little seems to have changed in the Anglo-Norman period in this respect. Although the jug form was developed, and the use of glaze more widely adopted, local wares were still largely handbuilt and inconsistently fired, unlike the Normandy Gritty and Seine Valley types that were being imported. By the high medieval period local pottery-makers had caught up and appear to have been capable of making pottery to the high standards achieved in the Saintonge,

at least in terms of methods of manufacture, use of glaze and firing. This is reflected in the wide range of vessel forms and decorative styles that characterise the local wares. There appears to have been a difference, however, in the organisation of the industry and the scale of output. It is likely that Saintonge pottery was made for export and thus a high rate of output, far beyond the requirements of local consumers, is indicated, while this is not the case for local products. The creations of many local producers, however, display a confidence and vitality that arises, perhaps, from an increased, if local, demand for ceramic vessels, and this surely prompted the extended repertoire that characterises the high medieval period. By the late-15th century that confidence had vanished and local pottery was uniformly drab and uncompromisingly functional. The delicate cups, mugs and jugs in Tudor Green may be classed as non-local wares, closer in character to imported types. In the late medieval pottery there was not only an increase in the range of sources for Continental imports but these also brought in a wide variety of technologically different ceramics. It was not possible for local producers to make stoneware and nor could they create tin-glazed or lustre-decorated pottery. It was a long time before English potters caught up.

Technique

A number of themes may be identified amidst the above summary. The most significant local technological development would appear to be the change from hand-built to wheel-thrown methods of manufacture, which may be dated to the first part of the 13th century. By the third quarter of the 13th century the wheel had been adopted universally, and this seems to have led to the production of an increased range of forms, which appear to have sprung from a technical freedom released by the new technology. In the high medieval period local pottery was being made in more shapes, sizes and decorative styles than ever before. It is proposed here to examine these products in an attempt to define characteristics of technology and technique, thus giving an insight into the ability and quality of local pottery-makers. Aspects of ceramic tradition will then be discussed, in an attempt to establish local cultural values and compare their development with those seen in the imported material.

There is more to be understood about vessel manufacture than determining the method of construction of the body wall. As has been shown in

London (Pearce 1984), techniques of applying components such as handles may differentiate vessels in the same fabric, and consequently allow identification of the products of different workshops or pottery-makers. Pearce's work is of course the study of a single ware type. The size and variety of the Southampton assemblage, and the scope of this examination of it, prevents any attempt at such a detailed analysis. Here it is possible only to note certain characteristics of technique within and between certain ware and vessel types as a way of illustrating the potential for this sort of analysis.

Characterising form types for the three ceramic periods has helped to define the most common vessels, in this case jar/cooking pots and jugs. Only these two vessel types are studied here. Jar/cooking pots are common to all three medieval periods, and by studying how they developed it is possible to see changes in technology and technique. Only jugs of the high medieval period are closely examined here. Aspects of vessel shape and decoration are compared in an attempt to differentiate local products on the basis of technique and these vessels are then compared with French jugs in order to examine cultural aspects of pottery making.

Jar/cooking pots

Table 18 shows the range of rim forms that may be seen among jar/cooking pots in the Major Wares of the early, high and late medieval periods. There are many different styles of rim among these vessels and each has been grouped into one of eight broad classes. In this way chronological variations in rim form and therefore manufacturing technique may be discerned. The comparison of base forms and styles of decoration are also discussed under separate headings.

Table 18. Occurrence by vessel number of cooking pot rim forms

Rim Form	Early Medieval	High Medieval	Late Medieval
Thumbed	142	12	0
Flat-topped	28	3	1
Lip-bead	43	34	2
Simple	40	46	1
Squared	19	50	0
Internal bead	3	167	1
Concave	1	17	0
Rounded	4	4	64
Total Vessels	280	333	69
No. of Rim Forms	36	33	20

Rims

All the rim forms classified into the groups listed in Table 18 are everted types, flaring out from the vessel neck. This is the most common form of jar/cooking pot rim in all three medieval periods. The classes of rim appear in Table 18 in order of chronological frequency, with those most common in only the Anglo-Norman period at the top of the table. It can be seen that thumbed and flat-topped rims are distinctive Anglo-Norman types. Simple everted rims and beaded forms are common in the early and high medieval periods. In the high medieval period rims with a squared profile, an internal bead and a concave shape are distinctive. The majority of late medieval jar/cooking pots had a rounded rim profile.

Thumbed rims are the most common Anglo-Norman type. These take a variety of forms, but all thumbed rims have been classed together here. This is obviously a deliberately executed technique but its purpose remains uncertain, especially given the range of patterns of thumbing. Potters usually thumb vertically down from the top of the rim to fix the final coil to the neck (J Hudson *pers comm*) but here, thumbing

around the edge of a rim is more common, and might be interpreted as a type of decorative embellishment and this is certainly suggested on examples where thumbing has resulted in little more than a delicate frill (4). On the largest scratch-marked jar/cooking pots (8), thumbing is distinctively deep, which suggests that its purpose in this instance was to ensure better firing of the thick rim.

Flat-topped rims appear quite different to the more common simple everted rim forms and were probably formed by trimming the top of the rim with a knife.

The simple everted rim has had no other treatment and retains a rounded profile. These are common in both the early and high medieval periods, showing that this form was produced in both hand-built and wheel-thrown pots and is not linked to any specific method of manufacture.

Beaded rims also appear on both early and high medieval jar/cooking pots. These were formed by pinching the upper edge of the rim to create a narrow ridge and may often be an accidental product of finishing a rim. The fact that this form occurs in both periods again suggests no technological connection.

More common in the high medieval period is the square-sectioned rim (28). The evidence from wheel-thrown pots is that this form was produced by knife-trimming. It would seem that this technique was adopted more readily by potters who used the wheel, perhaps because it is easier to execute when a vessel is revolving.

Southampton Coarseware is the most common fabric in this period and jar/cooking pots are typified by an internal bead in a form that is quite different from any of the Anglo-Norman types (29–37). This was probably created by the use of a rib to finish the rim (J Hudson *pers comm*), although the purpose of this form, if there was one, is unclear. It will certainly have strengthened the rim at the vulnerable point where it bends out from the neck, which may facilitate stacking, either in the kiln or in use. It is also the closest thing to a lid-seated form made in any local high medieval coarsewares. This form is rare in Anglo-Norman jar/cooking pots and must therefore be related to the use of the wheel.

Rims with a concave profile perhaps represent deliberate attempts at lid-seating, but the concavity is often slight and may in some cases be accidental. Local high medieval jar/cooking pot rims were never made with pronounced concave profiles, and although it is not possible therefore to suggest the regular use of lids, these vessels may have been stacked more effectively.

Jar/cooking pots in the Late Medieval Well-fired Sandy wares have a more upright form of rim, less obviously everted than those on earlier types. A wide variety of forms has been identified, but from a much smaller sample, due to difficulties in distinguishing jar/cooking pots from other types of vessel. These rims are quite different from earlier forms, having a tighter, rounded profile, which have very little in common with jar/cooking pots of the early and high medieval periods (143, 144, 145). It is significant that similar rims occur in several vessel types, for this is not the case in the early and high medieval periods. This perhaps serves to illustrate how the medieval tradition of coarseware jar/cooking pots was superseded by a different approach to pottery making, where a sandy ware was used for every type of vessel made by local producers.

There is no evidence that vessels with different rim forms were used for different purposes, nor can it be shown that they were more popular in different households. The identification of different rim forms is the observation of different potting techniques rather than modes of consumption. Technique can be related to the technology and organisation of pottery-making and the differences between the early and high medieval periods reflect the adoption of the wheel, those between the high and late medieval the assumption of different production values and the more utilitarian nature of the pottery produced in the 15th and 16th centuries.

Bases

No table showing different base forms has been reproduced here, as the range of forms is small enough to be discussed without recourse to statistical information.

The rounded base is universal on Anglo-Norman jar/cooking pots (eg 7). It is likely that this form was created by pushing the base out after drying the pot to leather-hardness. This is indicated by evidence that vessels were entirely constructed by coil-building. The round-based form proved effective for reasons related to both manufacture and use. Firstly, a round base gives stability when placing vessels on an uneven surface, whether in a cooking hearth or on an earth floor. Secondly, a round base allows heat to be distributed more evenly over the vessel surface and reduces stress during firing and when in use for cooking.

Rounded bases are difficult to identify in sherd form, and for this reason the sample is small compared to that for later periods. Jar/cooking pots of the high medieval period had sagging bases and a distinct basal angle (eg 28), which makes base sherds much easier

to identify. The spirit of the Anglo-Norman globular jar/cooking pot is retained in the way that the vessel walls flare out from the base towards rounded shoulders. Thrown vessels come off the wheel with flat bases and these were presumably deliberately pushed out when leather hard. The practical reasons for doing this are likely to have been similar to the reasons for producing rounded bases but it is possible also to suggest that this represents a nod of recognition towards earlier practice, thus indicating the cultural longevity of the coarseware jar/cooking pot tradition.

In the late medieval period the same type of flat base is found on jugs, pitchers, jars and even some bowls, which makes the identification of jar/cooking pot base sherds a difficult exercise. For want of a better approach, pieces that have sooting on them are the only ones that have been designated jar/cooking pots. Late medieval jar/cooking pots had flat bases with a more acute basal angle than is seen in the high medieval forms (eg 144). The fact that this form is repeated on different vessel types confirms the notion that pottery was becoming increasingly standardised in the late medieval period.

Decoration

Throughout the medieval period locally-made jar/cooking pots were plain unglazed vessels that were rarely decorated, although chronological distinctions can be made. Whether any of the techniques described below were a form of decoration is debatable and 'surface treatment' might be a more accurate term.

Scratch-marking is a characteristic Anglo-Norman technique. Both the method and purpose of this device are unclear. The depth, width and quantity of scratch-marking varies considerably from vessel to vessel (eg 1 and 7), suggesting that a variety of tools may have been employed by different potters. The technique may have been a method of ensuring that coils of clay were more effectively joined together, but smoothing is a more common way of doing this and here the result is anything but smooth. In theory scratch-marking would increase the total surface area of the outside of a pot, causing it to conduct heat more efficiently and become more resistant to sudden thermal change. This may have improved the chances of a successful firing and may also have made scratch-marked pots better for cooking with. It is difficult to see scratch-marking as a decorative technique, for to the modern eye it is not particularly attractive, but it was a very popular local style and it may have carried some cultural meaning.

Decoration of high medieval jar/cooking pots is rare, is confined to Southampton Coarseware vessels, and most frequently takes the form of a band of thumb-impressions around the neck or shoulder (**38–40**). This may have served a functional purpose, perhaps to aid lifting and holding, but this is by no means clear, and nor can it be proven that this device signifies the work of a single potter. More elaborate embellishment includes the addition of a thumbed applied strip, which may have served to strengthen the vessel wall (**42**).

Some late medieval jar/cooking pots have an incised wavy line around the shoulder, a motif seen also on jugs and the rims of open forms. This technique can be classified as decorative, but as it is so modest in intent it serves to confirm the basic functionality that lay behind the production of all medieval jar/cooking pots.

Summary

Round-based, everted-rim jar/cooking pots represent an established Anglo-Norman tradition that has its roots in Anglo-Saxon society, whatever the technical and practical aspects behind nuances of rim form and surface treatment. In the 13th century, technological change would bring in new rim and base forms, but the essence of the jar/cooking pot tradition remained embodied in the overall form. The jar/cooking pots of the late-15th century appear to owe little to this tradition and it is possible to see greater similarities of form between vessels with different functions.

Although there is little evidence that different rim, base or decorative forms denote different vessel functions it has been shown that particular forms are distinctive of different periods. This implies a technical progression, related almost certainly to methods of manufacture. There may also be cultural reasons for these developments, for it is possible that the changes in late medieval forms were related to different cooking methods. In the analysis of something as mundane as the rim form of medieval jar/cooking pots, however, aspects of cultural development are not easily addressed although these vessels certainly embody the development and decline of different ceramic traditions. In the Anglo-Norman period jar/cooking pots were the most common ceramic form and as such are an expression of ceramic tradition and contemporary culture. In the late medieval period jar/cooking pots represent a small component of an increased ceramic repertoire that is a reflection of technological and cultural developments. In the high medieval period jar/cooking pots seem to have been as significant, both in terms of function and

cultural meaning, as they had been in earlier centuries, although it is easier to see the changing values of this period expressed in a vessel type that rose enormously in popularity in the 13th century, the jug.

Jugs

The elaborate variety of form and decoration that is manifested in the medieval jug does not diminish the fact that all such vessels were primarily functional and ultimately disposable. The jug has enormous significance in medieval ceramic archaeology and perhaps this colours current perceptions of their value in medieval society. In the Anglo-Norman period in Southampton jugs were relatively rare local ceramic products but by 1300 they had become a national cultural tradition. In the late medieval period, however, the importance of jugs both to the potter and the user was perhaps diminished, as late medieval jugs are to the present day archaeologist. Comparison of jug forms between different ceramic periods is therefore more problematic than is the case with jar/cooking pots. The quantity of diagnostic sherds of Anglo-Norman jugs, or rather tripod pitchers, is unhelpfully small. Equally difficult is the identification of jug sherds in local late medieval fabrics. The development of technique throughout the medieval period has therefore not been attempted, although it may be observed in certain attributes of form. Base styles, for instance, developed from tripod types, through a variety of sagging/flat types that includes thumbed and turned examples, to become flat and usually plain or closely thumbed.

It remains possible, and profitable, however, to consider the high medieval jug tradition on its own and in comparison with imported forms, or more precisely those from France. High medieval local sandy wares have been classified together as a fabric group, broadly contemporaneous in production, distribution and use. Within this group are eight Major Wares in which the jug form predominates. Tables 19, 20, 21 and 22 compare the variety of rim, handle, spout and base forms, decorative techniques and motifs that appear in jugs of those fabrics and in high medieval Saintonge wares. The recognition here of stylistic similarities and differences may help to establish the technical identity of the production centres represented by these wares.

Rims

Jug rims are almost entirely upright types and varieties of this form are listed in Table 19. Four different classes of rim have been identified, into which specific types

Table 19. Occurrence of jug rim forms among Major Wares STWW, STS, SHRW, LOPS, LV, LOWW, LOWF, ANFG, HSO

Rim Forms	Major Wares STWW	STS	SHRW	LOPS	LV	LOWW	LOWF	ANFG	HSO
Simple									
R500			1	2	1				4
R518	2				1				
R576				1					
R604			1						
Thickened									
R501	15	19	14	8	6	5	3	1	17
R503		15	6	5					
R523	5				1				
R532			2						
R534		1	1						
Double-thickened									
R533	11	2	1	1	5		1		1
R558								12	
R565									1
Collared									
R519				1	1			1	
R520		1	4						
R530			4	2	1		1		
R561								1	43
R602									1
Total Vessels	33	38	34	20	16	5	5	15	67

have been placed. These are not the only forms of jug rim but they are the most common and are consequently regarded as the most useful in this analysis.

There are four types of simple upright rim, but all these are relatively rare among all fabrics. The most common form among the local wares is externally thickened with a squared inside edge (70). The well-defined right angle on the inside of the lip ensures that a jug will pour effectively (J Hudson, *pers comm*). The outer thickening was perhaps a natural product of finishing a vessel with a narrow neck but it would also have the effect of strengthening the rim, always vulnerable in vessels used for pouring, and may therefore have been deliberate. Several different types of thickened rim have been identified and some are obviously more common in certain fabrics. Rim form R503 has an internal bead, common in Southampton Sandy ware (69), while Southampton Whiteware jug rims have a distinctive ribbed profile (61, 62), formed by using a rib on a simple thickened rim, and this style is also common in Laverstock-type ware (104). This similarity may indicate a close relationship between Southampton Whiteware and Laverstock-type ware (see below). The ribbed form, as Table 19 indicates, may represent imitation of Saintonge collared rims (eg 198) or of similar forms seen in Anglo-Norman North French Glazed wares (eg Platt and Coleman-Smith 1975, illustration numbers 928, 929). The true collared rim does

not occur in Southampton Whiteware but is common in South Hampshire Redware (79, 82). A specific type of collared rim, R561, is typical of Saintonge jugs and is not reproduced in local forms (eg 198, 209) and it is possible that collared South Hampshire Redware rims were inspired by the Saintonge style.

Spouts and handles
Spouts have been classified as either pulled lips or those formed from applied clay. Table 20 shows that the former type is more common on local wares, where spouts are in any case rare, perhaps because the creation of a right-angle internal rim profile allowed satisfactory pouring. Applied spouts occur on some local forms, particularly Southampton Whiteware. Saintonge spouts were all applied, in a form known as 'parrot-beak' (eg 196) that is not represented among the local wares.

Handles have been classed firstly as rods or straps and within these two broad types different varieties have been identified. Neither class is typical of any local product but all the Saintonge vessels seen here have strap handles.

All local rod handles are solid and are either simple in form or have a groove down the upper surface that was presumably meant to open the clay and ensure a more thorough firing. This latter form is rare however and stabbing was a more common method of achieving the same end. Strap handles were made in a greater

Table 20. Occurrence of jug spout and handle forms among local high medieval sandy wares and Saintonge wares

| | Major Wares | | | | | | | |
	SWW	*STS*	*SHR*	*LOPS*	*LV*	*LOWW*	*LOWF*	*HSO*
Spout								
Pulled	1	5	2		2	1		
Applied	3		1			1		33
Handle								
Rod								
Plain	1	14	13	5	4	2	1	
Grooved	1		2	4				
Strap								
Plain	11	15	15	6	2	4	2	20
Ridged	1	2	1	1				
Thumbed	1	4	3		2	2		
Ridged & Thumbed		2	2	3				
Wheelthrown								46
Total Handles	15	37	36	19	8	8	3	66

variety of forms, but the simple type is most common in every fabric and it is not possible to relate a technique with any particular fabric. It is perhaps significant that those fabrics with the most handles, Southampton Sandy ware and South Hampshire Redware have examples of all but one of the forms listed here. The exception is the thrown strap handle, with its distinctive 'S-shaped' cross-section; this is exclusive to Saintonge jugs (**199** is a typical example).

Bases

Table 21 lists the main types of base form. Most high medieval local jugs had sagging bases, especially where thumbing was used. Here, the clay at the base angle was pulled down to form a frill which projects down and has the effect of stabilising vessels with sagging bases. Often the base may sag below the extent of the thumbing, but even then, although the vessel will not stand up straight, it will be more difficult to knock over. Several different forms of thumbing have been identified, and these have been placed into five main groups in Table 21. Type 1 represents single impressions spaced regularly and close together. It is most common in South Hampshire Redware (**72**), but occurs in all local wares. Type 2 is less common and consists of groups of thumb-impressions occurring at regular intervals (**75**). Type 3 has single impressions placed at wide intervals, and is most common in South Hampshire Redware (**78**). Type 4, overlapping thumbing, is most common in Local Pink Sandy ware. Here the base has continuous thumb-marks that overlap each other (**100**). As with the handles, all these forms occur in those fabrics which are best represented, Southampton Sandy ware and South Hampshire Redware. Type

5 comprises thumbed bases that cannot be classified into any particular type.

Beaded bases are flat and have a bead, or small foot-ring, around the base circumference (**64**, **105**) that was probably formed by shaving the underside of the base. The form is common in Laverstock ware and Southampton Whiteware and absent from the Southampton Sandy ware sample. Splayed bases, where the edge has a short acute angle before joining the vessel wall, are typical of Saintonge jugs (eg **199**, **200**, **202**), which are also all flat rather than sagging, and the technique was not copied locally. The splayed form may have been developed to provide stability to a tall, flat-based vessel and was therefore not replicated among local jugs that were more rounded and had bowed undersides. One other important aspect of the base is that it is what the potter holds on to when dipping the vessel into liquid slip or glaze mixtures (J Hudson *pers comm*). The distinctive splayed base of the Saintonge pots may be directly related to this, for it will prevent the pot from slipping out of the potter's grasp. Local jugs were apparently often glazed by dusting or brushing, for coverage is uneven both in thickness and over the surface of a vessel and a splayed base was therefore not necessary. Thumbed and beaded bases, however, would be equally effective in allowing safe handling.

Decoration

Table 22 shows the different types of decorative technique and motif grouped into broad categories. Decorative technique has been divided into seven separate types. If these occur in combination then this is entered into both techniques. For example, an instance of a thumbed applied strip would be counted as one

Table 21. Occurrence of jug base forms among local high medieval sandy wares and Saintonge wares

Base Form		Major Wares STWW	STS	SHR	LOPS	LV	LOWW	LOWF	HSO
Sagging		4	25	36	12	10	2	4	
Flat		5	2	2	2	11	1		62
Plain		2	7	11	3	12	1	1	20
Thumbed	1	1	8	13	4	3	1	3	
	2		2	1					
	3		1	2					
	4		1	1	5				
	5	2	8	9	2				
Beaded		4		1		6	1		2
Splayed									40
Total Bases		9	27	38	14	21	3	4	62

Table 22. Occurrence of forms of decorative technique and motif among local high medieval sandy wares and Saintonge wares

	Major Wares STWW	STS	SHR	LOPS	LV	LOWW	LOWF	HSO
Technique								
Applied	38	9	27	18	13	4	2	39
Incised	15	12	16	11	7	4	4	4
Combed	7	13	6	3	3	5		13
Ribbed	11		16	5	2	1		1
Impressed	7	1	3	1	2			14
Thumbed	2	6		1				8
Painted		17	5	1				15
Motif								
Vertical Lines	10	3	23	11	4	2	1	28
Horizontal Lines	6	19	9	10	3	4	1	18
Vert. & Horiz. Lines	4	2	1					
Misc. Lines		7	5	5	3	1	1	3
Complex Geometric	1				1			
Pellets	24	1	3	2	9	3	1	3
Morphic		1		1	1			7

applied and one thumbed example. These groups are placed in order of frequency.

Table 22 shows that the use of applied clay occurs in all the wares shown and especially so on Southampton Whiteware and Saintonge types. The use of incised decorative techniques, which includes stabbing, is also common to all fabrics but is not typical of any particular one. The ribbed category, which includes rilling, is usually confined to jug necks, and is common on Southampton Whiteware and South Hampshire Redware. Impressed decoration includes stamped and rouletted techniques. This again is common in Southampton Whiteware and also on Saintonge jugs, but is rare in the other fabrics. Thumbing is seen mainly on Southampton Sandy ware jugs, and the same is true of the use of brushed slips. In this analysis the term brushed slip refers solely to examples where a wash of a different colour has been applied directly to the surface of a vessel, and not where applied strips have

been covered in an iron oxide. On local wares this takes the form of a white slip, usually describing linear patterns (**70**), and is quite different from the polychrome technique seen on Saintonge pottery (**212–214**).

Decorative motifs have also been grouped into broad categories. Linear motifs predominate and are divided into vertical and horizontal types. Vertical lines are most common, being characteristic especially of South Hampshire Redware vessels. Horizontal lines are typical of Southampton Sandy wares, often occurring as thumbed applied strips around the neck; Table 22 shows that thumbing is more common in this fabric than any of the others. In all fabrics a combination of vertical and horizontal lines is rare. The use of pellets has been distinguished as a separate motif and Table 22 shows how common this is on Southampton Whiteware, although it occurs on all fabrics. Pellets are also relatively common on Laverstock-type pots which may be further evidence of a link with Southampton White-ware. Representative motifs are most common on Saintonge polychrome vessels and occur on only three local wares. In Laverstock ware there is an applied clay flower (108), one Local Pink Sandy ware vessel is a face jug in a recognisably English style (100) and one Southampton sandy ware sherd has a fleur-de-lys painted in a white slip (not illustrated). The other face jugs illustrated (84, 85) are not part of the quantified assemblage.

Vessel shape

It is difficult to undertake a comparison of vessel shape for most of the jugs that appear in Tables 19 to 22, as too many of them are badly fragmented or else repre-sented by only a few sherds. All the complete jug vessels have been illustrated in the catalogue above and the range of forms can be gauged from there. It is not possible at present to say that certain vessel shapes are particular to any local ware, but the Saintonge jugs seem to be made more consistently to conform to a particular style. The three illustrated polychrome jugs, for example, are very similar in shape, giving the appearance of having been made and transported, and perhaps acquired, as a single lot, or part of one. This notion may be reinforced by the fact that they all came from the same deposit. None of the local wares dem-onstrate comparable production values, and although certain attributes may be distinctive of particular fabrics, the overall impression is that local production was at a level somewhat below that of the Saintonge.

Summary

Tables 19 to 22 indicate the variety of potting techniques current in the high medieval period. Within this variety certain general trends can be discerned, and particular wares can be characterised.

Southampton Whiteware is perhaps the simplest local ware to characterise. Jugs have a distinctive notched rim, probably inspired by Anglo-Norman North French forms. Vessels do not usually have a spout or pouring lip, although applied spouts do occur. Handles are mainly plain straps. Although both flat and sagging bases occur, the flat, turned variety is common. The typical form of decoration is the applied pellet, usually arranged in vertical lines. Horizontal combing and vertical incised lines are also common. Vessel necks are often ribbed.

Southampton Sandy ware vessels also have distinctive features. Jug rims conformed to the typical plain thick-ened type, although examples with an internal bead are more common in this fabric than any other. All spouts are pulled pouring lips. Handles are less con-sistent, with most forms represented. Bases were usually sagging and thumbed in a variety of styles. Painted decoration is more common on Southampton Sandy ware than any other local fabric, usually taking the form of white slip linear motifs. Combing and other incised techniques are also common. Vessel necks often feature a thumbed applied clay band.

The remaining fabrics are less individual. The two most common, South Hampshire Redware and Local Pink Sandy ware share the same range of rim, handle and base forms and decorative styles. Vertical applied clay strips, often painted with an iron wash, are a common motif, as it is in Laverstock-type ware. In Local Pink Sandy ware, the use of white applied clay strips is also common. Pellets and painted slip motifs, the two distinctive techniques on the Southampton wares, are rare. These wares also have very similar fabrics, and it is possible that they are both products of the same production area. Diagnostic sherds of Local Whiteware, and Local Fine White Sandy ware are generally rare but conform to the styles seen in South Hampshire Redware and Local Pink Sandy ware.

Laverstock-type ware is similar to Southampton Whiteware, both in the ribbed rim form (eg 104) and in the type of base and the use of pellets. The highly decorated Laverstock types recovered from the kiln site (Musty *et al* 1969) are rare in this assemblage. Several of the kiln vessels had collared rims reminiscent of the Saintonge style (Musty *et al* 1969, fig 17) and some inspiration may have been drawn from those products.

The result of this analysis is that it is possible to identify different local types on the basis of form. Southampton Sandy ware has distinctive characteristics, such as the use of painted slips, which are rarely in evidence on other wares. Southampton Whiteware and Laverstock-type ware share certain aspects of form. The same is true of South Hampshire Redware and Local Pink Sandy ware. Local Whiteware and Local White Fine Sandy ware cannot be placed so easily in any stylistic group, but they undoubtedly belong within the local high medieval jug tradition. All these wares perhaps represent a southern rural tradition that is, overall, not well defined, and this perhaps reflects the level of production and the scale of demand. Simi-larities, as well as differences, between these products and those made further afield, particularly Dorset Whiteware can also be observed, widening the extent of this tradition still further.

The compact range of styles exhibited in Southampton Whiteware is perhaps due to the fact that waste kiln material forms the bulk of this material. It is also possible, however, that this was a relatively short-lived product within which a full range of forms was not developed. The same cannot be said of Southampton Sandy ware, which is one of the most common high medieval fabrics. Equally common is South Hampshire Redware where a full range of techniques and styles can be seen, perhaps because this was produced in large quantities over a long period of time. Nevertheless, this product and those akin to it are noticeably different from the Southampton wares.

Locally produced jugs seem to have been influenced hardly at all by the techniques and forms seen in contemporary Continental products. The exception would seem to be in the Southampton Whiteware rims. There is very little obvious similarity between local jugs and those of the Saintonge, which are much more consistent in form and technique and consequently simpler to characterise. The typical Saintonge jug had a collared rim, an applied bridge-spout, a thrown strap-handle and a splayed base. The most common decorative technique was applied clay, usually in the form of thumbed strips. The use of coloured oxides, in the polychrome style, is represented in this assemblage, but this form was probably the product of a single workshop, and remains a comparatively less frequent (albeit widely distributed) Saintonge type. Few local products reproduce these elements, although Southampton Whiteware and Laverstock-type rims and spouts recall Saintonge forms (**61**, **104**). The material excavated at the Laverstock kilns brings out further similarities, including splayed bases, but among the other local high medieval sandy wares collared rims are exceptional, applied spouts rare, there are no thrown strap handles and the Saintonge splayed base is not seen at all.

Different jug forms may be related primarily to differences in potting technique. In a comparison of local and Saintonge wares the quality of the clay must also be taken into account, especially in the absence of direct evidence for the technology of vessel manufacture. Saintonge jugs were thrown much thinner than their local counterparts, they were lighter, and details of form and decoration were more finely executed. In comparison, local jugs appear to be hefty, lumpen objects of little delicacy. These differences may be related to the skill of the potters but it would be fairer to suggest that they are more likely to be related to modes of production and firing. The consistency of technique evident in Saintonge jugs suggests a level of organisation beyond that of local pottery-makers, where manufacture perhaps took place all year round in extensive workshops with paid labour and high investment in technology. The quality of the local products is more suggestive of pottery-making as a seasonal activity in communal groups.

Some parallels in decorative technique can be drawn between local and Saintonge jugs, but rarely in motif. In both traditions the most common technique was the use of applied clay strips. These were usually thumbed on Saintonge vessels, or sometimes rouletted, and this is rare in local wares. Incised lines, including combing, are common on both local and Saintonge forms but ribbing is rare in the latter tradition. Local potters did not imitate the use of coloured oxides in the Saintonge polychrome style. Anthropomorphic motifs are present in local and Saintonge forms, but are quite different. There is a classic English face jug in Local Pink Sandy ware (**100**), and an unstratified example is also illustrated (**84**). This form uses the body of the pot as the surface of the face, with applied clay used to create the ears, nose and mouth. Faces were moulded and applied at the rims of Saintonge polychrome jugs and have details of the eyes and lips, and a band across the forehead, which may represent a head-dress, painted with an iron wash.

Differences in decoration may also have a technical significance. Although the same decorative techniques were employed in both traditions, the resulting styles are quite different. In Saintonge wares coloured oxides and glazes were used far more frequently as a decorative feature, perhaps due to the purity and whiteness of the clay. It is interesting to note that local whitewares also have more colourful glazes. The smoothness of the Saintonge clay also made it possible to apply coloured slips or oxides in a much more creative way than local potters could achieve. Local pottery-makers developed their own style of decoration, however, and produced some very elaborate vessels (**84**, **132**) and the jugs excavated at Laverstock (Musty *et al* 1969) are testament to this. The tradition of making colourful pottery was as strong in England as it was in south-western France and although local potters and those of the Saintonge were quite different in terms of organisation and technique, it is possible to discern more cultural similarities than initially seems apparent.

Tradition

It is not always necessary to undertake such a detailed analysis to establish the character of different ceramic cultures, for parallels and differences may be drawn at a fairly superficial level.

The character of local pottery-making has been fairly extensively dealt with above. The influences upon it are understood to have been largely external, and most obviously technological. One other important factor is local traditions of ceramic use, and this is discussed elsewhere. Here it is intended to show, in a broad sense, how the traditions that represent each ceramic period might be related.

It is not difficult to establish the relationship between local wares of the Anglo-Norman and Late Saxon periods. There seems to have been scarcely any change in methods of production, and the most common form remained the round-bottomed jar/cooking pot. The relationship between Anglo-Norman wheelthrown or glazed wares and any pre-Conquest types is less easy to establish. There is no evidence that Michelmersh-type ware, or the even less common glazed Winchester ware, were being produced at the time of the Norman Conquest. Perhaps unsurprisingly therefore, the Anglo-Norman tripod pitcher form apparently owes little to these types. Imported jug forms may have given impetus to the introduction of glaze and the local production of pitchers, but that would pre-suppose the widespread distribution of Continental pottery. It seems likely that local glazed wares were produced in response to a demand which itself was the product of imports, whether they be human or ceramic. Elements such as tubular spouts and round bases must originate from local practice, however, as they are rarely seen on contemporary imported forms. Anglo-Norman glazed wares should therefore be seen as the new product of a freshly stimulated market, and the beginning of a new local, indeed national, ceramic tradition.

A similar situation may be observed in northern France. There, the highly decorated green-glazed and Rouen style jugs developed out of an industry that had not significantly declined technologically since the Roman period. These types however, owe little to the more subdued decorative traditions observed in pre-Conquest products and continued in the plain Normandy Gritty wares. In Normandy also, it is possible to perceive the beginnings of a new ceramic style, stimulated perhaps by technological factors, the use of glaze, but also by cultural and political forces. Rouen-style jugs may be seen to be the ceramic em-bodiment of Norman artistic and cultural values, combining weighty practicality with a well-organised decorative style. If the same values were eventually brought to bear on local English pottery-makers there is little evidence for it in the unkempt appearance of tripod pitchers, or the naive exuberance of their successors.

The pottery of the high medieval period may be seen to develop out of these earlier traditions. Local jar/cooking pots conformed to the same basic form, although this was refined by the use of the wheel. The quantities of jugs that were produced and imported demonstrate the successful growth of the glazed ware industry, a result also of the introduction of the wheel. It is important to consider that the high medieval ceramic tradition has its roots in an earlier tradition that resulted principally from cultural rather than technological changes. Technological developments came later, and led to the flourishing of this tradition, rather than any significant alteration. The two ceramic strands which represent the essence of local ceramic production, coarse and glazed wares, were maintained and developed separately, perhaps by the same producers, throughout the 12th, 13th and 14th centuries. The breaking of this tradition, as with its foundation, was due to cultural rather than technological forces.

Few of the values of the local high medieval ceramic industry are apparent in the products of the 15th century. It is tempting to explain the emphasis on plain, utilitarian products as a result of a depressed economy and a decreased population, and this may be a more likely reason than any change in pottery-making methods. Whatever technological changes there were seem to have been improvements, the most obvious being increased kiln control, leading to more consistent firing at higher temperatures. These plain forms contrast markedly with the exciting range of Continental pottery that was being imported and avidly consumed. In the Anglo-Norman period, demand, and the presence of imported pottery, apparently stimulated a creative response from local potters; in the 15th century this does not seem to have been the case. Technological limitations no doubt played their part, for it was a long time before stoneware and tin-glazed ware were produced in this country. Many cultures are represented among the bewildering variety of late medieval Continental imports and perhaps this is one reason why local potters did not attempt to compete, although colourful finewares, for example Tudor Green, were produced in England. There is, however, no doubting the quality and durability of the pottery that was produced, nor the long-term effects of this new beginning. Verwood-type wares may justly be seen as a development out of the 15th-century ceramic tradition, and these continued in production into the 20th century.

5

PRODUCTION AND DISTRIBUTION

Having examined aspects of ceramic manufacture it is appropriate now to consider mechanisms of distribution and Southampton's role as a market and a port.

Archaeologists have often seen pottery as an indicator of exchange or trade, on the understanding that identifying the sources of the pottery types present in an assemblage will reveal patterns of ceramic distribution. These patterns are often taken to represent a wider system of exchange, for which pottery is often the only archaeological evidence. This will lead to an interpretation of the level of trading activity that took place in a settlement, and the extent of the commercial interests represented there. The evidence for local, national and international ceramic production and distribution is discussed here for the Anglo-Norman, high and late medieval periods. The likely location of production sites was considered in Chapter 2, and is not discussed here, but it may be worth recalling the definition of the term 'local' as it is applied to Southampton's pottery.

Local wares are those that conform to the geology of the region and occur frequently in this assemblage. They must have been made within easy reach of the town, and were regularly marketed here. It is considered unlikely that potters would regularly trade their goods at centres over a day's journey away, there and back, which probably limits the likely area of production for local wares to within twenty miles or so of Southampton. Local and other English sources are shown in Figure 1 and Continental production sites appear in Figure 2.

The Anglo-Norman period

The variety of pottery types produced locally in the late Saxon period is limited, implying a small number of production centres. A greater number of fabrics have been identified for the post-Conquest period, suggesting that more production sites were operating locally during this period. One reason for this may have been an increased demand as Southampton became established as a successful trading centre but it is also possible that crafts and industries were organised differently following the imposition of the new regime. Local products were mainly coarseware cooking pots and these were probably made principally for the people of Southampton, as it is unlikely that they were distributed over a very wide area outside the town. Scratch-marked ware, the most common Anglo-Norman coarseware, is found at settlements of this period all over the south. The author has observed that scratch-marked fabrics occurring at Winchester and Romsey, the towns closest to Southampton, are different in character from those in this assemblage. This indicates a localised production and distribution of coarse pottery at this period. The scale of production had perhaps increased since the late Saxon period, but it is unlikely that the potters making this material were able, or required, to produce pottery for a very wide market area.

This does not seem to be true of the Anglo-Norman glazed wares. These do not constitute a very large part of this assemblage, yet several different fabrics are represented, some of which have been given a Dorset source. It is likely that local potters did not begin producing glazed vessels as early as some others, and that Southampton was supplied from sources often situated some distance away. Similar wares have been noted at Poole (Brown 1992) and it seems most probable that the earliest glazed wares were brought into the town by traders who supplied several other centres. The growing importance of Southampton would have made it a worthwhile visit for any supplier. This in turn is likely to have stimulated production closer to the town. Splashes of glaze have been noted on a few scratch-marked sherds, indicating that glazed wares were produced locally, but a chronology for the introduction of glaze into this area is not easy to establish. There is little evidence either for the wider distribution of early glazed wares made in, or close to Southampton.

Anglo-Norman Continental imports came principally from Normandy. This is true also of the late Saxon period, and shows how well-placed Southampton was to receive cross-channel trade. The Norman Conquest must have strengthened what seems already to have been a healthy relationship between Southampton and the ports of northern France. The old political, economic and cultural boundaries were being altered, and if this is not immediately reflected in locally produced ceramics it can be seen in the range of imported wares. Highly decorated wheelthrown jugs of a quality and style not reproduced locally, characterise the Anglo-Norman imports, although the more prosaic Normandy Gritty ware products are more common. Pitchers and jugs are the principal imported form, answering a need for wine-serving vessels and it was probably the Norman appetite for wine that provided the mechanism for the importation of Normandy pottery. After the Conquest Southampton rapidly became established as one of the key ports on the south coast. Its prosperity was based on the trade in French wine (Platt 1973), which at this period was brought in mainly from the Normandy ports – with Barfleur and Rouen the best placed to deal with Southampton. Barfleur is on the Cotentin, close to, if not actually the likely production area for Normandy Gritty ware. Rouen, on the Seine, is known to have been a market for the highly decorated monochrome and Rouen-type jugs of the period. The quantity of north French pottery in this assemblage does not seem sufficient to suggest that it was brought to Southampton as a regularly traded commodity and evidence from the hinterland towns, the most important being Winchester, confirms that these ceramics were not re-distributed to other markets. Even in Southampton Normandy glazed wares occur in lesser quantities than the locally produced equivalent. Table 3 shows that imported wares account for seven percent by weight and nine percent by sherd count of all the Anglo-Norman pottery in this assemblage and most of that is Normandy Gritty ware. It is possible, therefore, to view these imported vessels as simply an additional element in the growing demand for glazed jugs (Brown 1997) and there is no reason to suppose that Normandy products were necessarily viewed as more desirable than local wares, for if they were than they were surely easy enough to acquire and one would expect them to occur in greater quantities. The low quantity of imported wares also perhaps reflects the low value of pottery and the poor profit-margin it represented at this time. It may have been cheap to buy, but it would have taken up valuable cargo-space and could not have been sold for much even in competition with technically poorer local products. This discussion must, however, be set against the unsettled history of Anglo-Norman relations in this period. The struggles for succession that followed the deaths of William I and especially Henry I may well have disrupted cross-channel traffic, and the anarchy of the latter period may have affected the comfort of Southampton's trading community. Indeed, Southampton narrowly escaped attack by Robert of Gloucester in 1142 (Platt 1973). Relative stability was achieved with the accession of Henry II, and the creation of the Angevin empire ultimately provided a different outlet for the commercial enterprise of the burgesses of Southampton.

The high medieval period

It has been suggested that the archaeological deposits of this period show Southampton to have been more densely settled than ever before and this is reflected in the quantity and variety of contemporary pottery. The range of high medieval local fabrics is correspondingly greater than preceding periods and can be related to a growth in the number of production sites serving Southampton.

The division between coarse and glazed wares persisted, but there is no reason why these should not have been made at the same production sites. Some wares, however, were distributed over a wider area than others. Southampton Coarseware is the most common cooking pot fabric in this assemblage and although this is the principal reason for its name, it is also apparent that it was produced mainly for sale in Southampton. It is a rare find in nearby towns such as Winchester, Romsey and Portsmouth. This is true of all the common coarsewares and also of the glazed pottery made in Southampton. Southampton Whiteware is one of only two high medieval fabrics associated with a kiln site. This is a distinctive type that certainly was distributed beyond Southampton, for sherds have been noted in Guernsey (Thomson 1980) and Aardenburg (B Hillewaert *pers comm*), but it has not been recognised elsewhere in Wessex. This distribution and the undoubted quality of the product raises questions about the Southampton Whiteware industry. Spoerry, in his chemical analysis of Wessex medieval pottery (Spoerry 1990) identified similarities between Southampton

Whiteware and Laverstock wasters. The stylistic similarity between the two products has also been established (see above) and it is possible that Southampton Whiteware was manufactured in the town by a potter who moved from Laverstock and perhaps imported clay from there. Southampton was undoubtedly a profitable market, with a distribution area that extended overseas, and must have been viewed as an excellent location for such an enterprise. It is hard to judge its level of success or failure, but it seems likely that production was short-lived. Southampton Sandy ware is more frequent in this assemblage, yet this has not been recognised on sites beyond the town and must be viewed, unlike Southampton Whiteware, as a very local product.

The remaining glazed wares have not been identified as Southampton products and were presumably distributed over a wider area. This is certainly true of the most common of them, South Hampshire Redware, which has been observed by the author in assemblages at Romsey, Winchester and Portsmouth. The high frequency of South Hampshire Redware in 13th- and 14th-century groups, both here and elsewhere, indicates that the kilns were sited within easy reach of all these centres. It also suggests that there was more of this pottery for sale than any other type. To modern eyes it was by no means the most superior pottery available. Both Southampton Whiteware and Laverstock ware seem more attractive and better made, yet South Hampshire Redware was most commonly used. As has been suggested, the Southampton Whiteware industry was possibly short-lived, while the one that produced South Hampshire Redware patently was not. Laverstock was perhaps too far away – twenty miles – to compete with more convenient producers, and in any case its main market was Salisbury. This may reinforce the suggestion that a Laverstock potter produced Southampton Whiteware. There was a regular traffic to and from the cathedral city throughout the medieval period. Salisbury was a major market for wool and cloth and Southampton the principal outlet, and this provides a ready context for the distribution of Laverstock wares to Southampton, even if they did not arrive in large quantities.

Few English ceramics made outside the range of the Southampton market seem to have been regularly available here. Dorset Whiteware and Dorset Sandy ware are the exception and these were possibly brought into the town by sea, a by-product of coastal traffic between Southampton and the Dorset ports. Although they occur regularly in deposits of this period these wares are by no means as common as those defined as local and it is unlikely that they were available here as regularly marketed commodities. English wares of more distant origin are very rare indeed. Cornish pottery perhaps reflects the traffic in slate that commenced in this period, while Ham Green ware and the Midland piece may be associated with the extensive commercial network that grew out of Southampton's mercantile prominence (Platt and Coleman-Smith 1975, Vol. 2, 18). The incidence of Scarborough ware perhaps requires less explanation than would its absence, for this material has a very wide area of distribution, and has been found on sites from Orkney to Exeter and also overseas in Scandinavia and the Low Countries, (Farmer P G and N C 1982). The established pattern is that coarsewares came principally from very local sources while glazed wares were brought in from a much more widely distributed range of production sites. The same observation may be made for most medieval settlements (Brown 1997a), urban or rural.

It is possible, if not probable, that many of the unidentified English wares of this period came from non-local sources, yet they represent a relatively small proportion of the total quantity of high medieval pottery and may similarly be accounted for as occasional by-products of regular traffic in other goods. Indeed, given the importance of Southampton as a port, and the extent of its communications with the wool-producing heartlands of the south and midlands, one might expect a greater quantity of non-local material. In response one only has to reflect that this serves as evidence for the pointlessness of transporting bulky, fragile, low-value goods over many miles of rough roads. Pottery may have been carried over substantial distances at this period, but rarely for commercial reasons. Moorhouse has reviewed some of the ways in which ceramics might have been moved around in medieval England (Moorhouse 1983). His comments on peripatetic households may perhaps be more relevant in an inland context. As a port, Southampton may have been more likely to play host to people travelling into or out of the country and already unburdened of domestic clutter. Furthermore, the sale of wool and grain, or the purchase of wine, were the principal reasons for visiting the town from inland. The fact that what little non-local pottery there is came from sites adjacent to established trade routes gives a context for their arrival in the town, but does not indicate trade in ceramics. This is powerfully emphasised by comparison with the quantity of Continental wares brought in at the same period.

As has been shown, 90% of the imported Continental pottery of the high medieval period came from the Saintonge. This reflects a shift in the emphasis of Southampton's trade from the Anglo-Norman period. The political and economic background to this is well-known. Gascony had become a possession of the Kings of England in 1154, with the accession of Henry II, but it was not until after the loss of Normandy in 1204 that it began to assume much importance in English affairs. Even then it only seems to have achieved prominence after it was confirmed as English property under the Treaty of Paris in 1259. The importation of Saintonge pottery into Southampton can be dated to the period following that event.

It is hard to over-estimate the significance of the Gascon wine trade to English commerce in the 13th and 14th centuries. In the 1300s up to 100,000 tonnes of wine were shipped out annually from Bordeaux, with England the principal market (Falkus *et al* 1981). Southampton was perfectly placed to handle much of the wine that came from Gascony, and indeed to market the wool, cloth and grain for which it was exchanged, but trade in other goods and to other centres was also important. Spanish interests are known (Platt 1973) and evidenced not only in Iberian coarsewares but also in previously published fine wares (Platt and Coleman-Smith 195 Nos 1274–77). Contact with northern France and Flanders was maintained, and is attested in the ceramics of the Seine Valley and the Low Countries highly decorated types.

The evidence of Southampton's extensive trading network provides a mechanism for the distribution of high medieval Continental pottery to the town, but does not suggest a reason for this phenomenon. It has already been shown that pottery from non-local English sources is rare, suggesting that there was little demand for such material. This may perhaps have been due in part to the reliable supply of fine imported products, but it is not necessarily the case that those were brought in as a marketable commodity. Saintonge pottery is rare even in towns in the immediate hinterland of Southampton, such as Winchester and this implies that it was not traded, but shipped here for use, or sale, within Southampton. Here again is evidence perhaps for the low profit margins involved in trading in pottery. The excavations from which this assemblage was recovered are concentrated in the merchant's quarter of the town, and therefore on the households of the very people who would have had easiest access to all the goods brought into port. It could be argued

that Saintonge pottery, as well as other imported wares, were acquired by merchants for their own use, but the evidence from other excavations shows that Saintonge wares occur regularly all over the town, including the poorest quarters (Brown 1997). It is possible, therefore, if only on the basis of its frequency, to characterise Saintonge pottery as another local ware. The quantities in which it is represented in this assemblage (see Table 4) show it to be a more common presence than Laverstock-type ware and even Southampton Whiteware. It is certainly likely that Saintonge wares were consumed at a greater rate by the wealthy inhabitants of the merchant's quarter, but this would have been true for all pottery, and indeed most other goods. It seems that everybody in Southampton had access to the same range of ceramic products, suggesting that they were available in the same markets, even if some people required them in greater quantities. The fact that local and imported vessels were broadly of the same type, namely jugs that were often highly decorated, indicates that there was little demand for something different from overseas suppliers. This might explain why so few imported wares reach inland markets, for local suppliers were presumably already providing what consumers required and there may have been little point in offering what was essentially more of the same, especially where profit margins were low. Saintonge pottery might therefore have been imported not because it was different but because there was a market for it in Southampton, and because it was easy to supply it. By this definition, Saintonge pottery may be described as a local ware.

There are exceptional vessels that run counter to this argument, however, and may indeed represent the exchange or acquisition of vessels that might have some higher value, whether commercial or cultural. The large Saintonge Redware pégau (**218**) with sgraffito decoration is an obvious candidate if only because there is no other vessel quite like it in Southampton. Saintonge mortars also, and the zoomorphic Seine Valley-type jug (**189**), may also be special pieces that one would not expect to find in poorer households, the same is probably also true of Scarborough ware knight jugs. There is therefore some suggestion that although most imported pottery is best viewed as an additional element to a wide range of local and non-local products, individual vessels could be exchanged or acquired outside the usual commercial mechanisms, perhaps for more personal reasons.

The late medieval period

The unrest that characterised the reign of Edward III undermined Southampton's economic security and heralded a period of recession, compounded by war and plague, which affected the town for almost a century. The effects of this recession on the archaeology of the town have been discussed above. In ceramic terms, the mid-14th century is when the importation of Saintonge wares seems to have ceased. The emphasis of Southampton's trade changed in the late medieval period, as did patterns of ceramic production and distribution.

Archaeological evidence for the last half of the 14th century is scarce, but this seems to have been a period of decline among local potteries. The emergence of different wares in the 15th century indicates a shift in the location of pottery kilns, for there are few similarities between these and the earlier products. The exception is Southampton Organic Sandy ware, which is made from similar clay to the high medieval Southampton Sandy ware, and may be a development of that type. Although it occurs regularly in 15th-century deposits this is not a very common type, and production may have been short-lived. It is certainly poorer in quality than the well-fired Sandy wares, and the influx of these may ultimately have ended its manufacture. There is no evidence for the distribution of Southampton Organic Sandy ware to centres away from the town and it is perhaps best to view this as a product that answered a local need created by the decline of the high medieval industries.

A variety of production sites has been suggested for the fabrics in the Late Medieval Well-fired Sandy ware tradition. Although these were not those that had operated in the high medieval period, it seems likely that they were located in the same areas, and utilised the same clays. Their products were regularly marketed in Southampton and similar wares are known at other settlements in the region. The consistency in fabric and form throughout the Late Medieval Well-fired Sandy ware tradition makes it difficult to show that certain types were produced for particular markets, or distributed over long distances, although it seems likely that those kilns that regularly supplied Southampton were not situated any great distance away.

Late medieval non-local English wares seem to have come almost entirely from the Surrey/Hampshire border. Tudor Green ware is not common, but it occurs regularly, in forms not produced locally and it is therefore likely that it was carried to Southampton as a marketable commodity. The 15th-century brokage books, which recorded the destination of imported goods leaving Southampton by road, show regular traffic to Farnham and Guildford (Lewis 1993), which in any case would have been passed through on the way to and from London. It was presumably in this way that Tudor Green ware, and occasionally Surrey Whiteware, was brought here.

The quality and variety of the Continental imports of the late medieval period not only mark the climb out of recession which began in the 15th century, but also signal a shift in the focus of Southampton's maritime interests. Recovery from the decline of the Gascon wine trade was principally due to an escalation of Italian influence from the beginning of the 15th century and the role of Italian merchants in late medieval Southampton is well documented (Ruddock 1951). It was the Genoese who first regularly used Southampton as a port, transporting goods to London overland and thus avoiding the heavy dues inflicted on foreign shipping in the capital. Soon the Florentine and Venetian trading fleets followed suit.

The port books, or customs returns, for the 15th century record the wide range of goods brought to Southampton by these merchants (Brown 1998). Pottery from both Italy and Spain features occasionally in the port books. A complete list showing all the references to ceramics in the port and brokage books is set out in Table 23, and a few examples are given here. On the 30 September 1448 '*165 jaretts olei cot' per jarre 3 lagen*' (165 jars of oil, each jar containing 3 'lagen') consigned to *Saldone Spla* were valued at *6s 8d* (Lewis 1993). On the 4 October in the same year '*4 duss' potts' de Malyk val' 5s*' (4 dozen pots of *Malyk*, perhaps Malaga, value 5 shillings) consigned to *Curro Moneto* carried a duty of 1*d* (*ibid*). In October, 1427 '*xv douzeine de peintepot, j pot de Sucre*' (15 dozen painted pots, and one pot of sugar), consigned to *Julian de Primenton* were brought in on a carrack from Genoa, owned by *Andre Spinol*. On the same vessel were loads of soap and dyestuffs consigned to the *Spinelli* and *Catan* families (Studer 1913, 43). On the 9 of January 1449 '*6 pott' argent*' (6 pots of mercury) consigned to *Georgio Karolo* were valued at 10*d* (Lewis 1993). '*vij jarres de gingebre verd*' (seven jars of green ginger) were imported by *Andre Spinol* on the 27 of March 1430 (Studer 1913, 112). In most cases, pottery brought in from the Mediterranean was consigned to Italian merchants and carried on vessels laden with the usual cargoes. The Genoese dealt mainly in dyes and soap, while the

Table 23. List of references to pottery in Southampton port books (£ s d)

Year	Description	Value
1427	15 dozen painted pots, 1 pot of sugar	£4
1428	4 jars of oil	
	4 cases (*coffyns plein*) of painted pots	—
	1 jar of oil containing 18 gallons	—
	17 pots of dates	6/8d
	4 pots of sugar *roset*	8/4d
	1 case of painted pots	
1429	26 pots of sugar	£6 10s
1430	8 pots of mercury (*argent*)	£28
	2 pots of sugar	6/8d
	1 case of painted pots	
	7 jars of green ginger	£30
	3 jars of dates *en confit*	50s
	3 cases of painted pots	1¾d
1435	1 jar of oil containing 16 gallons	
	2 pots of mercury	9¼d
1436	8 pots of green ginger weighing 20lb	26s
	1 case of painted pots	¾d
	6 jars of oil containing 1 pipe	
	6 jars of wine containing 1 pipe	
	7 jars of oil	
	22 small jars of oil containing 36 gall	
	1 jar of oil	
1439	8 jars of oil containing 1 pipe	
1440	1 pot of green ginger	
	4 cases of genoa (*gene*) pots	3¾d
1448	8 jars of oil containing per jar 3 *lagen*	
	6 jars of oil cont. per jar 15 *lagen*	
	1 *mawnd cu' oll' de malyk cot' v dos'*	5s
	2 jars of oil cont. per jar 14 *lagen*	
	13 jars of oil cont. per jar 3 *lagen*	
	2 *sport* cont. 10 dozen pots *de malyk*	10/10d
	5 dozen *oll' de Janua*	7/6d
	1 jar containing 12 *lagen*	
	4 dozen *potts' de malyk*	5s
	1 jar containing 15 *lagen*	
	3 jars of wine	

Year	Description	Value
	6 jars of wine	
	1 jar containing 10 *lagen*	
1449	6 pots of mercury	
	17 jars of oil	
	1 jar containing 10 *lagen*	
	16 pots of mercury	
	6 jars containing 9 gallons of oil	
	8 pots of sugar weighing 60 pounds	15s
1469	100 earthenware pots and pans	
	200 earthen pots	£1
	150 *warpe* earthen pots	
1470	500 *cruses*	£1
1480	100 earthen pots and goblets	6s
1481	200 *cruses*	£1
	300 earthenware pots	£1
	1000 beer *cruses*	£2/10s
	200 beer *cruses*	6/8d
	400 drinking pots	10s
	100 earthenware beer pots	—
	100 beer pots	—
	600 beer *cruses*	£1/6/8d
	200 beer *cruses*	—
	200 beer *cruses*	—
	100 earthen *bocal*	10s
1509	500 *oll' terr'*	3¾d
	100 earthen pots	20d
	600 Flanders *cruses* (*crus' flaundr'*)	20s
	300 *oll' terren'*	20s
1510	200 *crus'*	—
	400 Flanders *cruses*	2¾d
	100 *oll' terr'*	—
	500 Flanders *cruses*	20s
	1 *maund* of Flanders *cruses*	—
	100 Flanders *cruses*	2s
	100 *oll' eriis*	¾d
	5 jars of oil containing 5 gallons	—

Venetians and Florentines carried wine, oil, spices, silks, glass and luxury goods.

This pattern contrasts with the nature of the North Sea trade. It is apparent that this commerce was conducted by individuals rather than the large family concerns typical of the Italians. Coasting vessels in English, French or Low Countries ownership, were frequent visitors to Southampton, and these carried anything and everything, including pottery. In July, 1478, a Portsmouth coaster owned by *Thomas Yoxsale* brought in '*100 frying pans*' and '*200 earthenware beer pots*', along with 2 barrels of lathnails, 2 barrels of cork, 3 sacks of hemp and 20 dozen 'striped hats' (Quinn 1938).

The re-distribution of pottery is also recorded, in the brokage books, but these references are less frequent. On the 17 December 1448 '*2 cassys burnyes pott*', (2 cases of burnished pots, perhaps lustreware) consigned to *Frank Catan* left Southampton bound for London.

On the 17 January 1449 '*2 pott' pot sugr*' (2 pots of pot-sugar) were carried by *Wyll Lyghtefote* to Salisbury. On the 21 March of the same year '*1 jarr' oley cont' 12 lagen*' (1 jar of oil containing 12 'lagen') was carted to Romsey by *Wyll Parker*. The following June '*16 pott' argenti vivi*' (16 pots of mercury), consigned to *Galias de Nigro*, were taken to London (all Lewis 1993). A case and a little basket of painted Genoa pots were taken to Salisbury on behalf of *Andre of Pisa* in 1439 (Bunyard 1941). The Customs Books record goods taken out of Southampton by sea and include a few references to pottery. In 1428 '*j cofyns de peintepot*' (a case of painted pots) was recorded among a load consigned to *Bertholme Catan* and '*issant de ville pour Londres charge en dyuerses vessels*' (leaving the town for London, loaded on diverse vessels) (Studer 1913, 78) and another '*16 pott' argenti vivi*' were taken out on behalf of *Raphaell de Trapana* on the 4 June 1449 (Lewis 1993).

Table 24. List of references to pottery in Southampton brokage books

Year	Description	Destination
1439	1 little *mawnd* of painted Genoa pots	Salisbury
1440	1 barrel of pots	London
	2 cases of painted pots	London
1443	4 jars of oil	Alton
	4 jars of lemons	London
1444	16 jars of oil	London
	16 jars of oil	London
	10 jars of oil	London
	10 jars of oil	London
	1 jar of oil	Salisbury
	2 jars of oil	London
	7 jars of oil each 14 *lagen*	Winchester
	1 jar of wine	London
	1 jar of oil	London
	1 jar of wine	London
	1 jar of wine	London
	erthynpottes	Salisbury
1448	5 jars of wine	London
	1 case burnished pots (*burnies*)	London
	2 cases *burnyes pott'*	London
1449	2 pots of sugar. Value 12s	Salisbury
	5 pots of mercury	London
	1 basket of burnished pots	London
	1 jar of oil 12 *lagen*	Romsey
	16 pots of mercury	London
1478	Genoa pot of a galley-man	Salisbury
	1 basket of *cris'*	Salisbury
1527	1 basket of *crowses*	Lord Hyde
	100 *cruses*	Salisbury
	1 basket of *cruses*	Salisbury
	200 *cruses*	Salisbury
	100 *cruses*	Abington
1528	1 basket of *cruses*	Salisbury

These records provide some understanding of the relative commercial value of imported pottery in the 15th century. It might be expected that fine imported pottery would have a high market value, especially in the absence of any readily available alternatives, but this does not seem to have been the case. The port book of 1448–49 ascribes a customable value of ten shillings and ten pence to ten dozen '*pots de malyk*', or lustreware pots, which works out to a penny each (*ibid*, 9). In the same year five dozen '*oll de Janua*', probably Italian Maiolica jugs, were given a value of seven and six, or a penny-halfpenny each (*ibid*, 10). We might consider these tin-glazed types to represent 'luxury' pottery of the highest quality, but they evidently did not command a high monetary value or at least did not represent high value commodities. The same is true of the less decorative, but perhaps functionally superior, Rhenish Stoneware. In 1470 five hundred '*cruses*' or beer-mugs were valued at £1, or less than a half-penny each (Quinn 1937, 49). Comparison of these figures with the customable values of vessels in other materials and the

relative worth of pottery is more plainly exposed. In 1436 two dozen pewter vessels were valued at ten shillings, or five pence each (Foster 88) while in 1481 six cups of '*crystal*' or glass were valued at ten shillings, or one and eightpence each (Quinn 1938, 195). These values are far higher than those ascribed to any pottery, even if ceramics were subjected to a considerable mark-up in price after custom was paid. The profit margins for glass and metal must have been much greater. Wooden vessels, in fact, are more comparable in value to pottery. In 1510, six bottles '*lignorum*' were valued at eight pence, or almost a penny and a farthing each (James, 1990, 182). It seems clear that glass and metal were better indicators of wealth and status than even the most exotic pottery, and this is reflected archaeologically by the generally scant quantities of such material found in excavations, although factors of preservation and recycling should not be overlooked. Glass vessels occur with much of the late medieval pottery in this assemblage, showing that they were regularly acquired by Southampton residents, and no doubt greatly appreciated.

The port and brokage books also demonstrate some of the reasons for the importation of pottery into late medieval Southampton. References to jars of oil and ginger, also to pots of mercury, show how frequently ceramic containers were used and here it was the contents, rather than the pottery, that had commercial value. In March 1428, for instance, seventeen '*pot de dates*' were valued at six shillings and eight pence (Studer 1913, 53), nearly five pence a pot. A more extreme example is the value of £28 given to eight '*pot de argent vif*' in January 1430 (Studer, 110) and here it is clearly the mercury that was valued so highly and not the pottery containers. Painted pots, pots of Malaga, frying pans and beer pots, however, were all brought in as saleable goods in their own right, which marks a significant difference between this and preceding periods. There seems to be little evidence that in the Anglo-Norman and high medieval periods pottery was brought in for re-distribution elsewhere, yet 15th-century references show pots being taken out of the town for sale elsewhere. This is clear evidence for a trade in pottery during this period, and this may perhaps be one reason for the limited variety of the local products. It also serves to explain the high quantities of late medieval imported ceramics present in this assemblage. Table 5 shows that Continental pottery represents over 50% by weight and count of all late medieval pottery. It is surely no coincidence that this is the only period when local producers were not providing the vessel types represented by imported pottery. Consumers were forced to look further afield for all their tableware, including jugs, mugs, bowls and dishes, and a wide variety of sources was thus exploited, from the North Sea to the Mediterranean (see Brown 1997).

Summary

The pattern of local production and distribution seems to have changed little throughout the medieval period. Once a high demand for pottery had been established in the 13th century, it seems unlikely that the extent of the production area that regularly supplied Southampton would have altered. The limitions of travel time meant that producers closest to the town would have been more successful, as long as they could provide what their customers wanted. Coarsewares were not traded over as wide an area as glazed wares, the latter product being represented by a wider variety of fabrics. In the post-medieval period the number of local production sites that supplied Southampton seems to have decreased, and by the 18th century the kilns at Verwood were the principal providers. The early stages of this contraction can perhaps be detected in the late medieval period, when pottery fabrics and forms were far more standardised than they had been before.

Pottery from non-local sources is rare throughout the medieval period. In both the Anglo-Norman and high medieval periods Dorset types are most frequent. In the high medieval period, when the population and prosperity of Southampton was perhaps at its peak, pots from more distant sources reached the town, but with no apparent regularity. These have been inter- preted as occasional products of an established trade network. Wares from Surrey, mainly Tudor Green, occur most frequently in the late medieval period, and these were probably deliberately brought to the town to satisfy a demand for fine pottery that was not answered locally.

The pattern of the imported wares reflects the em- phasis of Southampton's commercial interests throughout the medieval period. At first, merchants dealt mainly with Normandy, before political and economic circumstances drew them to Gascony. In both periods the main form of imported vessel was the jug, which corresponded with the substance of local production. The means of recovery from the recession of the 14th century was found in the form of Italian trading fleets. These brought pottery containers, but also highly decorated wares that were quite outside the scope of local producers. The same is true of the stoneware mugs carried on the coasters that traded across the channel and into the North Sea and a ready market for these goods was easily established. It is significant that with the manufacture of stoneware and tin-glazed pottery in England, imported ceramics occur less frequently in Southampton.

6

FORM, FUNCTION, USE

Three ceramic periods have been identified, the fabrics that characterise each period have been described and their chronological relationships have been expressed in Figure 36. The same technique can be employed to study the development of vessel form throughout the medieval period. In Figure 40 all the Major Wares are arranged vertically in the same order as in Figure 36, and divided into the three period groups. Arranged along the horizontal axis are the identifiable vessel types that occur throughout the assemblage. The percentage of the total sherd number of each Major Ware that these vessel types represent is presented. See Table 1 for the total sherd number of each Major Ware. Figure 40 therefore shows how the range of vessel types used in Southampton increased through time.

As has been shown in Chapter 2, conditions of ceramic technology certainly contributed to the quantity, quality and range of vessels produced in each period. For example, the low fired, hand-built vessels of the Anglo-Norman period mainly took the form of cooking pots and bowls. Production and consumption are inevitably linked however, for artisans will make what they know people want and if potters perceive a demand for vessels being made in other materials they will try to produce them in ceramic form. Much of the impetus for change in the range of vessels produced therefore came from forces outside the limits of ceramic technique.

	Jar	Bowl	Jug	Lamp	Curfew	Dripping pan	Lid	Money box	Pipkin	Lantern	Cistern	Pan-cheon	Flask	Storage jar	Cup	Frying-pan	Col-ander	Mug	Chafing dish	Dish	Alba-rello	Unident-ified
EMFT	58	<1																				42
ACCW	72																					28
AXCWa	61	1																				39
AXCWb	44		1																			54
SMK	90																					10
ACWX	35		<1																			58
NOG			51																			47
ANG			68																			30
ADOQ			1																			44
AXCWc	36	4		6																		54
ANFG			61																			39
STWW	1		67		<1		<1															32
STHC	13	1	17					1														68
LOWW		1	36	2			<1		<1													60
LOWF			23	1																		76
LV		1	37				<1		<1													62
STCS	54	4	<1	<1	<1	<1																40
STCW	87	<1			1		<1		<1	2												9
SHR		<1	55					1			1											43
LOPS	1	1	46						<1		<1											51
HSO			63																			29
DOWW			81																			19
STS	7	<1	42			<1																50
HCSX	5		2		<1																	93
HDOQ	4		38																			57
STO		4	17								8											66
LWFS	10	5	7			<1	<1		<1		4	7				<1						67
IBR	4	2	1										11	29						<1		52
IBCW	1	1												89							<1	8
TDG		3	8												35							55
LCRD	35	8	<1				1	1								6	2			<1	<1	46
RARN			5															92				3
LSO		1	32																	23	6	35
SPTG																						
NST	1		18										4									77
ITMA		10	49										2							7		24
ITEW		44	1										9							4	21	21
BV		15	5															44	2	13		23
MCP													95									5

Figure 40. Matrix showing percentage of total sherd number of each Major Ware occurring as particular vessel types (see Table 1 for key to Ware Codes)

External forces similarly will affect the scale and focus of demand. Economic factors might affect the amount of money householders spend on all goods, limiting the choices between metal, glass and ceramic products. Changes in methods of cooking, eating and drinking – activities pottery (and archaeology) has always been closely related to – will have led to changes in the way pottery was used, and what it looked like. Thus, by examining the range of vessels present in each ceramic period, it may be possible to draw some conclusions concerning the relationships between ceramic technology, economic conditions and social custom. Finally, there is often a distinction between the functions a vessel is designed to perform, or for which modern archaeologists perceive it to have been made, and the purposes to which it was actually put. Evidence for vessel use is therefore also considered here.

The Anglo-Norman period

From the evidence of the pottery recovered from late Saxon deposits, the range of locally-produced vessels in the pre-Conquest period is confined mainly to jar/cooking pots, with some bowls (Brown 1995). This is understood to reflect not simply the limitations of the current ceramic technology, where pottery was hand-built and poorly fired, but also the limited demands of pottery users. Non-local forms were mainly pitchers, vessels apparently not attempted by local pottery-makers while imported vessels, mainly wheel-thrown pitchers and jars, were more sophisticated and even further beyond the repertoire of local manufacturers. The jars were used mainly for cooking, as evidenced by sooting at the base and this is perhaps further evidence of the limited uses to which ceramics were put at this time (Brown 1995a and Brown 1997).

Figure 40 shows that jar/cooking pots remained the most common vessel type in the Anglo-Norman period. Here again, perhaps the limitations of local potters are revealed, for although jug forms, which category includes pitchers, are represented they occur mainly in wares produced away from Southampton or imported from the Continent. Jar/cooking pots may have had a variety of uses, most obviously perhaps in storage or transport, but many of these vessels have sooting on the base, confirming their use primarily in cooking. Some Normandy Gritty ware pitchers also have sooted bases, which may indicate that they were used to heat liquids, perhaps in the mulling of wine or ale. The increased use in this period of jugs, which may be characterised as serving vessels, may reflect a post-Conquest increase in the consumption of wine and changes in mealtime custom, at least among the wealthier townsfolk. Such a change may have been brought in by the Normans, but similar changes are obviously in evidence within Normandy, as is shown by a comparison of the imported material in Southampton's late Saxon and Anglo-Norman assemblages, and it may simply be part of a general trend observable throughout western Europe. Both before and after the Norman Conquest, however, a variety of vessel types must have been required for purposes for which contemporary pottery was unsuitable, such as serving food and drinking. Other materials, for example basketry, wood, metal and horn, were most probably utilised, overall perhaps even to a greater extent than ceramics, and although these have not survived in the archaeological record it would be a mistake to place too much emphasis on the importance of ceramics in early medieval culture. It is possible, however, to identify the Anglo-Norman period as one of transition. The post-Conquest redevelopment of the town is shown in the building of a castle and the establishment of dwellings with cellars and halls. At the same time the comparatively informal social habits suggested by the late Saxon evidence were being reformed by more structured mealtime customs. The ceramic evidence for this is the introduction of the jug, where previously there had been little need for tableware.

The high medieval period

More emphatic evidence for the changing requirements of the post-Conquest consumer is found in the high medieval period, which saw an enormous increase in the local production of jugs. Although technological improvements doubtless facilitated this development, the implication is that there was a much greater demand than ever before. There is no doubt that jugs were used in many ways, including the fetching and carrying of water and the keeping of other liquids such as milk (McCarthy and Brooks 1988). A wide variety of jug forms were produced, from tall baluster-types to rounded, squat shapes but unfortunately, no correlation between shape and function can be discerned here. Many jugs of this period however, both locally made and imported, were often elaborately decorated, a feature that suggests their use at table rather than in the kitchen or dairy. This development, as well as the increase in the use of jugs, must be related to the changes in eating and drinking habits noted for the Anglo-Norman period.

Jar/cooking pots remain the most common locally produced form in the high medieval period. Figure 40 shows how these were made in a range of fabrics different to the jugs, as they were in the Anglo-Norman period. There appears to be no functional reason for making jar/cooking pots in coarse fabrics, and perhaps this represents the continuation of earlier medieval potting traditions. High medieval jar/cooking pots were wheelthrown, although their basic shape remained similar to earlier, hand-built types. New ceramic forms for use in the kitchen include pipkins, perhaps an indication of changes in food preparation and possibly related to a growing fondness for gravy and sauces. Dripping pans, used to collect the fats from roasting meat, may also be related to the making of gravy, and may indicate an increase in roasting rather than stewing, at least in households where meat was customarily consumed. Bowls were more common in this period, although whether these were used in the kitchen or at table is unclear. Some are certainly fine enough to be tableware. Other forms include curfews, lamps and a moneybox. These are comparatively rare but nevertheless evidence the extended repertoire of local potters and an increased demand for their products.

The most common type of imported vessel was the jug. Saintonge ware is perceived today to be more sophisticated than local products, and may have been similarly viewed as more desirable in the 13th century. Figure 40 does show that jar/cooking pots were rarely imported at this period, perhaps because these would not have been seen at table but as has been shown above, most coarsewares were produced locally, while glazed wares came from a much wider variety of sources. One of those sources happened to be the Saintonge (see also Brown 1997a and b) and the high quantities of those wares in Southampton may be testament more to its availability, and perhaps the marketing skills of those who purveyed it, than any notions of its superior usefulness.

Some pottery may have been imported because it performed a function not answered by local products. Saintonge pégaux for example, are quite unlike anything produced by English potters. Pégaux are large, unwieldy vessels with wide rims and large, open spouts that seem to make them unsuitable for the long-term storage of liquids, because they would be difficult to cover or seal. It is possible, therefore, that these vessels were used either to heat liquids, such as wine, or to mix or spice them. Ceramic mortars, too, were not available locally but stone ones were, and these were surely much more efficient. Pottery mortars might therefore have been a cheap alternative, yet they were highly decorated and are found on tenements where the occupants obviously had wealth and status. It is possible, therefore, to characterise these as vessels designed for use at table, perhaps again, in the spicing of wine, perhaps as chafing dishes or even in some ceremonial context.

The late medieval period

Figure 40 shows a further development in the range of vessels produced, and especially imported, in the late medieval period. Local pottery took on a more uniform appearance and there was now no longer any distinction between the fabrics used to make jar/cooking pots and jugs. Both were made in Southampton Organic-tempered Sandy ware, as well as new forms such as the bung-hole pitcher. This ware is probably earlier than the late medieval Well-fired Sandy wares that characterise late-15th-century groups and which take a greater variety of forms, including jar/cooking pots, bowls, jugs, pipkins, dripping pans and bung-hole pitchers; with new types such as pancheons and frying pans. No particular vessel type may be singled out as the principal product of the Well-fired Sandy wares

and the clear distinction between fabric types and vessel function apparent in earlier periods can no longer be made, for vessels for food preparation, storage and serving are all represented. This emphasises the uniformity evident in local 15th-century pottery-making.

Cooking vessels were probably used in the same ways as they had been in the high medieval period, although perhaps not for exactly the same purposes. The standard cooking pot had developed into a flat-based form, generally smaller than high medieval examples, and at the same time handled cooking pots, or pipkins, were also in use. This diminution in size, together with the introduction of more specifically designed vessels may represent a response to an increased use of metal cooking vessels, by providing for a different range of cooking activities, such as the making of sauces and the preparation of particular dishes. Bowls were more common and much larger than in the high medieval period. These include pancheons, deep wide-mouthed vessels that were probably used mainly for food preparation, just as similar vessels are used today. This would probably mainly involve mixing, but also the making of pastry and skimming milk (McCarthy and Brooks 1988). Bung-hole pitchers were probably primarily used to keep ale (Moorhouse 1978) and their appearance in the 15th century perhaps reflects an increase in the consumption of ale at this period. Jugs are rarely decorated and have a limited covering of glaze and it may seem on this evidence that the desire for ornate, highly decorated table wares had diminished in the late-14th century, perhaps an effect of the economic depression of that period. The evidence of the imported pottery contradicts this, however.

There is a clear absence in the local repertoire of vessels associated with drinking, an activity well-represented among the imported types. The majority of Tudor Green ware vessels are cups or small jugs or mugs, both probably used at table. Amongst the Iberian pottery there are two Seville Green and White cups but mugs are represented more frequently in the Beauvais Earthenwares and are the most common form in Rhenish Stoneware. South Netherlands Maiolica ring-handled vases, previously known as altar vases (Rackham 1939) and more recently as flower vases (Hurst 1986), may also have been used as drinking vessels. Plate 7 shows an illustration in a Flemish Book of Hours in the Southampton Museums collection. It represents a lady reclining in a boat and trailing one of these vessels in the water while supping from a bowl and an association with drinking is indicated, or at least a less decorous function than that normally associated with these objects. The highly decorated Italian Maiolica jugs must have been used for serving liquids at table and the same is perhaps true of Rhenish Stoneware jugs and possibly Martincamp flasks, which were apparently imported empty (Allan 1983). It is possible that stoneware mugs were used in drinking ale, while the tin-glazed forms were associated with wine.

A further range of imported decorated wares may be associated with drinking or eating. Bowls made in Beauvais earthenwares, late Saintonge Polychrome, Low Countries Slipped Redware, Valencian Lustreware, Seville Tin-glazed wares and Italian Maiolica, may all have been used for either purpose. Dishes, mainly in Iberian and Italian Tin-glazed wares are likely to have

been used at table either for presenting food or for eating from. Saintonge chafing dishes were also used in presentation.

It is also possible that many of these highly decorated types were not used at all, but simply displayed at mealtimes as symbols of the good taste, wealth and influence of their owners. This does seem unlikely, however, because it is likely that glass and metal vessels were regarded as much more potent class symbols than mere earthenware, which even at this time seems to have had a comparatively low value. Large quantities of glass were recovered from the same deposits that produced much of the late medieval pottery.

Imported vessels for food preparation occur almost exclusively in Low Countries Redware, in which the majority of vessels are cooking pots. These typically have two handles and three feet. These features, together with the rilled neck, suggest that these vessels were imitating contemporary metal forms. Other Low Countries Redware forms associated with cooking include frying pans, dripping pans and a colander. Much smaller cooking pots in Spanish and Italian Red Earthenwares are also present in this assemblage.

Imported storage vessels may have arrived containing foodstuffs. This is certainly true of the oil jars that form the bulk of the Seville Coarsewares, and perhaps also the Iberian Micaceous Redware flasks. It is not known whether, or indeed how, these vessels were used once their original contents had been emptied but it is unlikely that they were wasted. Albarelli were used to carry spices and ointments. Other types probably used for storage or transport include Martincamp bottles, Normandy Stoneware costrels, flasks, jars and jugs, and Saintonge pitchers.

The local products of the late medieval period suggest that pottery was used in Southampton in a greater variety of ways. Changes in the range of forms being made were perhaps due to competition from vessels made in other materials, or being imported from elsewhere. An improved availability of metal vessels may have influenced ceramic cooking pot forms, and metalware may also have affected local jug production. Imported vessel types were those that local potters did not produce, in contrast with the high medieval period, where the jug was one of the most common locally-made and imported forms. In the late medieval period decorative tablewares all seem to have been imported, either from outside the local region or from the Continent. The persistence of mealtime ceremony is evidenced in the range of fine tablewares of the 15th century. In the high medieval period, however, such pottery almost exclusively took the form of the jug and the popularity here of mugs, cups, bowls and dishes, in glass as well as pottery, suggests a refinement of eating habits and a requirement for fine ceramics to which local potters could not respond. There is no doubt that the period of recession affected local ceramic production, and for a time also local demand. It seems that the latter recovered before the former.

Summary

The role that ceramics played in medieval society would be better understood in comparison with a similar range of vessels of other materials. Basketry, wooden, leather and metal finds, unfortunately, are rare in the archaeological record. This does not necessarily indicate a corresponding rarity in medieval society. Earthenware is an unreliable material for many of the uses to which it seems to have been put, but it has always been relatively easy to make at a very low cost. It was thus extremely common and cheap. Furthermore, the plasticity of clay lends itself to the production of a wide variety of forms, decorated in any number of ways. The success of the highly decorated jug tradition in 13th-century England is testament not only to the colourful tastes of medieval society but also the versatility of both the potter and the ceramic medium. Yet potters are surprisingly derivative and many ceramic elements may be seen as reflections of products in other materials. The use of rilling, combing and applied pellets may be paralleled in metal vessels, while strap handles and the use of stabbing may have been inspired by leather forms. Whatever the origins of these and other features, they take on their own character in clay, and so the way in which a pot may be used must in part stem from the style and character of the vessel itself. This in turn, to some extent depends on the technological, technical and cultural limits imposed on its creator. Anglo-Norman pottery was essentially crude and limited in form, suggesting that it was not designed for a wide range of functions and that ceramics were not therefore central to contemporary material culture. In the high medieval period many new forms were introduced, in a range of wheel-thrown wares that were fired more consistently, and this reflects an increased demand to answer a greater variety of needs. Even so, the emphasis remains very much on the jar/cooking pot and the jug, and it was only in the late medieval period that pottery use developed further. The influence of new technologies is evident in the 15th century too, most obviously in the use of stoneware mugs, which emphasises the notion of a link between modes of manufacture and demand. From the Anglo-Norman to the late medieval period it is possible to see pottery increasing in domestic value, a trend that continued beyond the industrial revolution.

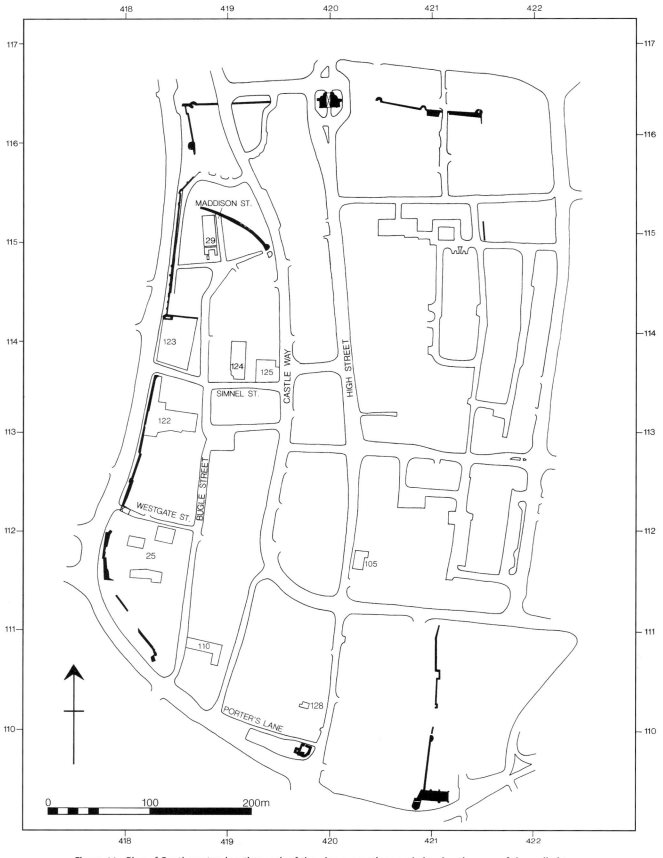

Figure 41. Plan of Southampton locating each of the nine excavations and showing the area of the walled town

7

CONTEXT

Having considered aspects of characterisation, manufacture, distribution and use, which are universal to all elements of this assemblage, it is time to consider the specific sites and various archaeological contexts from which this material was recovered. The location, extent and results of each excavation are presented first, followed by a discussion of the types of pottery-producing feature that characterise each settlement phase.

The sites

The locations of the nine sites from which this assemblage comes are shown in Figure 41. All but one of the excavations were situated on the west side of High Street, formerly English Street and of these eight, seven are south of the castle and the other within its walls. The south-western area of the town, where most of these excavations were located, was the wealthiest part of medieval Southampton. Merchants built their houses here, close to the quays on the south and western shorelines, and it was they who profited most from Southampton's status as one of the most important ports in medieval England. Today, the south-western quarter is noted for the number of vaulted cellars or undercrofts which survive as testament to the medieval prosperity of the town. From the same area was recovered most of the fine pottery previously published from excavations in Southampton (Platt and Coleman Smith 1975) and the medieval wealth of this part of the town seems to be reflected in the quality of the ceramic assemblages from these excavations, assemblages characterised by large quantities of imported pottery.

The pottery from the castle has been discussed in print with specific reference to stratified deposits (Brown 1986). This is a mixed assemblage, only a small part of which can be related to those living within its walls.

The only site situated east of the High Street, SOU 105, produced a very mixed ceramic assemblage that is notable mainly for the presence of wasters. South of this site was the Friary, while the north-east area seems to have been the poorer part of the town in the 13th and 14th centuries.

Each site will be considered individually below, with a brief description of the nature of the deposits and the quality of each ceramic assemblage. This information is also presented in the form of tables. Features or types of deposit have been grouped together in the following manner:

Structures: cellars, drains, garderobes, and wells. Deposits excavated from these are the fills that represent their closure.

Constructional: Features such as construction trenches, beam slots, postholes and walls.

Surfaces: Floor layers and cobbling, areas where, when in use, waste would probably not have been deliberately deposited.

Pits: External domestic features, presumably dug usually for the disposal of refuse.

Linear: Features such as ditches, gullies, slots and trenches, dug to demarcate areas or for unknown reasons.

Industrial: Mainly lime-kilns, although on one site (SOU 105) there was a stoke-hole.

Defensive: Features such as the castle rampart and ditches.

Miscellaneous: Features mysteriously referred to in site records as 'line of stones', 'stone base', 'hollow' and 'depression'; also others which are readily identifiable but are not easily classified elsewhere, such as graves, a road, or robber trenches.

Layers: General site layers, destruction layers.

Table 25 shows the amounts of pottery of each type for each period recovered from these sites. Pottery types have been divided into coarsewares, sandy wares and imports for each period. Tudor Green ware and Surrey Whiteware are specified among the late medieval types as non-local.

Each site appears in numeric order of site code as

Table 25. Quantities of ware groups on each site (the upper line represents sherd weight, the lower line shows sherd number)

Pot Type	SOU 25	SOU 29	SOU 105	SOU 110	SOU 122	SOU 123	SOU 124	SOU 125	SOU 128
Prehistoric and Roman	10	3	59	3	9	3	0	35	0
	2	2	4	1	1	1	0	5	0
Late Saxon	1534	3847	504	529	4	560	251	2303	0
	186	367	33	80	1	29	37	222	0
Anglo-Norman	9979	5091	7759	13094	2673	24378	14438	31225	262
	746	439	612	914	109	872	862	2021	15
Continental	1654	655	667	1723	762	1459	634	843	0
	115	54	104	142	27	97	61	78	0
Total Anglo-Norman	11633	5746	8426	14817	3435	25837	15072	32068	262
	861	493	716	1056	136	969	923	2099	15
HMed Coarseware	16498	14904	18590	1456	4204	9813	5579	17946	78
	896	1125	2142	102	276	705	511	871	3
HMed Sandy	21797	1939	26215	2625	26252	16721	6635	9525	377
	996	131	3147	299	1313	944	429	616	26
HMed Continental	17217	166	3862	2561	8521	1113	1316	3207	33
	650	18	833	376	394	122	140	211	5
Total HMed	55512	17009	48667	6642	35261	27647	13530	30678	488
	2542	1274	6122	777	1983	1771	1080	1698	34
LMed Sandy	1555	16134	6076	1130	4947	6259	14352	6160	38960
	130	511	466	66	200	281	347	230	1683
LMed Non-local	94	315	471	30	166	338	415	129	439
	14	52	128	3	29	57	14	22	41
LMed Continental	1719	5197	7775	5341	16520	2445	19226	3694	48505
	131	186	561	450	391	125	501	148	2482
Total LMed	3368	21646	14322	6501	21633	9042	33993	9983	87904
	275	749	1155	519	620	463	862	400	4206
Post-Medieval	226	2758	1954	454	3461	3276	6365	2640	5982
	24	92	138	48	111	107	175	58	332
Modern	11	262	67	2	38	10	86	5	0
	2	5	8	1	4	2	5	1	0
Unidentified	13	58	220	43	0	47	84	40	0
	2	3	28	5	0	5	10	5	0
Total	72307	51329	74219	28991	63841	66422	69381	77752	94636
	3894	2985	8204	2487	2856	3347	3092	4488	4587

designated in the Southampton City Council recording system, which adds the prefix SOU. The full name of each site is also presented along with the date of the excavation, the size of the area excavated and sources for the site information.

SOU 25: Westgate Street

Excavated 1979. Total area c 1000m.
Sources: Site Archive Report (P Blackman)

This site consisted of three trenches situated in the south-western quarter of the medieval town on the site of the 13th-century Bull Hall, south of Westgate Street and west of Bugle Street. Trenches A and B concentrated on the kitchen and yard areas to the rear of Bull Hall, while Trench C was sited in the garden of that

establishment. Part of the building itself was excavated in 1966 (Platt and Coleman-Smith 1975).

Four early phases of activity were identified. Pre-Conquest deposits were concentrated mainly in Trench C, where pits, postholes and a road surface lay preserved beneath medieval garden soil. The material from these late Saxon deposits is excluded from this publication. 11th- and 12th-century pits, and four graves dated to the 12th century comprise the remaining Anglo-Norman features. Bull Hall was constructed in stone in the early-13th century and most of the features in Trenches A and B are associated with the domestic activity of that household. The building phase is not well evidenced in the area of this excavation. What did survive was a series of rubbish pits, stone-lined cesspits, a garderobe and hearths belonging to the period of occupation of

Bull Hall up to *c* 1350. Many of the major rubbish pits are linked by cross-fitting pottery vessels, which suggest that they were roughly contemporaneous. One set of pits produced a fine group of vessels that is described in detail above, p 102). When the town wall was built in the late-14th century the gravel cliff on which Bull Hall stood was terraced and revetted. Two new buildings were erected on this terracing, and these were excavated in 1966 (Platt and Coleman-Smith 1975). In 1526 Bull Hall was rebuilt, although this phase and subsequent domestic activity did not badly interfere with the 13th- and 14th-century deposits that comprise the most significant aspect of this excavation.

Table 25 shows that most of the pottery from this site came from pits. The pre-Conquest deposits are excluded from this study and most of these features are contemporary with the 13th- and 14th-century occupation of Bull Hall. As Table 26 shows, 76% of the total weight of pottery examined from SOU 25 is high medieval in date, which corresponds with the date of most of the pottery-producing deposits. The presence of a number of cooking pots, dripping pans and curfews may suggest the proximity of these pits to kitchens. Imported wares represent 27% of the total pottery weight and 29% of the total weight of high medieval wares. These figures may be representative of the nature of the site and the status of the inhabitants of Bull Hall, for excavations on merchant houses such as this often produce relatively large amounts of Continental pottery. It is not surprising to find that most of the high medieval imported wares came from south-western France. Unusual Saintonge vessels were recovered including a Redware pégau (**218**), a Gritty ware mortar (**215**), and a lid (**217**). The best example of a Low Countries Highly Decorated Redware jug yet found in Southampton also came from this site (**261**). Local jugs are also well-represented. In ceramic terms this was a wealthy household indeed.

Table 26. SOU 25, distribution of pottery by feature type

Feature Type	Sherd Weight	Sherd Number	% Weight	% Sherd No.
Structures	14993	625	21	16
Constructional Surfaces	327	55	1	1
Pits	47867	2699	66	69
Linear	1011	52	1	1
Industrial	5441	199	7	5
Defensive				
Miscellaneous	106	17	1	1
Layers	2562	247	3	6
Total	**72307**	**3894**		

SOU 29: Maddison Street

Excavated 1980. Total area 600m.
Sources: Oxley 1986

This excavation, within the outer bailey of the castle, consisted of one large trench subsequently extended in two separate areas to the south. A pre-castle soil layer sealed late Saxon deposits that included the remains of a post-built structure. The earliest definite post-Conquest activity is represented by a ditch associated with a wall, which may itself have formed the original defensive boundary. At the north end of the site the tail of the 12th- or 13th-century rampart was excavated and into this a stone wall had been built. Almost certainly contemporary with the construction of this wall was a trefoil limekiln. When this fell out of use, and was partially back-filled, a pitch-kiln was set up in one of the pits. The pits of the limekiln also contained in their upper fills, six human skeletons. The last firing of the limekiln was TRM dated to 1270±20 (MF2 C2). Three pits, only one of which is likely to be a rubbish pit, post-date the disuse of the limekiln. Late medieval activity is represented by a series of rubbish pits and linear features cut into a soil layer which had built up over the site in the late 14th or 15th century. In the 15th and 16th centuries the bailey area became a rubbish dump for the townspeople and the digging of pits has been interpreted as part of a clearance process, probably in the 16th century.

Table 27. SOU 29, distribution of pottery by feature type

Feature Type	Sherd Weight	Sherd Number	% Weight	% Sherd No.
Structures				
Constructional Surfaces	540	48	1	2
Pits	10522	644	20	22
Linear	7092	379	14	13
Industrial	23234	1434	45	48
Defensive	285	46	1	1
Miscellaneous	1140	54	2	2
Layers	8426	380	16	13
Total	**51329**	**2985**		

Table 27 shows that most of this pottery came from the fills of the limekiln. Vessels associated with pitch-making, Southampton coarseware jar/cooking-pots that are covered in pitch (**29, 38, 39 40**), comprise 48% of the total pottery weight from the limekiln (Pieksma 1986). The remainder of the pottery from the limekiln is not associated with industrial processes, but is probably domestic refuse. The rubbish pits of the late medieval period also produced a great deal of pottery and account for most of the material indicated in Table 27 as coming from external domestic features.

As can be seen from Table 25 most of the pottery examined from this site is late medieval and this is associated with the period of dumping in the bailey by the townspeople. Apart from the vessels associated with pitch-making there is a relatively small amount of early and high medieval pottery. This is to be expected as the castle bailey would have been kept clear during the most active period of its occupation and the concentration of rubbish pits that typifies urban domestic back yards is absent here. The medieval assemblage is also comparatively poor in imported wares. These represent 12% of the total weight of the whole assemblage but only 5% of the total weight of high medieval pottery, excluding the pitch-making vessels. The pitch-covered pottery comprises 65% of the total weight of high medieval pottery.

Imported pottery represents 24% of the total weight of late medieval pottery, but most of this material was probably deposited in the bailey from the town and does not therefore reflect the quality of the ceramics in use in the castle at that time. Apart from the vessels associated with pitch-making the sherd size is small and few vessels can be reconstructed. Larger fragments were however, recovered from deposits associated with the later phase of dumping, including the complete profile of a bung-hole pitcher (140).

SOU 105: High Street

Excavated 1971. Total area *c* **450m.**
Sources: Medieval Archaeology, R G Thomson *pers comm*

Situated on the east side of the High Street and north of the site of the medieval Friary, this excavation comprised a single trench divided into separate areas. The area had been badly disturbed by post-medieval activity, and up until now attempts to stratify each context or to compile a meaningful sequence for these deposits have met with very little success. Context types have been identified, though it is very difficult to relate them to any of the broad phases of activity that were apparently identified. The earliest feature seems to have been a large ditch, which appeared in section and is possibly the eastern boundary of the 10th-century settlement. Later timber structures, fronting onto the High Street and with yards and cesspits behind, were built presumably in the 12th or 13th centuries. In the 14th or 15th centuries, a kitchen was built on stone footings.

The eastern part of the site revealed evidence of a waster dump and a feature interpreted as a stoke-hole was also excavated. Any kiln in the vicinity was probably operating in the last half of the 13th century, before the kitchen was built.

Making sense of the ceramic assemblage is as difficult as making sense of the stratigraphy, but the presence of wasters makes it worth the effort. Wasters represent 6% of the total sherd number. These are mostly in Southampton Whiteware with some Southampton High Street Coarseware. This material represents the only clear evidence for a pottery kiln in medieval Southampton and this factor alone makes this assemblage important. As the archaeology of the site shows however, this evidence is very slight and an excavation of the kiln itself rather than the fringes of the working area would be far more rewarding.

Table 28. SOU 105, distribution of pottery by feature type

Feature Type	Sherd Weight	Sherd Number	% Weight	% Sherd No.
Structures				
Constructional	1728	170	2	2
Surfaces	6850	468	9	6
Pits	15498	1466	21	18
Linear				
Industrial	119	12	1	1
Defensive				
Miscellaneous	664	100	1	1
Layers	49360	5988	66	73
Total	74219	8204		

Table 28 shows that most of the pottery came from site layers, with a relatively high proportion coming from miscellaneous deposits. High medieval pottery is clearly the most common, as Table 24 demonstrates. Although wasters do not form a very large proportion of these wares they are present throughout whatever sequence there is, and are thought to be residual in later contexts. Late medieval pottery is associated with the stone building, the construction of which must have disturbed the waster dumps.

The social status of the people living in the first phase timber building was almost certainly not at the level of the merchants who occupied the south-western quarter. The quality of the ceramic assemblage may support this view, but more persuasive evidence is the proximity of an industrial site. The later construction of a stone building may imply an increase in the wealth of the area in the 15th century. This is supported by the increased presence of imported wares in the late medieval period, which represent 56% of the late medieval pottery. It is unfortunate that the nature of the site and the lack of any stratigraphic sequence preclude any detailed examination of the pottery from the late medieval phase, or indeed from any phase, of the site's development. This assemblage gives us only a tantalising glimpse of the archaeology of this part of Southampton and of the potting industry in the town.

SOU 110: West Hall

Excavated 1970. Area *c* 123m
Sources: R G Thomson (*pers comm*), unpublished site archive.

This excavation was a single trench situated at the south end of Bugle Street and on its east side. Interpretation of this site also suffers from an incomplete archive. The earliest feature was a length of 10th-century ditch, possibly part of the Saxon settlement. In the 12th century a large stone house was constructed. One problem with this site is its identification as West Hall, for none of the SOU 110 features would appear to fit into the documented site of the tenement. Whether or not this excavation is on the site of West Hall, there seems to be little doubt that the deposits can be associated with a substantial medieval domestic dwelling. The excavation uncovered part of the south wing of a stone building, a stone-lined garderobe and a backyard area. In its earliest phase this yard contained a large pit (Pit 6), which produced 12th-century pottery from its lowest levels. It was filled in, probably in the 13th century, when the north wall of the south wing was extended to enclose the yard area, which was then floored over. The fills of Pit 6 were constantly subsiding, leading to a succession of floor levels appearing within it. In the late medieval period these floors became cobbled surfaces, perhaps because the walls of the extension were removed and this area became an external yard once more. Occupation continued into the post-medieval period.

Table 29. SOU 110, distribution of pottery by feature type

Feature Type	Sherd Weight	Sherd Number	% Weight	% Sherd No.
Structures	4317	287	15	11
Constructional	1993	136	7	5
Surfaces	275	68	1	3
Pits	13860	1187	48	48
Linear	156	8	1	1
Industrial				
Defensive				
Miscellaneous	188	24	1	1
Layers	8202	777	28	31
Total	**28991**	**2487**		

Table 29 shows that much of the pottery came from site layers, representing the build-up of deposits in the yard area. The pottery from the garderobe and Pit 6 together account for most of the total pottery weight of this assemblage and these are obviously the two most significant features on this site. Table 24 shows that Anglo-Norman pottery occurs in greater quantity by weight than that of any other period, although all periods are roughly equivalent in sherd number. This may be because most of the early material came from the garderobe and Pit 6, where sherds would be less susceptible to the forces of constant wear and breakage that affect pottery deposited in site layers, from which most of the later wares were derived. Imported wares of all periods represent 37% of the total assemblage weight. This may reflect the relative wealth of the household but the assemblage is not a large one. The excavation uncovered only a small part of the tenement, and it would be dangerous to read too much into the composition of this group. 'West Hall' was however, a large and wealthy establishment in the commercial core of the town and one would expect imported pottery to be in common use. Italian merchant families leased the property in the 15th century (Platt 1973), and the high quantities of late medieval imported pottery may reflect their occupation.

The pottery has not survived well, but among the fragmentary material are a nearly-complete tripod pitcher (**26**), a fine Seine Valley jug with zoomorphic decoration (**189**) and a decorated tubular spout of Andenne-type ware (**260**).

SOU 122: St Michael's House

Excavated 1972. Area *c* 2500m.
References: SARC Annual Report 1973.

This site consisted of a large single trench situated west of Bugle Street between Simnel Street to the north and Blue Anchor Lane to the south. The medieval town wall formed the western boundary. Once again, unfortunately, interpretation of this excavation is hindered by an incomplete archive, as well as an obscurely complex ceramic recording system. As a result, a small fraction of the great quantity of pottery recovered from this site has been examined. A very fine assemblage of post-medieval and early modern material was retrieved but none of this is presented here. The pottery that is considered came from deposits that can be identified as belonging to the medieval phase of the site's development. This represents most of the medieval pottery, though there is still a substantial quantity that cannot be accurately stratified at all, and must therefore be excluded from this study although certain vessels have been illustrated in the catalogue as unstratified.

The earliest activity on this site apparently dates from the early-13th century, although the ceramic evidence for this is hard to trace. Around 1250 the first stone buildings were constructed in this area and the archaeology becomes more easily understandable. Two buildings, on the western edge of the site, were founded on a gravel make-up that apparently sealed any earlier deposits. One stone house (House 3) was associated with a stone-built 'deep room', and areas of pits and middens to the north and south. Some of these pits may have been used for lime-burning, presumably during building. The plan of House 3 was completely revealed. The second building, to the north of House 3, was only partially preserved amidst later cellaring. In the 14th century two more houses (Houses 1 an 2) were built to the east of House 3. House 1 also contained a 'deep room'. The area between these two buildings contained cesspits and rubbish pits, one of which produced three Saintonge polychrome jugs (**21, 213, 214**) and was sealed by a burnt destruction layer. House 3 went out of use in the 16th century and was demolished to allow the final stretches of the town wall to be built across the site of it. The remaining houses continued in use. A stone-lined garderobe attached to House 2 was filled in around this time and its fills produced two Saintonge chafing dishes (**257**), a Spanish Oil Jar (**323**), a North Italian Sgraffito plate (**376**) and a Florentine Tin-glazed jug (**362**).

Table 30. SOU 122, distribution of pottery by feature type

Feature Type	Sherd Weight	Sherd Number	% Weight	% Sherd No.
Structures	15920	376	25	13
Constructional	70	2	1	1
Surfaces	99	5	1	1
Pits	40688	2081	64	73
Linear				
Industrial	108	6	1	1
Defensive				
Miscellaneous	4809	243	7	8
Layers	2147	143	3	5
Total	**63841**	**2856**		

The area of this excavation covered part of at least four medieval tenements and a length of the town wall. As might be expected on a large site with a good sequence of medieval domestic activity, most of the pottery came from pits. Table 30 shows that pits and the garderobe produced 89% of the total weight of this assemblage and 86% of all the sherds. This is partly

because these features are not only usually the most productive but they are also the most easily identifiable within the opaque remnants of this excavation archive. Most of the pits date from the 13th or 14th centuries. This is reflected in Table 24, which shows that 62% of the total pottery weight is of the same date. The low quantity of late Saxon and Anglo-Norman wares is evidence of the paucity of early deposits on this site. Late medieval pottery comprises 30% of the total pottery weight, and just under half of that came from the garderobe adjacent to House 2. Imported pottery comprises 38% of the total weight of 13th- to 16th-century material. The size and construction of the four houses, with two deep rooms and two stone-lined garderobes is evidence of the wealth of the inhabitants. This is emphasised by the range of pottery present on the site, for this assemblage contains imported pottery of a very high quality. These dwellings and this assemblage compare well with the evidence from other excavations in this part of the town.

SOU 123: Upper Bugle Street Phase 2

Excavated 1973–4. Area c 2739m.
Sources: Archive Report (D Devereux); Oxley 1986

Sited at the south-west corner of Southampton Castle this excavation encompasses part of the interior of the castle and the area outside. The site was divided into three areas. Area A was within the castle bailey wall and included a part section of the original motte ditch, the fills of Castle Hall and an associated garderobe. Area B was bounded to the north by the south wall of Castle Hall. The only feature associated with the castle was a fine tidal garderobe, but the rest of the trench seems to have covered an area of dead ground not associated with any extra-castle domestic activity. It did however include a limekiln, probably associated either with work on the castle or the town wall. The northern limit of Area C ran up to the south wall of the castle. Here a small gully and a pair of pits pre-date the curtain wall. Further south two buildings were excavated. Founded in the 13th century they were constantly modified into the late medieval period. Associated with these buildings were a few pits and a well which contained two bronze bowls.

The sequence of activity on this site begins with the excavation of the motte ditch in the late-11th or early-12th century and in the same period Castle Hall was constructed, with the earlier of the two garderobes. The south bailey wall was built slightly later. In the 13th century Castle Hall was modified by the insertion of a barrel vault that protruded above the original level of the first-floor hall and the early garderobe was filled in and replaced by the tidal latrine excavated in Area B. By the 16th century the castle had become virtually derelict and in the 18th century the vault was filled in, and finally collapsed. The area outside the castle was probably cleared of occupation during its construction. Domestic buildings were re-established here in the 13th century with houses fronting onto Bugle Street, though the only features of note in the area outside the castle were the limekiln in Area B and the well in Area C.

Table 31. SOU 123, distribution of pottery by feature type

Feature Type	Sherd Weight	Sherd Number	% Weight	% Sherd No.
Structures	30229	831	45	25
Constructional Surfaces	5336	359	8	11
Pits	2086	73	3	2
Linear	1790	78	3	2
Industrial	1444	108	2	3
Defensive	6100	400	9	12
Miscellaneous	2729	177	4	5
Layers	16708	1321	25	39
Total	66422	3347		

Table 31 shows that most of the pottery came from the two garderobes associated with Castle Hall. The earlier of these, Garderobe 1, produced 21kg of pottery, the best group from this site and indeed from the castle to date. Site layers comprise the second most productive type of context in this excavation. A wide variety of deposits were excavated here, as one would expect on a site that encompasses both the castle and extra-mural domestic buildings.

The pottery from this site is mainly 13th- and 14th-century. The material from Garderobe 1 is mainly early to mid-13th century in date and accounts for 75% of the total weight of Anglo-Norman pottery from this site. The area within the castle, including the motte ditch, the garderobes and Castle Hall, produced 52% of the total pottery weight of this assemblage. Most of the pottery from Areas B and C came from site layers. The limekiln produced only 1,254g of pottery, compared with 23,228g from a similar feature inside the castle bailey on SOU 29. The well produced 1,997g of material. The material from the well is perhaps representative of the quality of the ceramics used in the household on this tenement. It is mainly 13th- or 14th-century in date, with wheelthrown coarse and sandy wares present in the form of cooking pots and jugs. Highly decorated Dorset Whiteware and Saintonge products are evidence of a certain degree of

wealth but the bronze bowls, one of which is finely decorated, are far more obvious clues to the economic status of the occupiers of this area.

The material from the motte ditch and from Garderobe 2 is mixed in date. It is therefore the large group from Garderobe 1 that offers the best evidence for the type of pottery used in the castle. As with SOU 29 imports are rare and scratch-marked cooking pots and glazed tripod pitchers account for the greater proportion of this group, which may have been finally deposited in the Garderobe from another dump (Brown 1986). This group does nothing to contradict the notion that the occupants of the castle consumed fewer high quality ceramics than the wealthy occupants of the merchants' quarter, where imported wares are much more common. It is however, probably mid-13th century in date and thus slightly earlier than the pottery from the merchants' houses. This is one of the finest groups of this date yet excavated in the town and shows the castle to be a thriving establishment at this time.

SOU 124: Upper Bugle Street Phase 3

Excavated 1976–77. Area 575m.
Sources: Site Archive (M Shaw); Oxley 1986

This excavation was a single trench situated immediately south of the castle, north of Simnel Street and east of Upper Bugle Street. A section of late Saxon ditch, possibly the northern limit of the 10th-century settlement, was the earliest feature excavated. The earliest post-Conquest phase was the digging of the castle motte ditch in the 11th or 12th centuries and a section across this feature occupied the northern half of the site. Also in the 11th or 12th centuries a line of six rubbish pits was dug, which ran east-west, parallel to and outside the ditch. Occupation of the area outside the castle restarted in earnest in the late-12th or early-13th centuries but most of the evidence for this activity was destroyed in the mid-13th century by the insertion of two stone cellars. These also truncated the tops of the six earlier pits. The stone houses that topped these cellars would have had small back yards, due to the proximity of the motte ditch. By the middle of the 14th century however, the ditch had been filled in and this area was encroached upon from these tenements. A stone garderobe was built onto the back of the western house in the late-14th century and two ovens were built in an extension which extended over the now filled-in ditch. The motte ditch was partially re-cut in the late-14th century but by the 16th century it was completely filled in again. The garderobe in the western tenement was in-filled in the late-15th century and contained the marvellous group of pottery discussed in Chapter 3. In the 15th century the two tenements may have been combined, for access between the two was provided in a remodelling of the building. The extension to the western tenement was abandoned in the 16th or 17th centuries, probably due to subsidence of the ditch deposits. The buildings continued to be occupied into the post-medieval period.

Table 32. SOU 124, distribution of pottery by feature type

Feature Type	Sherd Weight	Sherd Number	% Weight	% Sherd No.
Structures	30344	690	44	21
Constructional	3046	327	4	11
Surfaces	4006	407	6	13
Pits	15973	805	23	26
Linear				
Industrial				
Defensive	7967	380	11	12
Miscellaneous	2134	140	3	4
Layers	5911	343	8	11
Total	69381	3092		

As Table 32 shows, only 11% of this assemblage came from the motte ditch. The remainder was recovered from domestic deposits, mainly pits and the garderobe. The pits are mostly early in date. During the occupation of the houses the motte ditch not only restricted the area available for the digging of rubbish pits, but also provided a ready dumping ground, thus making pits less necessary. The group associated with the garderobe comprises 44% of the total pottery weight and accounts for the high proportion of late medieval wares shown in Table 24. The high quantity of high quality pottery in this group, with complete profiles of French, Dutch, Rhenish, Spanish and Italian vessels, alongside some exceptional Italian glass, is testament to the wealth and status of the occupier of this property in the late-15th century. The social position of any previous occupiers is less easily determined. Anglo-Norman and high medieval wares are present in similar quantities with the Anglo-Norman material mainly derived from pits. The high medieval pottery was recovered from the motte ditch and floor and site layers, and is mixed and fragmentary. The material from the ditch was almost certainly deposited there by the inhabitants of these tenements and includes more imported wares than are usually associated with castle assemblages. This material is therefore viewed as a domestic group, and good quality local and non-local English wares are present along with Saintonge types. The ditch however was probably re-cut in the 14th century and much of the

high medieval material has therefore been lost, although some may have been re-deposited here (Oxley 1986). Imports comprise 11% of the high medieval pottery, which is compatible with domestic assemblages from other sites in the south-western quarter of the town. What really distinguishes this assemblage however is the late medieval group from the garderobe.

SOU 125: Upper Bugle Street Phase 3e

Excavated 1976. Area 352m.
Sources: Unpublished archive report; J Oxley *pers comm*

This excavation was a single trench sited east of SOU 124 on the junction of Simnel Street and Castle Way. A section of the 10th-century ditch observed on SOU 124 was also excavated here. Later than this feature, but possibly earlier than the foundation of the castle, are the remnants of timber structures and associated pits. These survive somewhat ephemerally amidst later disturbances and their stratigraphy is unclear. The area of the site covers parts of three medieval tenements that fronted onto the old line of Castle Lane at New Corner. The easternmost tenement was destroyed by a 15th-century cellar and the westernmost was not fully investigated, apart from a garderobe. The central property was examined in the most detail and the stone footings of the north-west wall of a building established in the 13th century were revealed. An outbuilding of this house was completely uncovered with part of the back yard area. An oven was situated in the yard and inside the outbuilding were two pits, one clay-lined and the other filled with sand. It has been suggested that these features were associated with brewing. All these buildings burned down in the early-14th century, possibly in the French raid of 1338, covering the site with a burnt layer. Thereafter, until the building of

Table 33. SOU 125, distribution of pottery by feature type

Feature Type	Sherd Weight	Sherd Number	% Weight	% Sherd No.
Structures	7769	406	10	9
Constructional	1837	241	2	5
Surfaces	125	26	1	1
Pits	34138	1856	44	41
Linear	74	9	1	1
Industrial				
Defensive				
Miscellaneous	321	46	1	1
Layers	33488	1904	43	42
Total	77752	4488		

the cellar in the eastern tenement this area lay open and layers of rubbish accumulated.

Table 33 shows that most of this assemblage came from site layers, representing build-up after the 14th-century destruction, and from pits, which were dug in the back yard area of the central tenement. As Table 24 indicates, there is a fairly high proportion of Anglo-Norman pottery, associated with the early activity on the site. Much of the pottery from the 13th- to 14th-century occupation is burnt and comes from those layers that covered the site after the building burnt down. From these layers comes the complete profile of a badly burned, highly decorated jug (132) in a local fabric. Imported wares represent 10% of the high medieval pottery, a figure that compares well with the assemblages from other sites in this part of the town. In terms of quantity and quality, a high status is implied here. The rubbish layers were very mixed and burnt pottery from the original destruction is present throughout the sequence. This is evidence that the site lay open for a long time, which explains the relatively low quantity of late medieval material.

SOU 128: Quilter's Vault

Excavated 1971. Area: *c* 256 sq. metres.
Sources: Walker 1979; site archive; R G Thomson
pers comm

The complex of structures that includes Quilter's Vault is situated at the south end of the modern High Street, north of Porter's Lane. Excavations undertaken in 1976–77 examined a series of buildings south of the 1971 trench that is discussed here. These have been published with reference to those earlier explorations (Walker 1979) and are not included in this analysis. What is included is a single phase of activity identified on Thomson's 1971 excavation, the closure of a stone-built cellar and associated garderobe in the late-15th century. The cellar, at the rear of the main vault, is thought to have been constructed *c* 1300. The masonry of the garderobe was bonded to the west wall of the cellar and presumably served the building that surmounted it. Table 34 shows the amount of pottery recovered from these structures.

In contrast to the material recovered in 1976–77, the 1971 finds are exceptional in quantity and quality. These deposits contained a massive quantity of late-medieval pottery and a fine group of glass of the same date. An extraordinary range of late-15th century ceramics is represented. Local late medieval Well-fired Sandy wares are present in a variety of forms, including

Table 34. SOU 128, distribution of pottery by feature type

Feature Type	Sherd Weight	Sherd Number	% Weight	% Sherd No.
Structures	94683	4587	100	100
Constructional				
Surfaces				
Pits				
Linear				
Industrial				
Defensive				
Miscellaneous				
Layers				
Total	94636	4587		

cooking pots, pipkins, dripping pans (149, 150), bowls and pancheons (155, 158), jars (146), jugs, and bunghole pitchers. There is a complete Tudor Green jug (168) and fragments of several cups. The range of imports is staggering. There is an unusual amount of late medieval French pottery. Beauvais Earthenware vessels include yellow and green bowls (238, 239, 244), mugs (235, 236, 242) and jugs, fragments of a chafing dish and a double-slipped sgraffito dish (247). There are several Martincamp flasks, five of which survive well enough to be illustrated here (230–233) and Normandy Stoneware is also present (226). Late Saintonge pottery includes a figurine (258), chafing dishes (255, 256), a large tubular-spouted pitcher (249), sherds of a basket-handled pitcher (250) and a polychrome dish (259). There are numerous Low Countries Redware vessels, including cooking pots (262, 269, 271), frying pans (279, 280, 281), two colanders (282, 283), a bowl (277) and a dish (276). There is also a South Netherlands Maiolica ring-handled vase, with a floral motif (294). Rhenish Stoneware includes Cologne-type mugs (315, 316, 317), several plain Raeren mugs (302–304, 307, 309–311) and two Siegburg vessels (299, 318). There is an extensive range of Iberian pottery, with coarseware oil-jars, a *lebrillo* (326), an Andalusian coarseware jar (330), a Micaceous Redware cooking pot (337) and an albarello (328). There are lustreware bowls and dishes (345, 346, 347, 348) and an albarello (349). Morisco ware vessels include a Seville Blue and Purple dish (350), a Seville Blue dish (351) a Seville Green and White cup (354) and a Seville Plain White bowl. Among the Italian Tin-glazed products are a small Faenza-type jug (364), Montelupo bowls or dishes (359, 360), and a Ligurian faience bowl (371). Italian Lead-glazed wares include North Italian Sgraffito and North Italian Red Earthenware bowls (377, 378) and albarelli (379, 381). There is also the base of a flagon (382).

The quality of this group indicates a prosperous household at least equivalent to those represented at the sites of Bull Hall, West Hall, St. Michael's House and the Upper Bugle Street property on SOU 124. The evidence from the finds suggests that the closure of the cellar and garderobe was a single event. Much of this pottery must therefore have been in use at the same time.

Feature types

The range of features on each site has been discussed and it is possible to establish a chronological pattern for ceramic deposition by relating feature types to the four settlement phases introduced in Chapter 3. Table 35 shows how the pottery in each settlement phase is distributed among groups of feature types.

Table 35. Relative quantities by weight and count of pottery by feature type for each phase

Feature Type	Phase 1	%	Phase 2	%	Phase 3	%	Phase 4	%	Unphased	%
Structures	30754	33	29822	18	2942	6	134500	71	190	1
	950	17	1174	12	167	5	5508	69	3	1
Constructional	1412	1	7310	4	1767	3	2620	1	1768	2
	250	4	623	6	131	4	159	2	175	2
Pits	58230	56	83553	49	9454	18	18260	10	16135	17
	3575	64	4648	47	436	14	653	8	1499	16
Industrial	1444	1	20308	12	680	1	7885	4	119	1
	108	2	1333	14	61	2	245	3	12	1
Miscellaneous	1043	1	4985	2	4818	10	12370	6	24705	26
	134	1	389	4	431	14	618	8	1555	16
Layers	6287	7	23955	14	31720	62	13348	7	51494	54
	570	10	1661	17	1969	62	768	10	6135	65

Phase 1

Most of the pottery in Phase 1 came from pit-fills. Fifty-two pits are represented in this phase, 33% of the total number of features. The large garderobe deposit at the castle, (see Chapter 3) accounts for the high proportion of material from structures. In comparison other feature types are poorly represented. Constructional features are mainly those associated with timber structures, including 49 postholes. These, unsurprisingly, yielded few finds. A limekiln at SOU 123, associated with the construction of the castle bailey wall is the only industrial feature. The miscellaneous group includes defensive features such as the castle rampart, gullies associated with the castle bailey and a road surface at Westgate Street (SOU 25).

Phase 2

The pattern of feature type distribution in Phase 2 is similar to that for Phase 1. Table 34 shows that half the pottery in Phase 2 was recovered from pits and most of the rest from structures. These principally represent the fills of stone-lined garderobes at Westgate Street (SOU 25) and St Michael's House (SOU 122), and stone-built drains at the latter. Constructional features include postholes, walls and wall-trenches, which again produced a relatively small quantity of material. The high proportion of finds from industrial features is explained by the inclusion of the pitch-making vessels recovered from the limekiln in the castle bailey (SOU 29; Pieksma 1986). A significant quantity of pottery was found in layers that are primarily located in the backyard areas of tenement plots.

The high percentage of pottery recovered from pits in Phases 1 and 2 reinforces the view that this was a period of intense occupation in Southampton. With space in the town at a premium, pits were dug in back yard areas for the disposal of domestic rubbish.

Phase 3

Layers produced 62% of the pottery in Phase 3, a pattern of deposition quite different from that for Phases 1 and 2. The most productive layers are those within the castle bailey (SOU 29) and a destruction layer at Upper Bugle Street 3e (SOU 125), but layers relating to this phase are present on every other site. Pits remain a significant source of material, but at a much reduced level. It is likely furthermore, that most of these were dug at an earlier phase as these finds came from secondary fills. Some material came from the closure of structures, but other feature types are poorly represented.

It is clear that at some time in the 14th century pit-digging declined in Southampton. Thereafter, domestic refuse was disposed of in other ways. The high proportion of material from layers however, does not indicate a propensity for spreading, rather than burying rubbish. Most of this pottery came from areas of open, neglected land, where the townsfolk dumped refuse in a desultory rather than an organised fashion. It is likely that at this time most domestic detritus was carted out of the town for disposal elsewhere.

Phase 4

Phase 4 has a different pattern again. Here, a very high proportion of pottery was recovered from structures. These include stone-lined garderobes, like that at Upper Bugle Street 3 (SOU 124) but most of this material came from back-filled cellars such as those at St Michael's House (SOU 122) and especially Quilter's Vault (SOU 128). Pits and layers comprise the next most productive feature groups. No new industrial features are represented and this group comprises mainly the latest fills of the limekiln in the castle bailey (SOU 29).

The deliberate closure of so many domestic structures suggests that the 15th century was a period of renewed activity in Southampton. There seem to have been major alterations within domestic properties. Although the relative paucity of finds from constructional features may indicate that little actual rebuilding was taking place, it should be noted that these have never proved very fruitful.

Conclusion

There is a clear chronological pattern to the deposition of pottery in Southampton, but a few other more general points may also be drawn out here. A comparison of the percentages given in Table 35 for weight and sherd number indicates relative sherd size between types of features. Structures generally show a higher weight than sherd number, suggesting that the vessels deposited were in large fragments. This implies that structures were filled relatively quickly with primary material. Pits show a different, and inconsistent pattern that implies that they were filled with material from a variety of sources, and perhaps over a longer period of time. The pattern for constructional and linear features, and surfaces and layers, is quite different, and indicates a small sherd size. This in turn suggests a high probability of residual or intrusive material being recovered from them.

8

INTERPRETATION

It is evident that the more ephemeral forces that affected past lives, those of a social, economic, political or cultural nature, are reflected in the physical representations of the past that archaeologists record. Medieval pottery is one of those physical representations, and the analysis of it provides a means of understanding those forces that affected the lives of the people who made, distributed and used it (Brown 1988). Previous chapters have classified, quantified and dated the medieval pottery of Southampton, shown how it was made, distributed and used, and described the sites and features from which it was retrieved. The purpose of all this has been to extend our understanding of medieval society; the life of the town and the way of life of its people.

Southampton

The four settlement phases introduced in Chapter 3 were created not only to provide a framework for chronological analysis but also as a means of characterising different periods of activity within Southampton. The archaeological manifestations of each phase were presented in Chapter 7 and it is intended now to show how the ceramic and depositional information for each phase can be related to the settlement history of the town.

The relative quantities of pottery types and the feature distribution for each phase are shown in tables in Chapters 3 and 7. In order to avoid constant reference to those tables, and to illustrate the interpretations made from them, they are presented here in pie-chart form in Figures 42, 43, 44 and 45. The percentages they show are based on the total pottery weight for each phase.

Phase 1 (late-11th to mid-13th centuries)
Settlement in the area that was to become the walled town of Southampton appears to have been unrestricted for at least part of the late Saxon period (Brown 1995). After the Norman Conquest, the construction of both the castle and the Bargate at the north end of the town, and the apparent establishment of a regular street pattern, initiated a more controlled period of development. This was a time of increasing prosperity for Southampton, for the town benefited hugely from enhanced trade links with Normandy. Such prosperity was made manifest, in the late-12th century, through the construction of stone houses, usually with vaulted cellars (Platt 1973). These merchant dwellings are concentrated in the south-west quarter of the town, where most of this assemblage was excavated.

At this period domestic refuse was regularly disposed of in backyard pits, as shown in Figure 42. This may reflect the growing pressure on tenement space in the town during a period when the population was increasing.

Although this was a period of growing commercial prosperity, when trade-links with Normandy had a more secure political foundation, this is not reflected in the pie-chart showing ware origins. North French pottery represents 5% of the total Phase 1 group, Continental imports as a whole about 8%. This is less than half the figure of 17% represented by imported wares in the late Saxon assemblage (Brown 1995). This difference may be explained by the fact that in the post-Conquest period local potters began making forms that previously could only be obtained from more distant English and foreign producers. In the Phase 1 group jugs represent 17% of the total sherd weight, an increase over the late Saxon period, where pitchers comprise 10% of all vessel types. This development may reflect a cultural change following the Norman Conquest, but it is clear that an increased demand for jugs or pitchers was being dealt with more by local potters than through cross-channel trade. Phase 1 may therefore be seen as a period when local pottery production was stimulated, as well as the development of the town. It is clear, however, that in terms of both production and demand, the jar/cooking pot remained

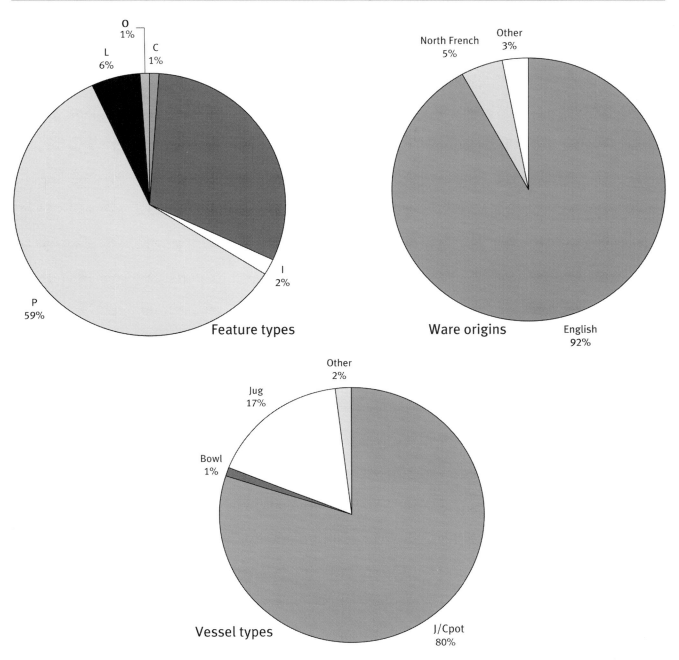

Figure 42. Pie charts showing proportions of Anglo-Norman pottery, for Phase 1, in each feature type, by origin and by vessel type
Key. Feature types: C = Constructional, S = Structures, I = Industrial, P = Pits, L = Layers, O = Others.
Vessel types: J/Cpot = Jar/Cooking pot

the most common ceramic product. Such a pattern harks back to the pre-Conquest period, and demonstrates that although changes were taking effect, the process was slow.

The overall picture for the Anglo-Norman period, therefore, is that far-reaching structural changes within Southampton were taking place more quickly than those that affected ceramic production. An increased demand for jugs may be indicated, but it was up to local producers to respond to it. This suggests that imported pottery at this period did not have any great significance but the importance of the trade links with

Normandy are reflected in the fact that North French pottery accounts for 86% of all the imported material.

Phase 2 (mid-13th to mid-14th centuries)

The profound cultural and political developments that characterise this period, and principally the reigns of Henry III, Edward I and Edward III, allowed ports such as Southampton to benefit from a flourishing economy. The acquisition of Gascony, and the subsequent enormous increase in the importation of Gascon wine, led to a shift in the emphasis of the port's commercial interests. Within the town, a multi-

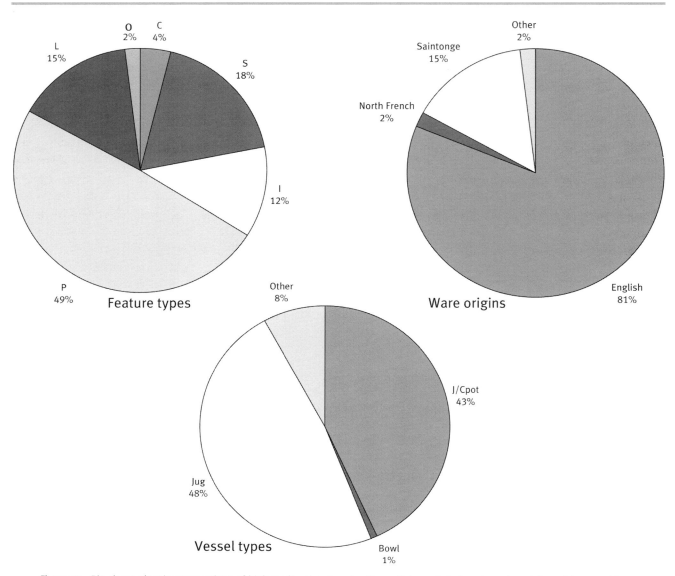

Figure 43. Pie charts showing proportions of high medieval pottery for Phase 2, in each feature type, by origin and by vessel type
Key. Feature types: C = Constructional, S = Structures, I = Industrial, P = Pits, L = Layers, O = Others.
Vessel types: J/Cpot = Jar/Cooking pot

cultural society seems to have flourished, with French and English merchants occupying the fine houses in the south-west quarter (Platt 1973), while by the mid-13th century the castle had been renovated to enhance the capacity of the king's cellars (Oxley 1986), a further indication of the increased intensity of the wine trade.

The pattern of ceramic distribution by feature observed for Phase 1 may also be seen in Phase 2. Pits remain the most productive feature type, suggesting that the town was densely populated, with space at a premium. An increase in the quantity of material recovered from layers may support this, showing that floors and yards were accumulating domestic debris.

This phase is represented by a high quantity of both archaeological deposits and ceramic finds, which indicates a period of increased consumption. The second half of the 13th century also saw English medieval

ceramics reach their creative zenith, especially in the form of the highly decorated jug tradition, most notably characterised nationally by the Scarborough-type Knight Jugs. The potteries local to Southampton at this period were hardly at the forefront of this tradition, but it is notable that both local coarsewares and jar/cooking pots represent just 43% of the Phase 2 sherd weight, nearly half the amount shown for Phase 1. The increased demand for jugs hinted at in Phase 1 becomes fully apparent in Phase 2. The response of local producers, who had by now fully adopted the technological improvements of the fast wheel and the flued kiln, was to meet that demand. This is further emphasised by the setting up of a pottery-making site on High Street (SOU 105), which hints at the entrepreneurial opportunities Southampton must have offered. There is also a significant increase in the quantity of Continental imports, which represent 19% of the total sherd weight. This came almost entirely from the Saintonge, reflecting the importance of the Gascon wine trade. Among the imported vessels were types not produced locally, including ceramic mortars and large pégaux, which perhaps answered a need not met locally. It is clear however that the most commonly imported vessel type at this period was the jug, a type that was available in large quantities from local potters. It is easy to see why Saintonge jugs were imported, for they seem to us to be finer and more attractive than most local wares, but it is probable that they did not represent an important commercial commodity for it surely would have been a relatively simple matter to import them in much larger quantities and also to

re-distribute them inland. It is apparent that pottery at this period, although consumed in large quantities, was not regarded as a very high class, or in other words expensive or profitable, commodity.

Phase 3 (mid-14th to early 15th centuries)
The busy society suggested from the archaeology and pottery of Phase 2 fell into recession in the late-14th century due, to put it simply, to the lasting effects of the Hundred Years' War and the Black Death. One effect of war was the disruption of trade with France and it probably at least halved imports of Gascon wine (Falkus and Gillingham 1981, 69). In 1338 Southampton fell prey to a French-instigated attack that left the town sacked, demoralised and probably empty of the French

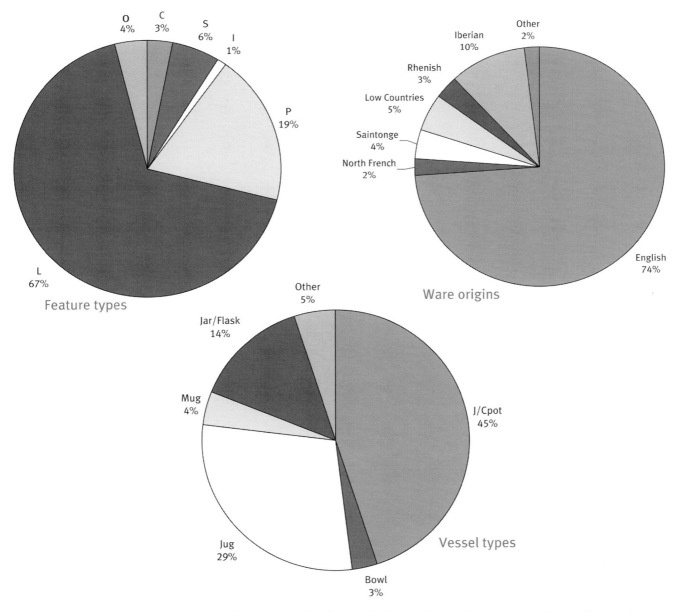

Figure 44. Pie charts showing proportions of high to late medieval pottery for Phase 3, in each feature type, by origin and by vessel type
Key. Feature types: C = Constructional, S = Structures, I = Industrial, P = Pits, L = Layers, O = Others.
Vessel types: J/Cpot = Jar/Cooking pot

merchants who had settled there. This event prompted the construction of a complete circuit of the town wall, a long and expensive process that almost bankrupted the town (Platt 1973).

Archaeologically, the depressed condition of South-ampton is reflected in the paucity of significant deposits. Pits were not being dug as frequently as they had been, reflecting both an awareness of the hygienic conse-quences of this practice and a decline in competition for space. During this period there was less domestic development and open areas of ground, such as the castle bailey were utilised as refuse dumps. A house excavated at Upper Bugle Street site 3e (SOU 125) had

burned down, possibly in the 1338 raid, and was not rebuilt until the late-15th century. The site was left abandoned and, inevitably, quantities of rubbish accu-mulated there. The same phenomenon has been noted in a site excavated at the Woollen Hall (SOU 393) on Castle Way in 1989 (White, unpublished site archive). The fact that 67% of the pottery in Phase 3 came from site layers emphasises the differences between this period and Phases 1 and 2. Pits are the second most productive feature type, but it is likely that many of those features were not dug during this period, and later fills are represented in this phase.

Evidence of the decline in trade with France may

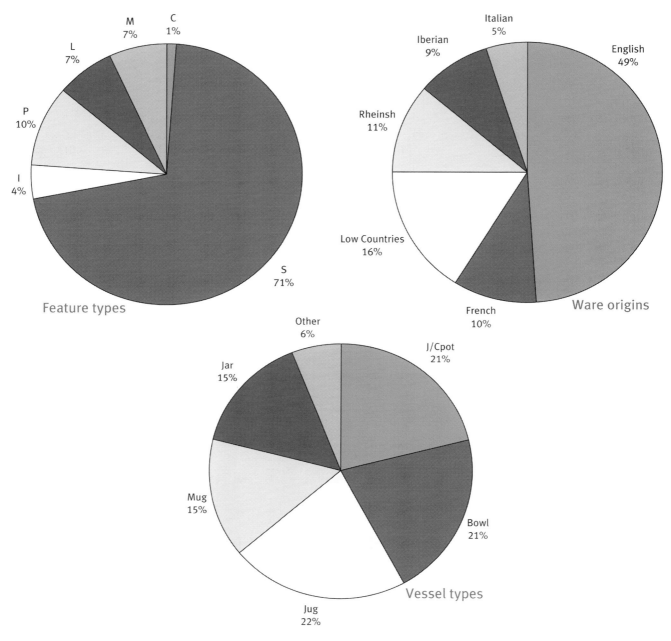

Figure 45. Pie charts showing proportions of late medieval pottery for Phase 4, in each feature type, by origin and by vessel type
Key. Feature types: C = Constructional, S = Structures, I = Industrial, P = Pits, L = Layers, O = Others.
Vessel types: J/Cpot = Jar/Cooking pot

be found in the hugely decreased amounts of Saintonge pottery from deposits dated to the mid-14th century or later. French wares represent a smaller proportion of all the Continental imports than ever before. Iberian wares are the most common imported type, mainly Seville Coarsewares and Micaceous Redwares and this perhaps indicates 14th-century origins for the trade with Spain and Portugal and suggests a source for the revival of Southampton's economic fortunes.

Phase 4 (c 1450 to 1550)

Phase 4 is the period that represents the revival in economic fortunes. Late medieval Southampton may never have been destined to achieve the levels of prosperity seen in the 12th and 13th centuries but the town did at least recover from intervening disasters (Platt 1973). French merchants did not return to settle in the same numbers, and a final blow to England's trade with Gascony was dealt by its loss to France in 1453. Southampton's fortunes were revived primarily by trade with the Mediterranean. Italian traders moved into the town, often representing large familial concerns with offices in London, as well as Italy. If Southampton had been cosmopolitan in the late-13th century, it must have been even more so now. A period of rebuilding ensued, evidenced by the redevelopment of the site at Upper Bugle Street 3e (SOU 125).

Phase 4 has a distinctive archaeological character that makes it quite different from any preceding period. The use of pits for the disposal of rubbish appears to have been rare, one reason for the good survival of Phase 2 features. Most of the pottery in Phase 4 has been recovered from deposits that mark the closure of structures, mainly garderobes and cellars. This occurs at St Michael's House (SOU 122), Upper Bugle Street 3 (SOU 124, Group 4 Chapter 3) and Quilter's Vault (SOU 128). It has also been observed in recent excavations at the Woollen Hall (SOU 393). All these deposits contain finds of the highest quality, not only exotic pottery but also fine vessels of Venetian glass. One can only guess at the activities represented by these groups (see below p 162).

Phase 4 is characterised by a far more even distribution of pottery types. Locally-produced pottery represents the most common single production area, but imports comprise over half the total sherd weight. This is a reflection of the fact that imported vessel types were not available from local potters and the utilitarian quality of all the local products meant that consumers had to go elsewhere for decorative ceramics. The contrasts between the 13th-century local jugs and those of the Saintonge were relatively slight, and this is reflected in their relative quantities. The contrasts between local pottery of the 15th century and imported types are far greater, and this is shown in the increased range and quantities of imported material. This point is further illustrated by examining the quantities of vessel types represented. Jar/cooking pots, bowls and jugs were the principal forms produced locally. They were also all imported: cooking pots from the Low Countries; bowls from France, the Low Countries, Spain and Italy; jugs principally from France and Italy. A variety of types are included here, from the utilitarian Normandy Stoneware and Low Countries Redware, to the colourful Spanish and Italian Tin-glazed wares, but they all seem to have been answering a demand that was not being met by local suppliers. This point can be even more clearly put when one considers that all mugs and cups were imported, and this includes the non-local Tudor Green types (which represent less than one percent of the total sherd weight in Phase 4). Jars and flasks are nearly all imported types, but this is less significant as in this case it was probably their contents that were being traded.

Profound cultural changes are represented in Phase 4. Although there seems to have been an equal demand for ceramics in Phase 2, this mainly was confined to a fairly narrow range of vessel types, jar/cooking pots and jugs. In Phase 4 a notable increase in the available range of wares and vessels, and in their consumption, may be observed. This may be related to the composition of Southampton's 15th-century society.

Domestic context

The Oak Book, a compilation of bylaws and regulations, records 'that no butcher or cook throw into the street any filth or other matter whereby the town or the street become more dirty, filthy, or corrupt; and if any one do this, and be attainted, he shall pay a fine of twelve pence' also 'No man shall have any pigs going about in the street, or have before his door, or in the street, muck or dung beyond two nights ... and he who shall have acted contrary to this statute shall be grievously fined.' (Studer 1910).

These records provide a background for any ceramic-based interpretations of medieval household management. It is clear that rubbish was often dumped in the street, but given the risk of fines, it is easy to see why back yard pits were so common. Here is a social context for the pattern of ceramic recovery seen in most urban tenement excavations. A lot of pottery comes from pits, but it is certain that what is found in these represents a fraction of the total consumption of a medieval household. Much will have been carried away, perhaps before lying in the street for two nights.

Studying the quantities of pottery found in different types of deposits adds more substance to this discussion. Thirty percent of this assemblage came from pits. The nature of the associated finds, with significant amounts of food waste such as bone and shell, show that these were, or became, domestic rubbish pits, and may have been constructed specifically for the management of waste. It is however, clear that householders would utilise any source available in disposing of refuse. The castle ditch was filled with rubbish from adjacent houses, and the castle bailey became a notorious dumping ground in the 15th century (Oxley 1986). The high proportion of pottery from general site layers shows that any area left open for some time would quickly become a target for people's rubbish. Indeed, the same behaviour can be observed in Southampton today. The pottery found associated with surfaces, mainly floor layers, can also be regarded as household waste, but this was presumably accidentally left behind. This point is reinforced by the fact that the average sherd weight for this material, along with that from construction features and layers, is six grams below the average seventeen grams that is achieved in features such as pits, limekilns and the castle ditch. There are suggestions here of the extent to which floor surfaces were maintained and kept clean.

The phenomenon observed in Phase 4 of closing garderobes and cellars suggests a different domestic event. The nature of the fills in these structures, and the cohesion of their artefact groups, suggests that each was closed in a single operation. The latrine at Castle Hall was filled in as part of structural alterations (Oxley 1986), and that may have been the reason for closing the other features. It is less easy to identify the source of the finds in these deposits. It has been suggested that the material in the Castle Hall garderobe may have come from a previous dump (Brown 1986), and this may also have been the case at Bull Hall, where ceramic cross-fits with other features have been found (see above p 102). This seems less likely for the late medieval features at SOU 122, St Michael's House, Upper Bugle Street, SOU124 and Quilter's Vault, SOU

128, where there was an enormous amount of pottery, along with other finds, especially glass, of high quality. The fact that sherds are missing from nearly every vessel supports the conclusion that whole pots were not deposited and this may indicate the exploitation of an existing dump of rubbish although that also might have accumulated rapidly. The number of similar deposits suggests that the closure of cellars and associated structures seems also to have been a common event in the late-15th century. Parallels have been found elsewhere in Southampton at the Woollen Hall (SOU 107 and SOU 393) and also at Barking Abbey, London (Jennings, forthcoming). The reasons for this spate of building alterations in the late medieval period are unclear, but there is no doubt that very high class goods were being disposed of. These may be associated with particular people or events, but very close dating is unachievable, and documentary evidence as yet unhelpful. At Acton Court, a large deposit of ceramics and other finds have been identified as the debris from entertaining Henry VIII (Courtney, *pers comm*, Vince and Bell 1992). A similar case cannot be made here, yet the Acton Court finds should encourage the search for less obvious reasons for this phenomenon. It is possible, for example that these finds represent possessions or middens left behind by former occupants and dumped by new tenants who were keen to rebuild.

One problem arising from dealing primarily with material deposited in pits or closed structures is that the fills represent their ultimate use. It is not known whether backyard rubbish pits were filled in once, or whether they were emptied out regularly before final closure. It is interesting to observe the frequency of inter-cutting among the sequence of pits at Westgate Street (SOU 25, Chapter 3, Group 3). There are two ways of interpreting this phenomenon. Firstly, it is possible that they inter-cut because when subsequent pits were dug nobody knew the position of previous features. This suggests that the occupants, or the people who dug pits for them, were different from those responsible for the earlier ones and/or that there was no trace of the pits that were cut into. Secondly, it is possible that the originators of the later pits were aware of the position of earlier diggings. If this is so then it was either because they were responsible for those as well, or because there was visible evidence of their location. It is hard to imagine anybody deliberately digging a new pit into an old one, if only because the sides of the new one would surely not be very stable. It is also hard, given the relatively narrow range of dates provided by the ceramic evidence, to believe that no trace of previous pits survived. The settling of pit fills usually takes place over a long period of time. One must conclude therefore that pits were deliberately inter-cut. This may have been due to lack of space. Also the frequency of inter-cutting, among features that can all be dated to a single phase, also suggests that when rubbish pits were dug they were filled in relatively quickly. The instability of the sides comprised of earlier pit fills may also be a factor here. Features that represent structures, such as cellars, garderobes or wells, were obviously originally created for specific, and

one must suppose less temporary, purposes and were thus kept free of detritus. Yet ultimately they became filled with rubbish and in this sense their fills can be compared to those of the backyard pits, although when in use these features were quite different. Both types of feature seem to have been filled rapidly, presumably in order to close them deliberately and finally. The fact that this was regularly achieved is surely an indication of the rate of consumption of household goods, or at least the extent of ownership of them. This is the subject of the next section in this chapter.

Economic context

In theory, the study of the waste from particular households should provide some understanding of the amounts of pottery consumed therein, leading to an appreciation of economic status. Only a small part of the overall back yard area of any dwelling has been investigated, however, so most discussion based on these assemblages is in some cases somewhat tentative. Tables 36, 37 and 38 present the relative quantities of pottery in each ceramic phase by origin and function. Vessels have been classified into one of five functional groups. Vessels used in the kitchen, a general term that includes sculleries etc, are those utilised in the storage, preparation and cooking of food or liquids, mainly jar/cooking pots, bowls and other forms such as

dripping pans. All jugs have been classified as table vessels although it is necessary to recognise that they may have been, in the same way as jars, multi-purpose vessels used for carrying a variety of liquids such as water, milk, ale, wine and probably also urine, as well as more solid substances. Also included among the tableware are mugs, in earthenware and stoneware, highly decorated bowls, such as Iberian and Italian tin-glazed types, chafing dishes and other specialised forms including the highly decorated Saintonge mortars, which are interpreted as display objects. Containers include storage and/or transport vessels such as olive jars, flasks and albarelli. The group of vessels used in heating and lighting includes curfews and lamps. The

Table 36. Weights of Anglo-Norman pottery in Phase 1 contexts, by vessel function and origin of each site

Site	Function	English	North French	Saintonge	Low Countries	Rhenish
SOU 25	Kitchen	7729				
Bull Hall	Table	926	1213		4	
	Unidentifiable	1324	425			
SOU 105	Kitchen	5369				
	Table	488	408		27	
	Heat/Light	12				
	Unidentifiable	1890	219			
SOU 110	Kitchen	9470				21
West Hall	Table	1661	1348	21	50	
	Heat/Light	34				
	Unidentifiable	1929	239			40
SOU 122	Kitchen	2430				
	Table	103	746			
	Unidentifiable	140	16			
SOU 124	Kitchen	13070				
	Table	188	364		16	
	Heat/Light	15				
	Unidentifiable	1165	251			3
SOU 125	Kitchen	23005				
	Table	2944	444		15	
	Heat/Light	66				
	Unidentifiable	5124	379			5
Castle	Kitchen	19244	296			
	Table	2820	574	82	20	
	Unidentifiable	1458	326			263

Table 37. Weights of high medieval pottery in Phase 2 contexts, by vessel function and origin for each site

Site	Function	English	North French	Saintonge	Misc.	French	Low Countries	Rhenish
SOU 25	Kitchen	14527	48		56			
Bull Hall	Table	15574	339	14751	823	749		
	Heat/Light	3621						
	Unidentifiable	4573	73	327	30			
SOU 105	Kitchen	14603						
	Table	7984	55	2376				
	Storage	245			5			
	Unidentifiable	14762	26	1114	44			
SOU 110	Kitchen	897						
West Hall	Table	1128	1588	711	39			
	Storage	46						
	Heat/Light	357						
	Unidentifiable	1653	4	124	75			
SOU 122	Kitchen	4064						
	Table	18186	234	7838			12	24
	Heat/Light	450						
	Unidentifiable	4040		332	54		27	
SOU 124	Kitchen	3601						
	Table	3973	23	814				
	Storage	14						
	Heat/Light	187						
	Unidentifiable	4439	54	335	83			
SOU 125	Kitchen	16058						
	Table	4530	267	2255	10			124
	Heat/Light	156						
	Unidentifiable	6505	17	477				
Castle	Kitchen	16054						
	Table	2135	22	187				
	Unidentifiable	3063	10	110	19			

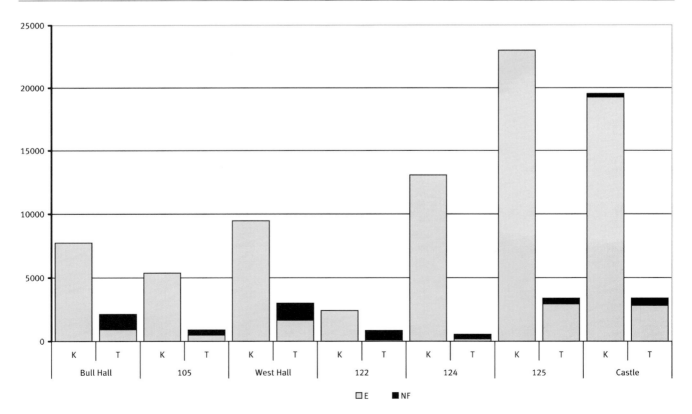

Figure 46. Stacked bar charts showing relative weights of English and imported pottery of different functional types in the Anglo-Norman period. E = English; NF = North French.

Key to vessel function codes: K = Kitchenware; T = Tableware; O = Other; C = Container

fifth group is comprised of sherds for which no function can be identified, although given the increased experience acquired by the author since sorting this assemblage, some pieces probably could be fitted into one of the other categories. A simplified version of the same data, without the unidentifiable material and in some instances grouping different origins together, is presented in graph form in Figures 46, 47 and 48.

An attempt has been made to get beyond the strictures of excavated areas and relate these data to specific properties or dwellings. SOU 25 is therefore referred to as Bull Hall, while SOU 110 is identified as West Hall. These, regrettably, are the only individual tenements that can be so named and SOU numbers are used for sites 105, 122, 124, 125 and 128. All of site 29 and parts of site 123 have been combined to form a single group that represents the castle. The non-castle material from SOU 123 has not been included in this analysis as it is unclear how it might relate to any property or properties.

The Anglo-Norman period

Table 36 and Figure 46 confirm what has previously been established, that English pottery was commonly used throughout the town, most of the imported material came from northern France in the form of jugs, and tableware comprised a relatively low proportion of the ceramic assemblage. The relatively low quantities of tableware might suggest that these products were used more conservatively, while kitchenware was consumed at a greater rate. This is perhaps to be expected, as most of the locally-produced jar forms are sooted at the base, which confirms their principal use as cooking pots. Imported jars, although rare, may for the same reason also be characterised as cooking pots. It may be supposed that earthenware cooking pots, subjected to heat and not easy to clean, had a shorter life than jugs, some of which might have been used at table only on special occasions. The relative quantities of the pottery from each dwelling are not significant, as they are more a reflection of the survival of Anglo-Norman deposits than an indication of the amount of pottery consumed during this period. It is likely that pottery was consumed at a relatively high rate, however, suggesting a comparable degree of prosperity amongst the inhabitants of these places. Only at SOU 124 is there a suggestion that more kitchen pottery than tableware was consumed and this might suggest a more lowly economic status. This may be undermined, however, by the presence of North French and

Table 38. Weights of late medieval pottery in Phase 4 contexts, by vessel function and origin for each site

Site	Function	English	French	Low Countries	Rhenish	Iberian	Italian
SOU 25	Kitchen	537		135			
Bull Hall	Table	12	4	227	86	96	33
	Transport					630	
	Unidentifiable	1100	27	217	22	231	
SOU 105	Kitchen	1566		513			
	Table	179	1270	497	953	30	85
	Transport			24		1879	
	Unidentifiable	4802	1319	642	79	686	11
SOU 110	Kitchen	684		2732			
West Hall	Table	4		64	339	30	19
	Transport			44		1188	50
	Unidentifiable	472	156	646	11	57	
SOU 122	Kitchen	3258		4660			
	Table	145	1580	238	2321	811	2494
	Transport/Store	211	476	366		2407	134
	Unidentifiable	1499	173	701	54	44	11
SOU 124	Kitchen	9427		2697			
	Table	280	512	742	4183	87	3420
	Transport		203	214		519	158
	Unidentifiable	1380	433	457	22		427
SOU 125	Kitchen	2559		562			
	Table	117	3		1126	45	89
	Transport/Store	23				716	
	Unidentifiable	3590	224	243	53	248	140
SOU 128	Kitchen	21738		7054		275	
Quilter's Vault	Table	381	7386	2162	11098	2464	1756
	Transport		4665	68		6969	449
	Unidentifiable	17280	978	2298	40	496	254

Andenne-type jugs. The overall picture is that in this period pottery is not a reliable indicator of economic status, perhaps because it did not play a very significant role in domestic material culture.

The high medieval period

Table 37 and Figure 47 offer a picture distinctly different to the Anglo-Norman period. There is more pottery, a larger proportion of it is imported and tableware is much more prominent. The yard area excavated at Bull Hall provides the best evidence for an analysis of the character of consumption at a single dwelling.

Trench A2 at SOU 25 revealed a dense concentration of pits that have been phased to the high medieval period and although they cannot be related to a single period of tenancy, the contents of these features can be associated with the 13th- and 14th-century occupation of Bull Hall. It is assumed that each of these pits was filled over a relatively short period of time. Cross-fits between a number of these features suggest that some were open simultaneously, and although some of those may result from the inter-cutting of pits, cross-fits between different fills of the same feature have also been noted (see above). Kitchen pots comprise 29% of the total sherd weight of identifiable vessel types, tableware 64% and lamps and curfews 7%. If table pottery was broken more frequently than kitchenware then it must have been more often in use. Jugs were not of course employed exclusively at the table, and this evidence suggests perhaps that they had a greater variety of functions than the jar/cooking pot. Highly decorated jugs, and imported types including Saintonge wares, figure as much in this group as in any other, and were obviously discarded regularly. It is apparent from this evidence that there was a consistently high turnover of all types of vessel, and few forms of pottery were very highly valued in the wealthy medieval household.

Table 37 suggests that the dwelling at SOU 122, and perhaps West Hall, and SOU 124, where the assemblages are much smaller, were at an equivalent level to Bull Hall in terms of the consumption of tableware. This is not true of SOU 105 or 125, where kitchenware is more prominent. This might simply indicate, however, that the deposits excavated were specifically used for kitchen waste, but the inclusion of some tableware counts against that interpretation. The castle group shows that the pottery used there was almost entirely English and that tableware was not consumed at a great rate. This might suggest that the Constable, although engaged in mercantile activity on behalf of

the king, may have had less use for imported or highly decorated tableware.

The overall picture for the high medieval period is of high rates of consumption of both kitchen and table pottery, suggesting prosperity and confidence.

The late medieval period

The large groups of pottery at SOU 122, 124 and 128, characterise this period and indicate a high degree of ceramic consumption by wealthy and extravagant individuals. The finds from Bull Hall, SOU 105, West Hall, and SOU 125 are all comparatively small. Bull Hall and West Hall were both occupied by Italians in the 15th century (see below) but this is scarcely reflected in the pottery. All four of these sites, however, match, in composition if not in quantity, the larger assemblages from the other dwellings and may be understood as typical late medieval assemblages. The late medieval assemblage from the castle has been interpreted as representing town rubbish and therefore is not included here because it will not relate to the character of ceramic consumption within the castle.

The three larger groups cannot be distinguished in terms of the origins or the function of pottery. Kitchen vessels are best represented at all of them, with tableware the next most common, then containers. These groups clearly represent the deliberate closure of stone-lined features and if the example of the castle garderobe is anything to go by (Brown 1986), secondary sources may well have been utilised (see preceding section, above). If pre-existing dumps of rubbish were exploited, then those dumps probably accumulated quickly, which suggests that these groups represent possibly single events, of either use or discard. If the former is true, then there is evidence here of lavish, highly visible consumption of high quality artefacts, including glass. If the latter is the case, then some sort of domestic clearance is suggested. Either way, it is possible to characterise these dwellings as places occupied by wealthy individuals who required large quantities of tableware, quite possibly to satisfy a typically late medieval penchant for entertaining and showing off.

If little concerning the actual rate of usage of pottery can be understood from this discussion, something of the value placed on it can. It is clear that status, or class can be understood from pottery analysis. The mere presence, however, of so-called 'luxury' or 'high class' ceramics, most often identified with Continental fine ware, is not sufficient in a port where they must have been relatively commonplace. The most astonishing aspect of the large deposits found at SOU

124 and 128 is the large quantity of material, not their specific components. These groups represent visible consumption on a grand scale, which is a reliable indicator of high status.

Identity

Pottery has long been considered a useful cultural indicator because it may be seen to reflect the background of the people who made and used it: witness Cunliffe's 'style-zones' (Cunliffe 1974, 129–57). A variety of pottery-producing areas and countries are represented in this assemblage and it may be that the preferences of individual residents reflect their own origins. It should therefore be, on the face of it, a relatively straightforward matter to associate different types of pottery from a consumer-site with people of different cultures. One might, for instance, expect the waste from an Italian household to include a high proportion of Italian pottery. Such an assumption lacks sensitivity however, towards both the nature of the archaeological record and the people who inhabited past societies and this issue will be examined for each ceramic period. The data used in the previous discussion, and set out in Tables 35, 36 and 37, and Figures 46, 47, and 48 serve also to inform this analysis.

The Anglo-Norman period

The purpose is to allow comparison of the ceramics from each dwelling in an attempt to characterise the cultural affinity of particular residents, but most sites exhibit a similar pattern. Nearly all the kitchenware is English in origin, which really means locally-produced, with exceptions at West Hall, and the castle. Most north French pottery took the form of tableware, although English jugs are usually more or less equally prominent. In the search for ethnic identities it seems, for several reasons, that tableware is a more promising indicator. It is pottery that is apparently designed for display during dining and as such will make more clear the cultural affinity of the householder, and it has been seen that there was regular, if low scale, importation of jugs from the Continent. If one accepts that a high proportion of North French tableware indicates a household with Norman or, at least Anglo-French origins it is possible to identify Bull Hall, West Hall and sites 122 and 124 as potentially the homes of merchants whose origins lay on the other side of the English Channel. The assemblage at SOU 125 does not conform to that pattern as there are higher quantities of English jugs, in one of the largest groups of tableware, and therefore an English resident is suggested. At SOU 105 the evidence is inconclusive. At most of these sites

pottery from the Low Countries or the Rhineland is also present. This perhaps testifies to the extent of Southampton's trading interests but it scarcely allows the identification of occupants who originated from the Low Countries. This pottery might, however, indicate the presence of merchants, for whom imported pottery was perhaps more readily available.

As with pottery, the quality of the documentary evidence improves through time and only one tenement history dating from the Anglo-Norman period is relevant here. West Hall, SOU 110, was built in the 12th century by the influential Gervaise le Riche (Platt 1973) and the large amount of Anglo-Norman pottery from this site may therefore be associated with the period of his occupation. Most of the pottery came from a large pit subsequently, and frequently, floored over (see above p 000), which must have been in the yard of the original building. This group mainly comprises Anglo-Norman coarsewares, but there are several imported vessels, with Andenne-type ware represented among the usual north French types. Bull Hall, SOU 25, was probably built by Thomas de Bulehouse in the early-13th century (Platt 1973, 267) and it is tempting to associate some of the Anglo-Norman material with his occupancy.

It is necessary for these dwellings to be placed into some historical context but during this period that is very difficult. The Domesday Book records the post-Conquest settlement of 65 Frenchmen and 31 Englishmen in Southampton. This certainly indicates a royal desire to build up the port and also makes valid the quest for archaeological evidence for French residents. Documents relating to specific tenements in the immediate post-Conquest period are, sadly, very rare and there is nothing that can underwrite any interpretations of the archaeological evidence. The castle, however, is surely the one site where occupation by Normans is a certainty, yet the pottery does not obviously reflect this; less than 5% of all the pottery, by weight, is of Norman origin. This is the only site, however, to produce North French kitchenware and on that basis it is possible to characterise this assemblage as originating from Norman occupants. This may affect the interpretations of the other groups however, for the unreliability of the ceramic evidence is clearly demonstrated. What is shown in the quantities laid

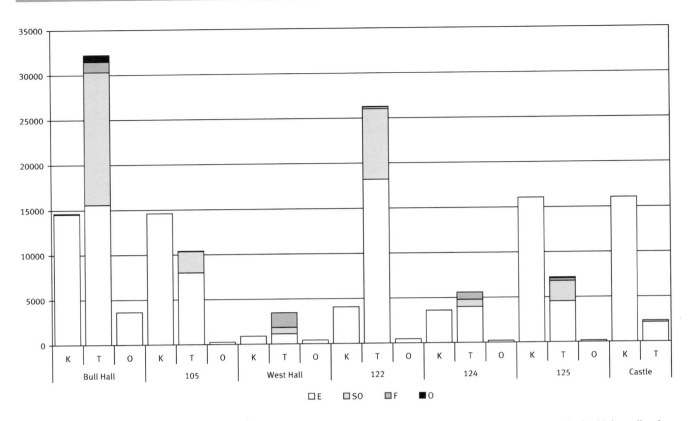

Figure 47. Stacked bar charts showing relative weights of English and imported pottery of different functional types in the high medieval period. E = English; SO = Saintonge; F = Other French; O = Other

out in Table 36 and illustrated in Figure 46, is that association of ceramic origin with cultural affinity is no simple exercise. There may be any number of alternative explanations for the high proportion of North French tablewares at, for instance SOU 122. It may be, for example, that the English occupants bought mainly Norman tableware in an attempt to align themselves, either socially, economically or politically, with those 65 French settlers and the reverse may also be true at SOU 125. There is also the factor of ceramic survival, for the pits at SOU 122 do not represent all the rubbish deposits made there during either the Anglo-Norman period, or the occupancy of a single household. That group gives only a partial picture, but even with all those provisos it must be recognised that it is at present the only evidence available to us, and the patterns shown by the data are there to be interpreted. More importantly, the evidence from the castle demonstrates the need for in-depth comparison and that must be done across periods as well as sites.

The high medieval period
Bull Hall, SOU 25, was owned in the high medieval period by Thomas le Halveknight, a wealthy English merchant and burgess who also owned West Hall (Platt 1973). The latter tenement was his *capital messuage* and

most likely where he actually lived and Bull Hall would therefore have been rented out, probably to a fellow merchant. The high medieval pottery from Bull Hall comprises, by weight, 69% English wares and 27% Saintonge types with other French and also Low Countries products present in much smaller quantities. All of the vessels related to heating or lighting are local in origin as is nearly all the kitchenware. Fifty-two percent of the tableware is Continental in origin. At West Hall a much smaller group of high medieval pottery was recovered and 62% of it is English in origin, a figure that includes all the kitchenware and 32% of the tableware. The latter quantity is perhaps distorted by the presence of a single, almost complete, highly decorated North French zoomorphic jug (189) and if it were possible to give an accurate vessel count then English jugs would comprise a much larger percentage of the tableware. The sample from SOU 105 has been reduced by the exclusion of the kiln waste, which, it is assumed, was not used in domestic activities. Documentary evidence for SOU 122 does not reveal the nature of the building or its inhabitants. The usual mix of vessel types is present however, in a large assemblage. All the kitchenware and heating/lighting pottery is English in origin, as is 69% of the tableware, although a wide variety of Continental types, including North French,

Saintonge, Rhenish and Iberian products are present. The high medieval pottery from SOU 124 is principally English, with 17% of the tableware originating from France. At SOU 125, also lacking good documentary evidence, a similar pattern may be observed. Once again, all the kitchenware and heating and lighting pottery is English, as is 63% of the tableware. Among the tableware, Saintonge products are the most common Continental type but there are also vessels from elsewhere in France, together with Iberian types. The material from Southampton Castle comes mainly from features in the bailey (SOU 29), including a back-filled limekiln. Here, imported wares are very rare and account for just 1.5% of the whole assemblage, including unidentifiable vessels.

It is possible, from these figures, to identify Bull Hall as the dwelling most likely to have been the home of a merchant who originated from what is now mainland France. Gascony was, at this period, governed from England but cultural differences were doubtless visible then and it is simpler now to distinguish people as English or French rather than group them together as Anglo-French. West Hall produced a similar percentage of French pottery but from a much smaller group. These two houses were the largest of the domestic sites presented here and it might reasonably be expected that the rubbish associated with wealthy merchants should include high quantities of highly decorated imports. This is certainly true at Bull Hall, perhaps less so at West Hall and it may be worth noting that West Hall is the likely home of the Englishman, Thomas le Halveknight, while Bull Hall was occupied by unknown tenants that may now be identified as French. That probability is enhanced by the fact that the Bull Hall assemblage is the only one that includes imported high medieval kitchenware, and it has also produced the only sherd of Céramique Onctueuse yet found in Southampton. The more modest houses at SOU 122, 124 and 125 both produced groups that are composed mainly of English wares. The presence of more obviously 'exotic' types, in the form of Iberian tableware suggests eclecticism, but their quantities are hardly sufficient to allow the suggestion that the householders were anything other than English. The variety among the tableware more probably indicates that they were merchants, but this may already be concluded from the location of the houses in the wealthy south-western quarter of Southampton. It has already been established that the house at SOU 105, situated close to a pottery kiln, was probably not of the highest order, but 23% of the tableware came from

France and tableware itself comprises 41% of the identifiable vessel types. This suggests a dwelling occupied by an individual with similar pretensions to his or her fellows on the other side of town. This is, therefore, likely to be the home of a merchant. The group from the castle seems to reinforce the interpretation of it as a Royal holding occupied at this period by a Constable who, although engaged in mercantile activity on behalf of the king, may have had less use for imported or highly decorated tableware. This is not an entirely satisfactory interpretation because the source of the pottery, from layers and back-filled features in the bailey, is not comparable with the deliberately dug back-yard rubbish pits that produced the other groups. Furthermore, the castle itself had perhaps a greater number of inhabitants, in the form of a garrison, than the town-houses, as well as a constant flow of workmen and labourers (as evidenced by the limekiln), all of whom might have used or brought in pottery of their own. These reservations notwithstanding, the impression given by the castle group is of a very English population and that is really no surprise.

The overall interpretation of the high medieval period, on the basis of this evidence, is apparently more predictable than it is for the Anglo-Norman. The pottery reflects a merchant society where French and English people had the same opportunities and shared similar cultural and social values. Saintonge pottery occurs on every site at this period and it is comparable with local wares in terms of its frequency. Similarly, the differences between French and English merchants may not have been so clear-cut as those we might envisage for the Normans and English of the twelfth century. It is less easy, for this reason, to look for 'incomers'. The analysis of ceramics remains useful however, for although the relative proportions of English and French wares have altered, the most commonly imported class of pottery was tableware, just as it was in the Anglo-Norman period. Once again, it is the presence of imported kitchenware that increases the likelihood that an assemblage might be associated with a foreign merchant

The late medieval period

Table 38 shows the quantities, by weight, of each vessel category by country of origin for each dwelling, and this is also shown, simplified, in graph form as Figure 48. The late medieval assemblage from Bull Hall is too small to inform this analysis, although the full range of ware types is represented. The Southampton Terrier, compiled in 1454, identifies Bull Hall as the capital

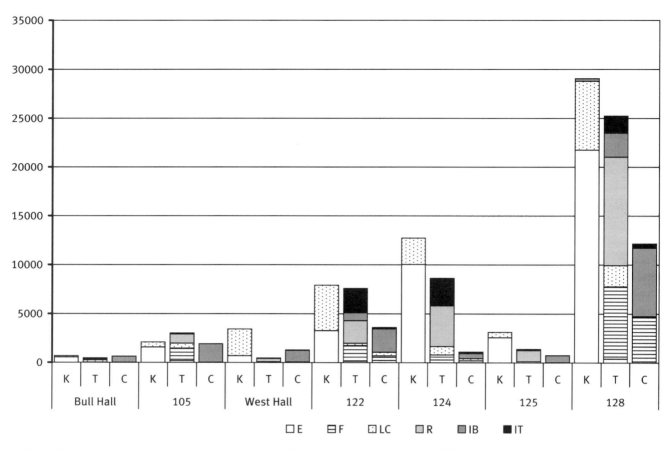

Figure 48. Stacked bar charts showing relative weights of English and imported pottery of different functional types in the late medieval period. E = English; F = French; LC = Low Countries; R = Rhenish; IB = Iberian; IT = Italian

tenement of John Serle, occupied by Galicius de Negro, a Genoese merchant (Burgess 1976, 99). The house remained in the ownership of the Serle family until at least 1507 (*ibid*), and may well have been leased to various other merchants. The size of this group is insufficient, unfortunately, to provide any insight into the ceramic preferences of those occupants. The house at SOU 105, where stone footings were uncovered in the later phases, also produced a relatively small assemblage that consists mainly of tableware, of which the largest percentage is French, which does not necessarily reflect the origins of the occupant. West Hall was still a major tenement at this period. In 1429 the property was leased to a Florentine merchant, Paolo Morelli (Platt 1973), and in 1454, when the Southampton terrier was compiled, the house was occupied by a Florentine, Angelo Aldebrandi (Burgess 1976, 84). It was subsequently taken over by the Genoese Marini family (Platt 1973). For most of the 15th century, therefore, West Hall was occupied by Italians, but this is not reflected in the ceramic record, which includes just two sherds of Italian pottery. Kitchenware is the most common type and most of that is of Low Countries origin. There is also a high percentage of

Iberian transportation vessels, primarily olive jars from Seville. These factors indicate that the late medieval group excavated at SOU110 represents kitchen waste. It is also a relatively small assemblage.

SOU 122 produced a large late medieval group from a range of features that included a back-filled cellar. The terrier of 1454 lists only English occupants within the dwellings that this site might represent (Burgess 1976, 105) but much of the pottery is probably later in date. This is a relatively large assemblage with a high proportion of Low Countries kitchenware.

At SOU 124, on Simnel Street, the large group of material from a stone-lined garderobe may be associated with the occupancy of Roger Machado between 1486 and 1497. That group is the only element of the late medieval material from SOU 124 included in this analysis. Roger Machado was a courtier to Henry VII and served as his ambassador in the courts of France, Naples and Spain. He was rewarded with the title Richmond herald and also with a grant to import Gascon wines free of duty, and this is perhaps one reason why he held a property in Southampton. The garderobe deposit includes some fine Venetian glass, which certainly testifies to Roger's wealth. Among the ceramics are Italian maiolicas, which comprise 16% by weight of all the pottery, a figure that is relatively high. The size of the group and the quantity of tableware, reflect the status and tastes of the occupant but, once again, not his cultural background. In fact Machado's cultural background is also confused. He was employed by the king as a French-speaker and it is suggested that he originated from Brittany but his travels made him apparently multi-national.

SOU 125 produced a small late medieval assemblage presumably associated with the re-development of the site after the previous dwelling was destroyed. The 1454 Terrier identifies a vacant plot (455), belonging to John Fifmark (*ibid*, 121), that may be the location of the excavation, but this does not help identify the later occupant of the site. The pottery includes mainly English kitchen vessels and Rhenish tablewares.

In the Terrier of 1454 the site at Quilter's Vault, SOU 128, was identified as the home of Philip Larcarius (Burgess 1976, 83), who was probably an Italian or perhaps a Spanish merchant, but the large group of pottery recovered from a stone-lined feature on this tenement was probably related to a later occupant of the house as it dates to around 1500. English wares comprise 45% by weight of the total assemblage. French pottery comprises 27% of the imported wares, 24% is from the Low Countries, Rhenish wares are at 23%, Iberian wares 21% and 5% is Italian. These figures are of little use in establishing cultural affinity although they may show that trade with North Sea, Channel and Mediterranean ports was carried out an equal level. The sheer quantity of pottery in this group, nearly 90kg, testifies to the extravagance and therefore the prosperity, of the householder but her or his character remains elusive. Based on the fact that almost the only tablewares available were those made on the Continent, one might preclude these from the discussion. That leaves kitchenware and transportation vessels. The latter

class might suggest a taste for less local foodstuffs and the presence of olive jars might indicate a liking for food cooked with olive oil but this is not sufficient to make any cultural interpretation, as olive jars occur in almost every late medieval group. The analyses of earlier periods have shown that kitchenware, and more specifically cooking vessels, might be a better indicator of cultural identity. In the late medieval period that is perhaps less likely. Nearly all the imported cooking pots came from the Low Countries in a form that was not made locally. Sherds of these vessels are present in every late medieval ceramic assemblage but it is unlikely that every one of those was from a Dutch or Flemish household. The group from SOU 128 however, is the only one that contains cooking vessels of Iberian origin and that might reflect the origins of the occupant.

The overall pattern for the late medieval period defies cultural patterning. The deficiencies of the local pottery industries forced consumers to buy imported wares and those products seem to have been universally available. The customs accounts, or port books, show that ships were bringing in all manner of goods, including clothing, cloths, foodstuffs, metalwork, dyestuffs, treen and glass and the ceramics must be viewed as one component in a vast array of goods on offer in the marketplace and at the quayside. The documentary evidence is more informative at this period than for any earlier time and helps in identifying particular dwellings and householders but there is little apparent difference between the pottery used at SOU 128 and SOU 124 although those houses may have been occupied by people of different nationalities. Small details, such as the presence of Iberian cooking pots at SOU 128, provide tantalising clues but they hardly clinch any argument at this level. What is required, for all periods of considered here, is a comparative study on a larger scale, between more Southampton sites and perhaps with sites in other places.

Conclusions

One aim of this analysis was to consider whether pottery can be used as an indicator of cultural affinity. This may be possible, but not at the superficial level of simply identifying a site which has, for instance, more French material than English. A more sympathetic and sophisticated approach is required, one which shows some appreciation of the nature of the material and the data.

The material evidence must be understood in terms of the meaning of pottery to the consumer, who will

have had a perspective different to the producer or the trader, or indeed the archaeologist. It is, for example, easy for us to identify pottery that was made in the Rhineland, but that does not necessarily mean that the consumer recognised it as such, or if they did, that they cared. In the acquisition of household goods the most important consideration was probably whether the goods would survive the uses to which they would be put. The relationship between local and imported wares is important here. Nearly all the groups considered above comprise mainly local pottery and the reason must be that it was not only plentiful and cheap but also that it was efficient. The relationship between vessels made of clay and those made of other materials must also be recognised. The reasons for obtaining particular types of pottery must be understood in respect of vessels made of basketry, wood, leather, glass and metal. Pottery cannot be viewed as the best expression available to the consumer of wealth, of social standing, or of cultural affinity. Archaeologically invisible phenomena such as language, clothing, diet and customs are all likely to be more potent cultural indicators. There is, furthermore, no evidence that the heads of any household were those who actually chose and acquired all the domestic items required. Servants would probably have been employed to equip the house, although they would no doubt have acted to instructions. What this leads to is an archaeology of choice and that requires an engagement with the past on a level above the recovery and analysis of data.

Respect for that data must be shown through an understanding of what our techniques of analysis really mean. This is a comparison of assemblages that have been sorted consistently and quantified to the same level but those techniques are not entirely objective. It is the author's understanding of the origin and function of a particular pot (albeit informed by experience and collective, accumulated knowledge) that has been quantified. That does not weaken the interpretation, indeed it strengthens it because it is couched in terms, and based on data, that others can understand. None of the groups that have been quantified, however, represent all the pottery that was used by a single family in a single house over the entire period of their occupancy. That can never be achieved and so the data represent a compromise; it is the best that can be achieved but it is not everything that is desired. Perhaps archaeologists need to try harder both to recognise what is needed and to attain it. In order to refine any similar

study it is necessary, therefore, to consider the ways in which excavations are located. In an urban environment at present, trenches are located with no respect for the arrangement of medieval towns. An archaeological site may intrude into a single tenement or it may extend over several. Interpretation of the structural and finds evidence must recognise this and it is therefore pointless to refer to a 'site' as a single unit as it is in reality nothing more than an imposition forced upon the deposits by the modern constraints of planning, services and resources. It is necessary now to study individual dwellings and it is also important that we should recover as much information about them as possible. That means that full excavation rather than sampling must be the preferred option. In support of this point it is hoped that the significance of small details, such as the possible meanings of imported kitchenware, has been made apparent in this search for cultural identity. The importance of documentary research must also be recognised as it provides a fuller context for archaeological analysis. The location of a dwelling within a settlement must also be understood together with whatever that may mean in terms of household management and social interaction.

With all those considerations in mind the overall conclusions of this analysis may be set out. What has been revealed by this analysis are cultures of pottery use. In the Anglo-Norman period pottery may have defined ethnicity but it was also perhaps a vehicle for change. In the high medieval town those changes had been established and pottery more clearly reflects trade patterns rather than identity. The late medieval period saw recovery from recession and the consequent rise of the proto-capitalist classes. Pottery assemblages reflect scales of consumption and the importance of display. Capitalism is a system of acquisition and at a ceramic level there would appear to be no obvious difference between an English capitalist and an Italian one.

9

Conclusions

The practice of pottery work involves the characterisation, quantification, analysis and interpretation of ceramic assemblages, and all of those stages have been completed here. It seems appropriate therefore, in this final chapter, to review those processes and consider possible directions for future research.

Characterisation

Exactly 466 different fabrics have been identified in this assemblage, and allotted ware names that group them together more meaningfully. This has been done without the consistent application of petrological or chemical analysis and a programme of more highly specified fabric analysis might be an appropriate next stage, most usefully to characterise and differentiate the various English wares and perhaps the Iberian coarsewares.

The result of such an exercise would be to consolidate a type series that already represents a considerable resource. Pottery assemblages from Southampton excavations are now recorded with reference to the type series, thus extending our understanding of the currency and distribution of particular ware types and groups. The next stage must be to provide a regional context for this reference collection by matching Southampton fabrics with other locally identified types. It has already been observed, for instance, that what is known here as South Hampshire Redware has been found also at Portsmouth, Winchester and Romsey, but archaeologists in those places do not necessarily refer to it by that term. Local type series have now been developed sufficiently to allow regional coordination of ware names and perhaps to encourage a concerted search for likely source areas.

The process of characterisation, naturally, is not unproblematic here. There are many fabrics that have not been traced more thoroughly to likely production sites or regions. Among the high medieval sandy wares, for instance, are 57 fabrics that are grouped together under a general ware name. The justification for this is that none of them occur in sufficient quantity to merit the effort, especially in an exercise that already involves the ordering of a large amount of material and data, of researching every possible provenance.

There remains, however, the likelihood that among these pieces a few fragments might harbour a surprise or two. The internal mercantile connections of medieval Southampton are reasonably well understood and have been shown to extend into the Midlands and the West Country (Platt and Coleman-Smith 1975, fig 117) but the quantities of English pottery from outside the immediate Wessex hinterland are perhaps surprisingly low. The sourcing of some of these less well researched fabrics may redress that.

Provenance, of course, is not the sole purpose of characterisation. Fabric analysis also relates to the technology of pottery making, as some inclusions are more suited to certain kiln conditions than others. It is noteworthy that the size of inclusions in local coarsewares diminishes with time from the Anglo-Norman Scratch-Marked and Flint-tempered types, through to Late Medieval Well-Fired Sandy ware. This has been related to methods of manufacture and kiln control but may also have some cultural significance.

Pottery is also characterised by form, and in this instance that seems less problematic. A comprehensive reference collection of form types has been set up, and some work has been done on relating forms to fabrics, although this could be developed further. Form may be viewed as a more useful indicator of chronology and provenance than fabric, because although clays do not really change, techniques and technical preferences do. Vessel forms, the shapes of component parts, methods of forming pots and decoration, all stem from the hands of the potter, and thus reflect human choices and actions. It is possible, therefore, given excavated groups that are sufficiently well stratified, to see shifting technical patterns that may show certain rim or handle forms, for instance, appearing and disappearing within the lifetime of a single fabric or ware. The lack of stratigraphic analysis on the sites that yielded this assemblage may have obstructed such an exercise, but now that the form series has been developed it may be worth applying form analysis to a different set of data. The examination of form that has been carried out here, however superficial it may be, has at least shown the potential value in collecting such information. The exercise of contrasting the forms of cooking pots and also the styles of jugs has provided a coherent basis for discussion of the chronological and regional development of potting techniques. As with the fabrics, future research could also be directed towards a regional form series and comparisons of groups from different localities. It has been hinted here, for example, that the forms of Saintonge vessels may have influenced the potters at Laverstock, but more rigorous analysis is required to elucidate that notion.

Form analysis may aid interpretations of chronology and provenance but its primary value is in determining vessel function. It has been shown how that developed through time, so that by the end of the 15th century a greater variety of vessels was being made than ever before. The potter's repertoire had expanded from two basic types in the 12th century, the jar/cooking pot and the jug, to include pipkins, skillets, pancheons, cisterns, cups and mugs. This reflects the increasingly important role pottery played in the household, resulting in a greater demand, that in Southampton was met either by local producers or through overseas trade. The characterisation of form is therefore linked to an understanding of aspects of supply, demand and use. The same is also true of fabric, and it is only through analysis of both ceramic attributes that the fullest understanding can be attained. It is doubtful that the fullest understanding has been reached here, but at least the establishment of fabric and form type series has created the potential for doing so.

The problems of ceramic classification however, extend far beyond the personal, chronological and geographical limits of this work. In adopting an accepted nomenclature of ware and vessel types the catalogue has an accessibility that makes it at once comprehensible and open to critical appreciation. The purpose of characterisation throughout every part of the recording process has been to provide data with which other assemblages may be compared. Recognition of the limitations of the language used to achieve this is necessary; but the fact that the central purpose has been attained means that, whatever its problems, that language succeeds.

Quantification

The ideal method of quantifying an assemblage would be to count exactly the number of vessels represented but this is not possible for such a large assemblage composed entirely of fragments. Three methods of quantification have been used here instead; rim percentage, weight and sherd count. Rim percentage has rarely been converted into estimated vessel equivalents here and most of the analysis has been based on weight and count, and simply compares relative quantities through the use of percentages. This is far from ideal, and may well be less revealing than the application of more refined statistical methods. Patterns of consumption and supply have been established however, using methods never before applied to post-Conquest medieval assemblages in Southampton. These three quantitative methods are also those used throughout pottery studies, and the collected data therefore represent a resource for further research, and indeed for more sophisticated statistical approaches, especially comparisons with other assemblages from Southampton and elsewhere. There is indeed, little more that could be quantified in an assemblage of this size and variety that would not compromise either the speed of processing or the simplicity of the analytical approach. That simplicity is crucial to making accessible both the data and subsequent interpretations, even if some of the analysis could be more securely founded in statistics, it is hoped that what has been shown is easily comprehended, and also understood to be of use in studying the development of pottery use in medieval Southampton.

Analysis

In the absence of good stratigraphic information for every site, analysis was focussed on establishing a ceramic chronology before engaging with more profound themes such as manufacture, distribution and use. This has led to the identification of three ceramic periods, Anglo-Norman, high medieval and late medieval. Chronological analysis has shown the validity of these divisions, and all subsequent investigations have centred on a comparison of each period. Differences between them, based on the character and quantity of pottery types, have therefore been examined and used to show how the technique of pottery making, routes of supply and the culture of pottery use changed through time. This exercise seems to have been fairly successful, and those changes may broadly be plotted and understood. Future work must concentrate initially on refining the chronology, perhaps through closer examination of certain groups and at least by unravelling the various stratigraphic sequences represented here. This chrono-logy is at present internally coherent but needs to be attached to a separate framework, both locally and regionally, to be fully tested and improved. If that can be achieved then further aspects of analysis will benefit, so that the somewhat basic level of this study will be replaced by more detailed research. After all, one purpose of this work has been to highlight the potential in Southampton for understanding many different aspects of pottery in the past.

Interpretation

'... the trade of clothing facts in words is bound by its very nature to fail'

Primo Levi

It is debatable whether any of the data set out here truly represent fact. The insecurities inherent in the exercise of attempting to analyse objectively a body of material so vulnerable to human caprice should, by now, be apparent. The sherds of pottery that survive as evidence of a medieval community may take on the aura of archaeological fact, but they have been sorted into types and recorded according to criteria that are wholly constructed by people with purposes quite different from the original makers and users. The universal languages of classification and quantification may have rendered aspects of this work comprehensible, but they also give the illusion of trustworthiness. Most readers will believe that what has been identified as Tudor Green ware is not really something else, and that there really are 291 sherds of it in this assemblage (they may also be relieved to learn that the author certainly does). The attempt to present collected 'facts' in a way that is comprehensible to those who cannot approach them first hand has led, therefore, to the creation of attendant ephemera, perceptive inferences and values, in the form of nomenclature, quantities, tables and graphs. The sherds may be fact, but the system of classification used to describe them is not. It is nothing but a language, subjective but not self-contained, wilfully idiosyncratic. If the systems of characterisation and quantification suffer from percep-tual, even perpetual, inconsistencies then the ultimate 'truth' of the subsequent analyses and interpretations must have similar failings.

This realisation, if not made before now, is no conclusion however, nor should it be a problem, for what should also have been appreciated is that this work has not been written solely as an examination of a ceramic assemblage. There seems little point in identifying and quantifying different pottery types and not offering any interpretation. Indeed, those under-standings that have been reached should extend far beyond an appreciation of simple ceramic types. The themes examined in Chapter 8 relate to the activities and concerns of the people living in a medieval town. It has been possible not only to illuminate their lives but also to examine the suitability of the evidence for such an undertaking. Social and economic differences, the practicalities of waste management, and the cultural identity of individuals, have all been explored through the pottery evidence with varying degrees of success. Further research might go deeper into the culture of pottery use, examining gender differences, colour sym-bolism and the relationship between ceramics and other materials such as metal, glass and wood. The archae-ological and historical resources of Southampton offer the potential to inform these issues, but only if they are properly exploited. At present, research is not conducted with the express purpose of extending our avenues of enquiry and this will not change until we address the conditions that currently govern the pro-cesses of archaeological excavation and data retrieval. What is certain, is that pottery has a potential for elucidating past societies that extends beyond the merely chronological. In presenting these interpreta-tions, and the supporting evidence, it is hoped that future work on the medieval pottery of Southampton will find an easily identifiable starting point.

Summary

Having identified some possible future directions for the study of medieval pottery in Southampton it seems appropriate to finish with a summary of the interpre-tations made here.

Three ceramic periods, Anglo-Norman, high medieval and late medieval, have been identified and characterised, together with four phases of activity for the medieval town. Anglo-Norman pottery consists largely of locally produced, handbuilt, jar/cooking pots with some jugs in the tripod pitcher tradition. Local coarsewares were probably made in, or very close to Southampton while jugs came from a greater variety of more distant production sites. Continental imports, mainly from northern France, (although there is some material from the Low Countries) comprise around seven percent by weight of the total material of this period. This pattern may be related to the ways ceramics were used in the pre-Conquest period, where a similar emphasis on jar/cooking pots may be observed. The arrival of the Normans strengthened existing cross-channel trade links, and this is reflected in the character of the imported material.

In the high medieval period, from the third quarter of the 13th century, local pottery was mainly wheel-thrown and a wider range of vessel types was in use. There were more jugs, some of them elaborately and colourfully decorated, being made and supplied to the town, together with the ubiquitous jar/cooking pot. Most of the latter were probably made very close to Southampton, which seems to have been the principal market for them. The majority of the jugs came from three local industries, the most common product being South Hampshire Redware, but a wide variety of other products, such as Scarborough ware, are also represented. There seems to have been an increased demand for pottery in the high medieval period, sufficient to encourage at least one potter to set up a workshop in Southampton itself, producing green glazed jugs that resembled Laverstock products, perhaps made from Laverstock clay. As a centre for trade, Southampton may have been seen to be a promising location for a kiln, but production seems to have been short-lived, despite evidence that vessels were distributed to the Channel Islands and Aardenburg. Southampton's merchants had shifted the emphasis of their commercial activities from northern France to Gascony, due in part to the loss of Normandy by King John, and the products of the Saintonge became the most common imported pottery, although northern French, Breton, Low Countries, Rhenish and Iberian types are all represented. Imported wares account for about sixteen percent by weight of the total high medieval assemblage. In the late medieval assemblage Continental imports are present in far greater proportions, over 50% by weight and sherd count, and more of it came from a wider variety of sources, including France, the Low Countries, the Rhineland, Portugal, Spain and Italy. Tudor Green ware was a common non-local English type. Many of these imports were decorative products quite unlike the utilitarian jars, pancheons and pitchers available locally, and it is apparent that for the first time local potters were not able to provide everything that the consumers required. The increased range of forms made locally may represent a response to this problem, so that, although decorated table ware was not being provided, an invaluable range of well-fired storage and cooking ware was on offer. The culture of pottery use seems to have changed in the fifteenth century, as there is less emphasis simply on the use of jugs and jars, with bowls and dishes more prominent than before. At the same time local pottery making was also in a state of transition, so although the high medieval highly decorated tradition was ended there was no other local equivalent. This period set the pattern for the post-medieval period, where local producers made plain earthenware, while more decorative pottery – be it stoneware, tin-glazed ware, or, later on, refined earthenware – was brought in from further afield.

It is possible to observe a relatively smooth transition from the Saxon period into the Anglo-Norman period and on into the high medieval, with the same types of jars being made and used. The shouldered, round-bottomed shape was current from the 8th to the 14th centuries, albeit with changes in the rim form, for instance, and those slight developments that can be seen, especially from the mid-13th century were probably due to use of the wheel in manufacture. There is far less similarity between the high and late medieval periods, and the recession, brought about by plague and war, which caused the end of the high medieval tradition, profoundly affected local pottery styles. These changes most likely resulted from the closure of individual potteries. Recession also affected Southampton's merchants, and the increase in pottery imported from beyond France reflects the widening of their commercial horizons, as well as the influence of Italian merchants and the North Sea ports of the Low Countries. Ceramic production, style, distribution and use in the late-15th century has more in common with the post-medieval period than with the preceding periods.

This broad pattern is reflected in the nature of the archaeological deposits that produced this material. Anglo-Norman and high medieval pottery has been recovered mainly from pits. Settlement Phase 3 is identified as one where archaeological deposits are scarce, and most of the pottery in this phase has come from site layers. In Phase 4, which corresponds with the late medieval ceramic period, stone-lined structures produced some enormous groups of pottery that included a wide range of spectacular imported vessels. These differences may be related to different ways of living within the town, where in the early phases rubbish was disposed of in back yards before a greater awareness of hygiene encouraged disposal of domestic refuse away from the home. The lack of activity indicated in Phase 3 may also be related to a period, perhaps of plague, when the population was low. At the end of the 15th century there seems to have been a time when structures such as cellars and garderobes were being closed off. The quantity and variety of pottery that appears to have been consumed in the late medieval period engenders the feeling that in the 15th century Southampton was undergoing a revival, and this is supported by evidence for structural redevelopment.

All these ruminations inevitably lead to a consideration of the relationship between pottery and living, pottery and people. Individuals are difficult to identify in the archaeological record, but a few names occasionally surface, such as Roger Machado, and it is tempting to match what we know of them with what we know of the pottery. It is more important, however, and easier, to look for evidence of how people in general lived, to consider how pottery can tell us what mattered to them, how they behaved. It seems that pottery became increasingly important in medieval Southampton, as both a marketable commodity and for use in the home. In the former context there is an increase in the amounts of pottery imported into the town, although it is not until the 15th century, it seems, that large quantities are redistributed into the hinterland. In the domestic context, pottery became better made, and more decorative, making it both more useful and more suited to display. The quantities of imported pottery in the 15th century indicate the decorative value of this material. The high medieval English decorated jugs, for instance, with their garish hues and exuberant forms, exemplify the relationship between pottery and those themes of cultural identity, shared artistic values, communal spirit, that archaeologists seek to illuminate. Those vessels were very much the product of their time, and the tragedy of how that way of life ended, through war, plague and deprivation, is expressed in the ceramic record. As usual, the subsequent revival is observed most clearly in the possessions of the wealthier classes, and the fates of the 13th-century potters who produced those wonderful objects were not recorded. The great thing about pottery though, is that everybody has some, uses some, and breaks some, and so everybody is revealed through archaeology, ourselves included. These vessels have taken on new meanings now, as museum pieces, as items for analysis, but most importantly they provide a way into the past. It is hoped that this work has done them justice.

Appendix 1

Concordance of Major Wares and Specific Fabrics

Major ware name	Code	Fabric numbers
Early Medieval Flint-tempered	EMFT	900, 1000
Scratch-marked ware	SMK	1007, 1008
Mixed Grit Coarseware	ECWXa	1011
Mixed Grit Coarseware	ECWXb	1014
Mixed Grit Coarseware	ECWXc	1095
Chalk-tempered Coarseware	ECWC	1055
Wessex Coarseware	EWQ	1016
Early Dorset Sandy ware	EDOS	1101, 1102, 1103, 1350
Anglo-Norman Glazed	EMG	1063, 1065, 1084, 1099, 1596, 1663, 1720, 1731
Normandy Gritty ware	NOG	1152, 1284, 1286, 1551
North French Glazed wares	NFG	1128, 1166, 1200, 1277, 1278, 1283, 1403, 1404, 1708
Southampton Coarseware	STCW	1123
Southampton Sandy Coarseware	STCS	1024, 1091
Southampton High Street Coarseware	STHC	1230
Mixed Grit Coarse Sandy	HCSX	1124
Southampton Whiteware	STWW	1044
Southampton Sandy ware	STS	1105, 1120, 1150
South Hampshire Redware	SHRW	1248
Local Pink Sandy ware	LOPS	1087, 1107
Laverstock ware	LAV	1034, 1053
Local Whiteware	LOWW	1118
Local Fine White Sandy ware	LWFS	1215
Dorset Sandy ware	DOQS	1430, 1729
Dorset Whiteware	DOWW	1156
High Medieval Saintonge	HMSO	1267, 1272, 1274, 1500, 1758
Southampton Organic-tempered Sandy	STOS	1130, 1136
Late Medieval Well-fired Sandy	LWFS	1027, 1110, 1115, 1133, 1161, 1170, 1203, 1263, 1264, 1356, 1359, 1365, 1381, 1496, 1524, 1574, 1577, 1607, 1633, 1643, 1648, 1651, 1694
Tudor Green	TDG	1193
Beauvais Earthenwares	BV	1195, 1316, 1319, 1436
Normandy Stoneware	NST	1349
Martincamp wares	MCP	1296, 1363, 1583, 1751
Late Saintonge ware	LSO	1454, 1770
Low Countries Redware	LCRD	1297, 1300, 1610
Raeren Stoneware	RARN	1245
Seville Coarseware	SVCW	1308, 1311, 1327, 1405, 1428, 1457, 1505, 1507, 1538, 1627, 1654, 1662, 1698, 1712, 1773
Iberian Micaceous Redware	IBMR	1304, 1305, 1337, 1355, 1371, 1470, 1471, 1476, 1484, 1512, 1617, 1766, 1776
Spanish Tin-glazed wares	SPTG	1070, 1348, 1448, 1472, 1765
Italian Maiolica	ITMA	1241, 1446, 1450, 1467, 1767, 1722
North Italian Red Earthenware	NITR	1768

Appendix 2

LIST OF ALL FABRIC NUMBERS AND WARE NAMES

A list of all the fabric numbers, in numerical order, with the ware codes, ware names and quantities by rim percent, weight in grams and sherd count.

Fabric no.	Ware code	Ware name	Rim %	weight (grams)	Sherd count
799	IA	Iron Age	0	3	1
799	IA	Iron Age	0	3	1
899	ROM	Romano-British	14	119	15
900	FTS	Flint-tempered Sandy ware	276	3382	363
901	LSCT	Chalk-tempered ware	21	372	22
902	SHT	Shell-tempered ware	0	166	14
903	LSV	Late Saxon Sandy ware	12	432	28
905	QTG	Late Saxon Sandy ware	46	684	46
906	OTS	Organic-tempered Sandy ware	249	4910	592
907	OTS	Organic-tempered Sandy ware	148	1961	167
908	LSSU	Late Saxon Sandy ware	0	7	1
909	LSSU	Late Saxon Sandy ware	0	67	3
910	MM	Michelmersh-type ware	0	62	3
911	MM	Michelmersh type ware	0	8	1
913	LSI	Late Saxon import	0	5	1
914	LSI	Late Saxon import	0	42	2
915	LSI	Late Saxon import	0	8	2
916	LSI	Late Saxon import	10	69	16
917	LSI	Late Saxon import	13	302	14
918	LSBV	Late Saxon Beauvais-type	0	68	4
919	LSI	Late Saxon import	0	76	10
920	LSI	Late Saxon import	0	4	1
921	LSSU	Late Saxon import	10	24	2
924	LSI	Late Saxon import	0	5	1
925	LSI	Late Saxon import	22	69	
926	LSI	Late Saxon import	0	3	1
929	LSI	Late Saxon import	14	45	5
930	LSI	Late Saxon import	0	25	1
934	LSI	Late Saxon import	0	6	4
935	MM	Michelmersh-type ware	0	13	1
936	LSI	Late Saxon import	0	4	2
937	LSI	Late Saxon import	0	5	2
1000	FTG	Flint-tempered Gritty ware	862	11923	55
1007	SMG	Scratch-marked Gritty ware	2620	52449	2870
1008	SMS	Scratch-marked Sandy ware	510	11374	42
1009	CIQH	Anglo-Norman Coarseware	7	186	16
1010	GFS	Unidentifiable Sandy ware	0	48	4
1011	ANWX	Anglo-Norman Mixed Grit Coarseware	112	3004	153

Fabric no.	Ware code	Ware name	Rim %	weight (grams)	Sherd count
1013	ANLF	Anglo-Norman Non-local Flint-tempered ware	0	763	28
1014	ANWX	Anglo-Norman Mixed Grit Coarseware	409	4672	225
1016	AWQC	Anglo-Norman Wessex Coarseware	180	3195	203
1024	STCS	Southampton Sandy Coarseware	630	15295	1312
1027	LWFS	Late Medieval Well-fired Sandy ware	106	573	36
1028	CWCX	High Medieval Coarseware	77	625	31
1030	GFS	High Medieval Sandy ware	13	274	12
1031	USIO	Unidentifiable Sandy ware	0	64	5
1032	CSIQ	High Medieval Coarseware	0	81	14
1033	CSXM	High Medieval Coarseware	7	197	10
1034	LV	Laverstock-type ware	145	4156	311
1036	PQCF	High Medieval Sandy ware	0	59	3
1039	WIQ	High Medieval Sandy ware		178	17
1040	WQL	High Medieval Sandy ware	0	24	3
1044	STWW	Southampton Whiteware	510	11484	35
1053	LV	Laverstock-type ware	211	2637	196
1055	ACWC	Anglo-Norman Chalk-tempered Coarseware	88	2337	58
1061	CWA	High Medieval Coarseware	21	725	36
1062	WIQF	High Medieval Sandy ware	5	272	30
1063	AGS	Anglo-Norman Glazed Sandy ware	20	866	21
1065	AWQC	Anglo-Norman Wessex Coarseware	0	1510	66
1066	SHR	South Hampshire Redware	42	2571	194
1067	ANDL	Andalusian Lustreware	10	124	17
1070	VALL	Valencian Lustreware	224	1666	33
1073	ANGT	Anglo-Norman gravel-tempered ware	0	17	2
1074	WFIQ	High Medieval Sandy ware	0	0	3

Fabric no.	Ware code	Ware name	Rim %	weight (grams)	Sherd count
1076	GSOF	High Medieval Sandy ware	0	182	14
1077	WSJM	Unidentifed Sandy ware	0	3	1
1078	MIDL	Midlands ware	30	214	1
1079	ULWS	Late Medieval Sandy ware	12	199	10
1081	CWAH	Anglo-Norman Coarseware	66	32	26
1084	AGCI	Anglo-Norman Glazed Coarseware with Iron	47	3851	142
1086	PFIQ	High Medieval Sandy ware	0	37	7
1087	LOPS	Local pink Sandy ware	501	10368	686
1092	SRWW	Surrey Whiteware	77	818	69
1095	ANWX	Anglo-Norman Mixed Grit Coarseware	178	2043	89
1096	ULSF	Late Medieval Sandy ware	0	108	11
1099	AGX	Anglo-Norman Mixed Grit Glazed ware	25	16	36
1101	ADOS	Anglo-Norman Medieval Dorset Sandy ware	6	308	15
1102	ADOS	Anglo-Norman Medieval Dorset Sandy ware	22	1141	88
1103	ADOS	Anglo-Norman Medieval Dorset Sandy ware	48	644	62
1104	CWAH	Anglo-Norman Coarseware	42	497	22
1105	STSW	Southampton Sandy ware	6	675	58
1107	LOPS	Local pink Sandy ware	59	3690	341
1109	WFQ	Late Medieval Sandy ware	0	36	6
1110	LWFS	Late Medieval Well-fired Sandy ware	342	3725	111
1111	RFIQ	High Medieval Sandy ware	0	160	17
1115	LWFS	Late Medieval Well-fired Sandy ware	222	5647	206
1116	VWTS	Late Medieval Sandy ware	0	781	55
1117	WFM	High Medieval Sandy ware	5	163	11
1118	LOWW	Local Whiteware	150	3120	219
1120	STSW	Southampton Sandy ware	263	4524	412
1121	GSIQ	High Medieval Sandy ware	19	477	51
1123	STCW	Southampton Coarseware	3622	67145	4766
1124	HCSX	Mixed Grit Coarse Sandy ware	132	1949	268
1126	WFSQ	High Medieval Sandy ware	0	20	5
1128	NFG	North French Glazed ware	0	18	3
1130	STOS	Southampton Organic-tempered Sandy ware	358	7646	335
1133	LWFS	Late Medieval Well-fired Sandy ware	579	11193	294
1134	RLPN	Late Medieval Sandy ware	18	558	16
1135	RSQO	High Medieval Sandy ware	19	761	69
1136	STOF	Southampton Organic-tempered Sandy ware	419	12609	409
1140	SLO	Late Medieval Sandy ware	0	184	13
1141	CSX	Anglo-Norman Coarseware	21	797	69
1143	RFS	Late Medieval Sandy ware	8	126	
1150	STSW	Southampton Sandy ware	764	18728	1701
1152	NOGD	Reduced Normandy Gritty ware	6	222	22
1153	RLSF	Late Medieval Sandy ware	26	163	
1154	WFM	High Medieval Sandy ware	0	27	5
1155	WIQ	High Medieval Sandy ware	0	108	13
1156	DOWW	Dorset Whiteware	139	3231	142
1159	RFLF	Late Medieval Sandy ware	0	31	2
1161	LWFS	Late Medieval Well-fired Sandy ware	306	4133	136
1162	GSIQ	Late Medieval Sandy ware	7	368	6
1166	NFG	North French Glazed ware	44	113	28
1170	LWFS	Late Medieval Well-fired Sandy ware	31	424	15
1174	RFLW	Late Medieval Sandy ware	0	391	17
1176	WLW	Late Medieval Sandy ware	13	308	12
1180	WLFW	Late Medieval Sandy ware	7	6	1
1184	GSU	Late Medieval Sandy ware	3	41	3
1185	CSIQ	High Medieval Coarseware	17	26	4
1187	ULWS	Late Medieval Sandy ware	15	50	4
1190	WSQ	High Medieval Sandy ware	0	58	
1191	ZWQI	French Whiteware with Quartz and Iron	13	141	14
1193	TDG	Tudor Green	574	1579	291
1195	BVMY	Beauvais Yellow-glazed	9	22	82
1196	WCQ	High Medieval Sandy ware	13	84	13
1198	WFQ	Late Medieval Sandy ware	0	6	3
1200	NFG	North French Glazed ware	10	748	71
1202	RSCT	Late Medieval Sandy ware	0	29	1
1203	LWFS	Late Medieval Well-fired Sandy ware	148	2209	71
1209	HMSF	High Medieval Sandy ware	18	383	5
1211	WFSQ	High Medieval Sandy ware	8	65	10
1212	WFSQ	High Medieval Sandy ware	17	36	
1215	LOWF	Local fine Whiteware	57	1478	157
1219	LFCT	Late Medieval Sandy ware	0	31	3
1221	ULWS	Late Medieval Sandy ware	32	541	44
1230	STHC	Southampton High Street Coarseware	8	2484	145

Fabric no.	Ware code	Ware name	Rim %	weight (grams)	Sherd count
1233	NFG	North French Glazed ware	0	103	4
1234	LIHF	Late Medieval Sandy ware	0	129	13
1240	RSIQ	High Medieval Sandy ware	0	61	4
1241	APM	Archaic Pisan Maiolica	106	753	47
1243	WFSQ	Late Medieval Sandy ware	0	3	1
1244	WIQ	High Medieval Sandy ware	0	25	5
1245	RARN	Raeren Stoneware	2007	18198	682
1246	SIG	Siegburg Stoneware	137	502	27
1247	RSOM	High Medieval Sandy ware	0	65	4
1248	SHR	South Hampshire Redware	72	28368	1671
1250	GSIQ	High Medieval Sandy ware	19	200	13
1251	WFSO	High Medieval Sandy ware	7	438	24
1252	GSIQ	High Medieval Sandy ware	0	3	1
1256	RFS	Unidentifiable Sandy ware	0	179	19
1257	LANG	Langerwehe Stoneware	0	521	17
1263	LWFS	Late Medieval Well-fired Sandy ware	157	4151	138
1264	LWFS	Late Medieval Well-fired Sandy ware	332	6144	144
1267	SORP	Saintonge Red-painted	0	130	16
1269	SOE	Early Saintonge Whiteware	0	82	2
1272	SOWW	Saintonge Whiteware	1134	18266	1825
1273	SORD	Saintonge Redware	87	3742	37
1274	SOPY	Saintonge polychrome	327	3210	219
1277	NFG	North French Glazed ware	0	277	8
1278	NFG	North French Glazed ware	41	206	43
1279	ZCMM	French Micaceous Coarseware	11	141	3
1281	NFG	North French Glazed ware	12	53	3
1282	WSQ	Late Medieval Sandy ware	0	45	4
1283	NFG	North French Glazed ware	2	138	13
1284	NOG	Normandy Gritty ware	155	4704	311
1285	NFRP	North French Red-painted ware	0	18	4
1286	NOGN	Normandy Gritty ware finer type	0	0	17
1288	NFG	North French Glazed ware	17	101	6
1289	IPQL	High Medieval imported ware	6	39	5
1290	ZPQ	French Pink ware	10	86	10
1291	NFPQ	North French Pink ware	0	318	30
1292	WSQ	High Medieval Sandy ware	0	5	2
1293	IMMQ	Late Medieval unidentified imported ware	0	1	1
1294	HMS	High Medieval Sandy ware	0	7	3
1296	MCPO	Martincamp-type Orange-pink	0	74	8
1297	LCRD	Low Countries Redware	2418	30332	1294
1298	SPGB	Iberian Green and Brown	0	24	1
1300	LCRB	Low Countries Slipped Redware	181	1092	49
1305	IBR	Iberian Micaceous Redware	0	25	5
1308	SPCW	Seville-type Coarseware	210	7756	164
1311	SPCW	Seville-type Coarseware	0	48	3
1316	BVDS	Beauvais Double-slipped Sgraffito	15	202	19
1319	BVSG	Beauvais Sgraffito	14	163	
1321	WRRA	Werra Slipware	0	46	1
1326	VER	Verwood-type ware	473	995	294
1327	SPCW	Seville-type Coarseware	53	3394	1
1331	RLS	Late Medieval Sandy ware	0	45	3
1336	RLS	Late Medieval Sandy ware	1	43	5
1344	WLW	Late Medieval Sandy ware	0	229	11
1346	RSTN	Rhenish Stoneware	64	60	67
1347	NSTP	Normandy Proto-stoneware	0	12	1
1348	IBMA	Iberian Tin-glazed	10	76	7
1349	NST	Normandy Stoneware	224	4071	205
1350	ADOS	Anglo-Norman Medieval Dorset Sandy ware	25	783	45
1355	IBR	Iberian Micaceous Redware	75	466	28
1356	BLL	Late Medieval Well-fired Sandy ware	116	1970	58
1357	WIQ	Late Medieval Sandy ware	0	69	
1358	CSQF	Late Medieval Sandy ware	74	695	33
1359	LWFS	Late Medieval Well-fired Sandy ware	21	660	45
1362	RSIQ	High Medieval Sandy ware	39	563	39
1363	MCPW	Martincamp-type White	109	1615	116
1365	BLL	Late Medieval Well-fired Sandy ware	200	6354	130
1367	GSIQ	Late Medieval Sandy ware	2	242	35
1371	IBR	Iberian Micaceous Redware	38	2270	165
1375	FRCN	Frechen Stoneware	126	691	23
1377	GLS	Late Medieval Sandy ware	15	139	8
1378	CLGN	Cologne Stoneware	29	648	40
1381	LWFS	Late Medieval Well-fired Sandy ware	41	174	15
1385	BLAG	Blaugrau ware	119	415	35
1387	RSIQ	High Medieval Sandy ware	15	829	35
1388	RFLW	Late Medieval Sandy ware	11	259	19
1390	ANN	Andenne-type ware	0	132	18
1402	RON	Rouen-type ware	60	286	50

Fabric no.	Ware code	Ware name	Rim %	weight (grams)	Sherd count
1403	ROND	Developed Rouen-type ware	62	320	48
1404	NFG	North French Glazed ware	0	45	1
1405	SPCW	Seville-type Coarseware	0	417	14
1406	WFQ	Late Medieval Sandy ware	0	1	1
1407	SNZO	Seine Valley Zoomorphic	100	1183	64
1413	ENFS	North French Sandy ware	54	362	16
1415	GSIQ	High Medieval Sandy ware	0	70	5
1419	RLWQ	Late Medieval Sandy ware	7	71	6
1420	MAI	Unidentified Tin-glazed ware	21	645	75
1421	SVBP	Seville Blue and Purple	6	56	3
1422	DTG	Low Countries Tin-glazed ware	181	429	84
1426	LCML	Low Countries Malling type	10	87	5
1428	SPCW	Seville-type Coarseware	0	60	2
1429	UFS	Unidentifiable Sandy ware	0	187	23
1430	DOQS	Dorset Quartz-rich Sandy ware	111	1649	1
1434	WSQ	High Medieval Sandy ware	0	13	1
1436	BVMG	Beauvais Green-glazed	194	751	74
1437	SPMV	Iberian Coarseware	0	202	18
1438	CWLO	Late Medieval Sandy ware	14	86	2
1439	ANDC	Andalusian Coarseware	25	3087	120
1440	ULWS	Late Medieval Sandy ware	0	11	1
1442	ISMM	High Medieval imported ware	0	3	1
1444	WW	Westerwald Stoneware	0	16	4
1445	DOQS	Dorset Quartz-rich Sandy ware	21	69	1
1446	MONT	Montelupo Maiolica	176	96	33
1448	SVB	Seville Blue	39	228	18
1449	MULB	Muel Blue	20	59	1
1450	FNZA	Faenza-type Maiolica	255	2539	134
1452	WFQ	Unidentifiable Sandy ware	0	13	4
1454	SOL	Late Saintonge Whiteware	291	8798	246
1457	SPCW	Seville-type Coarseware	0	19	2
1458	CONC	Ceramique Onctueuse	0	13	1
1459	WLFW	Late Medieval Sandy ware	0	8	2
1461	PSIQ	High Medieval Sandy ware	4	396	11
1464	SOGT	Saintonge Gritty ware	215	5813	38
1466	CWCR	Anglo-Norman Coarseware	11	257	8
1467	ITMA	North Italian Maiolica	192	1209	74
1468	VNMA	Venetian-type Maiolica	60	300	20
1470	IBR	Iberian Micaceous Redware	37	76	8
1472	SVW	Seville plain white	30	727	22
1476	IBR	Iberian Micaceous Redware	6	277	22

Fabric no.	Ware code	Ware name	Rim %	weight (grams)	Sherd count
1479	GFSH	Unidentifiable Sandy ware	0	11	2
1483	WSCP	High Medieval Sandy ware	0	174	15
1484	IBR	Iberian Micaceous Redware	14	229	27
1494	AARG	Low Countries Highly Decorated Redware	45	752	12
1496	LWFS	Late Medieval Well-fired Sandy ware	4	228	13
1500	SOBG	Saintonge Bright Green-glazed	270	1704	193
1501	ULWS	Late Medieval Sandy ware	0	51	6
1502	RFSV	Late Medieval Sandy ware	0	1	1
1503	CSFT	High Medieval Coarseware	0	31	1
1505	SPCW	Seville-type Coarseware	40	1475	184
1507	SPCW	Seville-type Coarseware	0	8	1
1509	WQT	High Medieval Sandy ware	0	205	25
1517	NFRP	North French Red-painted ware	23	63	4
1518	RFLW	Late Medieval Sandy ware	0	16	3
1523	PMR	Post-Medieval Redware	385	8469	326
1524	LWFS	Late Medieval Well-fired Sandy ware	0	19	5
1526	SCRB	Scarborough-type ware	10	494	18
1527	WFIQ	High Medieval Sandy ware	0	15	4
1528	IPCP	High Medieval imported ware	0	16	3
1532	PMGG	Post-Medieval Green-glazed Earthenware	295	6411	337
1533	HSMR	High Medieval Sandy ware	0	306	12
1534	HMS	High Medieval Sandy ware	0	308	1
1535	PQT	Late Medieval Sandy ware	0	7	1
1536	IBR	Iberian Micaceous Redware	15	135	14
1545	GSIQ	Late Medieval Sandy ware	7	45	3
1546	CSCF	High Medieval Coarseware	0	80	4
1548	SNWW	Seine Valley Whiteware	15	334	109
1549	CWCC	High Medieval Coarseware	0	86	2
1551	NOGO	Normandy Gritty ware Orange type	0	53	6
1552	HNFS	North French Sandy Whiteware	0	180	18
1553	GSOF	High Medieval Sandy ware	3	57	1
1555	IWQ	High Medieval imported ware	0	33	1
1556	MOD	Modern pottery	31	481	28
1559	PMS	Post-Medieval Sandy ware	81	1147	55
1563	CSXH	Anglo-Norman Coarseware	0	26	4

Fabric no.	Ware code	Ware name	Rim %	weight (grams)	Sherd count
1574	LWFS	Late Medieval Well-fired Sandy ware	7	686	21
1576	WSQ	Late Medieval Sandy ware	0	64	7
1577	LWFS	Late Medieval Well-fired Sandy ware	17	77	5
1580	NFRP	North French Red-painted ware	0	53	7
1581	UFS	Late Medieval Sandy ware	0	25	4
1583	MCPP	Martincamp-type Underfired Vitrified	106	704	80
1584	RLSF	Late Medieval Sandy ware	0	69	5
1589	RFSI	High Medieval Sandy ware	0	10	2
1592	CWCX	High Medieval Coarseware	0	290	27
1594	WQT	Late Medieval Sandy ware	0	2	1
1595	USTN	Late Medieval unidentified imported ware	0	8	1
1596	AGWW	Anglo-Norman Glazed Whiteware	0	44	3
1599	RSTP	Rhenish Proto-stoneware	0	41	5
1603	RCSO	High Medieval Sandy ware	0	44	4
1604	IVPN	High Medieval imported ware	0	12	4
1607	LWFS	Late Medieval Well-fired Sandy ware	160	765	25
1608	CRA	High Medieval Coarseware	0	16	1
1610	LCRG	Low Countries Redware Slipped and Green-glazed	25	302	21
1614	GSIQ	Late Medieval Sandy ware	0	68	6
1617	IBR	Iberian Micaceous Redware	0	10	1
1622	PQBI	Late Medieval Sandy ware	0	3	1
1633	LWFS	Late Medieval Well-fired Sandy ware	69	2513	53
1639	WIQ	High Medieval Sandy ware	0	218	7
1642	PMU	Post-Medieval Sandy ware	37	514	42
1643	LWFS	Late Medieval Well-fired Sandy ware	48	2496	154
1648	LWFS	Late Medieval Well-fired Sandy ware	15	136	14
1649	WFSQ	High Medieval Sandy ware	0	6	1
1650	CSOK	High Medieval Coarseware	0	36	3
1651	LWFS	Late Medieval Well-fired Sandy ware	0	18	2
1654	SPCW	Seville-type Coarseware	0	157	4
1663	AGX	Anglo-Norman Mixed Grit Glazed ware	34	193	13
1664	RFSO	Late Medieval Sandy ware	0	29	4
1665	PQT	High Medieval Sandy ware	0	27	5

Fabric no.	Ware code	Ware name	Rim %	weight (grams)	Sherd count
1666	RFLW	Late Medieval Sandy ware	8	38	2
1668	WFSQ	High Medieval Sandy ware	0	2	1
1669	WMQ	High Medieval Sandy ware	0	32	3
1672	CSOF	High Medieval Sandy ware	0	20	2
1675	WFN	High Medieval Sandy ware	8	15	2
1679	WIQ	High Medieval Sandy ware	0	11	1
1680	CWXO	Anglo-Norman Coarseware	0	25	1
1687	WF	High Medieval Sandy ware	6	24	3
1688	RQLH	Anglo-Norman Coarseware	0	6	1
1694	LWFS	Late Medieval Well-fired Sandy ware	5	109	5
1695	RQCS	High Medieval Sandy ware	0	13	2
1703	RFS	Late Medieval Sandy ware	0	49	5
1707	RFQL	High Medieval Sandy ware	0	8	1
1708	NFG	North French Glazed ware	4	22	4
1710	SIGG	Siegburg Green-glazed Stoneware	15	13	2
1711	NFWM	North French Micaceous Whiteware	0	275	17
1720	AGC	Anglo-Norman Chalk-tempered Glazed ware	0	56	6
1725	UFS	Anglo-Norman Coarseware	0	100	2
1726	CRNC	Cornish Coarseware	5	15	1
1728	WSQ	High Medieval Sandy ware	6	33	5
1729	DOQS	Dorset Quartz-rich Sandy ware	25	277	40
1731	CWQH	Handbuilt Quartz-rich Coarseware	10	79	2
1734	WFSO	High Medieval Sandy ware	4	11	1
1740	BRNT	Unidentifiable Burnt Medieval Sandy ware	68	2470	115
1741	LQWW	Late Medieval Sandy ware	0	392	17
1744	BVST	Beauvais Stoneware	70	44	4
1745	DLFT	Anglo-Netherlandish Tin-glazed	0	4	1
1747	RIQO	High Medieval Sandy ware	0	76	4
1749	NOPG	Normandy Pink-grey ware	0	15	2
1750	FRCB	Frechen Blue Stoneware	15	0	
1751	MCPV	Martincamp-type Vitrified	115	2613	235
1752	GFSG	Late Medieval Sandy ware	11	5	1
1753	BTCW	Breton Coarseware	0	54	1
1754	NOGL	Developed Normandy Gritty ware	22	133	14

Fabric no.	Ware code	Ware name	Rim %	weight (grams)	Sherd count
1756	WWQT	High Medieval Sandy ware	0	65	5
1757	FRCW	Frechen White Stoneware	100	625	4
1758	SOFD	Saintonge Highly Decorated Whiteware	0	8	1
1759	NFG	North French Glazed ware	0	3	2
1760	ITSG	North Italian Sgraffito	146	1276	37
1761	CRNS	Cornish Sandy ware	0	41	4
1763	NFBI	North French Bichrome	14	219	16
1764	NLFS	High Medieval Sandy ware	0	20	1
1765	SVGW	Seville Green and White	111	793	15
1766	SVCG	Seville-type Coarseware	10	89	2
1767	FLOM	Florentine Maiolica	75	1699	31
1768	NITR	North Italian Red Earthenware	177	34	62
1769	SPWC	Iberian Coarseware	0	125	1
1770	SOPL	Late Medieval Saintonge Polychrome	50	510	17
1772	LIGF	Ligurian Faience Maiolica	14	16	2
1773	SPGG	Seville-type Coarseware	19	446	4
1774	SIGL	Late Siegburg Stoneware	0	123	5
1775	LCSG	Low Countries Redware Sgraffito	0	26	2
1776	IBR	Iberian Micaceous Redware	28	275	17
1777	SPCW	Seville-type Coarseware	0	17	3
1779	CSFT	Anglo-Norman Coarseware	27	271	34

Fabric no.	Ware code	Ware name	Rim %	weight (grams)	Sherd count
1781	ZFWW	French Whiteware	100	815	40
2018	LWFS	Late Medieval Well-fired Sandy ware	24	12580	891
2026	SPCW	Seville-type Coarseware	0	87	10
2028	IBR	Iberian Micaceous Redware	10	24	5
2029	PMED	Post-Medieval miscellaneous	12	514	25
2040	EMCW	Anglo-Norman Coarseware	0	9	12
2041	EMS	Anglo-Norman Coarseware	0	67	6
2050	MCW	High Medieval Coarseware	0	41	6
2051	MCS	High Medieval Coarseware	6	17	1
2052	MEDG	High Medieval Sandy ware	5	293	45
2053	MNLO	High Medieval Sandy ware, Non-local?	0	15	3
2060	LMG	Late Medieval Sandy ware	49	1101	122
2062	MISC	Late Medieval unidentified imported ware	0	1	1
7002	LMU	Late Medieval Sandy ware	8	337	16
			33011	598878	35940

BIBLIOGRAPHY

Algar, D J, Light, A, and Treharne, P, 1979 *The Verwood and District Potteries*

Allan, J P, 1984 *Medieval and Post-Medieval Finds from Exeter 1971–1980*, Exeter Archaeological Reports **Volume 3**

Armstrong, P and Ayers, B, 1987 Hull Old Town Report Series No. 5, Excavations in High Street and Blackfriargate *East Riding Archaeologist* **8**

Baart, J, 1994 Dutch Redwares *Medieval Ceramics* **18**, 19–28

Barton, K J, 1963a The medieval pottery kiln at Ham Green, *Bristol Trans Bristol Gloucestershire Archaeol Soc* **79**, 95–126

Barton, K J, 1963b The medieval pottery of the Saintonge, *Archaeol J* **120**, 210–14

Barton, K J, 1966 Medieval Pottery at Rouen, *Archaeol J* **122**, 73–85

Barton, K J, 1979 *Medieval Sussex Pottery*, Phillimore

Barton, K J, 1980 Excavations at the Chateau des Marais (Ivy Castle), Guernsey, *Rep Trans Soc Guernesiaise* **XX**, 657–702

Barton, K J, 1984 Excavations at the Vale Castle, Guernsey, C.I., *Reports and Transactions of La Societe Guernesaise*, 485–538

Barton, K J, Cartwright, L, Jarvis, K S, Thomson, R G, 1992 *Catalogue of the Pottery*, in Horsey, 65–130

Beckmann, B, 1974 *The main types of the first four production periods of Siegburg pottery*, in Evison *et al* (eds), 183–220

Blackman, P, 1979 SOU 25 Site Archive Report, unpublished typescript, Southampton Archaeological Research Committee

Blake, 1987 *Archaeology and Maiolica*, in Wilson, T

Borremans, R, and Warginaire, R, 1966 *La ceramique d Andenne. Rechereches de 1956–1965*, Rotterdam

Brown, D H, 1986 *The Pottery* in Oxley, 85–108

Brown, D H, 1988 Pottery and Archaeology *Medieval Ceramics* **12**, 15–21

Brown, D H, 1992 *A Note on the Tripod Pitchers* in Horsey, 102–106

Brown, D H, 1995a Pottery and Late Saxon Southampton *Proc Hampsh Field Club Archaeol Soc* **50**, 127–52

Brown, D H, 1995b *Iberian Pottery Excavated in Medieval Southampton* in Gerrard *et al*, 319–328

Brown, D H, 1997a The Social Significance of Imported Medieval Pottery in Cumberpatch, C G and Blinkhorn, P W, *Not so much a pot, more a way of life*, Oxbow Monograph **83**, 95–112

Brown, D H, 1997b Pots from Houses, *Medieval Ceramics* **21**, 83–94

Brown, D H, 1998 Documentary sources as evidence for the exchange and consumption of pottery in 15th Century Southampton, *Actas das 2. as Jornadas de Ceramica Medieval e Pos-Medieval – metodos e resultados para o seu estudo*, 429–438

Bunyard, B D M, 1941 *The Brokage Book of Southampton from 1439–40, Vol 1 and 2*, Southampton Record Society

Burgess, L A, 1976 *The Southampton Terrier of 1454* Southampton Records Series **XV**

Burns, R, 1991 *Post-Medieval Normandy Stonewares from Guernsey* in Lewis, 104–127

Chapelot, J, 1983 *The Saintonge Pottery Industry in the later Middle Ages* in Davey and Hodges (eds), 49–53

Cobb, H S, 1961 *The Local Port Book of Southampton 1439–40*, Southampton Records Series **V**

Coleman, O, 1960 *The Brokage Book of Southampton 1443–44*, Southampton Records Series **IV**

Collis, J, 1978 *Winchester Excavations Volume II: 1949–1960, Excavations in the Suburbs and the Western Part of the Town*, City of Winchester

Cora, G, 1973 *Storia della maiolica di Firenze e del contado: Secoli XIV e XV*, Florence

Cunliffe, B, 1974 *Iron Age Communities in Britain*, Routledge and Kegan Paul

David, P and Gabet, C, 1972 La Poterie Medievale Saintongeaise *Archeologie Medievale* **II**, 221–252

Davey, P and Hodges, R (eds), 1983 *Ceramics and Trade*, University of Sheffield

Dufornier, D, and Fajal, B, 1990 Ceramologie et aspects de l artisanat potier dans l'Orne, *Empeintes l' Orne Archaeologique*, 86–90

Dunning, G C, 1968 *The trade in medieval pottery around the North Sea* in Renaud (ed), 35–58

Fairbrother, J R, 1990 *Faccombe Netherton, Excavations of a Saxon and Medieval Manorial Complex* British Museum Occasional Paper **No. 74**

Falkus, M, and Gillingham, J, (eds) 1981 *Historical Atlas of Britain*, Grisewood and Dempsey Ltd

Farmer, D H, 1992 *The Oxford Dictionary of Saints*, OUP, Oxford

Farmer, P G and N C, 1982 The Dating of the Scarborough ware Pottery Industry *Medieval Ceramics* **6**, 66–86

Fenelly, L R, 1969 A late medieval kiln at Knighton, IOW, *Proc Hampshire Fld Club Archaeol Soc* **88**, 97–110

Fichet de Clairfontaine, F (ed), 1996 Ateliers de potiers médiévaux en Bretagne, *Documents d archéologie Francaise* **55**

Foster, B, 1963 *The Local Port Book of Southampton for 1435–36*, Southampton University Press

Fox, R and Barton, K J, 1986 Excavations at Oyster Street, Portsmouth, Hampshire, 1968–71, *Post-Medieval Archaeology* **20**, 31–255

Gaimster, D, 1997 *German Stoneware 1200–1900*, British Museum Press

Gaimster, D (ed), 1999 *Maiolica in the North, the archaeology of tin-glazed earthenware in north-west Europe c 1500–1600* British Museum Occasional Paper **No. 122**

Gaimster, D, and Redknap, M, 1992 *Everyday and Exotic Pottery from Europe, Studies in honour of John G. Hurst*, Oxbow

Gerrard, C M, Gutierrez, A, and Vince, A G, 1995 *Spanish Medieval Ceramics in Spain and the British Isles* BAR International Series **610**

Giot, P R, and Morzadec, H, 1996 *La Poterie onctueuse* in Fichet de Clairfontaine, F, 114–125

Goggin, J M, 1960 The Spanish Olive Jar: an Introductory Study, *Yale University Publications on Anthropology* **LXII**

Goggin, J M, 1968 Spanish Majolica in the New World: Types of the Sixteenth to Eighteenth Centuries, *Yale University Publications in Anthropology* **LXXII**

Hinton, M, 1980 Medieval Pottery from a kiln site at Kingston upon Thames, *London Archaeol* **3**, 377–83

Holling, F, 1977 Reflections on Tudor Green *Post-Medieval Archaeol* **11**, 61–6

Horsey, I P, 1992 Excavations in Poole 1973–1983, *Dorset Nat Hist and Archaeol Soc Monograph Series* **10**

Hughes, M, and Gaimster, D, 1999 *Neutron activation analysis of maiolica from London, Norwich, the Low Countries and Italy* in Gaimster, D, 57–90

Hurst, J G, 1977 Martincamp Flasks, in DS Neal Excavations at the Palace of Kings Langley, *Medieval Archaeol* **XXI**, 274–6

Hurst, J G, Neal, D S, and van Beuningen, H J E, 1986 *Pottery Produced and Traded in North-West Europe 1350–1650*, Rotterdam Papers **VI**

Ickowicz, P, 1993 Martincamp Ware: a problem of attribution, *Medieval Ceramics* **17**, 51–60

James, T B, 1990 *The Port Book of Southampton 1509–10, Volume 1 and 2* (Weeks 1 to 26) Southampton Record Series **XXXII**

Janssen, H L, 1983 *Later Medieval Pottery Production in the Netherlands* in Davey and Hodges (eds), 121–185

Jarvis, K S, 1983 Excavations in Christchurch 1969–1980 *Dorset Nat Hist Archaeol Soc Monograph Series* **5**

Jarvis, K S, 1992 *Introduction to the Pottery*, in Horsey, IP, 62–65

Jennings, S, 1981 *Eighteen Centuries of pottery from Norwich*, East Anglian Archaeology Report **No. 13**

Jennings, S, forthcoming *Pottery from Barking Abbey*

Lewis, E, 1993 *The Southampton Port and Brokage Books 1448–9*, Southampton Records Series **XXXVI**

McCarthy, M R and Brooks, C M, 1988 *Medieval Pottery in Britain AD 900–1600*, Leicester

Moorhouse, S, 1978 Documentary evidence for the uses of medieval pottery: an interim statement, *Medieval Ceramics* **2**, 3–21

Moorhouse, S, 1983 Documentary evidence and its potential for understanding the inland movement of medieval pottery, *Medieval Ceramics* **7**, 45–87

Morris, M, Scobie, G, Zant, J, 1988 Winchester: The Brooks, *Current Archaeology* **110**, 98–104

Morton, A D (ed), 1992 *Excavations at Hamwic: Volume 1*, Counc Brit Archaeol Res Rep **84**

Musty, M A, Algar, D J, Ewence, P F, 1969 The Medieval Pottery Kilns at Laverstock, near Salisbury, *Wiltshire Archaeologia* **CII**, 83–150

Nicourt, J, 1986 *Céramiques médiévales parisiennes; classification and typologie* JPGF

Orton, C, 1980 *Mathematics in Archaeology*, Collins

Orton, C, Tyers, P and Vince, A, 1993 *Pottery in Archaeology* Cambridge

Oxley, J, 1986 *Excavations at Southampton Castle*, Southampton Archaeology Monographs **3**

Peacock, D P S, 1977 Ceramics in Roman and Medieval Archaeology in Peacock, D P S (ed), *Pottery and early commerce*, London: Academic Press, 21–34

Pearce, J, 1984 Getting a handle on medieval pottery, *the London Archaeologist* **5**, 17–23

Pearce, J and Vince, A G, 1988 *Surrey Whitewares, A Dated Type-Series of London Medieval Pottery, Part 4*, London and Middlesex Archaeol Soc

Pieksma, E, 1986 *A Group of Industrial Vessels from Context 980* in Oxley, J, 103–106

Platt, C, 1973 *Medieval Southampton The Port and Trading Community, AD 1000–1600*, Routledge and Kegan Paul

Platt, C and Coleman-Smith, R, 1975 *Excavations in Medieval Southampton, 1953–1969*, 2 vols, Leicester

Quinn, D B, 1937 *The Port Books or Local Customs Accounts of Southampton for the Reign of Edward IV, Vol. I 1469–1471* Southampton Record Society **No. 37**

Quinn, D B, 1938 *The Port Book or Local Customs Accounts of Southampton for the Reign of Edward IV, Vol. II 1477–1481* Southampton Record Society **No. 38**

Rackham, B, 1939 A Netherlands Maiolica Vase from the Tower of London, *Antiquaries Journal* **XIX**, 285–90

Reed, I, 1990 Meddelelser N R **25**; *1000 Years of Pottery, an analysis of pottery trade and use* Fortiden I Trondheim Bygrunn: Folkebibliotekstomten

Ruddock, A A, 1951 *Italian Merchants and Shipping in Southampton 1270–1600*, Southampton Record Series

Spoerry, P S, 1990 *The Chemical Analysis of Ceramic Fabrics from Medieval Dorset and its Region* unpublished PhD thesis, Dorset Institute

Stephan, H G, 1983 *The development and production of medieval stoneware in Germany* in Davey and Hodges (eds), 95–120

Studer, P, 1910 *The Oak Book of Southampton,* Southampton Record Society

Studer, P, 1913 *The Port Books of Southampton 1427–1430,* Southampton Record Society

Thomson, R G, 1980 *The Pottery,* in Barton, 677–86

Thomson, R G and Brown, D H, 1991 *On some earthenware curiosities from the Saintonge* in Lewis (ed), 62–80

Thomson, R G and Brown, D H, 1992 *Archaic Pisan Maiolica and related Italian wares in Southampton,* in Gaimster and Redknap (eds), 177–185

Timby, J, 1988 *The Pottery* in P Andrews (ed), Southampton Finds, Volume 1: the coins and pottery from Hamwic, 73–124, Southampton Archaeology Monographs 4

Verhaege, F, 1983 *Medieval pottery production in coastal Flanders* in Davey and Hodges (eds), 63–94

Veeckman, J, with Jennings, S, Dumortier, C, Whitehouse, D, and Verhaeghe, F, (eds), 2002 *Maiolica and Glass from Italy to Antwerp and Beyond* Antwerpen

Vince, A G, 1985 Saxon and Medieval Pottery in London: a review *Medieval Archaeol* **29**, 25–93

Vince, A G, and Bell, 1992 *Sixteenth-century pottery from Acton Court, Avon,* in Gaimster and Redknap (eds), 101–112

Vince, A G, and Brown, D H, 2002 'Characterisation and identification of tin-glazed ceramics using inductively-coupled plasma spectroscopy' in Veeckman *et al,* 2002, 465–473.

Walker, J S F, 1979 Excavations in Medieval Tenements on the Quilter's Vault Site in Southampton, *Proc Hampshire Fld Club Archaeol Soc* **XXXV**, 183–216

Watkins, J G, 1987 *The Pottery,* in P Armstrong and B Ayres, 53–181

Wilson, T, 1987 *Ceramic Art of the Italian Renaissance,* British Museum

Wilson, T, 1999 *Italian Maiolica around 1500: some considerations on the background to Antwerp maiolica,* in Gaimster, D, (ed), publisher?

INDEX

Notes

1. Main page references are in **bold**. Page references in *italics* indicate pages where figures/tables/plates are to be found. There may also be textual references on these pages.
2. Vessel illustrations are indexed by reference to pottery type only.

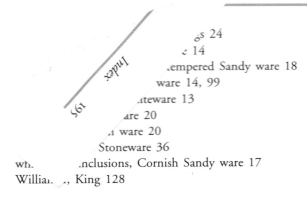